British Fami

Their origin and meaning, with lists of Scandinavian, Frisian, Anglo-Saxon and Norman names

Henry Barber

Alpha Editions

This edition published in 2019

ISBN : 9789353809362

Design and Setting By
Alpha Editions
email - alphaedis@gmail.com

BRITISH FAMILY NAMES:

Their Origin and Meaning,

WITH

LISTS OF SCANDINAVIAN, FRISIAN, ANGLO-SAXON, AND NORMAN NAMES.

BY

HENRY BARBER, M.D. (CLERK),

AUTHOR OF

'FURNESS AND CARTMEL NOTES,' 'THE CISTERCIAN ABBEV OF MAULBRONN,' 'SOME QUEER NAMES,' 'THE SHRINE OF ST. BONIFACE AT FULDA,' 'POPULAR AMUSEMENTS IN GERMANY,' ETC.

'What's in a name?—*Romeo and Juliet.*

'I believe now, there is some secret power and virtue in a name.'
BURTON'S *Anatomy of Melancholy*.

LONDON:
ELLIOT STOCK, 62, PATERNOSTER ROW, E.C.
1894.

CONTENTS.

PREFACE.

THE following pages are offered to the public in the belief that they will be found useful to those interested in the study of names or engaged in compiling family histories.

Although the vast catalogue of British surnames may not have been exhausted, yet by many years' labour more than eight thousand representative modern names extracted from directories, newspapers, voting lists, etc., have been traced to their source, and when it is remembered that this includes the numerous variations and ramifications of these patronymics, the extensive scope of this work will then be appreciated.

The utility of the lists of ancient names to the student of local etymology must at once be apparent, whilst to the genealogist (whether British, Colonial or American) the revelations as to the transformation of family names will be of the utmost service.

H. B.

Ravenstone,
Ashby-de-la-Zouch.

BOOKS CONSULTED.

Islands Landnáma-bók.

Domesday Book.

Rotuli Normanniæ. T. D. Hardy, 1835.

Rotuli Hundredorum, 2 vols., fol., A.D. 1273.

Rotuli de Oblatis et Finibus, *temp.* Regis Johannis. T. D. Hardy, 1835.

Lewis's Topographical History.

National Gazetteer of Great Britain. Virtue.

Kelly's County Directories of England.

Cleasby and Vigfusson's Icelandic-English Dictionary.

Ostfriesischen Sprache, 3 vols. Koolmann.

Directories of Belgium, Denmark, Germany, Holland, Normandy, Norway, Sweden.

Murray's Handbook of Normandy with Maps.

Bosworth's Anglo-Saxon Dictionary.

Edmund's Names of Places.

Taylor's Words and Places.

O'Hart's Irish Pedigrees.

Chambers' Etymological Dictionary.

Bailey's German and English Dictionary.

Wernick's Dutch and English Dictionary.

Rask's Icelandic Grammar.

Lenström's Swedish Grammar.

Halliwell's Dictionary of Archaic Terms, 2 vols.

Normandy and England. Palgrave.

Buchanan's Scottish Surnames.

Ellis's Introduction to the Study of Domesday Book.

Worsaae's Danes in England.

Lower's Patronymica Britannica.

INTRODUCTION.

'A painful work it is and more than difficult, wherein what toyle hath been taken, as no man thinketh, so no man believeth, but he that hath made the trial.'—ANTHONY À WOOD.

DURING a lengthened research in studying the place-names of the Danelagh (the district north and east of Watling Street, the old Roman road from London to Chester), the writer accumulated a great number of names from ancient sources necessary for unravelling the tangled skein of local etymology.

It occurred to him that these might be utilized in the treatment of British surnames, and his first idea was to publish the lists with an introductory chapter on the origin of surnames, for the use of students of this branch of archæology, who were in need of such things, for easy reference.

With this view the author wrote an article in the *Antiquary* (September, 1891), in order to draw attention to the subject, as Lower's 'English Surnames' is both out of date and altogether unreliable.

After this he met with, for the first time, the last-mentioned author's 'Patronymica Britannica,' a more ambitious work, and a great improvement upon the previous attempt, but still deficient in precise information and investigation.

The dictionary form, however, seemed to be the best for ready reference, and he thought a few examples, to show the way in which he had wrought out the names, would be of service to those who are interested in this important study. Hence it came about that this work has gradually grown until it assumes its present proportions.

The chief object has been to avoid anything like guess-work or fancy interpretation, and to seek for a definition among such sources as seemed likely to supply it, so that, when a word could not be referred to any reasonable origin, it was put on the shelf until time, experience, and discovery should verify it.

Besides the works of reference which he consulted, he found it necessary to prepare, for his own use, the lists of names already mentioned, and these have been of so much service that he trusts they will be found equally available for all those who wish to enter upon this arduous but fascinating task. They will certainly be more readily turned over now they are in type than when in manuscript.

In addition to these he has examined directories and maps of Great Britain, Norway, Sweden, Denmark, Holland, Flanders, Germany, Normandy, etc.

Many a name that seemed to defy all explanation was found to be that of some obscure village, so disguised as to be almost past recognition. Who, for instance, would expect to see Sevenoaks in Snooks, St. Olave's Street in Tooley Street, St. Etheldreda in Tawdry, Douglas in Diggles, Wilburgham in Wilbraham, Tuberville in Troublefield, Longueville in Longfellow, Longchamps in Longshanks, Blondeville in Blomfield, Adburgham in Abraham and Abram, Renshaw in Wrencher and Wrinch, Wymondham in Wyndham?

Indeed, as Mr. Lower truly says:

'Corruptions which many family names have undergone tend to baffle alike the genealogical and etymological inquirer.'

The following will serve as illustrations of the corruption to which names are liable. The family name of Weewall (N. *Vifill*, D. *Wivel*) occurs frequently in the parish register of Peckleton, Leicestershire, and between 1735 and 1750 there are many variations of the spelling, scarcely two entries being alike. It appears as Whewaugh, Whewvaugh, Wheevaw, Weway, Weewaa, Wheewhal, Whewwhaw, Whealwhal, Weewal, Wheelwall. In the North of England it took the form of Whewell.

The name of the great English dramatist is generally spelt Shakespeare, but there are many ways of spelling the name according to English orthography. Here are a few of them as appearing in old documents: Shakspere, Shaxpere, Shakspire, Shaxspere, Schaksper, Shakespere, Shakspeare, Schakespeyr, Shaxespeare, Shagspere, Shaxpur, Shaxsper, Shaksper, Shackspeare, Saxpere, Shakespire, Shakespeire, Shackespeare, Shakaspear, Shaxper, Shakspear, Shaxpeare, Shakspeere, Shaxbure, Shackspeyr, Shakespear, Schakesper, etc.

Goodwin is found in ancient documents as Godden, Goddin, Goddinge, Godewyn, Godin, Godwin, Godwyn, Goodden, Gooding, Goodyng, Gooden, Goodwen, Goodinge, Goodwin, Goodwyn, Goodwyne.

Bugge as Buci, de Bougy, de Bucy, Bugi, Boci, Bogge, Busse, Boge, Buggey, Bussey, Bogg, Boag, Boake, Bogue, Beucy, Beucey, Boogie, Buggy, Buggie, Bukie, Bouky, Boog, etc.

Mr. W. P. Phillimore, M.A., B.C.L., in 'Notes on Finnimore, Phillimore, and their Allied Surnames,' gives fifty-nine different ways of spelling the former, and thirty-four of the latter surname.

BRITISH SURNAMES.

'This is a subject which involves many curious questions of antiquarian interest, bearing upon the language, habits and pursuits of our countrymen in bygone days. It is one, also, that immediately concerns every man who feels an honest pride in being called by his father's name.'—*Notes and Queries*, vi. 201.

'To find out the true originall of surnames is full of difficulty.'—CAMDEN.

MUCH speculation has arisen as to the date when surnames were first used in this country. It is now pretty well admitted that they began to be adopted about A.D. 1000.

According to Lower, the practice commenced in Normandy, and gradually extended itself to this country; but the use of surnames was occasionally hereditary among the Anglo-Saxons before the Conquest, and the general adoption of family designations.

He quotes from a document referred to in Sharon Turner's 'History of the Anglo-Saxons as existing among the Cottonian MSS.' (No. 1,356 in Cod. Dipl.), bearing no date, but undoubtedly earlier than 1066.

It states that

'Hwita Hatte was a keeper of bees at Hœthfelda, and Tate Hatte, his daughter, was the mother of Wulsige, the shooter; and Lulle Hatte, the sister of Wulsige, Helstan had for his wife in Wealadene. Wifus and Dunne and Seolce were born in Hœthfelda. Duding Hatte, the son of Wifus, is settled at Wealadene; and Ceolmund Hatte, the son of Dunne, is also settled there; and Ætheleah Hatte, the son of Seolce, is also there; and Tate Hatte, the sister of Cenwald, Mæg hath for his wife at Weligan; and Ealdelm, the son of Herethrythe, married the daughter of Tate. Werlaff Hatte, the father of Werstan, was the rightful owner of Hœthfelda.'

In the time of King Edward the Confessor there was among the Saxon tenants in Suffolk one Leuric Hobbesune. Suert Magno or Manni, Godric Poinc, Tedricus Pointel, Siuuard Rufus, Stigand Soror also occur.

At the time of the Domesday Survey they were becoming more numerous, for both the tenants-in-chief and the under tenants possessed them. Thus we find Alwin Dodesune, Godric Cratel, William Goizenboded, William Hosed, Hugo Lasne, Walter Achet, Osmund Angevin, Roger Arundel, Bernard Barb, Walter Bec, Hugo Bolebec, William Bonvaslet, Aluin Coc (bedellus), William Denomore, Roger Deramis, etc.

Various writers have treated the subject of British surnames in different ways from Camden and Lower downwards. Some have produced very amusing articles by grouping the most extraordinary names they coul find together, as the names of birds, beasts, flowers, objects in common use, trades, etc.

A few have made some attempts to give the derivations of well-known names according to their own classification, ignoring altogether the possibility of many being traced to extremely ancient sources.

Names which betoken association with territorial possession and occupations, and Christian names also, are not difficult to distinguish ; but the oldest names of all are those which belong to the Norse or Frisian settlers, except such as are probably of Celtic or British origin.

It is a well-known fact that many family names are peculiar to certain localities, where they have remained for many generations, as can be proved from the old church registers. The spread of railways and the increased facilities for locomotion in every way are fast altering the old state of things, however, especially where there is a sudden development of one or more local industries, causing a great influx of strangers.

In remote country places, and particularly in agricultural districts, many of the old family names still remain—some, indeed, are seldom found in any other part of England.

In one district in England a marked peculiarity in the names of the people exists. This is known as the Danish Settlement (Danalagh), which, by agreement between Alfred and Guthrum, renewed by Edmund and Anlaf in 941, was divided from the Saxon kingdom by a line passing along the Thames, the Lea and the Ouse, following the course of Watling Street, the old Roman road running in a straight line from London by Stony Stratford to Chester.

Here, as might be expected, is a strong Norse element, and this distinction is more clearly marked the further east one goes from this line, as the names have not undergone the modification so often found in the west, since in many cases the original Scandinavian form prevails.

The family nomenclature of this part of the country undoubtedly requires particular treatment. It is not surprising, therefore, to discover many personal names, either of pure Norse patronymics or of places or qualities.

In East Anglia there is one remarkable peculiarity about the family names. A large proportion of them are monosyllabic. This singularity is so striking that it forces itself upon the most casual observer. Perhaps it is owing to the large infusion of names of Dutch and Flemish origin.

Moreover, strangely enough, the local pronunciation of names of persons and places has long outlived the many orthographical changes which took place in our written language while men spelt words phonetically, or as fancy dictated. Accordingly we find in old records, from Domesday Book to later times, some strange variations, in some cases making the derivation from the original source by no means easy.

All this is very interesting to the student of British surnames, who looks at the subject, not on the humorous side only, but in its historical, etymological, ethnological, and topographical aspect.

The language—dialect if preferred—of the North of England is to this day full of words and expressions which can only be explained by the help of the Icelandic as the representative of the old Northern languages spoken by the Scandinavian settlers in England. The colonization of

Iceland was included in that stream of emigration which began to leave Norway A.D. 852, and spread along the coasts of Normandy, England, Ireland, and Scotland up to the end of the eleventh century. For about four hundred years afterwards the old Norse tongue was locked up in that remarkable Northern island, and preserved almost incorrupt, while the mother country became affected and its original language considerably modified by contact with other European nations.

In a sort of Domesday Book, compiled by the authorities in Iceland (Islands Landnámá-bók), there was, among other matters recorded and deposited in the cathedral of Reykyavik, a roll of the names of the original settlers (of which perhaps a third are women) and the lands they occupied, making about five thousand proper names.

This remarkable document, which has been preserved, throws great light upon the derivation of many personal and local names in Scotland and Northern England hitherto considered to be obscure, and it is as necessary to the antiquary as the so-called 'Roll of Battell Abbey' or the Domesday Book of the Conqueror. It is, in fact, the chief storehouse for genealogical knowledge.

The study of the Icelandic in its relation to old and provincial English and its comparison with Swedish, Norwegian, Danish, Frisian, Flemish, and German, has opened out a wonderful field of never-ending interest, and made us acquainted with things we never before dreamed of in connection with this subject.

In the course of his researches the writer has picked up a few odds and ends of information which may perhaps be useful to others. It is possible to derive some instruction and to extract no little amusement from the carrying out of a train of speculation on the origin of names, so, if these details appear somewhat dry, it is to be hoped they will be set down as a humble effort to deal as carefully with a special and difficult subject as the nature of the materials within reach and limited qualifications for the task will permit of. It may appear to some, possibly, that the importance of the old Norse has been over-estimated, and not enough credit given to the Anglo-Saxon.

Perhaps it is so; but, besides the names of places, it must be admitted that very many modern English words show early Northern influence, and even in Anglo-Saxon times the language was so blended with Scandinavian words that there were often double expressions for the same thing. The fact is, we have no reliable Anglo-Saxon dictionary. No one can say with authority what the Anglo-Saxon language really was in its earliest stage, what it afterwards became when a great infusion of Scandinavian words was thrown into it, and what it was as it degenerated into Semi-Saxon after the conquest.*

It seems clear that the Frisian dialect of the Low German gives the best idea of the original so-called Anglo-Saxon, for it is the modern representative of the language of old Dutch Friesland, whence so many of those who settled in England (after the departure of the Romans) came.

This appears to be borne out by the fact that the early English missionaries (notably St. Boniface) made their way to that country because

* Taylor's 'Words and Places.'

it was the home of their fathers, and there was no more difficulty with the language than in the case of a citizen of the United States visiting Britain.

It will be seen that even at this early period names were derived from localities, occupations, personal and mental qualities and peculiarities as nicknames, social relations, etc. Further, in common with the Teutonic races, the Norse used diminutives, or pet names, which afterwards stuck to the individuals so designated and became family names.

The terminations ing, kin, and son, so common in English names, are derived from the Norse *ingr*, *kyn*, and *sonr*, the *r* being dropped in compounds. The Danish make the last *sen*. Also *kyn* must not be confounded with the diminutive-endings: Germ., *chen;* Fris., *ken* and *ke;* Flem., *kin;* which have quite a different meaning and are used in pet names chiefly.

The diminutives, Frisian, ken, ke, ock, and cock;* Norman French, et, ette, let, ot, otte, ell; Old Norse, i, a, ki, ka, gi, ga, ungr, ingr, lingr, should be noted.

Let us then apply the test of the old world sources to the family names of this country, comparing them in the first instance with those of the Northern nations, the Scandinavians (Danes so called), the Frisians (*i.e.*, Saxons), the Old English (Anglo-Saxon) in Domesday Book, and, in the second place, with existing names in Northern Germany, Sweden, Denmark, Normandy, Holland, and Flanders.

In addition to these quarries, which the writer will endeavour to work, it may be mentioned that there are many names which clearly bear the stamp of foreign origin and have not yet been so entirely metamorphosed but that their Continental source may be discovered. An Act of the Irish Parliament (5 Edw. IV., c. 3, A.D. 1465) ordained that every Irishman dwelling betwixt or amongst Englishmen in the counties of Dublin, Myeth, Vriel, and Kildare, should dress like Englishmen and take an English surname, of a town (as Sutton, Chester, etc.), or colour (as white, black), or art (as smith, carpenter, etc.), or office (as cook or butler), and he and his issue should use the same under a specified penalty. Thus, O'Gowan became Smith and MacIntyre Carpenter, etc. Most surnames will be found to come under one or other of the following heads:

1. Nicknames.
2. Clan or tribal names.
3. Place-names.
4. Official names.
5. Trade names.
6. Christian names.
7. Foreign names.
8. Foundling names.

* There has been much controversy over the termination 'cock.' It appears to be derived from the Frisian *gök* or *kök*, a foolish, silly, awkward person, hence the Scotch *gowk*. The Fris. *Jankök* (Johncock) is equivalent to the German *Hans Wurst*. At first applied to children as a check to thoughtlessness, it would become gradually used as a diminutive. *Cock* and *ock* are akin to *ke*.

I.—Nicknames.

'You had not your name for nothing.'—*Old Proverb.*

Unquestionably the oldest names of all are those derived from by-names, given on account of a strong peculiarity of figure, feature, or character, deed of prowess, eccentricity of dress, speech or carriage.

Among primitive nations the slightest deviation from the ordinary course of life or difference among his fellows was enough to mark a man, especially where a striking cognomen was readily applied. Fleetness of foot, a mighty hunter, skill in the use of a particular weapon, or the very opposite, gave rise to a name implying praise or contempt. Indeed, the most trifling cause served to invent a title by which a man was distinguished from his contemporaries. When King Magnus assumed the Highland dress he became known as Berbeinn (Bareleg) among his followers, and this is preserved to us in the modern though Puritan-sounding Barebones.

A man became notorious on account of a fearful scar upon his leg, hence he was called Orra-beinn (Scar-leg), which we see in Horrabin to this day.

In the Orkneys the Norse earl Einar gained the *soubriquet* of 'Turf-Einar' (Torf-Einarr) from having taught the Norsemen to dig peat, he having probably learnt it himself from the Gaelic tribes in Scotland.

Blund and Blunt (Blunðr, dozing, slumber), Brock (Bróki), Hannay (Hani, a cock), Hacker and Harker (Hákr), Harfoot (Héra-fotr, a Danish king), Read, Reader (Hreðr), Rell (Hrella), Rooke (Hrúkr), Root (Hrútr), Hook (Húkr), Carter (Köttr, a cat), Kemp, Camp, (Kampi, a champion), Capps, Capper (Kappi), Kitchen (Kikini), Kimber (Kimbi), Cropper (Kroppr), Maxey (Maxi), Masey, Macey (Mási), Monk (Munki), Orry (Orri, a moor fowl), Peak, Pick (Pík), Payne (Peini), Ramm (Ramr, strong), Spurr (Spörr, a sparrow), Stott (Stoti, foolish), Sandys (Sandi), Sellers, Sell (Selr, a seal), Silver (Silfri), Strong (Strangi), Scarth (Scarði, hare-lip), Skinner (Skinni), Scory (Skorri), Skeat, Skett (Skyti, a marksman, a shooter), Stubbs (Stubbi), Syers, Siers (Syr), Young (Ungi) Horrocks, (Örrek) are familiar names derived from old Norse nicknames.

Among these also may be classed pet names. In girls Sigga from Sig-riðr, Gunna from Guð-run, Inga from Ing-unn, Imba from Ingi-björg, Gudda from Guð-riðr, etc.

In boys Siggi from Sig-urðr, Gvendr from Guð-mundr, Simbi from Sig-mundr, Brynki from Bryn-jólfr, Steinki from Stein-grimr, Mangi from Magnus, etc.

A list of these will be found in the appendix to the Norse names.

Of later date may be mentioned that of Fortescue, said to have been bestowed on Sir Richard le Fort, one of the leaders of the Conqueror's army at the Battle of Hastings, who had the good fortune to protect his chief by bearing before him the *escue*, or shield.

The name of Plantagenet, borne by eight successive kings of England, originated with Fulke or Foulques, Count of Anjou, about the twelfth century, who went on a pilgrimage to Jerusalem, and wore in his helmet, as a mark of his humility, a piece of *planta genista*, or broom. Armstrong and Strongitharm arose from some feat of strength; Santerer was one who had been to the Holy Land (Sainte Terre); Romer, one who had been to Rome; Palmer, a pilgrim, etc.

Again, Applejohn, Brownjohn, Littlejohn, Micklejohn, Prettyjohn, Properjohn, Upjohn, etc., are probably of this class. The French have Beaujean, Bonjean, Grandjean, Grosjean, Henryjean, Klinjean, Mallejean, Neujean, Petitjean.

II.—Clan or Tribal Names.

'My foot is on my native heath and my name is MacGregor.'—Scott.

According to the Rev. Dr. Todd:

'Clan signifies children or descendants. The tribe being descended from a common ancestor, the chieftain, as the representative of that ancestor, was regarded as the common father of the clan, and they as his children.'

The Gaelic *Mac*, the Irish *O'*, the British *Ap*, the Norse *ungar*, the Frisian *ingar* and *en*, the Anglo-Saxon *ing*, the Norman *Fitz*,* are all indications of a family name.

'By Mac and O you'll always know
True Irishmen, they say;
But if they lack both "O," and "Mac,"
No Irishmen are they.'

The ancient tribe of Waring or Wearing, the Vœringi or Veringen, originally from what is still called the Vœringifjord in Norway, formed the celebrated Varangian Guard of the Byzantine Emperors, which was afterwards recruited largely from the North, and especially from Britain.

The following list, compiled from that excellent work, 'Words and Places,' by the Rev. Isaac Taylor, will be found to contain ancient Scandinavian and Frisian family names, with the Old English or Anglo-Saxon suffix.

A reference to and comparison with the Icelandic names of the Landnámábók and the Saxon tenants of Domesday Book will prove of great assistance to the reader.

Mr. Taylor points out settlements of these families in England, Normandy, and Germany.

A.

Ading	Arring	Æcling	Æscing
Aldring	Arting	Æfing	Æscling
Anning	Æbing	Ælcing	Æsling
Anting	Æbling	Æling	Æting
Arling			

* Verstegan is of opinion that the prefix Fitz originated in Flanders. It is remarkable that it is now unknown in France, and that it does not occur in the ancient chronicles of that country (Noble).

The generally accepted idea is that it is derived from the Latin *filius*, Fr. *fils*, old Norman Fr. *filz*, *fiz*, *fitz*. It has been used to distinguish the illegitimate children of kings and princes of royal blood. Many Irish families substituted Fitz for Mac in Norman times.

B.

Bæbing
Bæding
Bædling
Bæling
Bafing
Basing
Beccing
Belling
Belting
Benning
Beofing
Beoring
Beorling
Beorning
Berling
Bermating
Berring
Bessing
Billing
Bing
Birling
Bitering
Bobbing
Bocing
Bofing
Boling
Bonding
Bonning
Bosing
Brahcing
Branting
Bressing
Brimming
Brisling
Briting
Bucing
Buding
Bulling
Burring
Busling

C.

Cæding
Cæssing
Calling
Camering
Ceading
Ceadling
Cearling
Cenning
Cerring
Cofing
Colling
Coping
Coring
Cressing
Cridling
Cubing
Culling
Cylling
Cyrtling

D.

Darting
Dæfing
Dælling
Dedding
Deming
Diceling
Didding
Dilling
Dinning
Dinting
Dissing
Docing
Doding
During
Dycing

E.

Eadling
Eagling
Eardling
Earming
Eberding
Eding
Efing
Elcing
Elling
Elming
Elring
Emming
Eoring
Eorping
Epping
Ercensing
Essing
Etting

F.

Ferring. *See* Wæring
Feorming
Finning
Freling
Frescing
Fresting
Frilling
Fring
Fyling

G.

Garling
Gæging
Gedding
Gestinge
Gilling
Ging
Gipping
Gisling
Gystling

H.

Halling
Haning
Hæding
Hæfering
Hæsling
Hæssing
Hæsting
Hearding
Hearing
Helling
Helveling
Heming
Hensing
Heoring
Hereling
Hiceling
Hocing
Horing
Huding
Hunding
Huning

I.

Iceling
Ifing
Illing
Ipping
Iring
Ising
Isling

L.

Læcing
Læfering
Leafing
Leasing
Leding
Ledring
Lidling
Ling
Locing
Loding
Lofing
Lulling

M.

Malling
Manning
Mæding
Mægling
Mæring
Mæssing
Mæting
Mecing
Melling
Milling
Mincing
Minting
Molling
Motting
Mutling

N.

Næcing
Nolling
Nyding

O.

Ofing

P.

Pæccing
Pæfing
Pælling
Pæting
Pætring
Penning
Petling
Poling
Porning

R.

Ræding
Ratling
Renning
Ricing
Ricling
Rifing
Rilling
Rimming
Ripling
Rising
Rocing
Roding
Rowing
Rusting

S.

Sandling
Sæling
Seafing
Sealfing
Secging
Sepping
Serring
Sceacling
Sceading
Sceaning
Scearing
Sceding
Sinning
Sulling
Swanning
Swefeling
Sycling
Sydling
Syfing

T.

Tæting
Teorling
Ting
Toding
Torting
Tring

U.

Uffing
Uling
Upping

V.

Veorling (Feorling).

W.

Wading
Wælsing
Wæpling
Wæring
Wealding
Wealdring
Wealing
Wedering
Wendling
Weording
Wiccing
Wickling
Wipping
Wiscing
Witling
Witting

III.—Place-names.

'A local habitation and a name.'—*Midsummer Night's Dream.*

It was the custom of the Norsemen and the Saxons to give their names to the lands upon which they settled.

Hence it is that so many towns and villages in England as well as in Normandy show the name of the original occupier who appropriated the soil by right of conquest, and the prefix generally is found in the possessive case common to all Teutonic nations.

After the Norman Conquest the followers of William, among whom the land was divided, adopted the title of the manor or estate granted to them by the king.

These afterwards became their family names.

Ivo de Taillebois was made Baron of Kendal, but his descendant, William, assumed the style of de Lancaster. Robert de Tours became Robert de Lowick from his English estate, as, in like manner, William le Fleming was William de Aldingham from his lordship of that manor, and Nigel, younger son of Robert de Statford, inheriting the manor of Gresley, in the county of Derby, took the name and was known as Nigel de Gresley. This last family is one of the very few remaining of those who have retained their lands since the Conquest.

It is very likely that in after-years change of residence was usually the cause of the bestowal of the original abode as a surname.

About the fourteenth century another way of adopting place-names sprung up, as is seen from the registers of wills at Lincoln and other cities.

The word 'atte,' as implying residence, if not possession, crept in, and thereby arose such names as Atte Boure, Atte Brigg, Atte Hash, Atte Hay, Atte Kirkstile, Atte Lane, Atte Maydens, Atte Stile, Atte Well.

William Atwater was Bishop of Lincoln in 1574.

In course of time the *de* and the *atte* were dropped, as the persons using them lost their estates or changed their place of abode; but retaining the surname, they wandered into various parts of the country as fancy or necessity led them.

Hence it happens that many extraordinary surnames, which have been a puzzle to investigators hitherto, and almost defy derivation, are found to be traceable to some obscure spot in Great Britain or France.

It used to be said that

'In ham and by and ford and tun
Most of English suroames run.'

But it is only a partial statement, as we know. Also the old saw,

'By tre, pol, and pen,
Ye shall know the Cornishmen,'

is true as far as it goes, for many other local names in that county have given names to families.

Names derived from localities are more common in England and Scotland than in Wales and Ireland.

IV.—Official Names.

'I am become a name.'—Tennyson.

When the country became settled under Edward the Confessor, and the Norsemen, Saxon, and Welsh lived together with something like a suspension of their international feuds, the land was brought into a semblance of law and order, and, consequently, offices of influence and responsibility arose.

Bright, Steward, and Despencer are names of this period. They all mean the same thing. *Brýti* is the Norse and Dispensator the Latin equivalent of Steward.

Lagman (lawgiver), Fawcett (Forseti, judge), Alderman, Reeve, Sheriff, Tabberer (Tabarðr, a Tabard), Chamberlain (Camerarius), Chancellor (Canceler), Chaplain (Capellanus), Clerk (Clericus), Deacon (Diaconus), Beadle (Bedellus), Latimer (Latinarius, or interpreter), Miles (Miles, a soldier), Marshall (Marescal), Redman (Radman), Sumner or Somner (Chaucer's Sompnoure, a summoner or apparitor), Poynder (a bailiff), Parker (Park-keeper), Palliser (Park-pailings keeper), Franklin (a freeholder), Vavasour or Valvasour* (an office or dignity below a baron and above a knight), Arblaster (Balistarius), Botiler (Butler), etc.

V.—Trade Names.

'A rose by any other name would smell as sweet.'—*Othello.*

As might be expected, a man's occupation gave him notoriety, especially if he were skilled in his handicraft.

Even among primitive nations there seems to have been a tendency to adopt this mode of distinguishing an artificer by his calling.

The Norse *Skapti,* originally a shaft-maker, became a nickname, and afterwards a personal name as Scapti and Scafti, the Scotch form of which is Shafto. *Sneypir,* a snipper, gives us Snepp and Snape; *Dengir,* one who whets, Dangar, Danger, Dunger; *Kembir,* a comber, Kimber, Kimball, Kimbell, Kemble.

In Domesday Book occur Arbalistarius (a crossbowman), Aurifaber (goldsmith), Arcuarius (bowyer), Artifex (workman), Accipitrarius (falconer), Cocus (cook), Carpentarius, Censorius, Cubicularius (groom of the chamber), Dapifer (a server), Faber (smith), Forestarius, Harparius, Hostarius (ostler?), Ingeniator, Joculator, Larderius, Lorimarius (bridlemaker), Monialis, Machinator, Medicus, Porcarius (swineherd), Piscator (fisher), Pincerna (butler), Portarius (porter), Stalrus, Staller (groom), Stirman, Scutularius (page), Scriba, Tonsor, Venator (huntsman).

In Old English times we find, according to Lower, Massinger (Fr., Massager, a messenger), Pottinger (apothecary), Brownsmith (a maker of 'brown bills'?) Nasmith (nail-smith?), Ferrier and Farrier (horse-shoer),

* The Norman kings had an officer who kept ward at the entrances and borders of the realm, *ad valvas Regni.*

Jenner (joiner), Furner (Fr., Fournier, a baker), Lavender (Fr., Lavandier, a washerman), Pullinger (Fr., Boulanger, a baker), Pointer (a maker of 'points,' an obsolete article of dress), Pilcher (a maker of pilches, the great coat of the fourteenth century), Shearman and Sharman (one who shears worsteds, fustians, etc.—a 'cutter'?), Caird (a travelling tinker), Maunder (a beggar), Kidder and Kidman (a pedlar; N., *Kyta*, to hawk, deal), Crowther (one who plays upon the crowd; Welsh, *crwth*, a rude sort of violin), Arkwright (a maker of meal-chests?), Polter and Pulter (poulterer), etc.

It is open to question, however, whether some of the names popularly ascribed to occupations, such as Baker, Barber, Beadle, Botwright, Butcher, Carter, Cartwright, Cooper, Carver, Collier, Driver, Dyer, Glaisher, Iremonger, Packer, Painter, Pinder, Pointer, Plummer, Potter, Poulter, Plowright, Nailer, Osler, Sharman, Shearman, Sheppard, Skinner, Walker, Wheeler, Warrener, Tanner, Tinker, Tucker, Turner, Tyler, etc., will not bear a different interpretation. The reader is invited to study these names in their proper places.

VI.—Christian Names.

'What is your name?'—*Tempest*, Act III., Sc. 1.

When Christianity spread among the northern nations in the eleventh century, a baptismal name followed as a matter of course, and for a long time was the only one possessed by the individual upon whom it was conferred. Thus John, Peter, and Paul were great favourites, and those who were named in this way transmitted the Christian name to their descendants, who became know as Janson, Johnson, Peterson, Patterson, Polson, etc. (N. sonr, pl. synir.). In Wales and Cornwall, as well as in Flanders, the final *s* alone served to mark the fact that it had become a patronymic.

Of these names there are also many diminutives and modifications, as Jon, Ion, Jan, Jane, Jennis, Jenner, Jenkin, Jinks. In like manner we find Pete, Peet, Pate, Pett, Pitt, Pittar. Also Paul, Spaull, Powell, Pull, Pulley, Powley, Pollyn, Poll, Pole, Pullein, Pulleyne, Poole, etc.

VII.—Foreign Names.

I cannot tell what the dickens his name is.'—*Merry Wives of Windsor*, Act III., Sc. 2.

Some of these are undoubtedly Norman, others are more recent, and may presumably be set down to Huguenot and other refugee emigrants, or to the influx of followers of the Orange or Hanoverian Dynasties.

It is well known, moreover, that many French prisoners of war during the reign of George III. married or formed other ties during their captivity, and when peace was restored, remained in this country. To these may be added those who have been attracted to Great Britain by greater facilities of trade, or more political or individual liberty than they found at home.

Many names bear a close resemblance to such as are at present existing in the North of Germany and in the Low Countries—a large number, indeed, being very little changed.

The question arises, Are they direct importations, or are they derived through Frisian sources?

There is no doubt about many Frisian names having spread along the southern shore of the Baltic, for the prevalence of the diminutive 'ke,' in contradistinction to the German 'chen,' is transparently obvious. Nevertheless, there are many of them patronymics which are difficult to trace, either through the Frisian, or from those of ancient Scandinavia as found in Iceland.

Further research may possibly throw more light upon this interesting but complicated subject.

Of these foreign names many have become naturalized in this country. The earliest instances occur among the Norman tenants-in-chief in Domesday Book.

Those of more recent times will be readily distinguished as Aufrere, Beauchamp, Caux, Drew, Durrant, Frere, Grand, Jacques, Le Neve, Motte, Pettit, Roche, Sant, Vipond, etc.

VIII.—Foundling Names.

'Phœbus, what a name!'—Byron.

There is every reason to believe that we are indebted to the parish beadle and the workhouse officials for many extraordinary and even ridculous names which cannot be derived from any known sources. They have been evolved from the imagination of the bumbles of a past generation, as Charles Dickens shows us in 'Oliver Twist,' and they remain a puzzle to all who would attempt to clear them up, unless they are clăssed in this section.

Indeed, it is a convenience to have a receptacle of this sort in which to stow away, until further research comes to our aid, such names as philologists cannot yet account for, except upon the supposition that the ingenuity of the public servants has suggested them. Some of those which have been a source of wonder to many for a long time, and were supposed to be foundling names, can now be shown to possess a real historical signification.

Possibly, by-and-by, more may be rescued, but in the meantime they must be classified somehow, and it is better to put them on the unknown list rather than invent a fanciful origin which may be, after all, mere guess-work.

That there was a custom of naming foundling children after the parishes where they have been picked up is proved by the entries in the registers of several of the London City churches. Nicholas Acons, after the parish of that name, and Benetfink, Orgar, Sherehog, with many others, exist as surnames which may be all traced to this source. Other stray children have been named from the circumstances under which they were found.

Under the signature of 'Peter Lombard,' a writer in the *Church Times* has recently drawn attention to the registers of St. Mary Woolnoth where are these entries: 'A male child was found in our parish with a penny in his hand, and was named accordingly Henry Penny.' 'A child found in the alley between the church and the stocks on the morning of St. John's Day was named John Before Day.'

A girl who was so picked up was christened Anne Monday, after the day of the week, and a boy who was laid 'atte Mr. Garrett's dore' was christened 'John Bynight.'

Lower gives, among other instances, Jack Parish, Tom Among-us, and Napkin Brooker as the names bestowed by the parish authorities on foundlings. The last-mentioned, it is stated, was found by the side of a brook, tied up in a napkin.

Allbone (from Holborn ?) and such names as Lilywhite and Sweetapple may belong perhaps to this category.

A lady sends that of a family named Haycock. She was told that the father was found as an infant deserted under a haycock. The name is not uncommon, and may be otherwise accounted for. There is a hill in Cumberland called Haycock, and Hayo and Heie are Frisian personal names, to which may be added the diminutive 'cock.'

Indeed, Heij-Koch is a Dutch proper name.

Abbreviations.

N. Old Norse (Icelandic), S. Swedish, D. Danish, F. Frisian, Dch. Dutch, Fl. Flemish, Fr. French, G. German, A.S. Anglo-Saxon, D.B. Domesday Book, p.n. personal name, n.n. nickname, loc. n. local name.

LISTS OF ANCIENT PATRONYMICS.

OLD NORSE PERSONAL NAMES

FROM ISLANDS LANDNÁMA-BÓK (THE ICELANDIC BOOK OF SETTLEMENT) AND OTHER SOURCES.

A.

Abraham (Bp.)
Adam
Aðisl
Aðrianus
Afvaldr
Agnar
Agni
Aistein
Albert
Aldis (f.)
Alexius
Álfarinn
Álfdis (f.)
Álfeiðr (f.)
Álfgeirr
Álfgerðr (f.)
Álfjótr or Ulfjótr
Álfr
Álfarekkar or Halfrekkar
Áli
Alrekr
Álöf (f.)
Ámundi
Án
Áni
Anti-cristr
Are (Ari)
Arinbjörn
Armoðr
Arnaldr
Arnbjörg
Arnbjörn
Arndis (f.)
Arneiðr (f.)
Arnfinnr
Arnfriðr (f.)
Arngeirr
Arngerðr (f.)
Arngrimr
Arngunnr
Arnhaldr. *See* Arnaldr
Árni
Arnis
Arnkatla (f.)
Arnkel
Arnlaug (f.)
Arnlaugr
Arnleif
Arnljótr
Arnmoðr
Arnoddr
Arnóra (f.)
Arnórr
Arnriðr
Arnsteinn
Arnþjófr
Arnþóra. *See* Arnóra
Arnþórr. *See* Arnórr
Arnðruðr (f.)
Arun
Ása. *See* Æsa
Ásbera (f.)
Ásbjarnarsynir
Ásbjörg (f.)
Ásbjörn
Ásborg (Asbjörg)
Ásbrandr
Ásdis (f.)
Ásgautr
Ásgeirr
Ásgerðr (f.)
Ásgrimr
Áshildr (f.)
Ási
Áskell, n.n.
Askr
Áslákr, n.n.
Áslaug (f.)
Ásleif (f.)
Ásleikr
Ásmóðr
Ásmundr
Ásný (f.)
Ásolfr
Ásrauðr
Ásta (f.)
Ástriðr (f.)
Ásvaldr
Ásvarðr
Ásvör (f.)
Atli
Audolfr
Audr (f.)
Auðunn
Aun
Aungull
Aunundr. *See* Önundr
Aurlyger. *See* Örlygr
Auzor. *See* Özur
Ásvaldi
Ávaldr
Ávangr

From other sources.

Aðils. *A.S.* Eadgils (a king)
Akra-carl, cogn. (field-carle, ploughman)
Akra-spillir, cogn. (destroyer of fields)
Ali-karl, n.n. (fat carle)
Amb-höfði, n.n. *See* Hjart-höfði (hart-head), Orkn-höfði (seal-head)
Amloði (Hamlet)
Angan-tyr, p.n. *A.S.* Ongentheow
Aska-spillir, cogn. (a pirate)
Auðr, f. p.n.
Auðunn, p.n. *A.S.* Eâðvin (a charitable friend)
Aust-rænn, n.n. (a Scandinavian)

B.

Baldvini
Bálki
Barbara
Bardi
Bardr
Bárekr
Barna, n.n.
Baugr, n.n.
Baugssynir
Beda
Beinir
Beiskaldi
Bekan (Gaelic)
Bera (f.)
Berðlu, n.n.
Bergðis (f.)
Bergljót (f.)
Bergr
Bergþora (f.)
Bergþor
Bersi
Bjaðmakr (Gaelic)
Bjálfi
Bjargey (f.)
Bjarnaðr
Bjarneyja
Bjarnharðr
Bjarnheðin
Bjarni
Bjarnvarðr. *See* Bjarnharðr
Bjartmarr
Bifra, n.n.
Bjolan (Gaelic)
Bjólfr
Bjollok (f.), (Gaelic)
Birna (f.)
Birningr
Birtingr
Bitru, n.n.
Björg
Björn
Björnolfr
Blá-kinn
Blígr
Blót-már
Blund-Ketill
Blundr, n.n.
Blæingr
Bogi
Bolli
Borgillðr (f.)
Bót
Bótey (f.)
Bótolf
Bragi
Brandax
Brandi
Brandr
Brandönundr
Brattr
Braut-Önundr (Svia-Konungr)
Breidar-Skeggi
Breidr
Brennu-Kári
Bresasynir
Bresi
Briann or Brann (Gaelic)
Bryngerðr
Brynhildr (f.)
Brynjólfr
Brodd-Helgi
Broddi
Broddr
Brunda-Bjalfi
Bruni
Brunólfr
Brúsi
Bröndólfr
Budli
Burislafr
Bægifótr
Bödmóðr
Bódólfr
Bödvarr
Böggvir
Bölverkr
Börkr

From other sources.

Bak-skiki, cogn. (back-flap)
Barka-bazi, cogn.
Berbeinn, cogn. (bare-legged)
Beiskaldi, n.n.
Beit-stokkr, cogn.
Beli, cogn.
Berseker, n.n.
Bersi, p.n. (bear)
Bifr, cogn. (beaver)
Birtingr, n.n.
Bitra, cogn.
Blá-ber, cogn.
Blá-hattr, cogn.
Blá-siða, cogn.
Blá-tönn, cogn. (blue tooth)
Blígr, cogn. (staring)
Blunðr, cogn. (dozing)
Bog-sveigr, cogn. (bow-swayer)
Bófi, n.n. (knave)
Bragi, p.n.
Brák, n.n.
Brimstein, n.n.
Brikar-nef, n.n.
Bróki, n.n.
Bryti, p.n. (steward)
Bulla-fótr, p.n.

Buttr, p.n.
Buttraldi, p.n.
Bui. *D.* Boye ; *Icl.* Bogi
Bægi-fótr, cogn. (lame foot)
Boðvildr
Böggull, n.n. (a little bag)
Böl-viss, n.n. (detestable)

C.

Carlsefui
Cecilia (f.)
Christophor. *See* Kristofr
Colbeinn
Colr. *See* Kolr

D.

Dadi
Dagr
Dagrun
Dagstyggr
Dala-alfr
Dala-kollr = Hof-kolli (?)
Dalkr
Dalla (f.)
Darri
Digr-Ormr
Dís. *See* Dýs
Dofnakr
Dómaldr
Dómarr
Drafdritr (Gaelic)
Drafli
Drumb-Oddr
Dufan (Gaelic)
Dufnall (Gaelic
Dufniall (Gaelic)
Duf-þakr (Gaelic) = Dofnakr
Dugfus, (Gaelic Dúfgus)
Dygvi
Dýrfinnr (f.)
Dýri
Dýs (f.)

From other sources.

Dampr, p.n.
Dapi, n.n. (a fool)
Dengir, cogn. (one who whets)
Drettingr, cogn. (a loiterer)
Drótt (f.), p.n.
Dryllr, n.n.
Dyðrill or Dyrðill, n.n. (a tail)
Dyntill, cogn. (a dint)
Dytta, cogn. (a dint)

E.

Eadmund. *See* Jatmund
Edna (f.)
Egill
Eiðr
Eilífr
Einarr
Eindriði
Eireker
Eirný
Eldgrímr
Eldjárn
Elfraðr
Elina (f.)
Elliðagrimr
Endridi
Enoc
Erlendr
Erlingr (dim. of Jarl)
Erlygr
Erný (Eirný)
Erplingar
Erpr
Errubeinn
Evarr. *See* Ævarr
Exna-Þorir. *See* Yxna-Þorir
Eydis (f.)
Eyfreyðr
Eygerðr (f.)
Eyja (f.)
Eyjarr
Eyjolfr
Eylaugr
Eymundr
Eyrný (f.)
Eysteinn
Eyvindr (a jarl)
Eyvör (f.)
Eyþjófr

From other sources.

Eysill, n.n. (little ladle)

F.

Falgerðr (f.)
Falki
Fastný (f.)
Faxa-Brandr
Faxi
Feilan (Gaelic)
Fenkell
Fjarska = Fiska (?)
Fiðr
Filippus
Finna (f.)
Finnbjörn
Finnbogi
Finngeirr
Finni
Finnr
Finnvarðr
Fiska-Finnr
Fjölnir
Fjörleif (f.)

Fleinn
Flóki
Flosi
Flugu-Grimr
Foka
Fostolfr
Frayr (Freyr)
Freygerðr (f.)
Freyja. *See* Fraija
Freyleif. *See* Fjörleif
Freyer
Freysgyðlingr
Freysteinn
Freyviðr
Frið-Froði (Dana-Konungr)
Friðgerðr
Friðleifr = Odd-leifr
Friðmundr
Friðrekr (Frith-recr)
Fróði

From other sources.

Fasi, n.n.
Fisk-reki, n.n.
Fola-fótr, n.n.
Freys-goði, n.n.
Fuð-hundr, n.n.
Fugl, p.n.

G.

Galmi
Galti
Gamli
Garðar, or Garðarr
Garða-Snorri
Gaukr
Gaungu-Hrolfr
Gautr
Gautrekr
Geirbjörg (f.)
Geirhildr = Geir-riðr (f.)
Geiri
Geirlaug (f.)
Geirleifr
Geirmundr
Geirný (f.)
Geirolfr
Geirr
Geirriðr (f.)
Geirröðr
Geirsteinn
Geirþjofr
Geitir
Gellir (Gaelic)
Gerdr (f.)
Gerpir
Gestr (f.)
Gjaflaug
Gjafvaldr
Gils
Gisl
Gisli
Gisroðr
Gizur
Glædir
Glámr, or Glam-maðr, n.n.
Gleðill, n.n.
Gljómall (Gaelic)
Glíru-Halli
Glúmr
Gnupa
Góa (f.)
Goðormr-Goddi
Goðrun (f.)
Godun. *See* Jódis
Gollnir
Gormr
Gorr
Goti
Goðiscolkr (Bp.)
Goðmundr = Guðmundr
Goðröphr
Grafar-leifr
Granni
Graut
Greipr. *See* Gripr
Grelöd (f., Gaelic)
Grenjaðr
Grettir. *See* Ófeigr
Grima (f.)
Grímkell
Grímólfr
Grímr
Grimssynr
Grjótgarðr
Gripr
Gris
Gróa (f.)
Guðbjörg (f.)
Guðbrandr
Guðhormr. *See* Guttormr
Guðiskolkr. *See* Goðiscolkr
Guðlaug (f.)
Guðleif (f.)
Guðmund
Guðný (f.)
Guðriðr (f.)
Guðrikr
Guðrun (f.)
Guðröðr
Guðormr
Gufa (Gaelic)
Gufi
Gull-Þorir
Gunnarr
Gunnbjörn
Gunnhildr (f.)
Gunnlaugr
Gunnólfr
Gunnsteinn
Gunnvaldr
Gunnvör
Gunn-Þjólfr
Guttormr = Guð-hormr
Gyða (kona)
Gyðja
Gyrða

From other sources.

Galli and Gallaðr, n.n. (vicious)
Galpin, n.n. (merry fellow)
Gapa-muðr, n.n.
Geit-heðinn, p.n. (goatskin jacket)
Geit-skór, n.n.
Gellini, n.n.
Gestr, p.n.
Gisl, Gisli, p.n. by metathesis; Gils—as Þor-gils, Auð-gils, Spá-gils, Her-gils
Gleðill, n.n.
Glenna, n.n. (mummery)
Gloppa, n.n. (a big hole)
Glúmr, n.n.

Gnúpa = Gnufa, p.n.
Goddi, n.n.
Gormr, contr. of Goð-ormr. *A.S.* Guthrum
Grá-barði, cogn.
Graut-nefr, n.n.
Greifi, n.n.
Griss, n.n. (a young pig)
Gull-hjálmr, n.n. (golden helmet)
Gull-höttr, n.n. (gold hat)
Gull-knappr, n.n. (gold button)
Gull-kroppr, n.n. (gold body)
Gull-skeggr, n.n. (gold beard)
Gull-tanni, n.n. (gold tooth)
Gurpr, n.n.

H.

Hafgrimr
Hafliði
Hafljótr
Hafnar-Ormr
Hafr, n.n.
Hafrsteinn
Hafsteinn
Hafþora (f.)
Hafþorr
Hagbarðr
Haki
Hákon
Háleygar
Hálfdan (King)
Hálfr (K.)
Hálfsrekkar
Hallaðr (jarl)
Hallbera (f.)
Hallbjörg (f.)
Hallbjörn (f.)
Halldis (f.)
Halldora (f.)
Halldórr
Hallfreðr
Hallfriðr (f.
Hallgerðr (f.)
Hallgils
Hallgrima (f.)
Hallgrimr
Halli
Hallkatla
Hallkell
Hallormr
Hallr
Hallsteinn
Hallvarðr
Hallveig
Hallvör
Háls
Hamall
Hamundr
Haraldr (K.)
Hardrefr
Hárekr
Harri
Há-Snorri Oddson
Hásteinn
Haukr (bersekr)
Hávarðr
Hávarr
Heðin
Heggr
Heiðr
Heimir (jarl)
Heimlaug (f.)
Heimrekr (Bp.)
Helga (f.)
Helgi
Helgu-Steinarr
Helias
Hella-Björn
Hellu-Narfi
Herborg (f.)
Herdis (f.)
Herbrandr
Herfinnr
Hergils
Hergrimr
Hergunnr (f.)
Herjólfr
Herlaugr
Herleifr
Hermoðr
Hermundr
Herrauðr
Herriðr
Hersteinn
Hervarðr
Hertili
Hervör (f.)
Her-Þjólfr
Her-Þruðr (f.)
Hesta-Gellir
Heyjángrs-Björn
Heyjángs-Björn
Hjaldr (K.)
Hjallkárr
Hjalmgerðr (f.)
Hjalmólfr
Hjálmun-Gautr
Hjálp (kona)
Hjaltasynir
Hjalti
Hildi-björn
Hildi-brandr
Hildi-grimmr
Hildigunnr (f.)
Hildir
Hildiriðarsynir
Hildiriðr (f.)
Hildi-tannr, n.n.
Hild-ólfr
Hildr
Hjörleifr
Hjörr
Hjörtr
Hlenni
Hlif
Hlödverr
Hnaki
Hnokan (Gaelic)
Hofgarða
Hof-Kolli
Holbarki, n.n.
Hólmfastr
Hólmfriðr (f.)
Holmgaungu-Hrafu
Holmgaungu-Máni
Holmgaungu-Starri
Hólmkell
Holm-Starri
Holmsteinn
Holta-Þorir
Holti, n.n.
Hraði
Hrafn
Hrafna-Floki
Hrafnhilðr (f.)
Hrafnkell
Hrafsi
Hramn
Hrani
Hrappr
Hrefna (f.)
Hreiðarr
Hreinn
Hrifla
Hringr
Hríseyjar
Hrisi, n.n.
Hróaldr-hryggr
Hróarr
Hróðgeirr
Hróðmarr
Hróðný (f.)
Hróðólfr (Bp.)
Hroi
Hrojn, n.n.

Hrólfr
Hrollaugr
Hrolleifr
Hrómundr
Hrónarr
Hrossbjörn
Hrosskell
Hrútr, n.n.
Hrærekr
Hudar-Steinarr
Húnbogi
Hundi
Hundólfr (jarl)
Hungerð (f.)
Hunrauðr
Hvamm-Þorir
Hvamm-Sturla
Hvati
Hvítserkr
Hyrna, n.n.
Hyrningr
Hý-nefr, n.n.
Hængr, n.n.
Hæringr
Hæsna-Þorir
Hofða-Þórðr
Höggvandi, n.n.
Höggvin - Kinni, n.n.
Högni
Hörða-Kari
Hörðr
Höskuldr

From other sources.

Haddinja-skati, n.n.
Hak-laugr, n.n.
Hali, n.n.
Hamðir, p.n.
Hani, n.n. (a cock)
Harð-beinn, n.n.
Harð-jaxl, n.n.
Harð-magi, n.n.
Hausa-Kljufr, n.n.
Hákr, n.n.
Hálfr, n.n.
Há-fæta, n.n. (high leg)
Há-nefr, n.n. (high nose)
Heikil-nefr, n.n. (hook nose)
Heið-rekr (King)
Hein, n.n. *D.* King
Hemingr, p.n.
Hera-fótr, n.n. *D.* King
Herjan, p.n.
Herj-ólfr. *A.S.* Here-wolf
Hiði
Hildingr
Himaldi, n.n. (a laggard)
Hjálmr
Hjálmars
Hjálmgeirr
Hjálgrimr
Hjálmgunnr
Hjálm-týr
Hjalm-gerðr
Hjörr
Hjörtr
Hlöðr
Hnapp-rass, n.n.
Hnúfa, n.n.
Hólfs-rekkr, n.n.
Hol-muðr, n.n.
Horti, n.n. (a ruffian)
Hrani (a blusterer)
Hreða, n.n. (a bugbear)
Hregg-viðr, p.n.
Hreimr, n.n.
Hrella, n.n.
Hrókr, p.n. (a rook)
Hrúga, n.n.
Hrúkr, n.n.
Hugi, p.n.
Hundingi
Hundsfótr, n.n.
Húkr, n.n.
Hvitr, p.n. *D.* Hvid.
Hvit-beinn, n.n.
Hvita-skald, n.n.
Hvita-ský, n.n.
Hvita-kollr, n.n.
Hvita-leðr, n.n.
Hækill, n.n.
Hænsa-Þorir, n.n.
Hærn-kollr, n.n.
Höd-broddr, n.n.
Höttr, p.n.

I.

Idunn (f.)
Illugi
Indriði
Íngjaldr
Íngibjörg (f.)
Íngigerðr (f.)
Íngileif (f.)
Íngi-marr
Íngi-mundr
Íngimundarsynr
Íngiriðr (f.)
Íngolfr
Ínguðr (f.), or Ingvoldr
Íngunn (f.)
Íngunnr (f.)
Íngvarr. *See* Ýngvarr
Íngvildr. *See* Ýngvildr
Íngyoldr. *See* Inguðr
Ísgerðr (f.)
Ísleifr (Bp.)
Ísólfr
Ísrauðr
Ívarr

From other sources.

Ími, p.n.
Isja, n.n.
Ístru-magi, n.n. (paunch)
Ísungr, n.n.

J.

Jarngerðr (f.)
Jatmundr. *See* Eadmund
Játvarðr (Edward). K. of Eng.
Jóan. *See* Jón
Jódis (f.)
Jófreiðr
Jófriðr (f.)
Jóhann (Bp.)
Jólgeirr
Jón
Jóra (f.)
Jóreiðr (f.)
Jórunn (f.)
Josteinn
Jösurr
Jökull
Jörundarsynr
Jörundr
Jötun-Björn

From other sources.

Jarn-hauss, n.n. (iron skull)
Jarn-hryggr, n.n. (iron back)
Jarn-saxa, n.n. (iron knife)
Jarn-skjöldr, n.n. (iron shield)
Jólfr, p.n.

K.

Kaðall (Gaelic)
Kaðlin (f., Gaelic)
Kálfr
Kald-munnr, n.n.
Kali (Gaelic)
Kalman (Gaelic)
Kamban, n.n. (Gaelic)
Kampa-Grímr
Kári
Karl
Karli
Karlsefni
Kárr
Katla
Kaun
Ketilbjörn
Ketill
Ketilriðr (f.)
Kjallakr (Gaelic)
Kjallakssynir
Kjallæklingar
Kjarran (Gaelic)
Kjarfalr (Gaelic)
Kjartan (Gaelic)
Kjarvalr
Kimbi, n.n. (Gaelic)
Kjöl-fari, n.n.
Kjölvör (f.)
Kjötvi
Klaufi
Kleppjarn
Kleykir, n.n.
Klyppr
Klæingr
Klöku
Knappi, n.n.
Kneif, n.n.
Knútr
Knýtr, n.n.
Knörr
Knöttr
Koðrán
Kolbeinn
Kolbjörn
Kolbrún
Kolfinna (f.)
Kolgrima (f.)
Kolgrimr
Kolka, n.n.
Kolli (Gaelic)
Kollr
Kollsveinn
Kolr (Bp.)
Kolskeggr
Kolssynir
Koltherna
Kolumba
Konáll (Gaelic)
Kori (Gaelic)
Kórmakr (Gaelic)
Korni
Krafla
Krákneflingar
Kraku-Hreiðarr
Kristofórus
Krókr, n.n.
Kroppa, n.n.
Krumr
Kymlingar
Kræklingar
Krömu-Oddr
Kúgaldi
Kuggi
Kveld
Kvign-Þorleifr
Kvistr
Kýlan (Gaelic)
Kögurr, n.n.
Kögrssynir
Körmlöð (Gaelic)
Körtr, n.n. (Karta)
Köttr, n.n. (a cat)

From other sources.

Ká-beinn, n.n.
Ká-höfðaðr, n.n. (curly head)
Kaggi, n.n.
Kakali, n.n.
Kambari, n.n. (comb-maker)
Kamb-höttr, n.n.
Kampi, n.n. (bearded)
Kappi, n.n. (a hero)
Karls-ungi, n.n.
Kastan-razi, n.n.
Katrin (f.), p. n.
Kauða (f.), n.n.
Kaupungr, n.n.
Kausi, n.n.
Kegill, n.n.
Keikan, n.n.
Keis, n.n. (round)
Kekkja = Kökkr, n.n.
Kembir, n.n. (a comber)
Keppr, n.n. (a club)
Kerling, p.n.
Kesja, n.n. (a halberd)
Kiðlingr, n.n.
Kiðlings-munnr, n.n.
Kikini, n.n.
Kikr, n.n.
Kirjalax, p.n.
Kisi, n.n. (puss)
Kjötvi, n.n. (the fleshy)
Klaka, p.n.

Klápr = Kláfr, n.n.
Klemus, p.n. (Clements)
Kliningr, n.n.
Kló, n.n. (claw)
Knarra-bringa, n.n.
Knerra = Knörr, n.n.
Knúi, n.n. (a knuckle)
Kobbi, pet n. (Jacob)
Kolbeinn, n.n. (black-legged)
Konr, p.n. (noble)
Kráka, n.n. (crow)
Kráka-nef, n.n. (crow-nose)
Kregð, n.n.
Krepp-hendr, n.n. (cripple)
Krista, n.n.
Kristin (f.), Christina
Krist-röðr, p.n.
Krist-run, p.n.
Kroppr, n.n.
Kumbi, n.n.
Kúgaðr, n.n.
Kúgi, n.n.
Kúla-nefr (hump-nose)
Kussa, n.n. (cow)
Kutiza, n.n.
Kveld-úlfr, n.n.
Kylli-nef, n.n.

L.

Lambi
Langaholts-Þora
Laugarbrekku, n.n.
Lecný (Lækný), or Leikny
Leðrháls
Leggjaldi, n.n.
Leiðolfr
Leifr
Leik-goði, n.n.
Leó (Keisari)
Lina (f.)
Ljódarkeptr
Ljót (f.)
Ljótólfr
Ljótr
Ljótunn
Ljúfa (Kona)
Ljúfina (f.)
Ljoðhattr
Ljoðinn
Ljoðmundr
Loka-senna, n.n.
Loki, n.n.
Lón-Einarr
Loppæna (f.)
Loptr (Bp.)
Lunan (Gaelic)
Lunda-Steinarr (jarl)
Lýtingr
Lækný. *See* Lecný
Lög-Skapti
Löngu-bak, n.n.

From other sources.

Lafranz (Laurence)
Laf-skeggr, n.n. (wag-beard)
Lang-beinn, n.n. (long-legged)
Langa-spjöt, n.n.
Lang-brók, n.n.
Lang-höfði, n.n. (long-head)
Lang-nefr, n.n. (long-nose)
Láfi, pet n. (Óláfr)
Láki, pet. n. (Þorlákr)
Leggr, p.n.
Leira, n.n. (muddy shore)
Lindi-ass, n.n.
Lín-seyma, n.n.
Líri, n.n.
Ljóð-horn, n.n.
Ljómi, n.n.
Lundi, n.n. (puffin)
Lúfa, n.n. (rough hair)
Lúsa-Oddi, n.n.
Lúsa-skegg, n.n.
Lygra, n.n.
Lyngvi, p.n.
Lyrgr, n.n.
Lyrtr, n.n. (lurtr)
Lyst-Knappr, n.n.
Lysu-Knappr, n.n.
Lög-maðr, p.n.
Lömbungr, n.n. (lamb)

M.

Mábil (f.)
Maddaðr (K., Gaelic)
Magnús
Magr-Helgi
Mág-Snorri
Mána-Ljotr
Máni. *See* Menni
Már
Margret (f.)
Maria (f.)
Markús
Martein (Bp.)
Má-skári, n.n.
Mein-frettr
Mela-Snorri
Meldun (jarl Scot., Gaelic)
Melkorka (f., Gaelic)
Melpatrekr (Gaelic)
Miðfjarðr, n.n.
Mjöll (f.)
Móðólfr
Móðólfssynir
Moð-skegg
Moeiðr (f.)
Molda-Gnúpr
Molda-Gnúpssynir
Moldi, n.n.
Mos-hals, n.n.
Munnr, n.n. (the mouth)
Myra-Knjukr
Myrgjol (f., Gaelic)
Myrkjartan (K., Gaelic)
Mýrun

From other sources.

Magni, p.n.
Magr, n.n. (meagre)
Manar-menn (Manxmen)
Mangi (Magnus)
Manni, n.n.
Mar-drap, n.n.
Mat-Krákr, n.n.
Maull, n.n. (muncher)
Maxi, n.n.
Mág (Mac, Mc)
Málga, n.n. (chatterbox)
Mál-spakr, n.n.
Mási, n.n.
Mein-akr, n.n.
Mein-fretr, n.n.
Menni, n.n.
Mikill, p.n.
Mikla, n.n.
Mildi, n.n.
Mjo-beinn, n.n. (tapelegged)
Mjóvi, n.n. (the slim)
Mundi, pet n.
Murta, n.n. (a little fellow)
Munki, n.n. (monk)
Myntari, n.n. (mintmaster)
Mögr, p.n. *See* Mágr
Mör-landi, n.n. (suetman)
Mör-nefr, n.n.
Mör-strútr, n.n.
Möttull, p.n. (Finnish King)

N.

Naððoðr
Nafar-Helgi
Nagli
Narfi
Narvassynir
Náttfari
Nefsteinn
Nereiðr (jarl)
Nesja-Knjukr
Niðbjörg (f.)
Nikolás
Njáll (Gaelic)
Njörðr
Norr (K.)

From other sources.

Nef, n.n. (nosey)
Nefja (f.), n.n.
Nest-konungr, p.n.
Njosnar-helgi, n.n.
Næfra-maðr, n.n.
Nörtr, n.n.

O.

Óblauðr
Oddbjörg (f.)
Oddbjörn
Oddfriðr (f.)
Oddgeirr
Oddi
Oddkatla
Oddlaug
Oddleif (f.)
Oddleifr
Oddmarr
Oddný
Ǫddr
Ǫ́feigr
Ǫ́láfr
Ǫ́leifr
Ǫ́li
Ólöf
Órækja
Orð-lokarr, n.n.
Ormarr
Ormhildr (f.)
Ormr
Orms-tunga, n.n.
Ǫrný (f.)
Örrabeinn
Ǫrra-skáld, n.n.
Ǫ́sk
Ǫ́sku (f.)
Ǫ́spakr
Ósvaldr (K.)
Ósvífr (Osyfr)
Ǫ́tryggr
Óttarr

From other sources.

Opin-sjoðr, n.n. (open purse)
Orri, n.n. (moor fowl)
Oxi, p.n. (an ox)

P.

Páll
Papar (Gaelic)
Parak, n.n.
Paschalis
Patrekr (Gaelic)
Pétr
Petrus
Philippus

From other sources.

Paktin, n.n.
Pálnir, p.n.
Peini, n.n. (Payne)
Petarr, p.n.
Pík, n.n. (Peak)
Pitlor, n.n.
Plógr, p.n. (*D.*)
Plytr, n.n. (club foot)
Prest-mágr, n.n.
Prúði, n.n. (stately)
Pung-elta, n.n.

R.

Ráðormr
Rafn
Rafnkell
Raförta (f., Gaelic)
Rafsi
Raga-broðir, n.n.
Ragi
Ragnarr (K.)
Ragnheiðr (f.)
Ragnhildr (f.)
Rang-látr, n.n.
Rannveig (f.)
Rauða-Björn
Rauð-bekri, n.n.
Rauð-feldr, n.n.
Rauðr
Rauð-skeggr, n.n.
Rauðssynir
Rauðúlfr
Rauðum-skjaldi, n.n. (red shield)
Raumr
Raunguðr
Refr
Ref-skeggr, n.n.
Reginleif
Reidarr. *See* Hreidarr
Reistr
Reyðr-siða, n.n.
Reyni-björn
Reyr-Ketill
Rifla
Rjúpa (f.)
Rodolfr. *See* Hródólfr
Roðrekr
Rólf. *See* Hrólfr
Rotinn, n.n.
Rudolphus
Ruðu-Ulfr (Bp.)
Ruggi, n.n.
Runolfr
Rútr. *See* Hrútr
Rögnvoldr (jarl)

From other sources.

Rafa-Kollr, n.n.
Ramr, n.n. (strong)
Rand-eiðr (f.)
Rang-muðr, n.n.
Ranka (Ragnheiðr)
Rand-verr, p.n.
Rata-toskr, p.n.
Regg-búss, n.n. (Wendish)
Reikall, p.n. (a rover)
Remba, n.n. (a coxcomb)
Ruza, n.n.
Rykill, n.n.
Rympill, n.n.

S.

Salbjörg (f.)
Salgerðr (f.)
Samr
Saurr, n.n.
Saxi
Sela-Kálfr
Sel-Þórir
Semingr
Siðu-Hallr
Sigarr (K.)
Sigfastr
Sigfús
Sighvatr
Sigmundr
Signý
Sigriðr (f.)
Sigtryggr
Sigurðr (Bp.)
Sigvaldi
Sigvatr
Sigvör
Símon
Sjóni, n.n.
Skagi
Skáld-Helgi
Skáldhrafn
Skáld-Refr
Skalla-Grimr
Skálp-hæna, n.n.
Skamkell
Skapti
Skarpheðinn
Skati
Skefill = Skemill
Skegg-ávaldi
Skegg-broddi
Skeggi, n.n.
Skjalda-Björn
Skjaldbjörn
Skálgr
Skiði
Skinna-Björn
Skjöldólfr
Skolmr
Skopti
Skorargeirr
Skorri
Skota-Kollr, n.n.
Skrof-Skrofi
Skrof-uðr, n.n.
Skuli
Skúmr
Skútaðar-Skeggi
Skæringr
Sleitu-Helgi
Slettu-Björn
Smiðkell
Smiðr
Smiðskeggi
Snar-fari, n.n.
Snepill
Snertlingar
Snjallr. *D.* Snolde
Snjallsteinn
Snorri
Snæbjörn
Snækollr
Snælaug (f.)
Snörtr
Sokki, n.n.
Solveig (f.)

Sólvör
Sóti
Spá-Kona, n.n.
Spak-Böðvarr
Spana (f.)
Spörr, n.n. (sparrow)
Stafngrimr
Starkaðr
Starri
Steigar-Þorir
Steinbjörn
Steinfirðr
Steingrimr
Steini
Steinmóðr
Steinn
Steinnar (jarl)
Steinólfr
Steinrauðr
Steinuðr. *See* Steinunn
Steinvör
Steinþórr
Stephanus (Bp.)
Stigandi, n.n.
Stórólfr
Stoti, n.n.
Strangi, n.n.
Stúfr
Sturla
Sturlúngar
Sturlusynir
Styrbjörn
Styrkárr
Styrmir
Styrr
Sulki (K.)
Sumarliði
Sunnólfr
Súrr
Surtr
Svana (f.)
Svanlaug (f.)
Svanr
Svart-höfði
Svarðkell
Svarta-þurs, n.n.
Svartr
Svasi
Svavarr
Svegðir
Sveinbjörn
Sveinn
Sveinúngar
Svertingr. *A.S.* Swerthing
Svið-balki
Sviðu-Kári
Svigna-Kappi, n.n.
Svína-Böðvarr
Svinhaga-Björn
Svörfuðr
Sæbjörn
Sæhildr (f.)
Sælingr, n.n. (a wealthy man)
Sæmundr
Sæuðr (Sæunn) (f.)
Sæ-úlfr (Sjólfr)
Sökkólfr
Sölgi (K.)
Sölmundr
Solverr (Sölvarr), K.
Sölvi
Sörkvir-Svarkr
Söxólfr

From other sources.

Salt-eyða, n.n.
Samr, n.n. (swarthy)
Sandi, n.n.
Saup-ruðr, n.n.
Sel-byggr, n.n.
Selr, n.n.
Sels-eista, n.n.
Sepill, n.n.
Sið-nefr, n.n. (long nose)
Siggi (Sigurðr)
Signjótr
Silfri, n.n. (silver)
Sjaundi = Sjundi, p.n.
Skakki, n.n. (wry)
Skam-fótr, n.n. (short foot)
Skam-háls, n.n. (short neck)
Skammi, n.n. (the short)
Skarði, n.n. (harelip)
Skati, n.n.
Skat-Kanpendi, n.n.
Skála-glam, n.n.
Skáldi, n.n.
Skálf, p.n.
Skálgr, n.n. (squinter)
Skári, n.n. (sea mew)
Skemill, p.n. = Skefill (a scratcher)
Skeið-Kallr, n.n.
Skeifr, n.n.
Skekill, n.n.
Sker-auki, n.n.
Skerðingr, n.n. (shark)
Skerja-blesi, n.n.
Skin-hringr, n.n.
Skinni, n.n. (a skinner)
Skinn-vefja, n.n.
Skirvill, n.n.
Skíðungar (the descendants of Skíði)
Skífa, n.n.
Skjómi, n.n.
Skjöldr, p.n.
Skol-beinn, n.n. (brown-legged)
Skoppr, n.n.
Skorpa, n.n.
Skorri, n.n.
Skota, n.n.
Skota-Kollr, n.n.
Skotti, n.n. (a ghost)
Skógar-nef, n.n.
Skógungar, n.n.
Skólmr, n.n.
Skrafari, n.n.
Skratt-hauki, n.n.
Skrauti, n.n.
Skrápi, n.n.
Skreyja, n.n. *D.* Skryde
Skrill, n.n.
Skrukka, n.n. *D.* Skrog
Skrúð-hyrna, n.n.
Skúma (f.), n.n.
Skúmr, n.n.
Skvaðra, n.n. (jackdaw)
Skvaldri, n.n. *S.* squallia (a squatter)
Skúli, p.n.
Skyti, n.n. *D.* Skytte (a marksman, shooter, archer)
Skæla, n.n.
Slafsi, n.n. (slaverer)
Slagu-Kollr, n.n.
Slakki, n.n.
Slandri, n.n.
Slappi, n.n.

Slefa, n.n. (slaver)
Sleggja, n.n. (sledge-hammer)
Sleppi = Slappi, n.n.
Slinkr, n.n.
Slókr, n.n. (sloucher)
Slyngr, n.n. (skilled)
Smetta, n.n. *D.* Smutte
Snákr, n.n. (snake)
Snati, n.n.
Sneypir, n.n. (snipper)
Snjólfr (Snæ-úlfr)
Snoppa-langr, n.n. (long snouted)
Snókr, n.n. *See* Snákr
Snuin-bruni, n.n.
Snæ-þryma, n.n.
Soddi, n.n. (dampness)
Sopi, n.n. (sweep)
Spá-Kona, n.n. (spae-queen, a prophetess)
Spraka-leggr, n.n. (a dandy). *D.* Sprade
Spýtu-leggr, n.n.
Stag-brellr, n.n.
Stag-nál (f.), n.n. (darning needle)
Standali, n.n. (a post)
Stand-eykr, n.n.
Steðja-Kollr, n.n.
Steypir, n.n. (a caster ?)
Stigandi, n.n. (a stepper)
Stigr, n.n.
Stiku-bligr, n.n.
Storgr, n.n.
Storka, n.n.
Stoti, n.n.
Strangr, n.n. (strong)
Stri-nefr, n.n.
Strylltr, n.n.
Stubbi, n.n. (stump)
Stangar-högg, n.n.
Stöpuðr
Súrr, n.n. (a sour drink)
Svaði, p.n.
Svagi, n.n. (a gurgler)
Sveiði, n. of a sea king
Sveimr, n.n. (stir, bustle)
Sveinki, p.n. (Sveinungr)
Sveltir, n.n.
Sverrir, p.n.
Svið-balki, n.n.
Sviðandi = Sviðingr, n.n. (stingy)
Svín-höfði, n.n.
Syrja (f.), n.n. (sori, dress)
Sýr, n.n. (a sow)

T.

Talkni
Tanni
Tasaldi, n.n.
Teitr
Tindr
Tinforni
Tjörfi
Tófa (f.)
Tófi
Torf-Einarr (jarl)
Torfi
Torráðr
Tor-tryggr
Trandill, n.n.
Trefill, n.n.
Trolli, n.n.
Trumbu-beinn, n.n.
Tryggvi (K.)
Tumi
Túngu-Kári
Túngu-Oddr
Túngu-Steinn
Tunhani
Tvennum-brúni, n.n.
Tyrfingr

From other sources.

Tabarðr, n.n. (a tabard)
Tölu-sveinn, n.n. (chatterbox)
Tandri, n.n. (fresh as fire)
Tann-gnjóstr, n.n.
Tann-grisnir, n.n.
Tann-refill, n.n.
Tann-skári, n.n.
Tálgi, n.n.
Táta, p.n. (a teat)
Tin-forni, n.n.
Tin-teinn, n.n.
Titlingr, n.n. (a tit)
Tiðinda-Skopti, n.n. (the news teller)
Tjöru-skinn, n.n.
Tjúga-skegg, n.n.
Todda (f.), n.n.
Tosti, p.n.
Toti, p.n.
Tottr, n.n. *D.* Tommel-tot (Tom Thumb)
Tóki, p.n. *D.* Tyge, Lat. Tycho
Tónn, n.n. (tune)
Trausti, p.n.
Tré-bot, n.n.
Tre-telja, n.n.
Trúðr, n.n. (a juggler)
Trú-fast, n.n. of K. Athelstan (truthful, trusty)
Tronu-beinn, n.n. (crane leg)
Tulkari, n.n. (an interpreter)
Tungu-goði, n.n.
Tunni, n.n.
Tysti = Tosti, n.n.
Tyza, n.n.

U.

Uggi
Úlfarr
Úlfeiðr
Úlf-hamr
Úlf-heðinn
Úlf-heiðr (f.)
Úlf-hildr (f.)
Úlf-Kell
Úlfljótr
Úlfr
Úlfrun (f.)
Una (f.)
Uni
Unnr
Uppsala-Hrólfr
Urækja
Úspakr
Útryggr

From other sources.

Ubbi, p.n. *A.S.* Ubba
Uðr, p.n.
Ull-höttr, n.n. (wool hood)
Ulli, dim. of Erlendr
Ull-serkr, n.n.
Ull-strengr, n.n.
Ungi, n.n. (the younger)
Urðar-Köttr, n.n. = Hreysi-Köttr (wild cat)
Urðar-steinn, n.n.
Urka, n.n.
Úrr, n.n.

V.

Vaði
Valbrandr
Valdis (f.)
Valgarðr
Valgautr
Valgerðr (f.)
Vali
Valla-Brandr
Valla-Ljótr
Valþjoflingar
Valþófr
Valþýflingar (Valþýfingr)
Vand-raðr
Vanlandi (K.)
Vápni
Vatnarr (K.)
Vebjörn
Vébrandr
Védis (f.)
Véðormr. *See* Veþormr
Veðra-grimr
Veðr, n.n.
Véfreyðr
Végeirr
Végestr
Vékell
Vélaug (f.)
Véleifr
Vémundr
Vény (f.)
Vermundr
Vestarr
Vesteinn
Vestliði
Vestmaðr
Vetrliði
Véþormr
Véþörn
Viðarr
Vífill
Víga-Barði
Víga-Bjarni
Víga-Glumr
Víga-Hrappr
Víga-Skuta
Viga-Sturla
Víga-Styrr
Vígbjoðr
Vigdis (f.)
Vígfús
Viglundr
Vigsterkr
Vikarr
Vikinga-Kari
Víkingr
Vilbaldr
Vilburg (f.)
Vilgeirr
Vilgerðr (f.)
Vilhjálmr
Vilmundr
Vilraðr
Visburr (K.)
Vívill
Vorsar
Vorsa-Úlfr
Væpnlingar
Völu-steinn

From other sources.

Vaggaldi, n.n. (a waddler)
Vagn, p.n.
Val-frekr, n.n.
Vandill, p.n.
Vágr, p.n.
Véi, p.n.
Veðr, n.n. (a wether)
Veili, n.n. (ailing)
Veljungr = Vælungr, n.n.
Vendill, p.n.
Vendill-Kráka, n.n.
Vesall, n.n.
Vettir, n.n.
Við-finnr, p.n.
Við-leggr, n.n. (wooden leg)
Viggjar-skalli, n.n.
Vippa (f.), n.n. (a whip)
Víg-ólfr, p.n. (war wolf)
Væringi (the Warings)
Vörsa-Krákr, n.n.
Vöttr, p.n. (a glove)

Y.

Ýnglingar
Ýngvarr
Ýngvi
Ýngvildr (f.)
Ýr (Yri), (f.)
Yxna-Þori
Ysja (f.), n.n. (the bustler)

Þ.

Þángbrandr
Þengill
Þiðrandi
Þjóðarr
Þjóðgerðr (f.)
Þjóðhildr (f.)
Þjóð-mar. *G.* Ditmar
Þjóðrekr. *G.* Deitrich
Þjökka (f.), n.n.
Þjóstarr
Þjóstólfr
Þóra (f.)
Þórálfr
Þóralldr. *See* Þórhallr
Þórarinn
Þórarna (f.)
Þorbergr
Þorbjörg (f.)
Þorbjörn
Þorbrandr
Þorbrandssynir
Þórdis (f.)
Þórðr
Þórelfr (f.)
Þórey (f.)
Þorfiðr (Máni)
Þorfinna (f.)
Þorfinnr
Þorgautr
Þorgeirr
Þorgerðr (f.)
Þorgestr
Þorgils
Þorgnýr
Þorgrima (f.)
Þorgrímr
Þórhaddr
Þórhalla (f.)
Þórhalli
Þórhallr
Þórhildr (f.)
Þórhrolfr
Þóriðr. *See* Þuriðr
Þórir
Þorkatla (f.)
Þorkell
Þorketill
Þorlakr
Þorlaug (f.)
Þorleif (f.)
Þorleifr
Þorleikr
Þorljót (f.)
Þorljótr
Þormoðr
Þornjótr
Þórný (f.)
Þórodda (f.)
Þoroddr
Þórólfr
Þórormr
Þorsteinn
Þorsteinnsbjörn
Þórunn
Þorvaldr
Þorvarðr
Þór-vé (Þór-veig)
Þorviðr
Þórvör (f.)
Þráin
Þrándr
Þrasi
Þraslaug (f.)
Þróndr. *See* Þrandr
Þröstr
Þuriðr (f.)
Þussasprengir, n.n.
Þyna (f.), n.n.
Þöngull, n.n.

From other sources.

Þak-raðr = Þakk-raðr, p.n. *G.* Tancred
Þas-ramr, n.n.
Þausnir, n.n. (a romping fellow)
Þegjandi, n.n. (the silent)
Þenja, n.n. (an axe)
Þing-bitr, n.n.
Þing-höttr, n.n.
Þjálfi, p.n.
Þjóri, n.n. (a young bull). *D.* tyr
Þjóti, n.n. (the whistler)
Þórðr, p.n.
Þrjúgr, p.n. *D.* Tryge
Þruma, n.n. (a slow person)
Þrúða, Sig-Þruðr (f.)
Þumli, n.n. (Tom Thumb)
Þura, Þuriðr (f.)
Þurs, n.n. (a giant). *D.* Tosse (a fool)
Þvari, n.n.
Þveit, p.n. (Thwaite). *D.* Tvæde
Þyrni-fótr, n.n. (Thornfoot)
Þömb, n.n.

Æ.

Æði-Kollr, n.n.
Ægileif (f.)
Æsa (f.)
Ævarr

Ö.

Ögmundr
Ögurr
Ögvaldr. *See* Afvaldr
Ölfuss, n.n.
Ölmóðr
Ölmæðlingar
Ölver
Ön. *See* Aun
Öndott (f.)
Öndottr-Kraka
Öndottssynir
Öngr
Öngull. *See* Aungul
Önn
Önundarsynir
Önundr
Örlygr
Örn
Örnólfr
Örrek, n.n.
Örv-öndr, or Örvhendr, n.n.
Ösyfr. *See* Ósvifr
Öxna-megn, n.n.
Öxna-Þorir. *See* Yxna-Þorir
Özurr
Öþr. *See* Auðr

From other sources.

Ölbogi, n.n. (elbow)
Örðigr, n.n. (erect)
Örðig-skeggi, n.n.
Ör-eiðr, n.n. (the forsworn)
Örkn-höfði, n.n. (seal-head)
Ör-nefni, p.n.
Örra-beinn, n.n. (scar-leg)

Pet Names—Girls.

Ása, from Ás-laug
Ásta, from Ás-triðr
Disa, from Val-dís, Vig-dís, Her-dís
Dóra, from Hall-dóra
Friða, from Holm-friðr
Geira, from Geir-laug
Gudda, from Guð-riðr
Gunna, from Guð-rún
Imba, from Ingi-björg
Inga, from Ing-unn, Ingveldr
Jóka, from Jó-hanna
Jóra, from Jóreiðr
Kata, from Katrin
Lauga, from Guð-laug
Manga, from Margrét
Ranka, from Ragn-eiðr, Ragn-hildr
Sigga, from Sig-riðr
Sissa, from Sig-þruðr
Tobba, from Þor-björg
Valka, from Val-gerðr
Þrúða, from Jar-þrúðr, Sig-þruðr
Þura, from Þur-iðr

Pet Names—Boys.

Arni (Arne), from Örn
Ási, from Ás-mundr
Atli, from Attila
Bensi, from Benedikt
Bersi, from Björn
Bjarni, from Björn
Björsi, from Björn
Brynki, from Bryn-jólfr
Daði, from David
Erli, from Erl-indr (Erlingr)
Eyvi, from Eyj-ólfr
Fusi, from Víg-fús
Gamli, from Gamel
Goddi, from compounds in Guð
Grimsi, from Grímr
Gutti, from Guðormr
Gvendr, from Guð-mundr
Helgi, from Há-leygr
Ingi, from compounds in Ing
Jónsi, from Jon
Karli, from Karl
Keli, from Þor-kel
Kobbi, from Jacob
Láfi, from Óláfr
Láki, from Þor-lákr
Laugi, Gunn-laugr
Mangi, from Magnus
Mundi, from Ás-mundr

Ragni, from compounds in Ragn
Runki, from Rún-ólfr
Sebbi, from Sig-björn
Siggi, from Sig-urðr
Simbi, from Sig-mund
Snorri, from Snerrir
Steinki, from Stein-grímr
Sveinki, from Sveinn
Tumi, from Thomas
Valdi, from Þor-valdr

FRISIAN, PERSONAL, AND FAMILY NAMES.

A.

Abbo, m.; fam. n., Abben, Abena
Adde, m.; Adda, f.; fam. n., Adden
Ade, m.; fam. n., Aden, Adena
Afke, f. dimin. *See* Efke, Eveke, from Eva
Agatha, f.
Agge, m.; fam. n., Aggen
Agt, Agte, f. dimin. of Agatha
Aisso, Aisse, Eisse, m.; fam. n., Aissen, Eissen
Albert, Albarts, Albardus, Albertus (Albrecht), m.; fam. n., Alberts, Albers; f. Albertje
Alerk (Alarich, contraction of Athalarich), m.; fam. n., Alerks, Alers, Ahlers
Alle, m.; fam. n., Allen, Allena
Almôd, Almôth, Almt, f. (Allmuth)
Alt, m.; fam. n., Alts
Amel, m.; fam. n., Amels. Comp. Amala, Amalia, Amalung, etc.
Amke, m. and fam. n. *See* Hamke
Anke, f. (Antje), from Anna, as also Anken, Aennchen, Annechin
Anna, f.
Arend, Arnd, Arndt, m. (Arnold); fam. n., Arends
Arjen or Arien, m.; fam. n., Arjens, Ariens, Arjes
Arkonâ, Arkenâ, fam. n., from Arko
Arrel, Arl. *See* Harrel
Athe, m.; fam. n., Athen. *See* Ade, Atte
Atte, Atto, m.; fam. n., Attena

B.

Baino, Beino, m.; fam. n., Bainen, Beinen
Bantje, m.; fam. n., Bantjes, dimin. of Banno
Bärend, Bêrend, Bernd, m.; fam. n., Bärends, Berend, a contraction of Bernhard
Bauke, Bâwke, Bâfke or Bâvke, f. dimin. of Old *F.* Bavo; fam. n., Bavink
Beelke, Belke, dimin. of Bele
Beino. *See* Baino
Bela, f.
Bele, Behl, Beil, Bill, m.
Belemar, Biletrud
Bêner, m.; fam. n., Bêners
Benge, m.; fam. n., Bengen
Bêninga, Bênenga, fam. n.
Benno, m.; Benna, f.
Berend. *See* Barend
Bôdewîn, m. Comp. Bouduin, Balduin, Boldewin
Boko, m. *N.* Baugr
Boldewîn
Bôle, Boele, m.; fam. n., Bôlen, Bolema
Bôleke, Bôlke, Bolkes, dimin.
Bonno, m.; fam. n., Bonnen
Boys, Boye, Boy, m.; dimin. Boyke; fam. n., Boyen, Boyinga, Boyink, Boyunga
Brûno, m.; Brûnke and Brûntje f.; and fam. n., Brûninga, Brûns, Bronsema, and Brûnken

D.

Datter, m.
Dedde, m.; fam. n., Dedden
Dêtlêf, m.
Detmer, m.
Dever. *Dch.* Dieven
Deverke, dimin. f.
Dîderik, Dîdrîk, Dîdrîch, Dîderk, Dierk, Dirk, m. (Dietrich)
Dîko or Dyko, m.; fam. n., Dîken, Dyken, Dikena, Dykena
Dîle, Diele, m.; fam. n., Dielen (Dil.)
Dirk, Dierk, m.; f. Dirktje, Dirtje; fam. n., Dirks, Dirksen, Dirken, Dierken
Djure, m.; fam. n., Djuren; f. Djurke, Jurke
Djurelt and Durelt, m.
Dodo, m.; f. Doda; fam. n., Doden, Dodens, Dodena

E.

Ebbe, m.
Ebbo, m.
Ebo, Ebbo, Ebe, Eppo, Eve, m.; f. Ebbe, Eveke; fam. n., Eben, Even, Eppen, Ebeling.
Edde, m.; fam. n., Edden
Edo, m.; dimin. Edje; fam. n., Eden, Edinga
Edsard (Esdert ?), m.; fam. n., Edsards, Edzards, Esderts
Egbert, Ebbert, m.; fam. n., Egberts, Egbers
Egge, m.; fam. n., Eggen
Eibo, Eibe, m.; fam. n., Eiben
Eiko, Eike, m.
Eilert, Eilt, m.; fam. n., Eilerts, Eilers, Eilts, Eils (contraction of Egilhardt, Ailhardt)
Eimo, Eime, m.; fam. n., Eimers
Eint, Eent, m.; fam. n., Eints (Aginhardt ?)
Eka, Eke, Ekea, Eckea, f.
Ele, Ehle, m.; fam. n., Ehlen
Elle, m.; Ella, f.; Ellen, fam. n.
Eme, Emo, Ehme, and Eimo, m.; fam. n., Emen, Ehmen, Emminga; dimin. Emke; fam. n., Emken
Emmo, Emme, m.; Emma, f.
Emminga, Emmius, fam. n.
Eppo, m; Eppen, fam. n.
Ernst, m.
Esdert. *See* Edsard
Eta, Etta, f. dimin. Ettje
Eve, Ewe, Aeve, m.

F.

Fauke, m.
Feyen, fam. n.
Feyke, m; Feyken, fam. n.
Fekko, Fêko, Feyko, Fekke, m.; fam. n., Fekken, Feyken, Feikena
Fia, dimin. of Sophia, dimin. Fiake, Fîke
Fimmo, Fimme, m.; fam. n., Fimmen
Flamê, Flâm, a Fleming
Fôke, Fauke, m.; Fôken, fam. n.
Fokke, Fokko, m.; Fokka, f.; Fokken, Fokkena, fam. n.
Folerk. *See* Folrick
Foletta, f.
Fôlke, f.
Folkerd, m. (Folk-ward); Folkerds, Folkers, fam. n.
Folkmar, m.
Folpmer, m.
Folpt, Fulpt, m.; Folpts, fam. n.
Folrâd, Fulrâd, m. (Vollrath, Folkrâd)

Fôlrîk, Fôlrîch, Fôlerk, m.; Folrichs, Fôlerks, Fôlers, fam. n.
Frërk, Frêrk, m.; Frërksen, fam. n., from Frêrik, Frederik
Frese or Frêse, a *F.*
Fulbrand, m.
Fulf, m.
Fulke, f., or Fulka, Fulleke, from Fulla, Folla
Fulko, m., from Fullo

G.

Gaiko. *See* Geiko
Galt, m.
Gâlt, m., contraction of Garrelt, Garlt, Gerlt
Garbrand, Garbert, m.
Garrelt, Gerrelt, m.; Garrelts, Garrels, Gerrelts, Gerrels, fam. n. (Garhold, Gerhold)
Geiko, Gaiko, Gayko, Geike, m.; Geiken, fam. n., from Geio, Gayo
Gerd, m.; dimin. f. Gerdtje; fam. n., Gerdes, contraction of Gerhard. Also Gerjet, Gêjert, Gert, and Gerriet
Gerdrût, Gädrût, f. (Gertrude)
Gerke, m.; Gerken, fam. n.
Gërman, old fam. n.
Gêske, f. dimin. of Gêso, Gêsa, Giso (Gîsbert)
Grendel, Grennel; f. dimin. Grendelke, Grennelke
Greta (Margaretha), dimin. Grêtje
Grôn, fam. n.
Grönefeld, Grönfeld, fam. n.
Gronewold, Grônwold, fam. n.

H.

Habbo, m.; Habben and Habbinga, fam. n.
Haddo (Hatto), m.; Haddinga, fam. n. *See* Heddo
Hagen, m.; Hagena, fam. n.
Hamke, dimin. of Hamo; fam. n., Haming
Harm, m. (contraction of Hermann); f. dimin. Harmke; fam. n., Harms, Harmens
Hâro, Hâre, m.; Hâren, Haringa, Harringa, fam. n.
Harrell, Harle, m.
Hayo, m.; Hayung, Heyungs, Hayunga, fam. n.
Hebe, f. dimin. Hebeke, Hêbke, Hëpke
Heddo, Hedde, m.; Hedden, Heddinga, fam. n.; Heddo, *A.S.* Bishop, A.D. 676
Heie, Hei, m. *See* Hayo
Heiko or Haiko, m.; Heikens, Heiken, Heikena, Haiken, Hayken
Hein, m.; Heine, Heinen, fam. n. (from Heinrich)
Heini
Heink, m. *See* Hein
Heite, Heit, m.; Heits, fam. n.
Helmer, m.; Helmers, fam. n.
Herman, m.
Hêro, Hêre, Herre, m.; Hêren, Herren, fam. n.
Hester (Esther)
Hibbo, Hibbe, m.; Hibben, fam. n.
Hidde. *See* Hiddo
Hiddo, m.; Hidden, fam. n.
Hilke, f. dimin. of Hille, Hilla, Hilda
Hillerd, Hillerk. *See* Hillrich
Hillmer, Hilmer, m.; Hillmers, fam. n.
Hillrîch, Hillrik, Hillerk, Hillerd, m.; Hillrichs, Hillerks, Hillers, Hillern, fam. n.
Hima, f.
Himke, dimin. of Hima
Hinderk. *See* Hinrich

Hinrich, m.; Hinrichs, Hinnerks, Hinners, Hinnerssen, Hünerssen, fam. n.

Hiske, f.

Hoot, m.; Hoots, Hôting, Hooting (from Hotbert)

I.

Ibo, Ibe, Ihbe, m.; Iben, Ibben, Ibeling, fam. n.

Ide

Idje, Itje, f. dimin. of Ida

Idse, Itse, Idze, m.; Idsen, Itzen, Idsinga, fam. n.

Igge, m.; Iggen, Iggena, fam. n.

Ikke, Ikka, Ika, f.

Iko, Ike, m.; Iken, Ikena, fam. n.

Imel, m.; Imels, fam. n.

Imke, f., also Immeke, dimin. of Imme

Imme, Immo, m.; Immen, fam. n.

Ine. *See* Ino

Ing, Ingo, Inguio, m.

Inka, f.

Ino, Ine, Ihno, m.; dimin. Inke, Ihnke; fam. n., Inen, Ihnen; Ino, *A.S.* King, A.D. 727

Ippo, Ippe, m.; Ippen, fam. n.

J.

Jabbo, Jabbe, Jabe, m.; Jabben, fam. n.

Jak, m., also fam. n.; dim. Jäkchen

Jakub, Jakup, m.

Jan, m.; Janna, Jantje, f.; Jansen, Janssen, Jenssen, fam. n.

Jasper, m.; Jaspers, fam. n.

Jelle, m.; Jellen, Jellena, fam. n. (from Jellrich ?)

Jellrich, Jellrik, Jellerk, m.

Jetta, f. dimin. Jettchen

Jibbo, m.; Jibben, fam. n.

Jimme, m.; Jimmen, fam. n.

Jochem, Jofen, m. (Joachim)

Juist. *See* Jûst

Jürgen, Jürjen, contraction of Jürn, m. (Görgen), also Jörg; fam. n., Jürgens, Jürjens, Jürns

Jurke, f.

Just, loc. and fam. n.

K.

Karsten, Kersten, Karsen, Kassen, Kasjen, from Kristjan (Christian); fam. n., Karstens, Karsens, Kassens, Kasjens

Kasper, m.

Kâtje, f. dimin. of Kate, Catherina

Kês, m., contraction of Cornelius

Klâs (Klaus), Niklâs, m.

Klûn, Kluin, fam. n.

L.

Lambert, Lampert, Lambrecht, m.

Lanbert, Lanpert, Lantpert, m.

Lübbert, m.; Lubberts, Lübbers, fam. n.

Lübbo, m.; Lübben, Lübbena, fam. n.; dimin. Lübke; fam. n., Lübkes

Lûdowig, Lûdewig, Lûdwig, m.; Lûdowigs, Lûdewigs, Lûdwigs, fam. n.

Lûdo, m.

Lüitje, m.; Luitjens, fam. n.

Lüke, m.; Lüken, fam. n., contraction of Lüdeke, Ludeke, Liudeke, dimin. of Ludo, Lindo, etc.

Lükke, f. *See* Lüke

Lûks, m. (Lucas)

Lüppo, Lübbo, m.; dim. Lüpke; fam. n., Lüpkes

Lûth, m. (Lütet); Lûitje, f.

M.

Machelt, f. (Machtild)
Machtild, Mechtild, f.
Magrêta, f. (Margrêta)
Maike. *See* Marê
Mammo, Mamme, m.; Mammen, Memmen, Mamminga, Memminga, fam. n.
Manno, Manne, m.; Manninga, fam. n.
Marê (Maria), dimin. Marêken, Marêke, Maike
Margrêta, Margrêt, Magrêta, Magrêt, Megrêt, Mergrêt, contraction Grêta; dimin. Grêtje
Meinert, Mênert, contraction Meint, Meent, m. (Meinhard); Meinerts, Meiners, Meints, Meents, fam. n.
Meino, m. (Magino, Megino)
Memke, Mêmke. *See* Memmo. Memkes, Mêmkes, Mimkes, fam. n.
Memmo, Mémo, Méme, m.; Memmen, Memminga, fam. n.
Mêne, m.; Mênen, fam. n.
Menje, f. dimin. of Menna
Menko, Menke, m.; Menken, fam. n.
Menno, Menne, m.; f. Menna; Mennen, Menninga, fam. n.
Mense, Mens, m.; Mensen, Mensinga, fam. n.
Mês or Mêwes, contraction of Bartolomaeus
Meta, Metta, f. dimin. Metje
Mêwes. *See* Mês
Mia, f. (Maria); dimin. Mîke, Mîtje
Michel, m.
Mimke, Mimmke, m. (Mimeken, Mimmeken)
Mimste, m.

N.

Nanno, Nanne, m.; Nannen, Nanninga, fam. n.
Nâtje, f., contraction of Annatje, dimin. of Anna
Nôme, Nôm, m.

O.

Ode, Odo, m.; Odens, Odenga, Odinga
Okko, Ocko, Okke, m.; Okka, f.; Okken, Okkinga
Ommo, m.; Ommen, Omkes, fam. n.
Onke, Onneke, dimin. of Onno; fam. n., Onkes, Onnekes
Onno, m.; Onna, f.; Onnen, fam. n.
Ontje, m.; Ontjes, fam. n., from Onno
Ordgîs, Ortgîs, Oortgies, Oorthgies, Oordgiese, m.
Ortwin, Oorthwin, Ooordwin, m.
Otte, Otto, m.; Otten, fam. n.

P.

Paul, m.; Pauls, Paulsen, fam. n.
Peta, f.
Peter, m.; dimin. Peterke, f.; Peters, Petersen, fam. n.
Poppe, m.; Poppen, Poppinga, fam. n.; dimin. Popke, Popken
Poppe, Duke of Friesland, was slain in battle by Charles Martel in 734

R.

Reent, m.; Reents, fam. n.
Reimer, m. (Regimar); Reimers, fam. n.
Reiner, m. (Reinhard); Reiners, fam. n.
Reinhard, m.
Reint, m.; Reints, fam. n.
Rembold, m.
Remmer, m.; Remmers, Remmerssen, fam. n.
Rewert, m.; Rewerts, fam. n.
Rikkerd, Rikkert, m. (Richard); Rikkerts, Rikkers, fam. n.
Rôlf (Rodolf), m.; Rôlfs, fam. n.
Rötger, m. (Hrodgar); Rötgers, fam. n.
Rumke, m., contraction of Rumo or Hrom; Rumkes, fam. n.
Rummert, m.; Rummerts, Rummers, fam. n.

S.

Sebo, m.; Seba, Sebens, fam. n.
Sibet, m.
Sibo, m.; Siebens, fam. n.
Sikko, Sikke, m.; Sikkens, Sikkinga, fam. n.
Swêerd, Swêert, m.; Swêerds, Swêerts, Swêers, fam. n.
Swîthert, Swittert, Switer, m.; Switers, Switters, fam. n.

T.

Tado, Tade. *See* Thado and Tjado
Tako, m.; Takes, fam. n., contraction Tâks, Takens
Tale, Talea, f. dimin. Tâlke
Taletta, f.
Tammo, Tamme, m.; Tammen, Tamminga, fam. n.
Tanno, m.; Tannen, fam. n.
Tâtje, f.
Tebbo, Tebbe, m.; Tebben, fam. n.
Tetta, f. dimin. Tetje
Têwes, m., contraction of Matheus. Comp. Mes
Thado, Tado, Thade, Tade, m.; Thaden, Taden, fam. n.
Tjado, Tjade, m.; Tjaden, fam. n.
Tjârd, Tjard, Tjârt, m.; Tjârds, Tjards, Tjârts, fam. n.
Tjarko, m.; Tjarks, fam. n.
Tjetmer, m.; Tjetmers, fam. n. (Dietmar)
Tönjes, m. (Antonius)

U.

Ubbo, Ubbe, m.; Ubben, Ubbinga, fam. n.
Udo, Ude, m.; Uden, fam. n.
Ufo, Ufe, Uvo, Uffo, Uffe, m.; Ufen, Uven, Uffen, fam. n.; dimin. Ufke; Ufkes, fam. n.
Uko, Üko, Uke, m.; Uken, Ukena, fam. n.
Ulerk (Ulrich), m.; Ulerks, Ulers, fam. n.
Ulferd, Ulfert, m.; Ulferds, Ulferts, Ulfers. The Dutch form is Olferd, Ulferd, Ulverd, Ulverdus
Ulrîk. *See* Ulerk

W.

Warner, m. (Werner); dimin. Warntje; Warners and Warntjes, fam. n.
Wêert, m.; Wêerts, Wêers, Weiers, fam. n.
Wêrda, Wiarda, fam. n.
Wêt, m.; Wêts, fam. n.
Wilbert, m.; Wilberts, Wilbers, fam. n.
Wildert, contraction Wilt, m.
Wilhelm, contraction Wilm, m.; Wilms, fam. n.
Wilko, Wilke, m.; Wilken, fam. n.
Wît, Wiet, dimin. Witje, Wietje, m.; Wîts, Wiets, Wîtjes, Wietjes, fam. n.
Wîterd, Wîtherd, Wîthert, m.
Wobbo, Wobbe, Wobbi, m.; dimin. f. Wobbeke, Wobke; fam. n., Wobbena, Wobben
Wolbrecht, m.; Wolbrechts, Wolbergs, fam. n.
Wübbo, m.; Wübbens, Wubbena, fam. n.; Wübke, dimin. f.

NAMES OF PERSONS ENTERED IN DOMESDAY BOOK AS HOLDING LANDS *TEMP.* KING ED. CONFR.

A.

Aben
Abet
Abo
Achebranni
Achestanus
Achi
Achil
Achins
Acolf
Acum
Acun
Adam
Adeldreda
Adelmus
Adelid
Adelinge
Adeliz
Adelo
Adeold
Adelric
Adeluuald
Adelwoldus
Ademar
Adestan
Adjuuar
Adret
Adstan
Adstanus
Adulf
Æchebrand
Ædelflete
Ædeldreda
Ædgeua
Ædi
Ædmundus
Ædricus
Æduinus
Ædwardus
Æduui
Ædwoldus
Ægduuardus
Æileua
Æilmar
Æilmer
Æilmund
Æilric
Ællard
Ældeua
Ældid
Ældiet
Ældit
Ældred
Ældreda
Ældret
Ælfag
Ælfec
Ælfelm
Ælfer
Ælfeth
Ælfled
Ælfleda
Ælfric
Ælgar
Ælger
Ælget
Æli
Ælmar
Ælmer
Ælmund
Ælnod
Ælric
Ælsi
Ælstanus
Æluert
Ælueua
Æluin
Æluric
Æluuacre
Æluuard
Æluui
Æluuin
Ælwius
Æluuold
Ærefast
Ærgrim
Æstanus
Ætheldreda
Æthericus
Æthesi
Ætmarus
Ætnod
Agelmarus
Agebred
Agelricus
Ageluuard
Agemund
Agenulfi
Aghemundus
Aghete (Linc.)
Aieluert

Aifride
Ailad
Ailardus
Ailbernus
Ailbric
Ailbriht
Aildeig
Ailet
Aileua
Ailhalle
Ailid
Ailida
Ailiet
Ailith
Ailm
Ailmar
Ailmer
Ailmundus
Ailof
Ailred
Ailric
Ailsi
Ailuerd
Ailuert
Ailueua
Ailuuard
Ailward
Ailwi
Aimar
Ainar
Aiolf
Airaf
Airet
Aischil
Aisil
Aiulf
Aki
Ala
Alanus
Albani
Alberic
Albernus
Albertus
Albricht
Albus
Alcerl
Alchel
Alchemont
Alchen
Alcher
Alcheris
Alcherl
Alchetel
Alchil
Alcolm
Alcot
Alcude
Aldebert
Alded
Alden
Aldene
Aldeuuif
Aldgid (f.)
Aldi
Aldid
Aldiet
Adolfus
Aldred
Aldreman (Linc.)
Aldret
Aldvi
Alduin
Aldulf
Alebric
Alebrix
Alestan
Aluesdef
Alfa (Notts)
Alfac
Alfag
Alfah
Alfeg
Alfeih
Alfer
Alferd
Alfgerus
Alfhilla
Alfidis
Alfit
Alfled
Alfleda
Alflet
Alfnod
Alfric
Alfriz
Alfsi
Alfuuinus
Algar
Algerus
Algod
Algrim
Alham
Alid
Aliet
Alli
Allic
Allric
Almær
Almar
Almer
Almund
Almunt
Alnod
Alnoht
Alnold
Alnot
Alnoth
Alous
Alrebot
Alredi
Alreforda de
Alret
Alric
Alris
Alselmus
Alsi
Alsicus
Alsius
Alstan
Altei
Altet
Alti
Altor
Alwardus
Alued
Aluena
Aluene
Aluer
Aluerd
Aluerle
Alueron
Aluert
Aluet
Aluied
Aluiet
Aluin
Alun
Alunold
Aluol
Aluold
Aluort
Alur
Alured
Aluret
Aluric
Aluuacre
Aluuald
Aluuard
Aluuart
Aluuen
Aluui
Aluuid
Aluuin
Aluuol
Aluuold
Aluuric
Amod
Amund
Anand
Anant
Anaut
Ancholfus
Andrac
Andreæ
Andreas
Angarus
Angerus
Angot
Anschil
Anscot
Ansculf
Ansfrid
Ansfrig
Ansgar
Ansger
Ansgot
Ansketill
Anund
Anunt
Ape (Som.)
Appe (Wilts)
Arcebald
Arcenbald
Archel
Archetel
Archii
Archilbar
Archisti
Ardegrip

Arduin
Ardul
Ardulf
Aregri
Aregrim
Aret
Arfastus
Aric
Arich
Arling
Arnebrand
Arnegrim
Arnenger
Arnui
Arnul
Artor
Arulf
Asa
Ascer
Ascha
Aschi
Aschil
Aschilbar
Asci
Ascored
Aseloc
Asford
Asfort
Asgar
Asgot
Asi
Aslac
Asli
Assemann
Assorin
Asul
Asulf
Athelwold
Atilie
Atserus
Atsur
Attile
Atules
Audoen
Auduid
Audulf
Auegrin
Auelin
Aueue
Augustinus
Auic
Auitius
Aured
Ausgar
Austin
Autbert
Auti
Avigi
Awart
Azelinus
Azer
Azor
Azur

B.

Baco (Linc.)
Bada (Derb.)
Bade
Bain
Balchi
Baldeuin
Baldric
Balduin
Bar
Barch
Bardi
Bared
Baret
Barn
Barne
Basin (Yorks)
Basine (Yorks)
Batoc
Batsuen
Bedel
Bedling
Belam
Belehorne
Belrap
Benedict
Benne
Benz
Beorus
Ber
Berchinges de
Bercsi
Bere
Berguluer
Bern
Bernac
Bernard
Berne
Bernolt
Bernalf
Berrnar
Bers
Bertor
Bertunt
Besi
Beso
Besy
Beteslau
Bettice
Biche (Devon)
Biga
Bil
Bisi
Blac
Blach
Blache
Blacheman
Blachemer
Blacre
Blacsune
Blacuin
Blacun
Blacus
Blakeman
Blancar
Blund
Boche
Boda
Boddus
Bode
Bodin
Boding
Boi
Boia
Bole
Bolest
Bolla
Bolle
Bollo
Boln
Bolne
Bonde
Bondi
Bondo
Bondus
Borda
Boret
Borgered
Borgeret
Borred
Borret
Boso
Bosteinn
Bot
Boti
Botild
Botius
Botiz
Bou
Boui
Brand
Brandulf
Branduna
Branting
Branuuine
Breme
Bresibalt
Bretel
Bricfrid
Brichtmar
Bricmar
Bricmær
Bricnod
Bricsi
Bricsic
Bricsmar
Bricstan
Bricstec
Bricsteg
Bricstouuard (Som.)
Bricstual
Bricstuard
Bricstuin
Bricstul

Brictere
Bricteua
Brictic
Brictmar
Brictmer
Brictolf
Brictred
Brictric
Brictsuin
Brictuald
Brictuard
Brictui
Brictuid
Brictuin
Brictuold
Brictuolt
Brictuuard
Bricxtric
Brideuuold
Briford
Brihferd
Brihmar
Briht
Brihtman
Brihtmar
Brihtnoth
Brihtnot
Brihtric
Brihtuold
Brihtwald
Brinot
Brisid
Brismar
Brisnod
Bristec
Bristei
Bristeuuard
Bristoaldus (Devon)
Bristui
Bristuin
Bristuoldus
Bristuuard
Briteua
Britfleda (f.)
Britheue
Brithmar
Brithwold
Britmar
Britnod
Britric
Brixe
Brixi
Brixtuin
Brocles
Brode
Broder
Brodo
Brodor
Brodre
Bruhise
Brumage (Northants)
Bruman
Brumanbeard
Brumann
Brumar
Brun
Brune
Brunesune
Brungar
Brungart
Brunier
Bruniht
Bruning
Bruno
Brunus
Brunwin
Bu (Yorks)
Bubba
Buge (Notts)
Bugered
Bughered
Bugo (Notts, Yorks)
Bului
Bunda
Bunde
Bundi
Bundo
Burc
Burcard
Burch de
Burchard
Burchart
Burchric
Burkart
Burgel
Burgered (Devon)
Burli
Burnes
Burnod
Burred
Burrer
Burret
Burric
Burro
Busch (Herts)

C.

Cabe
Cadiand
Caduualent
Cædd
Caflo
Calpus
Camerarius
Camp
Campa
Campo
Cana
Canceler
Candovre
Cane
Canistre
Cano
Cantuin
Canud
Canus
Canut
Capellanus
Capin
Capus
Carentoch
Cari
Carle
Carlesone
Carleunda
Carlo
Carman
Caron
Caschin
Cassa
Caua
Cauua
Cecus
Cedd
Cedde
Celcott
Celeinus
Celestan
Cellinc
Celmar
Celred
Celric
Cerret
Certesyg
Ceruel
Cestre
Ceterith
Chelbertus
Chenegar
Chenestan
Cheneue
Cheneuuard
Chenias
Chenicte
Chening
Chenisi
Chenistre
Chenna
Chenp
Chenric
Chentis
Chentiscus
Chentuinus
Chenuard
Chenui
Chenuicelle
Chenvichelle
Chenvin
Chenut
Chepin
Cheping
Cheric
Cheteber

Chetel
Chetelbar
Chetelbern
Chetelbert
Chilbert
Chiluert
Chinesi
Chinestan
Chinias
Chiping
Chit
Chitel
Cild
Cille
Cilleham de
Cilt
Clac
Claman
Clarebold
Cliber
Clibert
Cloch
Cnud
Cnut
Cobbe
Coc
Code
Codolf
Codricus
Coduius
Cofsi
Cola
Colben
Colbert
Colbrand
Cole
Colebran
Coleg
Colegrim
Coleman
Colgrim
Colgrin
Colibertus
Colle
Collnic
Colne
Colo
Colocar
Coloen
Cols
Colsegc
Colsuan
Colsuein
Coluin
Colvin
Commend
Constabularius
Coolf
Coolle
Copsi
Corbun
Costellin
Couta
Crac
Crin
Croc
Crucan
Cubold
Cudulf
Cunlf
Cutbert

D.

Dachelin
Dacus
Dagobertus
Dainz
Dane
Danemund
Dedol
Dedou
Deincora
Delfin
Dena
Dene
Depekin
Derch
Derinc
Dering
Derolfus
Derstanus
Deule
Doda
Dode
Doding
Dodo
Dolesuuif
Dolfin
Domne
Domniz
Domno
Don
Done
Donne
Donning
Donno
Dons
Dore
Dot
Doth
Dotus
Dringlel
Drogo
Drondus
Duglei
Dunestan
Dunne
Dunniht
Dunninc
Dunning
Dunno
Duns
Dunstan
Durand
Durilda
Dustan
Duna (f.)
Dunen

E.

Eadmund
Eaduin
Ealgar
Earne
Ebrard
Eburg
Ecchebrand
Ecchefrid
Eculf
Edded
Eddeua
Eddeva
Eddid
Eddied
Eddiet
Edduin
Eddulf
Edeldreda
Edelmund
Edelric
Edeluuold
Edena
Ederic
Edestan
Edeulf
Edgar
Edged
Edgida
Edic
Edid
Ediet
Edilt
Edina
Edlouedief
Edmær
Edmar
Edmer
Edmund
Ednod
Ednoth

Edred
Edric
Eduin
Edunard (Cild, Cilt.)
Eduui
Edwin
Eduunus
Eduuold
Eduuolt
Edzi
Egbert
Egbrand
Egilfride
Egfride
Eghebrand
Eglesham, Abbatia de (Glouc.)
Eilaf
Eilsberie
Eileua
Eilmer
Eilric
Eingar
Einulf
Eiric
Eiulf
Elaf
Elded
Eldeua
Eldid
Eldildæ
Eldit
Eldred
Eldret
Elduif
Elduin
Eleua

Elfac
Elfag
Elfeg
Elfelm
Elfelt
Elfer
Elfgiva
Elfin
Elflet
Elfric
Elgar
Elget
Eli
Eliard
Eliert
Eliet
Elintone
Elmær
Elmar
Elmer
Elmund
Elnoc
Elnod
Elous
Elric
Elsi
Elstan
Elsuid
Eltor
Eluena
Eluin
Eluine
Eluolt
Eluret
Eluric
Elurilde
Eluuacre
Eluuar

Eluuard
Eluui
Eluuin
Eluuold
Engelri
Engelric
Enisan
Epy
Erchebrand
Erding
Erfast
Ergrim
Eric
Erich
Erlebald
Erlechin
Erlenc
Erne
Erneber
Ernebold
Ernebrand
Erneburne
Ernegrin
Erneis
Ernesi
Erneuin
Erneuui
Erni
Erniet
Ernold
Ernu
Ernui
Ernuin
Ernuit
Ernulf
Ertein
Eruastus
Esber

Esbern
Escelf
Eschet
Escul
Escule
Esgar
Esket
Eskmeld
Esmoda
Esnar
Esneburn
Essocher
Essul
Estan
Estarcher
Estmunt
Estori
Estorp de
Estred
Etgar
Etmar
Etnod
Etone
Etsius
Euchill
Eudo
Euing
Eur
Eureuuacre (Devon)
Euroac
Eustachius
Eustan
Euuacre
Ewen
Ewicman
Ezi
Ezui

F.

Faber
Fader
Fanchel
Fardan
Fardein
Fargrim
Fastolf
Fech

Feche
Feg
Fegarus
Felaga
Fenchel
Fenisc
Fin
Fin (danus)

Finegal
Fisc
Fitel
Fitheus
Floteman
Forn
Forne
Forst

Fot
Fradre
Frambolt
Fran
Frane
Frano
Franpalt
Franpold

Frauuin
Frebertus
Fredebern
Frederic
Fredghis
Fredgis
Fredgist
Fredregis
Fredri
Fregis
Fregist
Freowin
Freuuin
Fridebert
Friebern
Friebert
Frodo
Frogerus
Fuglo
Fulbert
Fulcard
Fulcher
Fulcheric
Fulchi
Fulchri
Fulcoi
Fulcui
Fulghel
Furcard
Fursa
Fyach

G.

Galterus
Gam
Game
Gamebar
Gamel
Gamelbar
Gamelcarle
Gangemere
Gardulf
Garle
Gellinge
Genret
Genuis
Genust
Genut
Gerinus
Gerling
Germund
Gernan
Gerneber
Gernebern
Gerold
Gert
Gest
Getda
Gethe (f.)
Gethne
Gheri
Ghida
Ghil (Yorks)
Ghilander
Ghile
Ghilebrid
Ghilemicel
Ghilepatric
Ghille
Gida
Gilemichel
Giraldus
Girardus
Giroldus
Gislebertus
Giso
Gitda
Gladewin
Gladuin
Gladuine
Gleuuin
Glouuec
Glunier
God
Goda
Godbold
Goddua
Gode
Goded
Godefrid
Godel
Godelent
Godeman
Godere
Goderic
Goderus
Godessa
Godestan
Godet
Godeua
Godeurt
Godeva
Godgeua
Godhit
Godid
Godil
Godinc
Goding
Godiva (Countess Warwick)
Godman
Godmar
Godmund
Godo
Godred
Godric
Godrid
Godton
Godtovi
Goduin
Goerth
Gogan
Gola
Golde
Golderon
Goldinus
Goldstan
Goldus
Golegrim
Golleue
Golnil
Golstan
Goltoui
Goluin
Gonchel
Gonchetel
Gondrede
Gonhard
Gonnar
Gonneuuate
Gonni
Gonnil
Gonuerd
Gort
Gos
Gosfrid
Gosp
Gospatric
Gotil
Gotild
Gotius
Gotlac
Gotone
Gotra
Gouti
Gozelin
Grene
Greslet
Greue
Gribol
Grichetel
Grifin
Griketel
Grim
Grimbald
Grimber
Grimbert
Grimbold
Grimchel
Grimchil
Grimmus
Grimolfus
Grimulf
Grimus
Grinchel
Grino
Grossus
Grud
Grunulf
Grut
Grutt
Guda (f.)
Gudda
Gudeta
Gudmund
Gudmunt
Gudret
Gueda
Guerd

Guert
Gueth
Guiolf
Gulbert
Guluert
Gunchil
Gundulf
Guneuuare
Gunnar
Gunner
Gunneuuate
Gunni
Gunnild
Gunning
Gunnor
Gunnulf
Gunre
Gunuer
Gunuert
Gunuuar
Gunward
Gurert
Guret
Gurt
Guthac
Gutmund

H.

Hache
Haco
Hacon
Hacun
Hademar
Hadeuui
Hadimar
Haduic
Hadulf
Haduuin
Haemar
Hagana
Hagane
Hagris
Haimer
Haiminc
Hairand
Hakena
Haldan
Haldein
Halden
Haltor
Hambe
Haminc
Haming
Handone
Hannart
Hapra
Har
Hard
Hardechin
Hardecnut
Hardewin
Harding
Hardul
Hardulf
Haregrim
Haregrin
Harold
Harparius (Camb. Aluui)
Hasten
Hauuard
Hauuart
Heche
Hedned
Hedul
Helewis
Helga
Helge
Helghi
Helghin
Helins
Helmelea
Heltor
Henricus
Her
Herald
Herbert
Herch
Herc
Heremannus
Hereuuard (Linc.)
Hereuuoldus
Herfast
Herfrid
Herfrind
Herleng
Hermann
Hernetoc
Herold
Herolf
Herueus
Herulfus
Hildeuert
Hobbesune Leuricus (Suff.). *See* Obbesune
Hoch
Hofward
Hoga
Holangar
Holchetel
Holefest
Holmo
Holt
Holund
Homdai
Honeuain
Horim
Horling
Horne
Horolf
Hosmund
Houden
Hugo
Humman
Huna
Hunchil
Hundic
Hundin
Hunding
Hundulp
Hune
Hunef
Hunepot
Huni
Huning
Hunneue
Hunni
Hunnic
Hunnit
Hunnith
Hunta
Hunus
Husteman
Huthtrad
Huthtret
Hveche

I. and J.

Jadulfus
Jalt
Jaul
Ilbert
Ineuuar
Ingar
Ingefrid
Ingelric
Ingemund
Ingeuuar
Ingolf
Ingrede
Inguare
Ingulf
Johannes (danus)
Joseph
Jouin
Iric
Judichel
Juin
Juing
Juo
Justan
Justin

K.

Kee (Norf.)
Keneuuard
Kenoldus
Kenric
Kerinc
Ketel
Ketelber
Ketelbern
Ketelbert
Keteluua
Keueua
Kochaga
Kochagana

L.

Ladulf
Lag
Laghemann
Lagman
Lambe
Lambecarl
Lambertur
Lanbecarl
Lanc
Lancfer
Lanch
Lanchei
Lang
Langabein
Lange
Langfer
Langfere
Lant
Lasciuus
Ledi
Ledman
Ledmar
Ledmer
Ledric
Leduui
Leduuin
Lefchil
Lefcill
Lefelm
Leffcilt
Lefflet
Lefled
Leflet
Lefmer
Lefolt
Lefquena
Lefric
Lefriz
Lefsi
Lefsida
Lefsinus
Lefsius
Lefstan
Lefsune
Leftan
Lefwin
Leimar
Leising
Leisini
Leit
Leman
Lemar
Lemer
Leodmer
Leofleda
Leofric
Leofsi
Leofstan
Leofsun
Leomer
Leonestan
Lepsi
Lesinc
Lesing
Lesius
Lestan
Leswin
Let
Letfled
Leua (f.)
Leuard
Leue
Leuecild
Leueclai
Leuecol
Leuedai
Leuefa
Leuegar
Leuget
Leueno
Leuenod
Leueric
Leueron
Leuestan
Leuesuna
Leuesunas
Leuet
Leuetuna
Leueua
Leuid
Leuiet
Leuiget
Leuild
Leuinc
Leuin
Leuing
Leuolt
Leured
Leuret
Leuric
(Leofric, the last Bp. of Crediton, transferred his seat to Exeter by permission of K. Ed. Confr, 1050.)
Leustan
Leuuard
Leuuare
Leuui
Leuuin
Leuuold
Leuuord
Leuuric
Ligul
Ligulf
Lihtwin
Linbald
Linxi
Liseman
Lisius
Liuing
Liuric
Liuuard
Lochi
Locre
Lodric
Lofe
Longus
Lord
Loten
Ludi
Ludri
Lufchel
Lurc
Lustuin
Luttin
Luuare
Luuede
Luuet
Luuetote

M.

Maban
Machel (Yorks, 332)
Machern
Machus
Macus
Madoch
Magbanec
Magne
Magno (Suert)
Mainard
Maino

Mal
Malet
Malf
Malgrim
Malgrin
Man (Yorks)
Mancus
Manegot
Manesuna
Manna
Mannicus
Mannig
Mannius (Swert)
Manno
Manstan
Mansuna
Mapesone
Marculf
Martinus
Maruaen
Maruuen
Matheld (Devon)
Mathila (Devon)
Mauna
Melc
Meldona
Melduna
Mellessam de (Suff., 409)
Melmidoc
Menleua
Merde
Merdo
Merefin
Meresuuet
Mereuin
Merken
Merlesuain
Merlesuen
Meruen
Meruin
Meurdoch
Micelenie
Michaelis
Michahel
Milda
Milegrim
Milnegrim
Modephefe (f.)
Modeva
Modgeva
Modinc
Moding
Moduin
Moithar
Molleve
Monulf
Morcar
Moregrim
Morewin
Morfar
Morganau
Moruant
Morulf
Mule (Yorks)
Mulo
Munding (Suff.)
Mundret
Munulf
Murdac
Murdoc
Muscham
Musla

N.

Nicholaus
Nigell
Niuelig
Niuelin
Noriolt
Norman
Novi

O.

Obbesune. *See* Hobbesune
Ocsen
Oda
Ode
Odeman
Oderus
Odeua
Odfrid
Odil
Odincar
Odincarl
Odo
Odulfus
Ofchetel
Offa
Offels
Offerd
Offers
Offo
Offram
Ofl
Oghe
Oin
Oiranti
Olbolt
Olf
Olgrim
Olketel
Olvva (f.)
Oluius
Oluuard
Oluuin
Olviet
Orde
Ordec
Ordgar
Ordin
Ording
Ordinc
Ordmær
Ordmar
Ordmer
Ordoff
Ordric
Ordui
Ordulf
Orduuold
Orgar
Orgrim
Orm
Ormar
Ormchetel
Orme
Ormer
Ornod
Orthi
Oruenot
Orulf
Osber
Osbern
Osbert
Oschetel
Oschil
Osfert
Osford
Osgar
Osgod
Osgot
Osiar
Osier
Osiet
Osketel
Oslac
Osmar
Osmer
Osmund
Ostebrand
Ostula
Osul
Osulf
Osuuald
Oswar
Osuuard

Osui
Osuid
Osuuol
Oswald
Otbert
Otburuilla
Ote
Othen
Otho
Othon
Otre
Otro
Otti
Oualet
Oudencar
Oudfride
Oudgrim
Oudon
Oudulf
Ouen
Ouiet
Oune
Outbert
Outi
Ouu
Ouuine

P.

Padda
Pagan
Pagen
Pallinus
Pat (Ches.)
Paulin
Pauli
Pbochestan
Perci
Perlo
Peurel
Phin
Pic
Pileuuin
Pin
Pinchengi
Pinslan
Poinc Godricus
Pointel Tedricus
Pur

R.

Rachenild
Rada
Radboda
Radolf
Radulf
Rænold
Rafrid
Rafuuin
Ragenal
Ragenald
Ragenalt
Ragenild
Ragenot
Rainald
Rainbald
Rainer
Ram
Ramechil
Rannulf
Rasrid
Ratho
Rauan
Rauecate
Rauechel
Rauechet
Rauechetel
Rauechil
Ravelin
Raven
Rauen
Rauenchil
Rauene
Rauengar
Rauensuar
Rauensuard
Raues
Rauesard
Rauesue
Raulfus
Rausnar
Rauuen
Rayner
Reder
Redulf
Rees (Ches.)
Regifer
Reider
Reimbald
Reinbald
Rembald
Renold
Restef
Restelf
Reuensuard
Reuer
Ricard
Rinbold
Ringul
Ringulf
Robert
Roc
Roches
Roger
Rold
Rolf
Rolft
Roschel
Roschet
Roschil
Rot
Rotbert
Rotlesc
Roulf
Rozo
Rufus Siuuard
Ruillic
Ruschil

S.

Sac
Sæmar
Sagar
Sagera
Sagrim
Saiard
Saied
Saiet
Sailt
Saisi
Saisil
Salecoe
Salomon
Salpus
Salvage
Samar
Saolf
Sared
Saric
Sarpo
Sauard
Sauin
Saul
Saulf
Sauord
Sauuard
Sauuata
Sauuin

Sauuold
Saxa
Saxi
Saxo
Saxulf
Saxwin
Sbern
Scaldefort
Scalpi
Scanchel
Scapius
Scelfride
Scemund
Scet
Sceua
Scheit (Norf.)
Scipti
Scireuold
Scirold
Sclula
Scotcol
Scotecol
Scotel
Scoua
Scroti
Scrotin
Scula
Scule
Sech
Seduin
Segar
Segrida
Seiar
Selecolf
Seleuuin
Selua
Semær
Seman
Semar
Semer
Sendi
Sercar
Seric
Serlo
Sessi
Seubar
Seuen
Seulf
Seuuar
Seuuard
Seuuart
Seuuen
Seuui
Seuuin
Seward
Sexi
Sibe
Sichet
Sidgar
Sigar
Sighet
Sigred
Simon
Simond
Simund
Sinod
Sired
Siret
Sireuuald
Sireuuold
Siric
Sirof
Sistain
Sistric
Siuard
Siuargent
Siuerd
Siuert
Siulf
Siuuard
Siuuart
Siuuin
Siuuold
Siuurad
Smail
Smalo
Smer
Smert
Smeuuin
Snellinc
Snerri
Snoch
Snode
Snot
Soartin
Sol
Sonneua
Sonulf
Sorches
Sorchoued
Soror Stigandi
Sort
Sorte
Sortebrand
Sortocol
Sota
Soteman
Sotinz
Sparhauoc
Sperhauoc
Sperri
Sperun
Spieta
Spille
Spirites
Spirtes
Sport
Spretman
Sprot
Sprotulf
Spuda
Spur
Staigrim
Stainulf
Stam
Stanard
Stanart
Stanchil
Stanfled
Stangrim
Stanhard
Stanhart
Stankar
Stanmar
Stannechetel
Stanuin
Stapleuin
Stari
Starling
Stauhart
Stein
Steinchetel
Steinulf
Stepi
Stepiot
Ster
Stercher
Stergar
Sterr
Sterre
Stichehare
Stigand
Stikestac
Stilla
Stille
Stingand
Stori
Stou
Strami
Stramun
Strang
Strangulf
Stric
Strui
Struostun
Stubart
Stur
Suain
Suan
Suardcol
Suart
Suartcol
Suartin
Suartric
Suaue
Sudan
Suein
Suert
Suerting
Suet
Sueteman
Sueting
Suetman
Suetth
Suga
Suglo
Sumersul
Summerde
Summerled
Suneman
Suuain
Suuarger
Suuen
Suwart
Swert
Syric

T.

Taini, Teini, Teigni
Taldus
Tallgebosc
Tarmoht
Tedgar
Tedric
Tedricus
Teit
Tela (f.)
Tenus
Teodric
Teolf
Teos
Tepechin
Tepekin
Terus
Thol
Thole
Tholi
Thor
Thoret
Thori
Thouus
Thuinam
Thurbern
Thure
Thuri
Thurmer
Thurmot
Tidulf
Tihell
Tisellin
Toc
Tocha
Tochæ
Toche
Tochi
Tochil
Tocho
Tof
Toiswald
Toka
Toke
Tokesone
Tol
Tolf
Toli
Tona
Tone
Tonna
Tonne
Tono
Tope
Topi
Topic
Tor
Toradre
Torber
Torbern
Torbert
Torbrand
Torbrant
Torchel
Torchetel
Torchil
Tord
Tored
Toret
Toreth
Torfin
Tori
Torif
Tormord
Torn
Toroi
Torol
Torolf
Torp
Torsus
Tort
Toruerd
Toruert
Torulf
Tosti
Tostil
Toti
Tou
Toue
Touet
Toui
Touilda
Toul
Toulf
Touni
Toxus
Trasemund
Trasmund
Trauuin
Trec
Trumin
Tube
Tuffa
Tuini
Tumi
Tumme
Tunbi
Tuneman
Tunna
Tunne
Turber
Turbern
Turbert
Turbran
Turbrant
Turch
Turchel
Turchetel
Turchil
Tureuert
Turgar
Turgis
Turgisle
Turgod
Turgot
Turgrim
Turi
Turketel
Turkil
Turlog
Turmod
Turmund
Turold
Turolf
Turorne
Turot
Turstan
Turstin
Turtin
Turued
Turuer
Turuerd
Turuert
Turuet
Turulf

U and V.

Vbe
Vctebrand
Vctred
Vdebrun
Vdeman
Vgelbert
Vgheta
Vibald
Vital
Vitel
Viulf
Vlbert
Vlbold
Vlchel
Vlchet
Vlchetel
Vlchil
Vlestan
Vlf
Vlfac
Vlfah
Vlfar
Vlfchetel
Vlfech
Vlfeg
Vlfeih
Vlfelm
Vlfenisc

Vlfer
Vlfert
Vlfenisc
Vlfiet
Vlfketel
Vlflet
Vlfmer
Vlfon (Sussex)
Vlfra
Vlfret
Vlfric
Ulfriz
Vlfstan
Vlfus
Vlfwin
Vlgar
Vlgrim
Vlketel
Vlmar
Vlmær
Vlmer
Vlnod
Vlnoth
Vlric
Ulsi
Vlsiet
Vlstan
Vlsuin
Vlsy
Vltain
Vltan
Vluara
Vluard
Vluer
Vlueron
Vluert
Vluerun
Vlueua
Vluied
Vluiet
Vluin
Vluoi
Vluret
Vluric
Ulwar
Vluuard
Vluuen
Vluui
Vluuic
Vluuiet
Vluuin
Vluuinchil
Vluuold
Vluured
Vlvi
Vnban
Vnfac
Unlot
Vnspac
Vntani
Vntan
Vnton
Vrleuuine
Vstred
Uthtret

W.

Wacra
Wada
Wade
Wadel
Wadelo
Wadels
Wado
Waga
Waih
Wailoff
Walduin
Walle
Wallef
Walleus
Wallo (Ches.)
Walraue
Walræuen
Walt
Waltef
Walteif
Walter
Walteu
Wana
Wand
Wants
Wardham
Warrena, Will de
Waso
Wateman
Wdebrun
Wege
Weghe
Weinhou
Weleret
Welgrim
Welland
Welle
Uuelp
Welp
Welrauen
Wenesi
Wenestan
Wenhou
Weniet
Wenning
Vueniot
Wenric
Werden
Wester
Westre
Wetman
Wgulafra
Whita
Wiber
Wibert
Wichigus
Wichin
Wicling
Wicnod
Wicolf
Wicstric
Wictric
Widard
Widegrip
Widenesci
Wider
Widuis
Wiet
Wifare
Wifle
Wiflet
Wig
Wiga
Wigar
Wige
Wigha
Wighe
Wiglac
Wigod
Wigot
Wihenoc
Wihtgar
Wightmar
Wihtred
Wihtric
Wiking (Suff.)
Wilac
Wilaf
Wilde
Wilegrip
Willa
Wimarc
Wimer
Wine
Winegod
Winemar
Winestan
Winge
Winterled
Wintrelet
Wintremelc (Alricus)
Wirelmus
Wiscar
Wisg
Wisgar
Wislac
Wistan
Wistric
Wit
Uuit
Uuite
Witg
Witgar
Wither
Withgar
Withmer
Withri
Witlac
Witric

Wiuar
Wiuara
Wiuelac
Wiulf
Wlbald
Wlf
Wlfah
Wlfric
Wlgar
Wlmær
Wlmar
Wlmer
Wlnod
Wlsi
Wlsin
Wlstan
Wluard
Wluar
Wleua
Wlui
Wluin
Wlured
Wluric
Wluuar
Wluuard
Wluuen
Wluui
Wlwi
Wluuin
Wnulf
Wordron

NAMES OF TENANTS IN CHIEF IN DOMESDAY BOOK.

A.

Abetot de
Achebranni
Adam
Adeldreda
Adeling
Adeliz
Adobod
Adrecide
Ældeva
Ældred
Agebric
Agemund
Ailmar
Ailrun
Ailunard
Aincurt de
Aiulf
Alan
Albamarla de
Albani
Alberic
Albert
Albingi de
Albus
Alden
Aldit
Aldred
Aldvi
Alestan
Alfhilla
Alfildis
Alfred
Algar
Alis
Almar
Almer
Almund
Alnod
Alric
Alselin
Alsi
Alverd
Aluers
Aluena
Alvied
Aluiet
Alured
Aluric
Alward
Alwi
Alwin
Alwold
Andeli
Anschetil
Ansger
Ansgot
Arches de
Archil
Arcis de
Aregrin
Areti
Artor
Arundel
Aschil
Ascuit
Asinus
Asne
Audoen
Autbert
Azelina
Azor

B.

Bade de
Badpalmas de
Baignard
Balduin
Balgiole
Bangiard
Bano de
Barbatus Hugo
Bastard
Batailge de la
Bech de
Bedford de
Belcamp de
Belet
Bella Fago de (Beaufoy)
Belmont de
Belot
Belvaco de
Benz
Benzelin
Berchelai de
Berchingis de
Bereville de
Bernai de (Normandy)
Bernard
Berneres de
Bernerus
Bersers de
Bertone de
Bertram de
Bevrere de
Bigot
Bituricensis
Blunders
Boci de
Bohun de
Bolebec de
Bolle
Bollo
Bomene de
Bonvalest
Bosch de
Boscnorman de
Breteville de
Bricteua
Brictoward

Brictric
Brictuin
Brimor de
Brismar
Brito
Bruis Robertus de (Yorks)
Brun
Bruning
Bucfestre de
Buci de
Budi de
Buenvaslet de
Buge (Notts)
Buiville de
Burci de
Burun de
Buruolt
Busli de

C.

Cadomo de (Caen)
Cahainges de
Cailgi
Cambrai de
Canut
Carbonel
Carentoch de
Carle
Carnot
Cedda, S.
Cernel de
Certesyg de
Cestre de
Ceterith de
Chana, Lewin
Chelbert
Chenvin
Cheping
Chetel
Chetelbern
Chetelbert
Chievre, Wm.
Chilbert
Cicestre de
Croches de
Claville de
Clec, Godwin
Clibert
Coci de
Cola
Colebern
Colegrim
Collinc
Colsvain
Colsuen
Colsuin
Columbels de
Colvin
Corcelles de
Cormelies de
Corniole, Wm.
Crass, Norman
Cratel, Godric
Credun, Wido de
Creneburne de
Crispin, Milo
Christina (f.)
Croc
Croiland de
Cudulf
Cvenild
Curbespine de
Curci de
Cutbert

D.

Dalari de
David
Derman
Dispensator
Dive de
Doai de
Dodesone, Alwin
Dodid
Dodo
Dolfin
Donne
Donno
Dons
Dovre de
Dowai de
Dreimes de
Drogo
Dunning
Durand
Dwai de

E.

Eadmund
Ebrard
Ebrulf
Eddeva
Eddid
Eddiet
Eddulf
Edeua
Edgar
Ediet
Edmund
Edred
Edric
Eduin
Eduard
Edwi
Edwin
Eglesham de (Eynsham, in Oxfordshire)
Eldild
Eldit
Eldred
Elfain
Elmer
Elnod
Elric
Elsi
Elward
Equarius
Erchenger
Eric
Erleching
Ernald
Ernebern
Erneis
Ernui
Ernuin
Ertald
Esnebern
Eudo
Eustachius
Exesse de

F.

Fafiton
Faleise de
Feireres de, or Ferieres
Fenisc, Ulf
Ferendon de
Flamme
Flanbard
Flandren
Flavus
Forne
Fossard
Fossart, Nigel
Fouuer, Ansger
Framen, Rudulf
Fresle, Richard
Frodo
Fulcher
Fulcred

G.

Galterus
Game
Gamel
Gand de
Gant de
Gerin
Gernio
Gernon
Ghilo
Gifard
Gilo
Girard
Girbert
Girold
Giselbert
Goda (f.)
Gode
Godebold
Godefrid
Godescal
Godeua
Godmund
Godric
Goduin
Goisfrid
Goizenboded, Wm.
Goismer
Golde
Gonduin
Gosbert, Hugo
Goscelmus
Gospatric
Gozelin
Granetarius
Greistein de (France)
Greno or Grenon. *See* Gernon
Grentebrige de
Grestain de
Gretuilla de
Griffin
Grimbald
Grim
Gudmund
Gunduin
Gunfrid
Gurnai

H.

Hagheburn
Hago
Haimeric
Haldein
Haluille de
Hamelin
Hamo
Handone de
Hardinc
Harding
Hardulf
Haregrin
Harold
Hascoit
Hascoith
Hascolf
Helion, Herveus de
Henricus
Heppo
Herald
Herbert
Herbrand
Hereford de
Herion de
Hermer
Herveus
Hesding
Hghbern
Hispaniensis, Alured
Holmo de
Hortone de
Hosed, Wm.
Hugo
Hugolin
Humfrid
Hunfrid
Hunger

I AND J.

Ida (Countess of Bologne)
Jeanio
Ilbert
Ilbodo
Illinge
Ingald
Ingania de (Engaine)
Ingulf
Insula de
Johannes
Isac
Iseldis
Judhel de Totenais (Totness)
Iveri de
Ivichel
Ivikel
Justen

K.

Ketel

L.

Laci de
Lanchei de
Landri
Landric
Lanfranc
Lanheie de
Lasne, Hugo
Latimarus
Launire de
Lawirce. *See* Wirce
Leduin
Lefstan
Legat
Leuena
Leviet
Levild
Leving
Leuric
Leutfrid
Leuuin
Ligult
Limesi de
Liof
Lira de
Liseman
Loges de
Lorz de
Losward
Lovet
Loveth
Luith
Luri de
Lusorüs de

M.

Madoc
Magnavilla (Mannwille)
Maigno
Maino. *See* Manno
Mal. *See* Malf
Malaopa
Malcolun
Maldoith
Maldred
Maldrith
Malet
Malf
Maminot
Mantel
Mappesone
Martin
Matheus
Mathild
Mauric
Mauritaniensis
Medehal de
Melchisan de
Mellend de
Merde de
Mereuuin
Merleberge de
Mert
Micelenie de
Moduin
Moion de
Molebec de
Monneuile de
Montagud de
Monteburg de
Montfort de
Montgomery de
Morin
Mortemer de
Mucelgros de
Musard

N.

Nicolaus
Nigel
Niger
Norman

O.

Oaura
Obarvilla de
Odard
Odburville de
Ode
Odin
Odo
Odolin
Oger
Oilgi de
Oirant
Olaf
Ordgar
Ordric
Ordui
Orlatelle
Orm
Osbern
Osgot
Osiet
Oslac
Osmer
Osmund
Ostreham de
Osward
Oswold
Otha
Otho
Otto
Ou de
Outi
Ouus
Ow de

P.

Pagen
Pagenel
Pancevolt
Parcher, Anschitil
Percehaie
Perci
Peret
Persore de
Peverel
Picot
Pictavensis

Pierani de
Pilardintone de
Pincerna
Pinel
Piperellus. *See* Peverel
Poillgi de
Pointel de
Pomerei de
Porth de
Pugnant
Puingiant
Puintel

Q.

Quintin, S. de

R.

Rabellus
Radulf
Ragenald
Rainald
Rainbald
Rainburgis
Reinbuedcurt de
Ramechil
Rames de
Ramesy de
Ramis de
Rannalf
Ravelin
Raven
Ravenchil
Rayner
Reinbald
Restold
Ricard
Riueire
Robert
Rodmund
Roelent
Roger
Rolf
Romenel de
Rotbert
Rothais (f.)
Ruald

S.

Saiet
Saieva
Saisselin
Salceid de
Salceit de
Salebi de
Salmur de
S. Quintin de
Sanson
Saric
Sariz
Sasford
Sasselin
Saulf
Saward
Sawin
Sawold
Sbern
Scalers de (or d'Echallers)
Schelin
Scohies de
Scrope
Scudet
Sedret
Seric
Seuard
Sibold
Sigar de Cioches
Siric
Siuard
Soartin
Sortebrand
Spech (or Espec ?)
Sperri
Stanard
Starcolf
Stefan
Steinulf
Stigand
Stirman
Stratfort de
Sturmid
Suain
Suarding
Suarting
Suen
Sueno
Surdeual de
Suuen
Svain
Swan

T.

Tailgebosch
Tedfort de
Tehell
Teodric
Tetbald
Tezelin
Theodric
Thomas
Tison
Tisun
Tochi
Todeni de
Toenio de
Tona
Tor
Torber
Torbern
Torchil
Tored
Tornyg de (Thomey)
Totenais de
Tovi
Turbern
Turbert
Turchil
Turstui
Turstun

U and V.

Valbadon de
Valonges de
Valonis de
Vctred
Vdi
Veci de
Ver de
Verdun de
Verli de
Vernon de
Vis de Lew
Vlbert
Vlchel
Vlf
Vlfric
Vlgar
Vlmar
Vlnod
Ulsi
Vluiet
Vluui

W.

Wadard
Wado
Walchelin
Waldin
Waleram
Waleran
Waleric
Walter
Wanz
Warene de
Warwell de
Wateman
Wateuille de
Waula
Wibert
Widuile de
Wielard
Wigar
Willelm
Wiltune
Winemar
Wintremelc
Wirce de
Wislac
Wit
Wlmar
Wluin
Wlwi
Wrehantune de

NAMES OF UNDER-TENANTS OF LANDS AT THE TIME OF THE DOMESDAY SURVEY.

A.

Aba (Northts.)
Abba (Norf.)
Abel (Kent)
Abernon de
Abetot de
Abraham
Acard
Achet, Walterus
Acun
Adam
Adelard
Adeledmus
Adelelmus
Adelina
Adelold
Adelolf
Adelulf
Adelwin
Adeluuold
Adestan
Adolf
Adret
Ældeua
Ældred
Ælfelm
Ælgot
Ælmer
Aelons
Ælric
Ælueue
Æluuard
Ærnold
Agemund
Aguet
Agenulf
Aghemund
Agnes
Ailbold
Ailmar
Ailric
Ailuard
Ailuuacre
Aincurt de
Airard
Aistan
Aitard
Aiulf
Alam
Alan
Albengi de
Alberi
Alberic
Albert
Albin'
Albold
Albus
Alcher
Alde
Alded
Aldelin
Alden
Aldi
Aldred
Aldrie
Alelm
Alencun
Alestan
Alflet
Alfred
Alfric
Alfrid
Algar
Alger
Alich
Allic
Almær
Almar
Almer
Almfrid
Almod
Alno
Alnod
Alnulf
Alred
Alric
Alselin
Alsi
Altet

Aluerad
Aluered
Aluena
Aluiet
Alulf
Alured
Aluric
Aluuard
Alward
Alwart
Alwewe
Aluui
Aluuin
Aluuold
Amalric
Ambrose
Amelfrid
Amelger
Amerland
Aman
Amund
Anchitill
Andeli de
Andreas (Cornw.)
Anger
Angevin, Osmund
Anschetill
Anschill
Anschitil
Ansegis
Ansel
Anseredus
Ansfred
Ansfrid
Ansgar
Anger
Ansger
Ansgered
Ansgot
Anslepe de (Northampt.)
Ansleuile
Appeuile
Archil
Archis
Arcis de
Arda de
Ardulf
Arling
Armenteres
Arnald
Arnegrim
Arni
Arnulf
Artur
Arundel, Roger
Asc' (Ascelin)
Aschil
Ascolf
Aselin
Asford
Asfort
Aslac
Aslen
Asne
Asso
Asuert
Avenel
Auesgot
Augustin
Avigi
Auigi
Auti
Azelin
Azo
Azor

B.

Baderon
Bagod
Baignar
Baignard
Bainard
Baingiard
Bainiard
Baldeuin
Baldric
Balduin
Balt
Barb, Bernard (Heref.)
Barbes de
Baret
Baro
Basset
Basuin
Beatrix
Bec, Walter
Bech de
Belcamp de
Belencun' de
Belet
Belfago
Belfou
Bellafago
Beluard
Benedict
Benthelm
Benzelin
Berard
Berchelai de
Berdic
Berengarius
Bereuuold
Berger
Bernai de
Bernar
Bernard
Berner
Bernulf
Berold
Berruarius
Bertran
Beruold
Beuerde
Beulf
Big
Bigot
Blach
Blacheman
Blancard
Blancus
Blechu
Bleio
Blize
Blohin
Bloiet
Blon
Blond
Blosseuille de
Blund
Bodin
Bolebec, Hugo
Bollo
Bondi
Bono
Bonuaslet, Willm.
Borci
Bordin
Borel
Boret
Borghill
Bosc de
Boscroard de
Boselin
Boso
Boteric
Boter
Boti
Botild
Braiboue de
Braiose de
Brant
Bretel
Breteuile de
Bricmær
Brictmar
Brictmer
Brictolf
Brictred
Brictric
Brichelf
Brictuin
Brictuuard
Brien
Briend
Brienz
Brion
Brisard
Brismer
Bristeua
Bristist
Bristoald
Bristoard
Brito
Brixi

Brodo
Bruman
Brun
Brunard
Brunel
Brungar
Bruning
Brunnuin
Bruno
Bucard
Buci de
Buerd
Bueret
Buissel
Bundo
Burci de
Burdet
Burghard
Burnard
Burnart
Burneuill de
Bursigni de
Busch
Busli de
Buter

C.

Cada' de (de Cadamo)
Cadio
Cadomi
Cadomo de
Caflo
Cahainges de
Caisned de
Calpus
Caluus
Calvus
Candos de
Cardon
Cardun
Carnot'
Caron de
Carun de
Cedde
Celric
Celsi de
Cepe
Chacepol
Chemarhnec
Chenesis
Chenret
Cheping
Chernet de
Chetel
Chetelbar
Chetelbern
Chetelburn
Cheure
Cioches de
Clarebald
Clarenbald
Claron
Clauile de
Clavilla de
Clodoan
Coc, Aluuin (bedellus)
Coci de
Cola
Colbert
Colegrim
Colevil de
Colgrim
Collo
Colo
Colsuain
Colsuan
Coluin
Colvin
Conded
Constantin
Corbelin
Corbet
Corbin
Corbun
Corcel de
Co'rp
Credun, Wido de
Crispin, Milo
Croc
Cruel
Cudhen
Culling
Curcan de
Curci de
Cus

D.

Daniel, Roger (Suss.)
Dauid
David
Denomore, Wm.
Denuers, Wm.
Depeiz, Guerno
Deramis, Roger
Dereman
Dereuuen
Derinc
Derisbou, W.
Derman
Deuais, Robt.
Deuernu' (De Vernon)
Doda
Doddus
Dodeman
Dodemund
Dodesone, Aluuin (Herts.)
Dodin
Dodo
Dolfin
Domnic
Donecan
Doneuuald
Donno
Douenold
Douuai de
Dreuues, Amalric de (Wilts)
Drogo
Dudeman
Dunning
Dunstan
Dur'
Durand
Dynechaie

E.

Eadvuun
Ebrard
Ecchebrand
Eddeua
Eddid
Eddiet
Eddille
Eddulf
Edelo
Ederic
Edgar
Edied
Edmar
Edmund
Ednod
Edred

Edric
Eduin
Eduuard
Eduui
Egbert
Egbriht
Ehelo
Eideua
Eileua
Eiluuard
Einbold
Elbert
Eldeid
Eldred
Elduin
Elfin
Elfric
Elfrid
Eli
Elinant
Elmar
Elmer
Elmui
Elmund
Elnod
Elric
Elsi
Eluard
Elward
Eluui
Eluuin
Engelbric
Engeler
Engenold
Engenulf
Enisan
Enisant
Er (Ermen-hald)
Erchebrand
Erchenbald
Erenburgis
Erfast
Erluin
Ermenhald
Ermenfrid
Erm'iot
Ernald
Ernegis
Erneis
Ernold
Ernolf
Ernucion
Ernui
Ernuin
Ernulf
Ernuzen
Ertein
Escalers de
Ettard
Eudo
Euen
Euerwin
Eurard
Eurold
Euruin
Eustachius

F.

Fabri
Faderlin
Fadrelin
Faeicon
Faeto
Falcus
Farman
Fastrad
Fatat
Fech
Feggo
Felcher
Felger
Ferme
Ferron
Firmat
Fla'bard
Fla'mart
Fla'mens
Flanbard
Flandr'
Flavus
Flint
Floc de
Folcheran
Folcran
Folet
Forist
Fragrin
Frane
Franco
Frano
Fredgis
Fredo
Frodo
Froger
Froissart, Wm.
Frumond
Fulbert
Fulbric
Fulcard
Fulche
Fulcher
Fulchered
Fulcho
Fulco
Fulcoin
Fulcold
Fulcran
Fulcred
Fulcui
Fulcuin
Fulkered
Fulo
Furic

G.

Gadinc
Gadio
Gadomo de
Galicer
Galt'
Galterus
Gamas
Game
Gamel
Gamelin
Gand de
Gaosfrid
Garenger
Garin
Garmund
Garner
Gatelea
Gaufrid
Gaurinc
Gausfrid
Gerald
Gerard
Gerbodo
Gerelm
German
Germund
Gerneber
Gernon
Gerold
Geron
Gherui
Gifard
Gifart
Gildre
Gingom
Girald
Girande
Girard
Girold
Giron
Gisbert
Gislebert
Gislold
Giso

Glauill
Gleduin (Leic.)
Gleu (Bedf.)
Glodoen
Godard
Godebold
Godefrid
Goderet
Goderun
Godescal
Godeue
Godid
Godinc
Goding
Godman
Godmund
Godric
Goduin
Godzelin
Goisbert
Goisfrid

Goislan
Goislen
Goismer
Goldwin
Goleman
Gollam
Golstan
Gondran
Gonfrid
Gonther
Gosbert
Goscelin
Goscelm
Goselin
Gosfrid
Goslin
Gospatric
Gotwin
Goze
Gozel
Gozet

Grai de
Grando
Grantcurt
Grapinel
Greno
Grentmaisnil de
Grento
Greslet
Grichel
Grichetel
Grifin
Griketel
Grim
Grimbald
Grinon
Gros
Gualter
Guarin
Gudhen. *See* Cudhen

Gudmund
Gueri
Gveric
Guerlin
Guert
Guibert
Gvihu'mar
Gulaffra
Gulbert
Gulfer
Gulfered
Gummar
Gunduin
Gundulf
Gunequata
Gunfrid
Gvnhar
Gunner
Guntard
Gunter
Gutbert

H.

Hacun
Hadeuuin
Hadulf
Hagebert
Haimard
Haimer
Haiming
Haimo
Halanant
Halsard
Hame
Hamelin
Haminc
Hamo
Hamon
Hardeuuin
Harding
Harold
Hato

Heldered
Heldred
Heldret
Heldric
Helduin
Helgod
Helgot
Helio
Helmer
Helto
Hengebald
Henric
Herold
Herbert
Herbrand
Herding
Hereberd
Hereuuard
Herfrid

Herion, Tihell de
Herlebald
Herlebold
Herleuin
Herman
Hermenfrid
Hermer
Hernold
Herold
Herolf
Herpul
Heruen
Hesdinc
Hesding
Hezelm
Hildebrand
Hosdena de
Hosdenc de

Hosed
Hotot de
Houard
Huard
Hubald
Hubb'
Hubert
Hubold
Hveche
Hugo
Hugol'
Hugolin
Hunald
Hunfrid
Hunger
Hunnit
Hunulf
Hurant
Huscarle

I and J.

Jacob
Jagelin
James

Jarnacot
Idhel
Ilbert

Ilbod
Ildebert
Ilduin

Ingald
Ingelra'n
Ilgerus

Inganie
Ingelbald
Ingelbert
Ingelram
Ingelran
Ingelric
Ingenulf
Ingrann
Ingulf
Johais
Joh's
Johannes
Jouin
Iric
Isac
Iseldis
Isenbard
Iseuuard
Ispania de
Judhell
Judichel
Juhell
Junain
Junan
Junen
Iuo
Ivo
Iuran
Iurei
Iuri
Ivri
Iward
Iuuein

K.

Keresburg de

L.

Lacei de
Lachelin
Laci de
Lambert
Lanbert
Landri
Landric
Langetot de
Langhetot de
Lanzelin
Lardarius
Latin
Latinarius
Latinus
Laurentius
Ledman
Ledmar
Leflet
Lefric
Lefsi
Lefsun
Leftan
Lemar
Lemei
Lepsi
Lestan
Letard
Lethelin
Letmar
Leucilt
Leuegar
Leuenot
Leueua
Leuiet
Leuinc
Leuing
Leuric
Leusin
Leuuard
Lewes
Leuui
Leuuine
Leuuric
Liboret
Ligulf
Limesi de
Lincole de
Liof
Lira de
Liseman
Lisoisus
Locels de
Loder
Lodouuin
Loeruic
Lof
Loges de
Loher
Losoard
Losuard
Louel
Louet
Ludichel
Ludo
Lundonie de
Lunen
Lungus
Lusorio de

M.

Machar
Machinator
Machus
Maci
Madoc
Maigno
Mainard
Mainfrid
Maino
Maiulf
Malauill
Malbedeng
Maldoit
Malet
Malf
Malger
Malus Vicinus
Maminot
Manasses
Manbodo
Manneuille de
Mara de
Marcher
Marci de
Marcud
Marescal
Martel
Mascerel
Mascherell
Mater
Mathild
Matheus
Mechenta
Medicus
Meinard
Meinfrid
Mellend de
Melling de
Merc de
Merde de
Mereuin
Merlebey
Miles
Modbert
Moion de
Molebec
Monetar
Monfort de

Monulf
Moran
Morcar
More de
Morel
Moriland
Morin
Moriton de
Mortemer de
Mortuing
Morua
Moruant
Moruuin
Mosters de
Motbert
Moyses
Mucedent de
Mucelgros de
Muceull
Mundret
Murdac
Musard

N.

Nardred
Nauuen
Nemore
Nepos
Nicol
Nicolaus
Nigel
Noiers de
Noies de
Nogiold
Norgiot
Norgot
Norman
Norun
Noui
Nouuers de
Nubold

O.

Oburuilla de
Odard
Odarus
Odbert
Odburcuilla de
Oddo
Odelin
Odin
Odmus
Odo
Odon
Offa
Offels
Offran
Oger
Ogis
Oidelard
Oilard
Oilgi de
Oismelin
Olaf
Olbald
Ole de
Olf
Olgi de
Oliuer
Olnei de
Oluu'
Orbec de
Ordmær
Ordmar
Ordric
Ordulf
Orduui
Orenet
Orenge de
Orgar
Orger
Orm
Ormar
Orme
Ornod
Osbern
Osbert
Osgot
Oslach
Osmund
Osulf
Oswald
Oswar
Osuuard
Osuuic
Osuuold
Otbert
Otbold
Otburville de
Othelin
Othem
Othingar
Otho
Otto
Oudchel
Ouethel
Outi
Ow de
Ou

P.

Pagan
Pagen
Paisfor
Paisforere
Pancefold
Pantul
Pantulf
Papald
Parisiac
Parisiacenis
Parler
Passaq'
Peccatu'
Perapund de
Perci de
Periton de
Pertenai de
Pesserara
Peteuin
Petrus
Peverel
Peurel
Phanexon
Picot
Pictavensis
Pincerna
Pinchengi de
Pinc'u'n'
Pinel
Pipe (Som.)
Piperell
Pipin
Pirot
Piscator
Pistor
Pleines
Poingiant
Pointel'
Polchehard
Pomerei de
Ponther
Ponz
Port de
Pugnant
Pungiant

Q.

Quintin

R.

Rabboda
Rabel
Rademar
Rademer
Radfred
Radman
Radulf
Radus
Rafri
Raimar
Raimund
Rainald
Rainalm
Rainbald
Rainbert
Rainbold
Rainelm
Rainer
Rainfrid
Rainold
Ramis de
Randulf
Rannulf
Rardulf
Rasrid
Ratho
Rauemer
Rauen
Rauengar
Rauenot
Raynald
Rayner
Raynold
Raynouuard
Reduers de
Reger
Reimund
Reinbald
Reinbert
Reiner
Reinfrid
Reinold
Remir
Renald
Renbald
Renelm
Reneuuald
Renold
Renuuar
Restald
Restold
Restolt
Ret
Ribald
Ricaiard
Ricar
Ricard
Richer
Ricoard
Ricolf
Rictan
Ricuard
Riculf
Rippe
Risboil de
Riset de
Riuold
Riuualo
Roald
Robert
Rodbert
Rodeland de
Roder
Rodulf
Rog'e
Roger
Rogo
Rogus
Rohard
Roic
Rold
Rolf
Rolland
Romenel de
Roric
Ros de
Rotbert
Rotroc
Rozel'
Rozelin
Ruallon
Rualon
Rufus
Rumald
Rumbold
Rumold
Runeuille

S.

Sacheuilla de
Sæfrid
Safrid
Sagar
Sagrim
Saiet
Saieua
Sais de
Salmur de
Salo
Salomon
S. Leger
S. Quintin
S. Sansone de
Sanson
Sasfrid
Sasgar
Sasuualo
Sasuuard
Saucnie de
Sauigneio de
Sauigni de
Saulf
Sauuard
Sauuold
Saxlef
Schelin
Schelm
Scohies de
Scolland
Scoua
Scriba
Scudet
Scutet
Sedred
Segrim
Seibert
Seifrid
Semar
Semer
Sencler de
Sent Cler de
Sentebor de
Seolf
Septniuels de
Seric
Serlo
Sessibert
Seward
Seuuen
Seuui
Sigar
Silua de
Silvester
Simon
Simond
Simund
Sinod
Sired
Sireuuold

-Siric
Siuert
Siuuard
Siuuate
Smalavill de
Soies de
Sotus
Spec
Spech
Sprottulf
Stable
Stanard
Stanart
Stannechetel
Stantone de
Stauhart
Stefan
Stenulf
Stirman
Stoches
Sturm'
Sturmid
Sturstan
Suain
Suan
Suarting
Suartric
Suausey de
Suauis
Suen
Suertin
Suerting
Suetin
Sueting
Suetman
Sufreint
Suin
Sumeri de
Sund
Surd've
Suttuna
Suuan
Suuen

T.

Taccham de
Tædald
Tailgebosc
Taissel de
Talebot
Talliebosc
Tame de
Tascelin
T'chetel
Tebald
Tedald
Tedbert
Tedbold
Tedric
Tehel
Teher
Teodbald
Teoderic
Teodric
Teodulf
Terbert
Tetbald
Tetbaud
Tezelin
Tham de
Thochi
Tidbald
Tiger
Tinel
Tirel de
Tirus
Toche
Tochi
Tochil
Todeni de
Toeni de
Toka
Toli
Tonne
Tor
Torchill
Tored
Toret
Torgis
Tornai
Torold
Torstin
Tosard
Tosti
Toui
Touilt
Traillgi de
Tralgi de
Trauers
Troard de
Troarz de
Tual
Tuder
Tumbi
Tur
Turald
Turbat
Turbern
Turchetil
Turchil
Turgar
Turgis
Turi
Turlauillade
Turmit
Turold
Turstan
Tursten
Turstin

U and V.

Vagan
Valbadon de
Vallibus de
Valonges
Valongies de
Valonis de
Vals de
Uctebrand
Vctred
Veci
Venables de
Venator
Ver de
Verley de
Verli de
Vernon de
Vill'o de
Vinitor
Uis de Leun
Uisdelups
Visolupi
Vitalis
Vitard
Vlchel
Vlchetel
Vlestan
Vlf
Vlfac
Vlfchetel
Vlketel
Vlmar
Vlmer
Vlnod
Vloi
Vlric
Vlsi
Vlstan
Vltbert
Vluard
Vlueua
Vluiet
Vluric
Vluuard
Vlwart
Vluui
Vluuin
Vmfrid
Vrfer
Vrso
Vruoi
Uttal
Uual' de

W.

Wachelin
Wadard
Wal' de
Wala
Walbert
Walchel
Walchelin
Walcher
Walcin
Waldin
Walen
Walenn
Walenses
Waler'
Waleram
Waleran
Walicher
Walifrid
Wallef
Walo
Walon' de
Waloniencis de
Walo de
Walscin
Walter
Waluille de
Wanceio de
Wanz
War' de
Waras de
Wareger
Warene de
Wareng'
Warenger
Warenna de
Wares de
Waribold
Warin
Warinbold
Warinc
Warmund
Warner
Wast
Wasunic
Wateuile de
Wazelin
Wazo
Wenelinc
Weneuc
Wenric
Werelc
Werenc
Werestan
Wert
Wesman
Westone
Wgulafra
(W. Gulafra)
Wiard
Wibald
Wiberg
Wibert
Wicard
Wichin
Widald
Widard
Widelard
Wido
Widr
Wielard
Wigar
Wigemore
Wiger
Wighen
Wigot
Wihanoc
Wihomarc
Wihtmar
Wihuenec
Wihumar
Wihvmarc
Wilard
Willac
Willelm
Wimarcæ
Wimerus
Wimund
Wineman
Winemar
Wintrehard
Wiscand de
Wisgar
Wissand de
Witbert
Witburg
Witsand de
Wituile de
Hugo
Wizo
Wlb'tus
Wlric
Wlsi
Wlueua
Wluuard
Wluui
Wluuold
Wodeman

Y.

Ymfrid (Humfrid)

NORMAN NAMES.

A GREAT deal has been written about the Roll of Battell Abbey and the companions of the Conqueror which is doubtless of great interest to those who claim to be descendants of the persons therein recorded.

There was such a roll suspended in the great hall of the building, and it bore the names of 645 knights, but it has disappeared long ago, as well as the other relics of the battle, which were removed to Cowdray, and perished in the great fire there in 1793.

There are several copies more or less imperfect. The lists which appear to be the most authentic are: Duchesne's list, taken from the abbey charter, containing 405 names; Leland's collection, with 498 names; Magny's catalogue, with 425 names; Delisle's, with 485 names. These are all of a much later date than the Conquest.

Of the great array of time-honoured names very few are now borne by direct representatives. They exist rather among the old gentry than in the peerage. In the majority of cases the later descendants of illustrious families have sunk into poverty and obscurity unconscious of their origin, and this was more likely to be the case with the younger branches, since the name or title of the family went with the elder line that inherited the estates.

The following names have been collected from the lists above mentioned. Many of them will be found in Domesday Book, and where such is the case they may be considered to be genuine followers of the Conqueror. It is obvious that those which compare favourably with Domesday Book are the most reliable, and others which do not stand that test may be looked upon as of later date. The names of some of the Flemings who accompanied William are also included in this list.

Much doubt has long existed as to the authenticity of the several versions which have appeared at different times claiming to be a roll of the names of the Norman invaders who survived the battle of Hastings, but it is manifest that many of those recorded, even if they were ever upon the original document deposited with the monks of Battell Abbey, are not found to correspond with either the tenants-in-chief or the under-tenants of Domesday Book at the time of the Survey (A.D. 1086). On the other hand, the last mentioned—of whom there are a great number—have hardly a place upon the roll.

It is well known that the heralds of the fourteenth and fifteenth centuries were not scrupulous in adding names to the list.

Queen Isabella of France, the consort of Edward II., introduced in her train many personages bearing surnames previously unknown in England.

The Rotuli Normanniæ, R. Hundredorum, and R. de Oblatis et Finibus, *temp.* Regis Johannis, are valuable evidence as to Norman names. The place-names of Normandy have been added.

The asterisk denotes a tenant-in-chief.

A.

Abbevile. Appeville; a loc. n. *D.B.* Appeuile de Oburvilla
Abell. *D.B.*, Kent
Aimeris. *D.B.* Haimeric*
Aincourt. *D.B.* de Aincurt.* Agincourt; a loc. n.
Akeny. *D.B.* Acun (?). Acquigny, Aucun, loc. n.
Albeny. *D.B.* Albani*
Amay (Johannes Ame). Amécourt (?), loc. n.
Amerenges
Amouerduile, Aumarill, Amundeville (?)
Angenoun. Angennes; a loc. n.
Angers, Aunwers. *D.B.* Anger. Angers; a loc. n.
Angewyne. *D.B.* Angevin Osmund
Angilliam, Aungeloun. Angoulême; a loc. n.
Anuay. Aunay, loc. n.
Archere. *D.B.* de Arcis,* de Arches
Arcy, D'Arcie, Darcy,* from de Ardreci. *D.B.*, T.C. (Lincs.)
Argentoune. David de Argentomo in *D.B.* Reginald de A., Sheriff of Camb. 5 Rich. I., Argentan; a loc. n.
Arundel. *D.B.**
Arwerne
Aspermound
Aspervile
Audeley. *D.B.* Andeli* (?). Andelys; a loc. n.
Audeville or Adryelle (?). Adervielle; a loc. n.
Auenant, Avenele. *D.B.* Avenel
Aumarle. *D.B.* de Albamarle*
Avereris
Aybeuare (John Aubry). Aubevoye, loc. n.

B.

Bagott. *D.B.* Bagod
Bailif. *D.B.* Belfou or de Belfaco. Bellevue; a loc. n.
Baillol. *D.B.* Balgiole.* Bailleul; a loc. n.
Bainard, Byngard. *D.B.* Bangiard*
Baious, or Baus. Bayeux; a loc. n.
Baloun. Bâlines, loc. n.
Banastre, Banestre
Banet or Benny. *D.B.* de Bano* (?)
Barchampe. Beauchamp, loc. n.
Bardolfe
Barduedor
Barnivale, Berenvile, Burneville, Burinell. *D.B.* de Burneuill. Barneville; a loc. n.
Barrett, Baret. *D.B.* Baret
Bary, Barre, Barry. Berry; a loc. n.
Bascoun. *D.B.* Basuin (?)
Baskerville
Basset or Bassey. *D.B.* Basset
Bastard. *D.B.**
Baudewin, Baudin, Baldwin. *D.B.* Balduin,* Count of Flanders
Baupere. Beauport; a loc. n.
Beauchamp. *D.B.* de Belcamp
Beaumont. *D.B.* de Belmont (?), de Bomene*; a loc. n.
Beauvise or Bevers. Beauvais; a loc. n.
Beelhelme, Bealum. Bellême; a loc. n.
Beisin. Bessin; a loc. n. *D.B.* Basuin (?)
Beke. *D.B.* de Bech.* Bec-Hellouin; a loc. n.
Belefroun. Beauvron; a loc. n.
Belesur. Bellecourt; a loc. n.
Beleuers. *D.B.* Beluard. Belliére (?); a loc. n.

Bellet. *D.B.* Will. Belet (Hants). Harvey Belet lived *temp.* K. Steph.
Bellew. *D.B.* Belot.* Bellou, loc. n.
Bellire. Balleroy; a loc. n.
Berners. *D.B.* de Berners.* Bernières; a loc. n.
Bernon. *D.B.* Bernar (?)
Berteuilay. Berthouville (?), loc. n.
Bertin. *D.B.* de Bertone.* St. Bertin; a loc. n.
Bertram. *D.B.* de Bertram,* Robert Vicomte, 1047
Beteruile or Breteville. *D.B.* de Breteville. Bretteville; a loc. n.
Beurey or Bevery. *D.B.* de Bevrere* (a Fleming)
Bevill, Belevile. Belleville; a loc. n.
Bigot. *D.B.**
Bikard, Bekard. *D.B.* Brictoward.* Briquesart; a loc. n.
Biroune. *D.B.* de Burun.* Biron; a loc. n.
Blondell or Blundel. *D.B.* Blunders* or Blond (?)
Bluet. *D.B.* Bloiet
Blunt, Blundet, or Blounte. *D.B.* Blunders.* Blandain; a loc. n.
Bodin, Bidin. *D.B.* Bodin. Beaudéan; a loc. n.
Boels. Bouelles, loc. n.
Bohun. Bohon, a loc. n. *D.B.* de Bohun*
Bois. *D.B.* de Bosch* (*Fl.*), Busch, or Boscherville, loc. n.
Bondeville. Bonneville; a loc. n. *D.B.*
Bonett. Bonnat; a loc. n., *Fr.*
Bonrett
Bonueier. Bonnières; a loc. n.
Boranvile. Bérengeville (?), loc. n.
Botelere
Botevile or Boyville. *D.B.* Botild (?). Bouille; a loc. n. (?)
Boundes. *D.B.* Bondi (?) or Bundo (?)
Bounilaine
Bourcher. *D.B.* Borci (?)
Brabason or Brabaion. *D.B.* de Braibone
Bracy. Brecy; a loc. n.
Braibuf. *D.B.* de Braiboue
Braine. *D.B.* Brien. Brionne; a loc. n.
Brand. *D.B.* Brant
Braunch
Bray, loc. n.
Brazard, de Braiosa (?). *D.B.* Suss., Hants, Berks, Wilts, Dors.
Brebus
Brent. *D.B.* Brant
Breton. *D.B.* Brito*
Brette. Bretteville (?); a loc. n.
Broilem. Breuilpont (?), loc. n.
Broleuy. Broglie; a loc. n.
Brouce, Brus, Brutz, Bruys. *D.B.* Robertus de Bruis* (Yorks). Breux, loc. n.
Browe, Broy. Breux, loc. n.
Bryan. *D.B.* Brion. Brionne; a loc. n.
Buffard. Bouffey; a loc. n. Or Beaufour
Burdett. *D.B.* Burdet
Burdon. *D.B.* Buerd (?). Beaudoin, loc. n.
Bures. *D.B.* Buret (?). Bures; a loc. n.
Burgh, Bourg; a loc. n.
Busard. *D.B.* Bucard
Bushell. *D.B.* Buissel. Buscel; a loc. n.
Bushy or Bussey. *D.B.* de Buci.* Bougy, Buchy, loc. n.
Busseuille, Boseville. *D.B.* de Buiville.* Boscherville, Beuzeville, loc. n.
Buttecourt. *D.B.* Buter. Butot, loc. n.
Bysey. *D.B.* de Buci.* Buzy; a loc. n.

C.

Cammile. *D.B.* de Cormelies.* Cormeilles; a loc. n.

Camois, Camoys. Camous; a loc. n.

Camvile, Cameville. Campneuseville; a loc. n.

Caperoun

Carbonelle. Chabannes; a loc. n. *D.B.* Carbonel

Carevile, Coruyele. Courville; a loc. n.

Cateray, Cartrait. *D.B.* de Ceterith.* Cauterêts; a loc. n.

Cauncy, Chauncy. Canchy; a loc. n.

Chaiters, Chartres. Chartres; a loc. n.

Challouns. Challones; a loc. n.

Chamberay. Chambrais; a loc. n.

Chamberlain

Chambernoun or Chaumberoun. Cambernon; a loc. n.

Champney, Champnais, Chawnes. Champigny, loc. n.

Chanduit, Chaudut. Chanday; a loc. n.

Chantelow (Cantelupe ?), Cauntelow. Canteloupe; a loc. n.

Charles, Chaleys. Chalais; a loc. n.

Chaumont, a loc. n.

Chaundos. Chanday; a loc. n. *D.B.* de Candos

Chaward, Chaworth. Chauvincourt (?), loc. n.

Chawent, Chauunt. Chaumont (?); a loc. n.

Cheine, Cheines, Cheyni. *D.B.* Chenesis. Chênée and Chiny, Flanders. Chaignes, Le Chesne, loc. n., *Fr.*

Chereberge. Cherbourg; a loc. n.

Cherecourt

Cholmeley. Chamblac, loc. n.

Chopis, Chapes. *D.B.* Chepin

Clarell. *D.B.* de Claville (?) Clavelle, Cléville, loc. n.

Cleremaus, Clerevals

Clerenay

Clifford. *D.B.* Clibert (?)

Clinels

Coinvile. Cornouailles (?); a loc. n.

Columber. *D.B.* de Columbels.* Colomby; a loc. n.

Colvile. *D.B.* de Colevil. Colleville; a loc. n.

Comin, Comeyn. Comines; a loc. n.

Conderay. Connerré; a loc. n. (?)

Conestable

Corbett, Corbet. *D.B.* Corbet

Corbine, Corby. *D.B.* Corbin. Corbie; a loc. n.

Coville. Couville; a loc. n.

Cressy, Crescy. Crécy; a loc. n.

Creuquere, Crevecuer. Crevecœur; a loc. n.

Cribett

Cuily

Curly

Curson, Courson. *D.B.* de Curcan

Curtenay, Courteny. Catenay, loc. n.

D.

Dabernoune. *D.B.* de Abernon

Dabitott. *D.B.* de Abetot*

Dakeny. Daguéniere (?); a loc. n.

Dalseny

Dambleton

Damnot, Damot. Motteville (?), loc. n.

Damry, Damary. Dame-Marie, loc. n.

Daniel. *D.B.* Roger Daniel (Suss.)

Danway. Hanouard (?), loc. n.

Darell

Daubeney. *D.B.* de Albingi.* Aubigné; a loc. n.

Daueros, Deveroys
Dauntre, Dautry
Dauonge, Daverenge. Avranches; a loc. n.
Davers. *D.B.* Denvers (?); *Fl.* Anvers
Deheuse, De la Huse. Héas and La Hisse; loc. n.
De la Bere. Labouheyre (?); a loc. n.
De la Hill
De la Hoid, De la Hay. La Haye; a loc. n.
De la Linde. Lindebeuf, loc. n.
De la Planche. Planquery; a loc. n.
De la Pole. St. Pol de Léon; a loc. n.
De la Vache, De Wake. La Vacherie, loc. n.
De la Vere. *D.B.* de Ver.* Ver; a loc. n.
De la Ware. Wierre; a loc. n.
Delaund. La Londe, loc. n.
Delaward. *D.B.* de War'
Delee, Del Isle. Ille; a loc. n.
Denaville. Dénestanville, loc. n.
Derey. *D.B.* Derinc
Desny, Diseny. Isigny; a loc. n.
Devaus. Vaux; a loc. n.
Deverelle
Devereux. Évreux; a loc. n.
Devile, Deyville. Déville; a loc. n.
Devise. *D.B.* Devais
Disard, Disart. Izards; a loc. n.
Dispencere, Dispenser. *D.B.* Dispensator*
Dive. Dives; a loc. n. *D.B.* de Dive*
Dodingsels, Dodingle. *D.B.* Dodid* (?)
Doiville. Ouville, loc. n.
Druel. Ruelle; a loc. n.
Drury
Duilly, Duylly. *D.B.* de Oilgi (?). Ailly; a loc. n.
Dulce. Dolcé; a loc. n.
Dunchamp. Encamp; a loc. n.
Dunstervile. Dénestanville, loc. n.
Durand, Durant. *D.B.* Durand.* Douvrend (?), loc. n.
Durange

E.

Engaine. Enghien; a loc. n. *D.B.**
Estrange, Destranges
Estriels
Esturney
Estuteville, Estoteville. Etréville (?), loc. n.

F.

Facunburge. Fauquembergues, loc. n.
Fauecourt. Fallencourt, loc. n.
Fenes. *D.B.* Fenisc Ulf. Fains, loc. n.
Fermbaud. *D.B.* Ferme (?)
Ferrerers. *D.B.* de Ferieres.* Ferrère; a loc. n.
Fichet, Fichent
Filberd, Filebert. St. Philbert; a loc n.
Finere
Fingez
Fitz Aleyn. *D.B.* Alan*
Fitz Auger
Fitz Browne, Bryan
Fitz Eustach
Fitz Fitz
Fitz Fouk
Fitz Geffrey
Fitz Henrie
Fitz Herbert

Fitz Hugh
Fitz John
Fitz Laurence
Fitz Marmaduke
Fitz Morice
Fitz Otes
Fitz Pain
Fitz Peres
Fitz Philip
Fitz Rainold
Fitz Rauf, Rafe
Fitz Rewes
Fitz Roand
Fitz Robert
Fitz Roger
Fitz Simon
Fitz Thomas
Fitz Walter. *D.B.* Walter*
Fitz Waren
Fitz William
Flamville. *D.B.* Flamme.* Flamanville; a loc. n.
Fleschampe
Fleuez or Flevez
Folioll, Filiol. Folleville (?), loc. n.
Foliot, Filiot. *D.B.* Folet
Folville. Folleville; a loc. n.
Formay. Formerie; a loc. n.
Formibaud
Forz, Forges (?), Belgium
Fouke. *D.B.* Fulche
Fourbeville
Freville, Fryville. Fréville, loc. n.
Frisell, Fresell. *D.B.* Fresle, Richard.* Fresville; a loc. n.
Frisound, Frisoun
Front de Bœf. Daubeuf (?), loc. n.
Furnieueus, Forneux. Furnaux, Belgium
Furnival, Furnivaus

G.

Gamages. *D.B.* Gamas (?). Gamaches; a loc. n.
Garre, Karre
Gaugy, Gorgeise, Georges, Gourges
Gaunson
Gaunt, Kaunt. *D.B.* de Gand,* *Fl.* Gand; a loc. n.
Gernoun. *D.B.* Gernon.* Guernanville (?), loc. n.
Giffard, Gifard. *D.B.* Gifard*
Glateuile. *D.B.* Glauill
Goband, Gobaude. *D.B.* Godebold* (?)
Gobion, Gubioun
Golofre, Galofer. *D.B.* Gulaffra, Gulfer. Goulafrière, loc. n.
Gower
Grammori, Grymward (?)
Graunson. Grandchain (?), loc. n.
Graunt. *D.B.* Grando. Grand-Camp (?), loc. n.
Gray. *D.B.* de Grai
Greile, Greilly
Grendon, Graundyn
Grenet. *D.B.* Granetarius. Grenade; a loc. n.
Greneuile, Geneville. Granville; a loc. n.
Grensy
Gressy, Gracy. Graçay; a loc. n.
Griuel. Greuville, loc. n.
Guines, a loc. n.
Gurdon, Gerdoun
Gurley
Gurnay, Gurney. *D.B.* Gurnai, Gournay. Gurney, loc. n.
Gurry. Gueures, loc. n.

H.

Haket. *D.B.* Walter Achet. Achiet; a loc. n.
Hamelin. *D.B.**
Hamound. *D.B.* Amund, Hamont (?) loc. n., Belgium
Hanlay, Haulley. Aulnay (?), loc. n.

Hanville. Anneville, loc. n.
Hardell
Harecourt, Harcord. Harcourt; a loc. n.
Harewell, Hareville. Ardouval (?), loc. n.
Hastings. Hastingues; a loc. n., island in the river near Bayonne
Haunsard. Hanouard, loc. n.
Haurell, Hurel. Eurville (?), loc. n.
Hauteny, Hautein. Autigny, loc. n.
Hayward. Hauwaert, loc. n., Belgium
Henoure
Hercy, Herey. Herseaux (?), Belgium
Herioun, Heroun. *D.B.* de Herion.* Héron le, loc. n.
Herne. Hern, loc. n., Belgium
Heryce
Houell. Oherville (?), loc. n.
Husee. Ussé, or Houssaye; a loc. n.

J.

Januile
Jarden, Jardyn
Jasperuile
Jay. Jouy-sur-Eure (?), loc. n.
Jeniels
Jerconuise

K.

Kancey
Karrowe
Keine, Kanæs. Kain, loc. n., Belgium
Kenelre
Keveters
Kimaronne, Kymarays
Kiriell

L.

Lacy, Lascy. *D.B.* de Laci.* Lessay; a loc. n.
Lane, Lenias. Lens; a loc. n.
Lascales, Lascels
Latomer, Latymer
Laumale, La Muile. Lamballe (?); a p.n.
Leded
Lemare, Lymers (?). *D.B.* Lemar. Limours; a loc. n.
Liffard
Limers, Limesey, Limousin; a loc. n. *D.B.* de Limesi.* Limours; a loc. n.
Linnebey. Lindebeuf, loc. n.
Lisours. Lisieux (?); a loc. n., *Fr.*
Loious
Longechampe. Longchamps; a loc. n., Belgium
Longespes
Longueuale, Longville, Logevile. Longueville; a loc. n.
Lorancourt
Loriage
Loterell. Loudervielle; a loc. n., *Fr.* (?)
Loueney, Loveyne, Lovein, Lovan. *D.B.* Leuuin.* Lieuvin; a loc. n., *Fr.* Louvain, loc. n., Belgium
Louerace, Loverak. Louvres; a loc. n.
Loveday, Leuetot, Lovetot. *D.B.* Leviet* (?) or Lovet (?), Louvetot, loc. n., France
Lovell. *D.B.* Laval; a loc. n.
Lownay. Luynes; a loc. n. (?)
Loy, Loif. Louye, loc. n.
Lucy, Luse. Lucy; a loc. n.

M.

Maiell. *D.B.* de Medehal*
Maine, Maoun. *D.B.* Maino.* Mayne; a loc. n.
Mainell. Ménilles, loc. n.
Maingun (?). *D.B.* Maigno
Mainwaring, Mesnil-Warin
Malebranch, Malebys (?)
Maleheire
Maleherbe, Maleberge. Malesherbes; a loc. n.
Maleluse. Malause; a loc. n.
Malemaine, Maumasin. Malmaison; a loc. n.
Malemis
Malet. *D.B.* Malet*
Maleuile. Maleville; a loc. n. *D.B.* Malauill
Malevere. *D.B.* Malavill (?). Maulévrier; a loc. n.
Mallony. Malaunay; a loc. n.
Mallop. *D.B.* Mala opa
Mandut, Maudiet (?)
Mangisere
Maniard, Mainard. *D.B.*
Manlay
Manse, Monceus (?). *D.B.* Manasses (?). Mantes; a loc. n.
Manteuenant. Maintenon; a loc. n.
Mantolet, Mantelent. *D.B.* Mantel.* Manthelon, loc. n.
Manuile, Meneville. *D.B.* de Manneuille. Mainneville, loc. n.
Marceaus. *D.B.* de Marci.* Marsous; a loc. n.
Mare, Marre. *D.B.* de Mara. St. Maure; a loc. n. (?)
Marmilon
Marny. Mauny, loc. n.
Marteine. *D.B.* Martin.* St. Martin; a loc. n.
Martinaste. Martinvaast; a loc. n.
Massey. *D.B.* Maci. Massay; a loc. n.
Matelay. Madeleine de - Nonacourt (?), loc. n.
Mauches. Monchaux (?), loc. n.
Mauclerke
Maularde
Maulay, Maule, Morley. Marley; a loc. n.
Maulicerer
Maunchenell, Mauncel
Maundervile, Maundeville. *D.B.* de Manneville.* Mondeville; a loc. n.
Maurewarde
Mauveysin. Mauvezin; a loc. n.
Meintenore
Meletak
Meller. Mélicourt (?), loc. n.
Melun. *D.B.* de Mellend.* Melen, loc. n., Belgium
Menere, Maners (?). Le Manoir, loc. n.
Menpincoy, Mounpinson
Merke, Merkenfell. *D.B.* de Merc. Marques (?), loc. n.
Miriel. Mirville; a loc. n.
Mohant
Monchenesey, Mountheusey
Monhout. Manéhouville (?), loc. n.
Montfichet
Monthermon, Maihermer
Montrauers, Mountravers. Montaure (?), loc. n.
Morell. *D.B.*; a loc. n.
Moren. *D.B.* Morin.* Morainville, loc. n.
Moribray, Mowbray. Moutbray; a loc. n. Maubray, loc. n., Belgium
Morleian. *D.B.* Moriland (?)
Morreis, Mourreis, Murres. *D.B.* Mauric.* Marais, loc. n.
Mortimere. *D.B.* de Mortemer; a loc. n.
Mortiuale, Mortivaus. Motteville (?); a loc. n.
Morville; a loc. n.
Mouett, Movet. Mouettes, loc. n.
Mouncey. Monchy (?), loc. n.
Mountagu. *D.B.* de Montagud.* Montaigu; a loc. n.
Mountbother. *D.B.* Manbodo

Mountford. Montfort; a loc. n. *D.B.* de Montfort*

Mountgomerie. *D.B.* de Montgomery

Mountlovel, Maulovel. Malleville (?), loc. n.

Mountmarten, Mortimaine. Montmain, loc. n.

Mountsoler, Mounsorel (?)

Mourteney, Morteyn. *D.B.* Mortuing. Mortain; a loc. n.

Mowne, Mooun, Moine, or Mohun. Moyon; a loc. n. *D.B.* de Moion

Musarde. *D.B.* Musard.* Mousseaux (?), loc. n.

Muse. *D.B.* Musard.* Moux (?); a loc. n., *Fr.*

Musegros. *D.B.* de Mucelgros

Musett, Muschet. Muchedent (?), loc. n.

N.

Navimere. *D.B.* Nemore (?)

Nefmarch, Newmarch. Neufmarché, loc. n.

Neile, Fitz-Nele. *D.B.* Nigel. Nagel, loc. n.

Neiremet

Nembrutz

Nermitz

Neville, Nereville. Neuille and Néville, loc. n.

Newborough, Newburgh. Neubourg; a loc. n.

Noers, Neuers. Nevers; a loc. n. (?). *D.B.* de Noiers

Norbet, Newbet. *D.B.* Nubold (?)

Norice. Norrey; a loc. n.

Normaville. Normanville, loc. n.

Nusetys

O.

Oisell. Oisel; a loc. n.

Olenel, Otinel (?). *D.B.* de Olney (?). Aulnay (?), loc. n.

Olibef. Elbœuf; a loc. n.

Olifant

Olifard. *D.B.* Oliver

Orioll. Orival (?), loc. n.

Otevell. Octeville, loc. n.

Ounall. Ouainville, loc. n.

P.

Paifrere. *D.B.* Paisforere

Paignel or Panel. *D.B.* Pagenel*

Paiteny

Pampilium

Pantolf. *D.B.* Pantulf

Patefine, Parthenay; a loc. n.

Pauey. Poey le Houn; a loc. n.

Pavley, Paveley. Pavilly; a loc. n.

Peccell

Peche. *D.B.* Peccatu (?). Le Pecq; a loc. n.

Peito. Poitou; a loc. n.

Pekeny. Picquigny; a loc. n.

Penecord. Piencourt, loc. n.

Percelay, Perechay. *D.B.* Percehaie.* Perche, loc. n.

Percivale. Puisenval (?), loc. n.

Percy. *D.B.* Perci.* Percy; a loc. n.

Perepound, Pierrepoint. *D.B.* de Perapund

Perere, Perrers. Perrières, loc. n.

Pershale

Pery, Perot. *D.B.* Peret*

Petiuoll. Petiville, loc. n.
Pevrell. *D.B.* Peverel.* Pierre-val (?), loc. n.
Phuars, Fours, loc. n.
Picard. Picardy; a loc. n.
Pigot, Pygot. *D.B.* Picot.* Pierre-court (?), loc. n.
Pinchard, Punchardoun, Pinka-doun. Punchardon or Pincher-doun, loc. n.
Pinel. *D.B.** Pinterville (?), loc. n.
Pinkenie. *D.B.* de Pinchengi
Placy, Place. Plessis; a loc. n.
Plukenet. Plangenoit, loc. n., Belgium
Pomeray. *D.B.* De Pomerie.* Pommeraie; a loc. n.
Poterell. La Poterie (?), loc. n.
Pounce, Poynce. *D.B.* Ponz. Pon-toise (?); a loc. n.
Power, Poer. *D.B.* de Porth* (?). Portes, loc. n.
Preaus. Preaux, loc. n.
Preulirlegast
Pugoy, Pugoys. *D.B.* Pugnant (?) Puchay (?), loc. n.
Putrill

Q.

Quinci, Quyncy
Quintini. *D.B.* de St. Quintin.* St. Quentin; a loc. n.

R.

Raband. *D.B.* Rabbada
Raimond. *D.B.* Raimund
Rait. *D.B.* Ret. Retz; a loc. n.
Randvile. Ranville; a loc. n.
Rastoke
Richmound. Richemont, loc. n.
Ridell
Rie, Ry. Rhuys, loc. n.
Rigny
Rinuill, Reynevile. Regneville, loc. n.
Ripere, Ripers. *D.B.* Rippe
Risers, Rysers. *D.B.* de Riset
Rivell. *D.B.* Rivvuls. Riville, loc. n.
Rivers. Reviers, loc. n. *D.B.* Riveire*
Rochford. Roquefort, loc. n.
Rokell. Rocheville; a loc. n.
Romilly; a loc. n.
Ronde
Ros. *D.B.* de Ros. Rosay (?), loc. n.
Roselin. *D.B.* Roselent,* Rozelin. Rouisillon; a loc. n.
Rougere. *D.B.* Roger. Rochers; a loc. n.
Rous, Rothais (?) or Roic (Roys). La Roussiere (?), loc. n.
Rushell, Rozel, Russell. Risle; a loc. n. *D.B.* Rozel
Ryan. Royan, loc. n.

S.

Saluin. *D.B.* Sawin* (?)
Sanctes, Sainct Tesc. St. Eus-tache (?), loc. n.
Sandvile. Sandouville, loc. n.
Sanford. Sancourt (?), loc. n.
Sauay. *D.B.* de Sais (?), or de Soies (?)
Saulay, Souley. Soule; a loc. n.
Saunay. *D.B.* de Sauigni. Savigny; a loc. n.
Sauncey. *D.B.* de St. Sansone
Saunsouerre. *D.B.* de Saucnei. St. Saire (?), loc. n.
Say. Sées; a loc. n.

Seffe. *D.B.* Seifrid (?)
Seguin, Sengryn. Serquigny, loc. n.
Senclere. *D.B.* de Sencler. St. Clair; a loc. n.
Sent Albin. St. Aubin; a loc. n.
Sent Amond. St. Amand, loc. n.
Sent Barbe. *D.B.* de Barbes. St. Barbe-sur-Gaillon; a loc. n.
Sent Cheveroll, Soucheville. *D.B.* de Sacheuilla. Sacquenville, loc. n.
Sent George. St. Georges-sur-Fontaine, loc. n.
Sent John, St. Jean. St. Jouin, loc. n.; Sent Jean, Flanders
Sent Legere, St. Ligiere. St. Léger, loc. n.
Sent Les. Lez; a loc. n.
Sent Martin; a loc. n.
Sent More. *D.B.* de More. St. Mards (?), loc. n.
Sent Omere. St. Omer, loc. n.
Sent Quintin. *D.B.* de St. Quintin*
Sent Scudemore
Sent Vile. Sainneville, loc. n.
Sheuile. Seuilly (?); a loc. n.
Sieward. *D.B.* Siuuard
Sirewast
Snylly. St. Helier (?), loc. n.
Somerey, Someray. *D.B.* de Sumeri. Somery; a loc. n.
Somerville
Soreglise
Sorell. Surville (?), loc. n.
Souch. Sauchay (?), loc. n.
Sourdemale, Surdevale. *D.B.* Sourdeval; a loc. n.
Sucheus
Sules, Soules, Solers. Selles (?), loc. n.
Suremounte. Saumont, loc. n.

T.

Talbot. *D.B.* Talebot
Taket or Takel. Tocqueville (?), loc. n.
Tankervile. Tancarville; a loc. n.
Tanny, Tany
Tardevile
Tarteray
Tavernez
Tenwis
Tercy. Tessé (?); a loc. n.
Thorney. *D.B.* Tornai. Tournay; a loc. n.
Thornille
Tibtote
Tinel. *D.B.* Tinel
Tinevile
Tirell. *D.B.* Tirelde
Tisoun. *D.B.* Tisun*
Toget, Tuchet
Tolet
Tollemach, Tolimer
Tolous. Toulouse; a loc. n.
Tomy
Torell. *D.B.* Torchill (?). Tocqueville (?), loc. n.
Tortechappell
Totelles
Touke, Tuk. *D.B.* Tochi.* Touques; a loc. n.
Touny, Tony. *D.B.* Tona.* Tonnay; a loc. n.
Tracy
Traies, Thays
Trainell
Travers. *D.B.*
Travile. Trouville, loc. n.
Tregos
Trenchevile
Trenchilion
Treverell, Treville (?)
Trison
Trivet
Trousbut
Trussell
Trylly. *D.B.* de Traillgi
Turbevile. *D.B.* Turberv. Touffreville (?), loc. n.
Turley
Turvile. Tourville; a loc. n.
Tyriet. Turretot (?), loc. n.

V.

Vaberon
Valence ; a loc. n.
Valenger, Valenges. *See* Wallangy. Valognes ; a loc. n.
Valers. Valois ; a loc. n.
Valingford
Valiue. Valliquerville (?), loc. n.
Vanay. Vannes ; a loc. n.
Vancorde, Venecorde
Vasderol
Vauuruile. Varaville ; a loc. n.
Vaux, loc. n.
Vavasour
Veirny. Vernet ; a loc. n.
Venables, loc. n.
Vendore, Venour. Vendres ; a loc. n.
Veniels. Vénesville (?), loc. n.
Verdeire, Verders, Verdour
Verdoune. Verdon ; a loc. n.
Vere. Ver ; a loc. n.
Verland. Verlaine, loc. n., Flanders
Verlay, Werlay. Verlée, loc. n., Flanders
Vernoun. Vernon ; a loc. n.
Vernoys
Veroun. Verune ; a loc. n.
Verrere. *See* Ferrer
Vesey, Vessay. *D.B.* de Vesci*
Vian. Vienne ; river
Viez. *D.B.* de Uis (?)
Vilan. Vilaine ; a river. Villainville, loc. n.
Vinoun
Vipont
Viville, Wyville, Wivell. Virville (?), loc. n.
Umfravile. Amfreville, loc. n.
Vnket
Vrnaful
Vrnall. Verneuil ; a loc. n.
Vschere

W.

Wacely, Wely. Vesly (?), loc. n.
Wafre. Wavre, loc. n., Belgium
Walangy, Valenger. *D.B.* de Valonges.* Valognes ; a loc. n.
Waloys, Valers (?). *D.B.* de Wals. Valailles (?), loc. n.
Wake, Wace (?). Wace ; a loc. n.
Wamerville
Ward. *D.B.* Wiard
Wardebois, Warroys (?)
Wareine, Warrene. *D.B.* de Warene,* Warenger. Varengeville, loc. n.
Wate
Watelin
Watevil, Waterville. *D.B.* de Wateuile.* Vatteville ; a loc. n.
Werdonell
Wermelay
Wespaile. Wespelaer, loc. n., Flanders

ALPHABETICAL LIST OF BRITISH SURNAMES.

A.

ABBOTT. Dimin. of Abb. *See* Abbs, or *Fr.* Aubert; a p.n.

ABBS. *F.* Abbo; *D.B.* Api, Appe, Aba, Abba, Abo; *G.* Aber, Ahber, Haber; *Dch.* Abas, Abbing, Appij; *Fl.* Abas, Abs, Abts; *D.* Aabye, Abo; p.n.

ABDALE. From Abbeydale; a loc. n., Yorks

A'BECKETT. From Beckett; a loc. n., Berks

ABELL. *D.S.G.* Abel; *Fl.* Abbeele, Abeels; *Dch.* Abels, Eble; *G.* Abel, Ebel; *D.B.* Abel; p.n.

Abell is on the Roll of Battell Abbey. Abel, tenant in *D.B.* (Kent). *See* Abbs.

ABERCORN. A loc. n., Linlithgow

ABERCROMBIE. A loc. n., Fife

ABERNETHY. A loc. n., Perths., Elgin, Fife, Moray

ABIGAIL. From Abinghall; a loc. n., Glost.

ABLE. *See* Abell

ABLETT. Dimin. of Abb, or *see* Ablewhite

ABLEWHITE. From Applethwaite; a loc. n., Cumb., Westmd.

ABLEY. From Abberley; a loc. n., Worcest.

ABNEY. A loc. n., Derbysh.; *D.B.* Habenai

ABRAHALL. From Aberhale; a loc. n., Mongomeryshire

ABRAM. A loc. n., Lancs., formerly Adburgham

ABSELL. *Fl.* Absil; a p.n.

ABY. A loc. n., Lincs.

ACKERS. *Fl.* Hakkars; a p.n.

ACLAND. A loc. n., Devon.

De Acland was settled there *temp.* Hen. II.

ACORNS. *Dch.* Akens; a p.n.

ACRES. *See* Ackers

ACTON. A loc. n., Middlx., Chesh., etc.

ADAMS. *Fr.* Adam; *Fl.* Adams; p.n.

ADCROFT. From Addiscroft; a loc. n., Cornw.

ADDERLEY. A loc. n., Salop

ADDERTON. From Atherton; a loc. n., Lancs.

Or Edderton, Ross.

ADDICOTT. From Adcott; a loc. n., Salop

ADDINGTON. A loc. n., Kent, Surrey

ADDISON. *N.* Haddingr; *S.* Adde; *F.* Ade, Adde; *Fl.* Adan; *Dch.* Adee; *G.* Hader; p.n.

ADDLEY. *See* Adderley

ADDY. *F.* Ade; *S.* Adde; *G.* Hader; *Dch.* Ade, Addicks, Aders, Adee; p.n.

ADE, ADEY. *See* Addy

ADEANE. From Atte-Dean. Dean; a loc. n., Glost., Hants, etc.; or *F.* Adde, Adden; p.n.

ADENEY. *See* Adney
ADLINGTON. A loc. n., Lancs.
ADNEY. A loc. n., Salop
ADSHEAD. From Adsett; a loc. n., Glost.
AFFECTION. *Fr.* Afchain; a p.n. (?)
AFFLECK. A loc. corruption of Auchinleck, Ayrshire
AGACE. *See* Aggis
AGATE. *G.* Agath; a p.n. *See* Aggs
AGGAS. *See* Aggs
AGGER, AGAR. *See* Aggs
AGGS, AGGIS, AGGUS. *N.* Ögurr (Ahgurr); *F.* Agge; *D.B.* Agnet, Agenulf, Aghemund, Achebrand, Aghete; *D.* Ager, Acker; *Fl.* Hager, Hacker; *G.* Hager, Hake, Hakus, Ache, Acker; p.n.
AGNEW. *Fr.* Agneau; *Fl.* Agnier; p.n.
AIKEN. *See* Eykin
AILSBY. From Aylesby; a loc. n., Lincs.
AINGER. *See* Angier
AINSLIE. *Dch.* Enslie; a p.n.
AINSWORTH. A loc. n., Lancs.
AIREY. *N.* Eyjarr; *Fl.* Eyer; *D.B.* Airet; p.n.
AISHFORD. *See* Ashford
AISTROP. From Aisthorpe; a loc. n., Lincs.
AKEHURST. *See* Akhurst
AKERS. *See* Ackers and Aggs
AKHURST. From Hawkhurst; a loc. n., Kent
AKISTER. From Acaster; a loc. n., Yorks
ALABASTER. *See* Arblaster
ALBAN. *N.* Hallbjörn; *D.* Allbahn; *Fl.* Albouin; *D.B.* Alban; p.n.
Or Albourne; a loc. n., Suss. Aldborne, Wilts.
ALBIN. *See* Alban
ALBRIGHTON. A loc. n., Salop
ALDERTON. A loc. n., Wilts
ALDHAM. A loc. n., Ess., Suff., Yorks
ALDINGTON. A loc. n., Kent
ALDIS. *N.* Aldis; *F.* Alt, Alts; *D.B.* Alti, Aldi, Altor, Aldin, Alis; *G.* Alder; *Dch.* Alders; p.n.
ALDOM. *See* Aldham
ALDRED. From Aldreth; a loc. n., Camb., or *see* Alfred
ALDRICH. *See* Aldridge
ALDRIDGE. A loc. n., Staff., Suff.
ALDWINCKLE. A loc. n., Northants
ALDWORTH. A loc. n., Berks
ALECOCK. *N.* Áli, or Halli, dim. Ali-Karl; *F.* Alle; *G.* Alker; *D.* Halck; *Dch.* Alchen, Ali, Alink; *D.B.* Alcerl, Alchel, Alchen, Alcher, Alcot
Allcock, dim. of Halli.
ALESBURY. *See* Aylesbury
ALEXANDER. *Dch. G.* p.n.; *Fr.* Alexandre; a p.n.
ALFORD A loc. n., Lincs., Somers.
ALFRED. *N.* Hallfreðr, or Elfraðr; *D.B.* Alured, or Alvred, Aldred; *Fl.* Alleweireldt; *D.* Allert; p.n.
ALFREE. *See* Alfred
ALGAR, ALGER. *N.* Álf-geirr; *D.* Ellegaard; *Fl.* Allegaert; *Dch.* Algie, Allgäuer; *D.B.* Algar, Ælfgar, Elfgar, Elgar; *G.* Allger; p.n.
ALINGTON. A loc. n., N. Wales, Wilts
ALKER. From Altcar; a loc. n., Lancs.
ALLAN. *N.* Áli; *F.* Alle, Allen; *Fl.* Allen; *S.* Alin; *D.B.* Alan, Aline; *Fr.* Allain; p.n.
ALLANBY. *See* Allonby
ALLARD. *D.* Allert; p.n. *See* Alfred
ALLARDYCE. A loc. n., Kincardineshire
ALLAWAY. A loc. n., Ayrshire
ALLBERRY. From Alderbury; a loc. n., Wilts
ALLBON. *See* Alban
ALLBROOK. A loc. n., Hants
ALLCARD. *See* Allgood
ALLCHIN. *Fl.* Halkin; *Dch.* Halk; *D.B.* Alchen; p.n.
Dimin. of *N.* Halli; a p.n.

ALLCHURCH. From Alvechurch; a loc. n., Worcest.

ALLCOCK. *See* Alecock

ALLCORN. From Alchorne; a loc. n., Suss. (?)

ALLDAY. *See* Halliday

ALLDIN. From Halden; a loc. n., Kent

Or Aldon, Kent, Salop (?).

ALLDRITT. *See* Aldred

ALLEN. *N.* Ali; *F.* Alle, Allen; *Dch.* Alink; *D.B.* Alan; *Fr.* Allain; p.n.

ALLENGAME. *See* Allingham

ALLERTON. A loc. n., Yorks

ALLERY. *See* Elleray

ALLETT. *See* Alured

ALLFLAT, ALLFAT. *N.* Alf-jótr; *D.B.* Adelfiete, Alfiet, Alvert; *Fl.* Aelvoet; *Dch.* Alphert; p.n.

ALLGOOD. *N.* Hallgerðr; *G.* Alger; *D.* Hallegar; *Fl.* Allegaert; *Dch.* Allgäuer; *D.B.* Algar, Algod; p.n.

ALLINGHAM. A loc. n., Kent

ALLINGTON. A loc. n., Devon, Dorset, Lincs., Salop, Hants, Wilts

ALLKIN. From Halkyn; a loc. n., N. Wales; or *see* Allchin

ALLMAN. *N.* Ölmóðr; *D.S.* Ahlman; *Fl.* Aleman; *G.* Hallman; *D.B.* Almund; p.n.

ALLNATT, ALLNUTT. *D.B.* Alnod; *A.S.*, p.n.

ALLONBY. A loc. n., Cumb.

ALLOTT. *N.* Hallaðr; *S.* Allart; *D.* Allert; *Dch.* Allot; *Fl.* Allard, Allart, Hallart, Hallet; p.n.

Aluiet, a tenant in chief; and Aliet, a Saxon tenant in *D.B.*

ALLPASS. *D.* Alpers; a p.n. *See* Alpe

ALLPRESS. *See* Allpass

ALLUM. From Hallam; a loc. n., Derbysh.

ALLWARD. *See* Aylward

ALLWAY. *See* Alloway or Holloway

ALLWOOD. *N.* Hallvarðr; *S.* Allard; *G.* Altvater; p.n.

Alward, a tenant in chief in *D.B.*; also a Saxon tenant.

ALLWORK. *See* Aldworth

ALLWORTH, ALLWORTHY. *See* Aldworth

ALLWRIGHT. From Aldreth or Alderwith; a loc. n., Camb. (?)

ALMACK. From Almeneches, a loc. n., Normandy (?)

There is a tradition that a Scotchman, coming to London, changed his name from MacAll to Allmack! It may be so.

ALMENT. *See* Allman

ALMOND. *See* Allman

ALNWICK. A loc. n., Northbd.

ALPE. *N.* Hjálpr; *D.* Alpers; *Fl.* Alpen; *Dch.* Alphen; *G.* Hallop, Hallup; p.n.

ALPORT. A loc. n., Derbysh.

ALSFORD. *See* Aylesford

ALSOP. A loc. n., Derbysh.; *D.B.* Elleshope

ALSTON. A loc. n., Cumb.; or *N.* Hallstein; *Fl.* Alsteens; *D.B.* Alstan, Alestan; p.n.

ALTHORP. A loc. n., Lincs.

ALTMAN. *G.* Altmann; a p.n.

ALTON. A loc. n., Staffs.

ALURED. *See* Alfred

ALVEY. *N.* Halveig; *Dch.* Halfweeg; *G.* Hallwig; p.n.

ALVIS. From Alves; a loc. n., Elgin

AMAS. *See* Ames

AMBLER. From Amberley (?); a loc. n., Suss.

AMEN. *See* Ames

AMER. *See* Hamer

AMERY. *Fl.* Emery; *G.* Emerich; p.n.

AMES. *N.* Eymundr; *F.* Emo, Eme; *D.B.* Haimo, Haimer, Hamo, Humez; *Dch.* Ameaz, Amsen, Emous, Amen; *Fl.* Ameys, Haemer; *D.* Ham, Hemme; *G.* Ameis, Emmes, Hems, Hemme; p.n.

AMESS, AMIES, AMIS, AMISS. *See* Ames

AMHERST. A loc. n., Kent

AMMAND. *See* Hammond

AMMON. *See* Hammond

AMOORE. *See* Armer or Hamer

AMOR. *See* Amer

AMPHLETT. From Amflete; a loc. n., Normandy

AMPS. *Dch.* Ampers, Hampe; p.n.

AMYS. *See* Ames

ANDERTON. A loc. n., Cornw., Yorks

ANGEL. *D. Dch.* p.n.

ANGIER. *Fr.* Anger; *D.* Anger, Ankjer; *D.B.* Anger; p.n.
Angers in Roll of Battell Abbey; Anger or Auinger (venator) in Rot. Obl. et Fin., K. John.

ANGLE. A loc. n., S. Wales; or *see* Angel

ANGUIN. *N. Fr.* Angevin in *D.B.* From Anjou

ANKER. *D.* Anker; *G.* Anke; *Dch.* Hankart; p.n.
Or Aincourt in Roll of Battell Abbey.

ANLEY. From Hanley; a loc. n., Staffs.

ANNABLE. *D.* Hannibal; *Fl.* Hennebel; p.n.

ANNAN. A loc. n., Scotl.

ANNES, ANNESS. *See* Annis

ANNIS, ANNISON. *N.* Áni; *F.* Onno and Enno; *D.B.* Enisan; *G.* Hanus, Hannsa; *Dch.* Annes, Ansel; *S.* Hane, Hanner, Henne; *Fl.* Hanes, Hanneson, Anhes, Annez; *D.* Hanisch, Annise; p.n.

ANSAR. *See* Ensor

ANSELL. *Dch.* Ansel; a p.n. *See* Annis

ANSLEY. From Annesley; a loc. n., Notts

ANSON. *See* Hanson

ANSTEAD. From Henstead; a loc. n., Suff. (?)

ANSTEY. A loc. n., Devon, Hants, Herts, Warw., Wilts

ANSTRUTHER. A loc. n., Fife

ANTILL. From Ampthill; a loc. n., Beds
Or *Fr.* Antieul, Antil; p.n.

ANTROBUS. A loc. n., Chesh.

ANYON. From Aniange; a loc. n., France. *See* Onions

APPERLEY. A loc. n., Glost., Yorks

APPLEBEE. *See* Appleby

APPLEBY. A loc. n., Westmd., Leicest., Lincs

APPLEGARTH. A loc. n., Dumfries

APPLEGATE. *See* Applegarth

APPLETON. A loc. n., Lancs, Norf., Yorks

APPLEYARD. *See* Applegarth

APPS. *See* Abbs

APRILE. *Fl.* April; a p.n.

APTHORPE. A loc. n., Notts

AQUS. *See* Ackers

ARBER. *N.* Há-bjarðr; *Dch.* Harbord; *D.* Harboe; p.n.

ARBLASTER. *D.B.* Arbalistarius, a cross-bowman

ARBOURN. From Harborne; a loc. n., Worcs.

ARBUCKLE. A loc. n., Lanark

ARBUTHNOT. A loc. n., Kincardineshire

ARCH. *Fr.* Arques; *D.B.* de Arches, de Arcis; p.n.
Tenant in chief in *D.B.* Henry de Arches held land in Yorks *temp.* K. John.

ARCHARD. *Fr.* Achard; a p.n. Or *see* Orchard

ARCHBELL. From Archibald; a p.n.

ARCHBOLD. From Archibald; a p.n.

ARCHDALL. From Arkendale; a loc. n., Yorks

ARCHDEACON. From the office

ARCHER. *Fr.* Archier; a p.n.
Richard le Archer and Nicholas Archer in Rot. Obl. et Fin., K. John.

ARDEN. A loc. n., Lanark, Yorks

ARDILL. From Ardle; a river, Perth (?). Or Hartell, Worcs.

ARDLEY. A loc. n., Herts

ARGLES. *Dch.* Arkel; a p.n.; or *see* Arkle

ARGYLE. A loc. n., Scotl.

ARKCOLL. *See* Arkle

ARKELL. *See* Arkle
ARKILL. *See* Arkle
ARKLE. From Acle; a loc. n., Norf.
Or Ercal, Salop.
ARLESEY. From Arlsey; a loc. n., Beds
ARLIDGE. From Arley; a loc. n., Warw. *D.B.* Arlege (?)
ARLINGTON. A loc. n., Suss.
ARLOSH. From Harlosh; a loc. n., Skye
ARMER. *N.* Ormr, Ormarr, Arm; *G.* Armer, Hermer; *D.B.* Harmer, Orm, Ormer; *Fl.* Harmer; p.n.
ARMES, ARMIS. *D.* Harms; *Dch.* Armes; p.n. *See* Armer
ARMFIELD. *S.* Armfelt; a p.n.
Or Amfield; a loc. n., Hants.
ARMITAGE. A loc. n., Staff.
ARMON. *Fr.* Armand; a p.n.
ARMSBY. *See* Ormsby
ARMSTEAD. *See* Hampstead
ARMSTRONG. From Armston; a loc. n., Northants (?)
Or from the Irish Lamb Laidir (strong arm); a n.n.
ARMSWORTH. A loc. n., Hants
ARNALL. *See* Arnold
ARNE. A loc. n., Dorset; *D.* p.n.
ARNELL. *See* Arnold
ARNOLD. A loc. n., Notts, Wilts, Yorks; *D.B.* Ernehale
ARNOTT. *See* Arnold, or dimin. of *N.* Örn
ARRINDELL. *See* Arundel
ARSCOTT. A loc. n., Salop
ARSTON. From Harston; a loc. n., Leics., Northants, Camb., etc.
ARTER. *Fl.* Artur; a p.n.
ARTHY, ARTHEY. *See* Artis
ARTIS. *N.* Hjörtr; *D.B.* Arte, Artor; *G.* Harter, Hart, Harte; *Fl.* Art, Arts, Artus; *D.* Hartig; *Dch.* Arts; p.n.
ARUNDELL. A loc. n., Suss.
ASBURY. From Ashbury; a loc. n., Berks, Devon; or *see* Astbury
ASCOITH. *See* Askew
ASCOTT. A loc. n., Cornw.
ASH. A loc. n., Derbysh.; *D.B.* Eisse
ASHBEE. *See* Ashby
ASHBRIDGE. From Agbridge; a loc. n., Yorks
ASHBURNER. *N.* Ásbrandr, also Asbjörn; *D.B.* Esbern, Osbern; p.n.
ASHBY. A freq. loc. n.
ASHCROFT. A loc. n., Yorks
ASHDOWN. From Ashdon; a loc. n., Ess.
ASHENDEN. A loc. n., Herts
ASHFIELD. A loc. n., Suff.
ASHFORD. A loc. n., Derbys., Devon, Hants, etc.
ASHLEY. A loc. n., Hants, Wilts
ASHMAN. *N.* Ásmundr; *D.* Asmund; *G.* Assman; *Dch.* Asman; *D.B.* Asseman, Osmund; p.n.
ASHMORE. A loc. n., Dorset, Wilts
ASHPITEL. From Ashbrittle; a loc. n., Somers.
ASHPLANT. *See* Aspland
ASHPOLE. From Aspull; a loc. n., Lancs
ASHTON. A loc. n., Lancs, Hants, Herts, Glos., Wilts
ASHURST. A loc. n., Kent, Lancs, Suss.
ASHWELL. A loc. n., Herts, Rutl., Somers.
ASHWIN. *N.* Ás-vinnr (?); *A.S.* Oswin; p.n.
ASHWORTH. A loc. n., Lancs
ASKER. *N.* Askviðr; *D.* Askov; *S.* Asker; *Dch.* Asscher; *D.B.* Ascuit; p.n. Comp. Askew, Ascoith, etc.
ASKEW. A loc. n., Yorks; *D.B.* Ascwith, Hascoith; p.n.
ASKHAM. A loc. n., Notts, Lancs
ASKWITH. *See* Askew
ASMUS. *G.* Assmus; a p.n.
ASPDEN. From Aspenden; a loc. n., Herts
ASPINALL. *Dch.* Espagniol; a p.n.

ASPINWALL. *See* Aspinall

ASPLAND. *S.* Asplund, Espelund; a loc. and p. n.

ASPRAY. *Fr.* Esprit; a p.n.

ASSHETON. A loc. n., Ess.

ASTBURY. A loc. n., Ches.

ASTELL. From Astwell; a loc. n., Northants

ASTLEY. A loc. n., Lancs, Salop, Warw., Worc.

ASTON. A loc. n., Glos., Hants, Heref., Salop

ASTROP. From Asthorpe; a loc. n., Herts

ATHAWES. From Atte-Hawes; a loc. n.

ATHERLEY. From Hatherleigh; a loc. n., Devon

ATHERSMITH. *F.* Athe; a p.n., and Schmid; or *F.* Atteschmid, the obsolete form of Ritterschmid, an armourer, who belonged once to the lower orders of nobility.

ATHERSTONE. A loc. n., Warw.

ATHERTON. A loc. n., Lancs

Robert de Atherton, Sheriff of Lancs, A.D. 1206.

ATHORNE. From Atte-Horn; a loc. n.

Horn was a corner or triangular piece of land.

ATHORPE. *D.* Attrup; a loc. and p. n.; or from Authorpe; a loc. n., Lincs

ATHOW. From Hathow; a loc. n., Lincs; or *see* Atto

ATKINS, ATKINSON. *See* Atto

ATLAY. *N.* Atli; *S.* Atler; a p.n.

Atilie, a Saxon tenant in *D.B.* Or from Atlow; a loc. n., Derbys. *D.B.* Etelaw.

ATTENBOROUGH. A loc. n., Notts

ATTERBURY. A loc. n., Devon

Or Atterby, Lincs.

ATTERSLEY. *See* Attlee

ATTFIELD. *See* Hatfield

ATTHEL. *See* Atthill

ATTHILL. From Atte Hill

A surname adopted as early as the fourteenth century from place of residence.

ATTLE. *See* Atthill or Attley

ATTLEE. From Atterley; a loc. n., Salop

Or Hatley, Camb.

ATTMORE. From Atte-moor, at the moor

ATTO, ATTOE. *N.* Höttr (Hattr); *F.* Athe; *D.B.* Atre; *G.* Hattin, Hatto; *Fl.* Athée, Attout; *D.* Hatting; *Dch.* Ates, Atten, Atkins; p.n.

ATTREE. Atte Tree; loc. n.

ATTRIDGE. Atte Ridge; loc. n.

ATTS. *Dch.* Ates; a p.n. *See* Atto

ATTWATER. Atte Water; loc. n.

ATTWOOD. From Atte-wood

ATTY. *F.* Athe, Atte; *Fr.* Athée; a p.n. *See* Atto

ATWELL. From Atte Welle; a loc. n.

Adopted as a surname 1258-1358, Court of Husting, London.

AUCHINLECK. A loc. n., Ayr

AUCOTT. From Hawcoat; a loc. n., Lancs (?)

AUDLAND. From Audlem; a loc. n., Ches. (?)

AUDLEY. A loc. n., Ess., Staffs.

AUDSLEY. From Audley; a loc. n., Staffs.

AUGER. *G.* Augar; a p.n. *See* Aggs

AUKER. *N.* Haukr; *F.* Arko; *G.* Hauk, Hauke; *Fl.* Haucq; *Dch.* Aukes; *D.* Harke; p.n.

AUKLAND. A loc. n., Dur.

AUSTEN, AUSTIN. *D.* Augustin; *D.B.* Augustin, Austin; p.n.

AUSTWICK. A loc. n., Yorks

AVANT. From Havant; a loc. n., Hants

AVELEY, AVELING. *Fl.* Evely; *Dch.* Evelein; *D.B.* Avelin; p.n.

AVENELL. Norman, *Fr.*; p.n.; *D.B.* Avenel

W. Avenel, in Rot. Obl. et Fin., K. John.

AVERELL. From Haverhill; a loc. n., Suff.

AVERY. From Evreux (?); a loc. n., Normandy
Cecil de Evereus in Rot. Obl. et Fin., K. John.

AWDRY. From St. Awdry (St. Etheldreda, Ely)

AXFORD. A loc. n., Wilts

AXHAM. From Hexham; a loc. n., Northd.

AXON. *Dch.* Haksteen; p.n.

AYBEL. *See* Abel

AYERS, AYRES. *Fl.* Eyer, Eyers; p.n.

AYLESBURY. A loc. n., Bucks

AYLETT, AYLOTT. *D. F.* Eilert; *D.B.* Ailet; p.n.

AYLIFFE. *N.* Eilífr; *D.B.* Ailof, Eilaf; p.n.

AYLING. From Hayling; a loc. n., Hants
Or *Fl.* Elen, Eylen; p.n.

AYLIVARD. *See* Aylward

AYLMER. *F.* Helmer; a p.n.
Ailmar, a tenant in chief, *D.B.*

AYLWARD. *N.* Egil-hjörtr; *F.* Egilhardt, Eilart; *D.* Ellegaard, Eylard; *Fl.* Allegaert; *D.B.* Ageluuard, Aieluert, Ailuuard; *G.* Ehlert; p.n.

AYRE. From Ayr; a loc. n., Scotl.; or *see* Avery

AYRTON. A loc. n., Yorks

AYSCOUGH. From Aysgarth; a loc. n., Yorks

AYTON. A loc. n., Berwick, Yorks

B.

BAALAM, BAALHAM. From Baylham; a loc. n., Suff. *See* Bellamy

BAAS. *D.* Basse; *Dch.* Baas, Bas; *Fl.* Baes; p.n.

BABBAGE. *See* Burbage

BABBINGTON. A loc. n., Cornw., Northd., Notts, Somers.

BABBS. *G.* Babisch, Babst; p.n.

BABER. A loc. n., Norf.

BACCHUS. *See* Backhouse

BACK. *Dch.* Bac, Bak; p.n. *See* Bagge

BACKHOUSE. *Dch.* Backhaus; a p.n.

BACON. *N.* Bekan; *D.B.* Baco; p.n.

BADCOCK. *D.* Badock; *G.* Badke, Batke; p.n.

BADDELEY. From Baddiley; a loc. n., Ches.

BADGER. A loc. n., Salop

BADHAM. A loc. n., Cornw.

BADKIN. *Fl.* Batkin; a p.n.

BADLEY. A loc. n., Suff.

BAGGALLAY. *See* Baguley

BAGGE. *N.* Bögvir; *S., D.* Bagge; *G.* Baake, Backe; *Fl.* Bagge, Baguet; *Dch.* Bagge, Baggers; p.n.
D.B. Baco, Bagod.

BAGLEY. A loc. n., Berks, Salop, Somers.

BAGNALL. A loc. n., Staffs.

BAGOT. *Fl.* Bygodt; *Fr.* Baguet; *D.B.* Bagod; p.n.
Baggard, Bagod, Bagot, Bargard, Bigard, Bigod, Bigot, in Rot. Obl. et Fin., K. John.

BAGSHAW. From Bagshot; a loc. n., Surrey, Wilts

BAGULEY. A loc. n., Ches.

BAGWELL. *See* Bakewell

BAIGENT. *See* Bezant

BAILEY. From Beeleigh; a loc. n. (Ess.); or *G.* Behlau; *Dch.* Beeling; *Fl.* Beeli; p.n. *See* Bales

BAINBRIDGE. A loc. n., Yorks

BAINES. *N.* Beinir; *F.* Baino, Beino; *D.* Behn; *S.* Been; *Fl.* Bayens, Beine, Beyns; *Dch.* Beens; *G.* Bens; *D.B.* Bain, Benz; p.n.

BAKE. *See* Beck

BAKEWELL. A loc. n., Derbysh.

BALCHIN. *D.* Balchen; *Fl.* Balcaen; *N.* Bálki; *D.B.* Balchi; *G.* Balcke; p.n.

BALCOMBE. A loc. n., Suss.

BALDERS. *N.* Baldr; *D.B.* Baldric; *G.* Balder; *D.* Bald, Balle, Boldt; *Dch.* Balder, Bols, Bolt; p.n.

BALDERSON. *See* Balderston

BALDERSTON. From Balderstone; a loc. n., Lancs

BALDING. *See* Baldwin

BALDOCK. A loc. n., Beds

BALDRY. *See* Balders

BALDWIN. *N.* Baldvinni (friend of the god Baldr); *G.* Baldin; *D.* Bolding; *Dch.* Bolding; *Fl.* Bauduin, Boldewin

The name of the Counts of Flanders. Bawdwin is on the Roll of Battell Abbey, and Baldwin among the tenants in chief in *D.B.*

BALE. A loc. n., Norf.; also Beale, Yorks. *See* Bell

BALFOUR. A loc. n., Fife

BALLANTYNE. *See* Bannatyne

BALLARD. *Fl.* Balat; a p.n. (?)

BALLENGER. *See* Ballinger

BALLINGER. From Ballingham; a loc. n., Heref.

Or *Dch.* Baldinger; a p.n.

BALLS. *See* Balders

BALMER. From Balmire; a loc. n., Cumb.

BAMBER. *See* Bambury

BAMBRIDGE. From Bembridge; a loc. n., Camb., Hants

BAMBURY. From Bamburgh; a loc. n., Lincs, Northd.

BAMFORD. A loc. n., Lancs., Derbysh.

BAMFYLDE. A loc. n., Somers.

BAMPTON. A loc. n., Cumb., Devon, Oxf., Westmd.

BANBURY. A loc. n., Oxon

BANCROFT. From Brancroft; a loc. n., Yorks

Or Bangrove, Glos. (?).

BANE, BANEY. *N.* Beinir; *F.* Baino, Beino; *D.B.* Bann, Bain; *S.* Béen; *Fl.* Beine; *G.* Bein, Bens; *D.* Beine, Behn, Been; *Dch.* Banen, Beien, Benier, Benner, Beno; p.n.

BANFATHER. *See* Pennefeather

BANGER, BANGERT. *Dch.* Bangert; a p.n.

BANGHAM. *See* Banham

BANGS. *D.* Bang; *G.* Banke; *Dch.* Bank, Bangert; *D.B.* Bangiard; p.n.

BANHAM. A loc. n., Norf.

BANISTER, BANNISTER. From Banstead; a loc. n., Ess., Surr. (?)

Adam Banastr in Rot. Obl. et Fin., K. John.

BANKS. A loc. n., Yorks; or *D.*, *S.*, *Dch.* Bancke; *Fl.* Banker; p.n.

BANNATYNE. From Bannocktine; a loc. n., Scotl.

BANNER. *Dch.*; p.n.

BANNERMAN. *Dch.* Bonnerman; a p.n.

BANTIN, BANTING. *Dch.*; p.n.

BANYARD. *D.*, *Dch.* Bangert; a p.n.

BARADALE. A loc. n., Ayrsh.

BARBEN. *See* Barbon

BARBER. From St. Barbe sur Gaillon; a loc. n. in Normandy, where was the celebrated abbey of St. Barbara; or *Fr.* Barbe, Barbiaux, Barbry; *Dch.* Barbe; *G.* Barber; p.n.

Bernard Barb and de Barbes, tenants in *D.B.* St. Barbe is on the Roll of Battell Abbey. William de St. Barbara, Bishop of Durham, A.D. 1143. Barber or Barbour, a hamlet in Dumbartonshire; or *Fr.* Barbier, Barbieur; p.n.

BARBEY. *Fr.* Barbé, Barbet, Barbey; p.n.

Hugo Barbatus in *D.B.* (Hugh with the beard.)

BARBON. A loc. n., Westmd.

BARBOUR. *See* Barber

BARCLAY. *See* Berkeley

BARDELL, BARDILL. *See* Bardwell

BARDSLEY. A loc. n., Lancs

BARDWELL. A loc. n., Suff.

BARE. *See* Bear

BAREFOOT. *See* Barfoot

BARFF. A loc. n., Lincs

BARFITT. *See* Barfoot

BARFOOT. From Barford; a loc. n., Worc., Norf., Camb., Oxf.
Or Barforth, Yorks; or *D.* Barfod; a p.n.

BARGE. *Dch.*; p.n.

BARGMAN. *Dch.*; p.n.

BARHAM. A loc. n., Kent, Suff.

BARKER. *N.* Börkr; *S.* Barck; *Dch.* Barger; *Fl.* Barker; *G.* Barche; *D.B.* Barch; p.n.

BARKLEY. *See* Berkeley

BARKSHIRE. From Berkshire; the county

BARKUS. From Bargus; a loc. n., Cornw.

BARKWAY. A loc. n., Herts

BARKWORTH. From Barkwith; a loc. n., Lincs

BARLEE. *See* Barley

BARLEY. A loc. n., Herts

BARLOW. A loc. n., Derbysh., Yorks

BARNABY. From Barnby; a loc. n., Suff.

BARNACKLE. From Barnacre; a loc. n., Lancs

BARNARD. *N.* Bjarnarðr; *Fl.* Barnard; *D.B.* Bernard; p.n.

BARNBY. A loc. n., Yorks

BARNES. A loc. n., Surr.

BARNETT. From Barnet; a loc. n., Herts; or *N.* Bjárni; *G.* Barnatt, Barnert; *Fl.* Bernert; p.n.

BARNEWALL. *See* Barnwell

BARNEY. A loc. n., Norf.

BARNICLE. *See* Barnacle

BARNSDALE. A loc. n., Yorks

BARNSLEY. A loc. n., Dorset, Yorks

BARNWELL. A loc. n., Ayr
Or Barneville, Normandy.

BARON. A loc. n., Normandy

BARR. A loc. n., Ayrshire; or *N.* Bangr; n.n. *D.* Barr; *Fl.* Bar; *Fr.* de la Barre; *D.B.* Bar; p.n.

BARRADALE. From Borrodale; a loc. n., Cumb.

BARRELL. *Fl.* Barel, Bareel; *D.* Baruël; a p.n.

BARRIE. A loc. n., Forfar

BARRINGTON. A loc. n., Camb., Lincs, Somers.
Or from Barenton; a loc. n., Normandy.

BARROW. A freq. loc. n.; or *D.* Barroe; *Dch.* Barrau; *Fl.* Baro; p.n.

BARRY. *See* Barrie

BARSBY. A loc. n., Leics.

BARSTOW. From Barstone; a loc. n., Kent

BARTER. *N.* Bardr; a p.n.

BARTH. *D.*, *Dch.*. *Fl.*, *G.*, p.n.
A contr. of Bartholomew.

BARTHORP, BARTHROPP, BARTROP. From Barthorp; a loc. n., Lincs

BARTINGTON. *See* Partington

BARTLETT. *G.* Bartelt; *Fr.* Bartalot; p.n.
Dimin. of Bartholomew.

BARTLEY. A loc. n., Hants, Worcs.

BARTON. A freq. loc. n.

BARWELL. A loc. n., Leics.

BARWIS, BARWISE. *Fr.* Barvais; *G.* Barwisch; p.n.

BASAN. *See* Bezant

BASCOMB. From Boscombe; a loc. n., Hants, Wilts

BASCUM. *See* Bascomb

BASE. *See* Bayes

BASEY. *See* Beazer

BASHALL. A loc. n., Yorks

BASHAM. From Barsham; a loc. n., Norf.

BASHFORD. From Bassford; a loc. n., Staffs.

BASKETT. From the *Fr.* Bassecourt; a loc. n. Or Bosquet; a p.n. Or *Dch.* Bastet; a p.n.

BASS. A loc. n., Invury, Haddington
Or *D.*, *Fr.* Basse; a p.n.

BASSANT. *See* Bezant

BASTABLE. From Barnstaple; a loc. n., Devon

BASTARD. *Dch.* Bastert; *Fl.* Batard; p.n.
In Roll of Battell Abbey and in *D.B.* Wm. le Bastard held land in Yorks *temp.* K. John.

BASTIN. *Fr.* Bastien; *Fl.* Bastin; p.n.
BASTING. *Dch.* Basting; *D.* Bastian; *Fl.* Bastin; p.n.
BASTOW. From Baston; a loc. n., Lincs
BATCHELDER. *See* Batchelor
BATCHELOR. *Dch.* Baggelaar; *Fr.* Bachelet; *G.* Bachaly; p.n.
BATE, BATES. *N.* Beda; *D.B.* Beda; *D.* Betz; *Dch.* Beets; *Fl.* Bette, Beths, Beetz, Bets; p.n.
BATELEY. *See* Batley
BATEMAN. *S.* Betjeman; *Dch.* Betman; p.n.
BATGER. *See* Badger
BATH. A loc. n., Somers.
BATHE. *Dch.* Bethe, Beth; p.n.
BATHURST. A loc. n., Suss.
BATHY. From Bartholomew
BATLEY. A loc. n., Yorks
BATSFORD. A loc. n., Glost., Suff.
BATSON. *See* Bathy
BATT, BATTYE. *Fl.* Batta, Batteux; p.n.
BATTCOCK. *See* Badcock
BATTELL, BATTLE. A loc. n., S. Wales, Suss.
Or *Fr.* Battaille; a p.n.
BATTEN. From *Fl.* Batkin; a p.n.
Or *Fr.* Bethune or de Bethune; a p.n.
BATTERHAM. *See* Buttram
BATTERSBURY. From Battlesbury; a loc. n., Wilts
BATTERSBY. A loc. n., Yorks
BATTERSHALL. From Patishull; a loc. n., Staffs.
BATTISCOMBE. From Bettiscombe; a loc. n., Dorset
BATTOCK. *See* Badcock
BATTRUM. *See* Buttrum
BATTY. *See* Bathy
BAULY. From Beoley; a loc. n., Worcest.
BAYE. *Fr.* Bavay; a p.n.
BAVEN, BAVIN. From Bavent; a loc. n., Normandy
Or *Fl.* Bawin; a p.n.
BAWDEN. A loc. n., Cornw.
BAWN. *D.* Baun; *Fl.* Bauwen; p.n.
BAWTREE. From Bawtry; a loc. n., Yorks
BAXENDEN. A loc. n., Lancs
BAXTER.
The Scot. and N. Engl. form of Baker.
BAYES, BAYS. *Fl.* Baye; *D.* Beyer; *Dch.* Bes, Bey, Bies; p.n.
BAYLISS. *Fl.* Bellis; a p.n.
BAYNES. *See* Baines
BAYNHAM. *See* Banham
Or Benholme; a loc. n., Kincardine.
BAYNTON. A loc. n., Northants, Oxf., Yorks
BAZELEY. *See* Beasley
BEACHAM. *Fr.* Beauchamp; a p.n.
BEACOM. *Dch.* Beckünn, Beekum; p.n.; or *see* Beacham
BEADLE. From Bedale; a loc. n., Yorks; or *see* Biddulph
BEADSMORE. From Birdsmoor; a loc. n., Dorset
BEAK. *G.* Bick; *Fr.* Bické, Bicqué; p.n.
BEAL. A loc. n., Yorks
BEALE. A loc. n., Dur.
BEALES. From Bealings; a loc. n., Suff.
BEALEY. From Beeley; a loc. n., Derbysh.
BEAMENT. *See* Beaumont
BEAMISH. A loc. n., Dur.
BEAN. *D.*, *Dch.* Biene; a p.n.
BEANHAM. *See* Baynham
BEANLANDS. A loc. n., Cumb.
BEAR. *N.* Bera; *D.* Bjerre; *D.B.* Bere; *Dch.*, *Fl.* Beer, Behr; *G.* Behr; p.n.
BEARCHELL. From Bircholt; a loc. n., Kent
BEARD. A loc. n., Derbysh., Devon
BEARDMORE. *See* Beadsmoor
BEARDSLEY. From Bardsley; a loc. n., Lancs
Or Buwardsley, Ches.
BEARDWELL. From Bardwell; a loc. n., Suff.
BEASANT. *See* Bezant

BEASEY. *See* Beazer

BEASLEY. From Beazley; a loc. n., Warw.

BEATON. *Fr.* Bethune; a p.n.; or *see* Beeton

BEATTIE or BEATTY. From the Irish Betagh (biadhtach), a public victualler; a p.n.

BEAVEN. *Fl.* Beving; a p.n.

BEAVIN, BEAVON. *See* Bevin

BEAZER. *Fr.* Bisez; a p.n.

Bisi or Bysey in the Roll of Battell Abbey. *D.B.* Besi, Besy; p.n.

BECCLES. A loc. n., Suff.

BECK. *N.* Bekan; *D.S.G.*, *Dch.* Beck; *Fl.* Baeck; p.n. Or from Bec-Hellouin; a loc. n., Normandy

Beke on the Roll of Battell Abbey. De Bec a tenant in chief, Walter Bec at the time of the Survey, in *D.B.* Bec and Bek in Rot. Obl. et Fin., K. John.

BECKFORD. A loc. n., Hants

BECKHAM. A loc. n., Norf.

BECKLEY. A loc. n., Hants, Suss.

BECKWITH. A loc. n., Yorks

BED. *N.* Beda; *Fr.* Béde; *Fl.* Bette; *G.*, *Dch.* Beth; p.n. *See* Bate

BEDALL. From Bedale; a loc. n., Yorks

BEDDOE. *G.* Beddau; *Fr.* Bidaut; p.n.

BEDFORD. A loc. n., the county town

BEDINGFIELD. A loc. n., Suff.

BEDWELL. A loc. n., Beds

BEE. *D.*, *Dch.* Bie, Bye; *N.* Bui; p.n. *See* Bugge

BEEBEE. From Beeby; a loc. n., Leics.

BEECH. A loc. n., Staffs.

BEECHEY. *See* Beeching

BEECHING. A loc. n., Suss., Wilts

BEEDELL. *See* Bedall

BEEDEN. From Beeden; a loc. n., Berks

BEEFORTH. From Beaford; a loc. n., Devon

BEER. *D.*, *Dch.*, *Fl.*, *G.*, p.n.; or a loc. n., Devon

BEESLEY, BESLEY. *See* Beasley

BEESTON. A loc. n., Norf., Notts

BEETHAM. *See* Betham

BEETLES. *See* Bedall

BEETON. From Beighton; a loc. n., Norf.

BEETS. *See* Bates

BEEVER. *Fr.* Biver; a p.n.

BEGBIE. From Bigby; a loc. n., Lincs

BEGG. *See* Beck

BEHAG. *Fl.* Behagel; a p.n.

BEITH. A loc. n., Ayr, Renfrew

Or *G.* Bieth; a p.n.

BELCHAM. From Belchamp; a loc. n., Ess.

D.B. De Belchamp; p.n. Or *Fr.* Beljambe; a p.n.

BELCHER. From Bellecourt; a loc. n., Normandy, near Perrone

Bellesur in Roll of Battell Abbey.

BELDAN. *See* Belding

BELDEN. *See* Belding

BELDING. From Beltinge; a loc. n., Kent

BELFRAGE. From the Norman French Beaufoy, Latinised into de Bella Fago. *D.B.* Belvaco, Belvou; p.n.

BELHAM, BELHOMME. *See* Baalam

BELL. *N.* Beli; *F.* Bela, Bêl, Bele; *S.* Bell; *Dch.* Bel; *Fl.* Baele, Beli; p.n.

BELLAIRS. *See* Bellares

BELLAMY. A *Fr.* p.n. from Bellème; a loc. n. in Normandy

Beelhelme in Roll of Battell Abbey, Belam in *D.B.* *D.* Beilum; *Fl.* Belemme; *Dch.* Bellm; p.n.

BELLARS, BELLARES. *Fl.* Bellers; a p.n.

Beleuers in Roll of Battell Abbey. Hamon Bellars was a hostage to K. John, A.D. 1216 (Whitwick, Leics.).

BELLASIS. A loc. n., Cornw., Northbd., Yorks

Ballisise in Roll of Battell Abbey.

BELLEW. *Fr.* Bellot; a p.n.

Bellew in Roll of Battell Abbey; Belot, a tenant in chief in *D.B.* Gaufrid Belewe and Robt. de Baleewe in Rot. Obl. et Fin., K. John.

BELLIN. *Fl.* Belin, Bellen, Belyn; p.n.

BELLOE. From Belleau; a loc. n., Norf.; or *see* Bellew

BELLOWS. *See* Bellairs

BELSHAM. *See* Belchamp

BELSHAW. *Dch.* Belser (?); or *see* Belcher

BELSTEN. *See* Belston

BELSTON. A loc. n., Devon

BELTON. A loc. n., Leics.

BEMROSE. From Penhrôs; a loc. n., Wales

Or Penrose, Cornwall.

BENBOW. From Benningborough; a loc. n., Yorks

BENCE. *N.* Bensi, *Dch.* Bense; p.n.

BENDALL. *D.* Bendahl, Bendal; *Dch.* Bendel; p.n.

BENDELOW. *Dch.* Bentelaar; a p.n.

BENDER. *D.*, *Dch.*, *Fl.*, *G.*, p.n.

BENDING. *D.* Benthin; *Dch.* Bendien, Bentinck; p.n.

BENDON. From Benton; a loc. n., Northmbd.

BENDY. *G.* Bendig; a p.n.

BENFIELD. From Benefield; a loc. n., Northants

BENFORD. From Bainsford; a loc. n., Stirling

BENHAM. From Benholme; a loc. n., Kincardine

BENN, BENNY.

Dimin. of Benedict.

BENNINGTON. A loc. n., Lincs

BENSLEY. A loc. n., Ayr

BENSON. *N.* Benni and Bensi; *F.* Benne (dimin. of Benedict); *S.* Benzon; *D.* Bengtsen, Bendsen, Benzen; *Dch.* Bense; *D.B.* Benz; p.n.

BENSTED, BENSTEAD. From Binstead; a loc. n., Hants, Suss.

BENTHALL. A loc. n., Salop

BENTHAM. A loc. n., Staffs.

BENTLEY. A loc. n., Yorks

BENWELL. A loc. n., Northbd.

BERBIDGE. *See* Burbage

BERKELEY. A loc. n., Glos.

BERRETT.

Barrett in Roll of Battell Abbey. *See* Borret.

BERRICK. *See* Berwick

BERRIDGE. From Berwich; a loc. n., Ess.

BERRY. A loc. n., Normandy; or from the Irish O'Beara; a p.n.

BERWICK. A loc. n., Ess., Northbd., Wilts

BESANT. From *Fr.* Baisant; a Huguenot n.

BESFORD. A loc. n., Worc.

BESSELL. *D.* Bestle; a p.n.

BESSEY. *See* Beazer

BEST. *D.*, *Dch.*, *Fl.*, *G.*, p.n.

BESWICK. A loc. n., Yorks

BETHAM. A loc. n., Westmd.

Ralph de Betham was a benefactor to Furness Abbey, Hen. II.

BETHELL. *G.* Bethel; *Fl.* Beethel; p.n.

BETSWORTH, BETTESWORTH. From Betchworth; a loc. n., Surr.

BETT. *Fl.* Bette; *Dch.*, *G.* Beth; p.n.

BETTELEY. From Betley; a loc. n., Staffs.

BETTERIDGE. From Pettridge; a loc. n., Kent

BETTERTON. A loc. n., Berks

BETTS. *See* Bates

BEVAN. *Fl.* Bevenot, Beving; p.n.

Bevan and Bevin occur in Rot. Obl. et Fin., K. John.

BEVINGTON. A loc. n., Lancs

BEVINS. *Fl.* Beving; *D.* Bevensee; p.n.

BEVIS. From Beauvais; a loc. n., France. Or *Fl.* Bevers; or *Fr.* Beaufils (?); p.n.

W. Beaufiz de Rya in Rot. Obl. et Fin., K. John.

BEW. *D.* Beu; a p.n.

BEWICK. A loc. n., Yorks

BEWLEY. A loc. n., Westmd.

BEWSHER. *N.* Buðker; *D.* Bödker; *G.* Böttcher (a cooper); *S.* Bottger; *Dch.* Bodekke; *Fl.* Buker, Buscher; *Fr.* Bucher; *D.B.* Boscher; p.n.

BEX. *Fl.* Bex; *D.* Becks; p.n.
BEYNON. *Fr.* Binon; a p.n.
BEZANT. *Fr.* Baisant; a Hugonot n.
BIBBY. *See* Beebee
BICK. *Fr.* Bické, Bicqué; *G.* Bick; p.n.
BICKELL, BICKLE. *Fr., Dch.* Bickel; *D.* Bichel; p.n.
BICKER. A loc. n., Lincs. *See* Bigg
BICKERSTETH. From Bickerstaffe; a loc. n., Lancs
BICKERTON. A loc. n., Norf.
BICKFORD. A loc. n., Staffs.
BICKLEY. A loc. n., Kent, Worcest.
Or Bickleigh, Devon.
BICKMORE. From Bicknor; a loc. n., Glos., Heref., Kent
BICKNELL. From Bickenhall; a loc. n. Somers.
Or Bickenhill, Warw.
BICKTON. From Bicton; a loc. n., Cornw., Devon, Hants
BIDDLE. *See* Biddulph or Bedell
BIDDULPH. From Biddulph; a loc. n., Staffs.
BIDGOOD. From Bidacott; a loc. n., Devon
BIGG. *D.* Big; *G.* Bick; *Dch.* Bicker; a p.n.
BIGGAR. A loc. n., Lanarks
BIGGINS. A loc. n., Derbysh.
BIGGS. *See* Bigg
BIGNALL, BIGNELL. A loc. n., Staffs.
BIGSBY, BIXBY. Erom Bigby; a loc. n., Lincs
BILBOROUOH. A loc. n., Notts, Yorks
BILBY. A loc. n., Notts
Or Beilby, Yorks.
BILLETT. *N., Fr.* Belet; p.n.
BILLING. A loc. n., Lancs, Northants, Yorks (contr. of Billingham); or *D.S.* Billing; *Fl.* Billen; *Dch.* Bille; p.n.
Billing, an ancient noble northern clan.
BILLINGTON. A loc. n., Staffs.
BILTON. From Bilston; a loc. n., Staffs.
BINDLEY. A loc. n., Hants
BINDLOSS. *G.* Bindlos; a p.n.
BINDON. A loc. n., Hants
BINGHAM. A loc. n., Notts
Hugo and Robert de Bingeham in Rot. Obl. et Fin., K. John (Notts).
BINGLEY. A loc. n., Yorks
BINKS. *D.* Bing, Bink; *A.S.* Bings; *S.* Bing; *G.* Bieneck; *Dch.* Bing, Binger, Bink, Binns, Binnen; p.n.
This patronymic gives the names to Bing (Suff.), Bingham (Northants), Bingley (Yorks), Bingen (Rhine), Binges (Burgundy).
BINLESS. *See* Bindloss
BINNEY. From Binnie; a loc. n., Linlithgow
BINNS. A loc. n., Roxburgh; or *Dch., Fl.* Bins; *G.* Binas; p.n.
BINSTEAD. A loc. n., Hants, Suss.
BINYON. *See* Beynon
BIRCH. A loc. n., Ess., Lancs, Salop, Yorks; or *see* Burch
BIRCHALL. From Bircholt; a loc. n., Kent
BIRCHAM. A loc. n., Norf.
BIRCHENOUGH. *Dch.* Berkenhoff; a loc. and p. n.
BIRCHINGTON. A loc. n., Kent
BIRD, BIRT. *N.* Birtingr; n.n. *D.* Bird; *Fl.* Burdo, Burth; *G.* Burde, Berto, Berdie; *D.B.* Berdic, Buerd, Burdet; p.n.
BIRKETT. *N.* Birkiviðr; or *Dch.* Berkhout; *Fl.* Burkard; *G.* Burchardt; *D.B.* Bucard, Burkart; p.n.
BIRKIN. A loc. n., Yorks
De Birchinges, a tenant in chief in *D.B.* John de Birkin held land in Yorks *temp.* K. John.
BIRKLE. From Birkhall; a loc. n., Aberdeen
Or Birkhill, Fife.
BIRLEY. A loc. n., Heref.
BIRTHWRIGHT. From Birthwaite; a loc. n., Westmd.
BISPHAM. A loc. n., Lancs
BISS. *S.* Bishe; a p.n.
BISSELL. *See* Buscall

BISSETT. *Fr.* Bissot; *G.* Bissert; p.n.

BISSMIRE. *Fl.* Pessemier; a p.n.

BITTLESTON. From Biddlestone; a loc. n., Heref.

BIXBY. *See* Bigsby

BIZLEY. *See* Beasley

BLABY. A loc. n., Leics.

BLACK. *D.* Black; *Fl.* Blake; *Dch.* Blaak, Blak; p.n.

BLACKABY. From Blackfordby; a loc. n., Leics.

BLACKADDER. From Blackheath; a freq. loc. n.

D. Black; a p.n., *hede*, heath.

BLACKALL. From Blackall; a loc. n., Devon

BLACKBORN. *See* Blackburn

BLACKBURN. A loc. n., Lancs

BLACKFORD. A loc. n., Devon

RLACKGROVE. From Blagrave; a loc. n., Berks

BLACKLOCK. From Black Loch; a loc. n., Lanark, Renfrew, Stirling

BLACKMORE. From Blackmoor; a loc. n., Somers.

BLACKTIN. From Blackden; a loc. n., Ess.

BLACKWELL. A loc. n., Derbysh., Dur., Worc.

BLADE. *N.* Blaudr; *A.S.* Bleâde; *D.* Blad, Bladt; *S.* Blad; *Fl.* Bled; *Dch.* Blad, Blatt; *Scot.* Blate; p.n.

BLADES. A loc. n., Yorks

BLADON. From Bladen; a loc. n., Dorset

BLAGBURN. *See* Blackburn

BLAGDEN. *See* Blagdon

BLAGDON. A loc. n., Devon

BLAGG. *See* Black

BLAGROVE. From Blagrave; a loc. n., Berks

BLAKE. *Dch.* Bleek; *Fl.* Blieck; p.n.

BLAKEMORE. From Blakemere; a loc. n., Heref.

BLAKENEY. A loc. n., Glos., Norf.

BLAKESLEY. A loc. n., Northants

BLAKISTON. From Blackstone; a loc. n., Worcest.

BLAMIRE. *D.* Blumer; *Dch.* Bloemer; *Fl.* Bloemart; a p.n. Or *N.* blaamyr (blue moor), a poetical name for the sea

BLANDFORD. A loc. n., Dorset

BLANKLEY. From Blankney; a loc. n., Lincs

BLATCH. *D.* Blache; *G.* Blach, Blasche; a p.n.

BLATCHLEY. From Bletchley; a loc. n., Oxon, Salop

BLATHERWAYT, BLATHWAYT. From Bleathwaite; a loc. n., Cumb.

BLATHERWICK. A loc. n., Northants

BLAXALL. A loc. n., Suff.

BLAXLAND. From Blackland; a loc. n., Suff.

BLAY, BLEY. *G.* Blei; *Dch.* Bleij; p.n.

BLAYDON. *See* Bladon

BLAYNEY. From Blaney; a loc. n., Fermanagh

BLAZY. *N.* Blá-siða, cogn.; *Fr.* Blaise; *Dch.* Blaze, Blazer, Bles; *Fl.* Blaes, Blazy; *D.B.* Blize; p.n.

St. Blazey; a loc. n., Cornw. Bleiswijk; a loc. n., Holland.

BLEACKLEY. From Blakeley; a loc. n., Lancs

BLEASBY. A loc. n., Lincs

BLEASDALE. A loc. n., Lancs

BLEASDELL. *See* Bleasdale

BLEBY. *See* Blaby

BLECHYNDEN. A loc. n., Hants

BLENCOE. From Blencow; a loc. n., Cumb.

BLENKARNE. From Blencarn; a loc. n., Cumb.

BLENKINSOPP. A loc. n., Northbd.

BLESSLEY. *See* Blatchley

BLEW, BLOW. *G.* Blüh; a p.n.

BLEWITT. *Fr.* Bluet; *D.B.* Bloiet; p.n.

Bluat in Roll of Battell Abbey. Robert Bloet, Bishop of Lincoln, 1093. Robert Bloet held land in Wilts *temp.* K. John, 1201.

BLEZARD. *See* Blizard

BLICK. *N.* Blígr; *S.* Blix; *D.* Blicker; *Fl.* Blieck; *G.* Blicke; *Dch.* Bleeker; p.n.

BLIGHT. *D.* Blyt; a p.n.

BLISS. *Dch.* Bleijs; a p.n.

BLIZARD. *D.* Blichert; *D.B.* Blize; p.n.

BLOCK. *D.* Blok; *Dch.*, *Fl.* Block; *Fr.* Bloc; p.n.

BLOCKIN. *See* Block

BLOCKLEY. A loc. n., Worcest.

BLOGG. *Dch.* Blog; a p.n. *See* Block

BLOMEFIELD. *G.* Blumenfeld; a p.n.

BLOOM. *S.* Blom; *D.* and *Fl.* Blom, Blum; *Dch.* Bloem, Blom, Blum; *G.* Bluhm, Blum, Blume; p.n.

BLORE. A loc. n., Staffs.

BLOSS. *See* Blowers

BLOSSOM. *See* Bloxham

BLOTT. *S.* Blad; *Dch.* Blöte; p.n.

BLOWERS. *D.* Bloes; a p.n.

BLOWEY. *See* Bloye

BLOXAM. From Bloxham; a loc. n., Lincs

BLOY, BLOYE. From Blois; a loc. n., Normandy

BLUETT. *See* Blewitt

BLUNDELL. *Fr.* Blondel; a p.n.
Robert Blundel in Rot. Obl. et Fin., K. John.

BLUNT. *N.* Blundr; *D.B.* Blund; p.n.

BLY. *G.* Blei, Bloy; *Dch.* Bleij, Bloys; *D.B.* Bleio; p.n.

BLYTH. A loc. n., Northbd., Notts

BOAG, BOAK. *N.* Bogi; *D.B.* Boche; *D.* Boeck, Booek; *Dch.* Bock, Boeg, Bok; *G.* Bock, Böge; p.n.

BOARBANK. *See* Bowerbank

BOARD, BOORD. *Dch.* Bordes; *D.B.* Borda; p.n.

BOAREE. *Dch.* Boeree; *G.* Boerey; p.n.

BOASE, BOAZ. *D.* Boas, Boese, Bohse; *Dch.* Boas; *Fl.* Boes; *Fr.* Bous; *G* Boas, Boos; *D.B.* Boso; p.n.

BOAST. *Fr.* Bost, Boust: p.n.

BOATWRIGHT. *See* Boothroyd

BOBBIT. *Dch.* Bobbert; a p.n.

BOBBY. *N.* Bófi (?); *D.B.* Bubba; *G.* Bube, Bober, Bobisch; *S.* Bobberg; *D.* Bobe; *Dch.* Bobbe; *Fr.* Bobée; p.n.

BOCOCK. *See* Boocock

BODDINGTON. A loc. n., Glos.

BODENHAM. A loc. n., Wilts and Heref.

BODGER. *See* Boger

BODGINER. *Fr.* Bodinier; a p.n.

BODILLY. *See* Baddeley

BODKIN. *D.* Bodecker; *Dch.* Boddeke; p.n.

BODLE. *See* Boodle

BODLEY. *See* Badley

BODY. *N.* Boddi (dimin. of Bödvarr); *D.B.* Boda, Bodin, Boddus, Boding, Boter, Boti, Bot; *Fr.* Bodé; *D.* Bodi, Bodin, Bott; *Fl.* Bodhy, Body; *G.* Bods, Bode, Böde; *S.* Bode, Bodin; *Dch.* Boddé, Bode, Boddaert, Bodt, Botter, Bott; p.n.

BOFFIN. A *Fr.* p.n.

BOGER. *G.* Böger; a p.n.

BOGERT. *Dch.*, *Fl.* Bogaert; *Dch.* Bogaardt; p.n.

BOGGERS, BOGGIS. *Dch.* Bogers; a p.n.

BOLDERS. *See* Balders

BOLITHO. A loc. n., Cornw.

BOLLAND. A loc. n., Yorks

BOLLARD. *Fr.* Boulard; a p.n.

BOLLINGTON. A loc. n., Ess.

BOLSHAW. From Balsham; a loc. n., Camb.

BOLSTER. From Bolsterstone; a loc. n., Yorks; or Boulstone, Heref.

BOLT. *D.*, *Dch.*; p.n.

BOLTON. A freq. loc. n.

BOMPAS. *Dch.* Bombach; a loc. and p. n.

BONALLACK. From Banhaglog; a loc. n., Montgomeryshire

BOND. *N.* Bondi; *D.* Bond; *S.* Bonde; *Fl.* Bondue; *D.B.* Bonde, Bondi, Bundi; p.n.

BONE. From Bohon; a loc. n., Normandy. Or *Fr.* Bouhon; *Dch.* Boon; *G.* Bohn; *D.*, *Fl.* Bon; p.n.

BONEHILL. A loc. n., Staff.; or Bonhill, Dumbarton. Or *Fl.* Boncels; *Fr.* Bonnel; *Dch.* Bonel; p.n.

BONFIELD. *See* Bonville

BONHAM. A loc. n., Somerset

BONIFACE. *Dch.*, *G.* Bonifacius; *Fr.* Boniface; p.n.

BONIWELL. *See* Bonville

BONNER. *Fr.* Bonnard, Bonneau, Bonheur; p.n.

BONNETT. *Fr.* Bonnet; p.n. Bonnat and St. Bonnet; loc. n., France

BONNEY, BONNY. *Fr.* Bonné; a p.n.

BONVILLE. A loc. n., near Rouen, Normandy

BOOBY. *See* Boobyer

BOOBYER. A loc. n. (from *N.* Buíbýr)

BOOCOCK. *Dch.* Boock; *D.*, *S.* Book; p.n. Dimin. of *N.* Búi; p.n. *See* Bugg

BOODLE. From Bootle; a loc. n., Lancs, Cumb.

Bodele in *D.B.*

BOOKER. *See* Boucher

BOOL. *Fr.* Boulle; a p.n. *See* Bull

BOOME. *Dch.* Boom; a p.n.

BOON. *Dch.*; p.n. *See* Bone

BOORMAN. *Dch.*, *Fl.*, *S.* Borman; a p.n.

BOORN. *See* Bourne

BOOSEY. From Bowsey; a loc. n., Staff. Or *D.* Boese, Busse; *Dch.* Bosse; *G.* Böse; *Fr.* Bussy, Buzi; *D.B.* Buci; p.n.

BOOT. *See* Butter

BOOTH. A loc. n., Derbysh. Or *D.*, *Dch.*, *Fl.* Bude, Budde; p.n. *See* Butter

BOOTHBY. A loc. n., Lincs

BOOTHROYD. From Bodewryd; a loc. n., Anglesey

BOOTON. *See* Button

BOOTY. *G.* Buthy; *Fr.* Boutez; p.n.

BOOW. *N.* Búi; *D.* Boye; *F.* Boyo; *Fl.* Boey, Bohy; *G.* Boy; *D.B.* Boui, Boi, Bou, Bu; p.n.

BOOY. *See* Boow

BORHAM. From Boreham; a loc. n., Wilts, Ess., Suss.

BORKING. From Barking; a loc. n., Surr.

BORLAND. From Burland; a loc. n., Yorks

BORN. *D.*, *Dch.*, *G.* Born; a p.n.; or *see* Bourne

BORNER. *Fr.* Borné; a p.n.

BORRET. *N.* Berg-harðr (?); *D.B.* Borgeret, Borgret, Borret, Burghard, Burred, Burret, Borred; *D.* Borregaard; *Fl.* Boret; *G.* Burchardt, Burghardt; *Fr.* Bourret; p.n.

BORRINGTON. *See* Barrington

BORTHWICK. A loc. n., Edinburgh

BORWELL. *See* Barwell

BORWICK. A loc. n., Lancs

BOSCAWEN. A loc. n., Cornw.

BOSS. *Fr.* Bosse; *D.* Boss; *G.*, *Dch.* Bos; p.n.

BOSSEY. *Fr.* Bossis or Bosuet; p.n.

BOSSOM. *Dch.* Bosboom (?); a p.n.

BOSTEN. *See* Boston

BOSTOCK. A loc. n., Ches.

BOSTON. A loc. n., Lincs

BOSWELL. *Fr.* Bosseville; a p.n. Bosville; a loc. n., Normandy

BOSWORTH. A loc. n., Leics.

BOTFIELD. A loc. n., Salop

BOTHAM. From Bodham; a loc. n., Norf.

BOTHAMLEY. From Barthomley; a loc. n., Ches.

BOTHERWAY. *Dch.* Botterweg; a p.n.

BOTHWELL. A loc. n., Lanark; or Botwell, Middlx.

BOTT. *See* Body
Brien Bot in Rot. Obl. et Fin., K. John.

BOTTEN, BOTTING. A loc. n., Lancs

BOTTENHAM. From Bodenham; a loc. n., Wilts

BOTTERIL. *Fr.* Bottrel; a p.n.

BOTWRIGHT. *See* Bootheroyd
Boteric in *D.B.* (?)

BOUCHER. *Fr.;* p.n. *See* Bowker

BOUGEN. *See* Buggins

BOUGHEN. *See* Buggins

BOULT. *D., Dch.* Bolt; a p.n.

BOULTBEE. From Boulby; a loc. n., Yorks

BOULTER. *Fr.* Bolté; a p.n.

BOULTON. From Bolton; a freq. loc. n., Lancs, etc.

BOUND, BOWN. *Fl.* Bawen, Bawin; *D.* Boun; p.n.

BOUNDY. *D.* Bonde; a p.n. *See* Bond

BOURKE, BURKE. *Fr.* de Burgo; a p.n.

BOURNE. A loc. n., Devon, Lincs, Norf., Somers., Suff.

BOUSTEAD. A loc. n., Cumb.

BOUTTELL. *Fr.* Boutel, Bouteille; a p.n.
Boteville in Roll of Battell Abbey.

BOVER. *N.* Bödvarr (?); *Fl.* Bouffard, Bouvier; *Dch.* Bouwer, Boeve; *Fr.* Beaufour; p.n.

BOVILL. *See* Boswell

BOWCH. *Fr.* Bouche; *G.* Bauch; p.n.

BOWCHER. *See* Bowker

BOWDEN. A loc. n., Ches., Leics., Northants, Roxburgh

BOWEN. *Fl.* Boen; *Dch.* Bowen; p.n. *See* Bugg

BOWERBANK. A freq. loc. n.

BOWERS. A loc. n., Staffs.

BOWES. *See* Boase

BOWGEN. *See* Buggins

BOWGIN. *See* Buggins

BOWHILL. *See* Bull

BOWKER. *Fr.* Boucquet, Bouché, Boucher; *G.* Bauke; p.n. *N.* Baugr; n.n. (?)

BOWLER. *Fr.* Boulard; *G.* Buller; p.n. *See* Bull

BOWLES. *F., Dch., Fl.* Boels; a p.n. *See* Bull

BOWLEY. A loc. n., Heref.

BOWMAR. *See* Beaumont

BOWRING. *Fl.* Bauraing; a p.n.

BOWSER. *Fr.* Beaussieu or Boussard; p.n. Or *see* Boucher

BOWSKELL. From Bouskall; a loc. n., Cumb.

BOWSTEAD. *N.* Bú-stað; *S.* Bostad, Bystedt; *G.* Baustatte; loc. and p. n. *See* Boustead

BOWYEAR, BOWYER. *Dch.* Bowier; a p.n.

BOX. A loc. n., Wilts. Or *D., Fl.* Bock; *G.* Bochs; *Dch.* Box; *D.B.* Boche; p.n.

BOXALL. A loc. n., Herts

BOYACK. *F.* Boyke (dimin. of Boy); *D.* Boëck; *Fl.* Boek; *D.B.* Boche (?); p.n. *See* Boy

BOYCE. *D., Fl.* Boyes; a p.n. *See* Boow

BOYCOTT. A loc. n., Salop

BOYD. *Fr.* Boyard; a p.n. Or Gaelic *boidh*, fair-haired

BOYDELL. *G.* Beudel; a p.n.

BOYER. *Fr.;* p.n. *See* Bowyer

BOYLE. From the Irish O'Baoighill; a p.n.

BOYNTON. From Boyton; a loc. n., Lancs

BOYS. *See* Boyce

BRABBS. *Dch.* Braber; *Fl.* Brabandt; *G.* Brab, Brabender; p.n.

BRABY. From Brawby; a loc. n., Yorks

BRACEBRIDGE. A loc. n., Lincs

BRACEY. *See* Breese

BRACHER. *Fl.* Brachert; a p.n.

BRACKENBURY. A loc. n., Lincs

BRACKETT. *Fl.* Brachert; *Fr.* Braquet; p.n.

BRACKLEY. A loc. n., Northants

BRADBROOK. From Bradbridge; a loc. n., Suss.

BRADBURY. From Bradberry; a loc. n., Devon

BRADBY. A loc. n., Derbysh., now Bretby

BRADDOCK, BRADOCK. From Broadoak; a loc. n., Cornw., Ess.

BRADDON. From Bradden; a loc. n., Northants, Somers.

BRADDYLL. From Bradwall; a loc. n., Ches.; or Bradwell; a loc. n., Derbysh. (?)

Radulph de Bradel held land in Lincs *temp.* K. John.

BRADE. *N.* Breidr; *S.* Brate, Bratt; *D.B.* Brodos, Broder, Brode, Brodo, Brodre; *G.* Breit, Breede; *Fl.* Breda, Bret; *Fr.* Brodier; *D.* Breede, Brede, Bret; *Dch.* Brade, Brat, Briedé, Breda, Bredée; p.n.

BRADING. A loc. n., Isle of Wight

BRADLAUGH. From Bradley; a loc. n., Lincs (*D.B.* Bredlow). Also Broadlaw, a mountain in Peebles.

BRADLEY. A loc. n., Yorks, Glost., Lincs, Wilts, Staffs.

BRADNAM. From Braddenham; a loc. n., Norf.

BRADSELL. From Breadsall; a loc. n., Derbysh.

BRADSHAW. A loc. n., Lancs

BRADWELL. A loc. n., Derbysh., Ess., Suff.

BRADY. From the Irish O'Braidaigh; a p.n.

BRAGG. *N.* Bragi; *S.* Brag; *D.* Bracker; *Dch.* Brakke; *Fl.* Brack; *Fr.* Bracq; p.n.

BRAHAM. A loc. n., Camb.

BRAIDLEY. A loc. n., Yorks

BRAIKENRIDGE. From Brackenrigg; a loc. n., Cumb.

BRAILEY. *See* Braidley

BRAILSFORD. A loc. n., Derbysh.

BRAIN. *Fr.*; a p.n.

BRAITHWAITE. A loc. n., Yorks

BRAKE. *Fl.* Braecke; a p.n.

BRAKSPEAR. From Braceby (?); a loc. n., Lincs. *See* Shakespeare and Winspear

BRAMALL. A loc. n., Ches.

BRAMBLE. From Brambeley; a loc. n., Middlx. Or *see* Brimble

BRAME. *D.* Bram; *D.B.* Breme; *S.* Brehm; *Fl.* Brame, Brems; *Dch.* Brehm, Brem; *F.* Bremer; p.n. Or *see* Braham.

BRAMLEY. A loc. n., Yorks

BRAMMER. *G.* Bramer; *Fr.* Brame; *D.* Brammer; p.n.

BRAMWELL. *See* Bramall

BRAN. *G.* Brann; a p.n.

BRANCH. *Dch.* Branse; *Fl.* Brants; p.n.

Braunch in Roll of Battell Abbey. *See* Brand.

BRANCHFLOWER. *Fr.* Blanchfleur; a p.n.

BRAND. *N.* Brandr; *D.* Brandt; *S.* Brander; *Dch.*, *G.* Brand; p.n.

Brand in Roll of Battell Abbey and *D.B.*

BRANDER. *See* Brand

BRANDON. A loc. n., Norf., Suff.

BRANDRAM. From Brandrum; a loc. n., Monaghan

BRANDRETH. A loc. n., Cumb.

BRANDUM. From Brantham; a loc. n., Suff.

BRANFORD. A loc. n., Worcest.

BRANSCOMBE. A loc. n., Devon

BRANSGROVE. From Bransgore; a loc. n., Hants (?)

BRANSTON. A loc. n., Hants, Lincs, Staffs.

BRANWHITE. From Brandthwaite; a loc. n., Cumb.

BRAS. *Dch.* Bras, Brass; *Fr.* Brasse; p.n.

BRASIER, BRAZIER. From Bressuire; a loc. n., France. Or *Fr.* Brasseur; a p.n.

BRASSEY. From Brachy or Brecy; loc. n., Normandy

Bracy in Roll of Battell Abbey. Robert de Brasey in Rot. Obl. et Fin., K. John.

BRATBY. *See* Bradby

BRATTLE. From Braithwell; a loc. n., Yorks. Or *see* Braddyll

BRATTON. A loc. n., Devon, Somers.

BRAUNSTON. A loc. n., Leics.

BRAY. A loc. n., Normandy; also in Berks. Or *Fr.* de Bray; *Dch.*, *G.* Bree; p.n.

Bray in Roll of Battell Abbey. Radulph de Bray in Rot. Obl. et Fin., K. John.

BRAYBROOK. A loc. n., Northants

BRAYSHAW. *See* Brasier

BREACH. *Fr.* Briche; a p.n.

BREAM, BREAME. A loc. n., Glost.

BREARLEY. A loc. n., Yorks

BREDDY. *See* Brady

BREE. *Dch.*; p.n. *See* Bray

BREEDEN. *See* Breedon

BREEDON. A loc. n., Glost., Leics., Worc.

BREEKS. *See* Briggs

BREESE. *N.* Bresi; *S.* Braise; *D.* Bræs; *Fl.* Brees; *Dch.* Bres, Breys; *G.* Briese; p.n.

BRELY. From Brilley; a loc. n., Hunts

BRENCHLEY. A loc. n.. Kent

BRERETON. A loc. n., Ches., Staffs.

BRETHERTON. A loc. n., Lancs

BRETT. *Fr.* Bret; a p.n. *See* Brade

BRETTON. A loc. n., Yorks. Or *see* Britton

BREWER. *Fr.* Bruyère; a p.n.

William Briwere, a favourite of Hen. II., descended from Drogo de Bevreire, a Fleming, who held lands in Northants, Leics., Lincs, Norf., Suff., Yorks, *D.B.* Briwer in Rot. Obl. et Fin., K. John; or *see* Bryer.

BREWSTER. The Scot. and N. Engl. form of Brewer

BRICKDALE. From Birkdale; a loc. n., Yorks

BRICE. *Fl.* Brys; a p.n. (?)

BRICKNELL. *See* Brignall

BRICKSTOCK. *See* Brigstocke

BRIDGES. *D.* Brügge; *Dch.* Brigg; *G.* Brieger; *Fl.* Bruges; a p.n. *See* Briggs

BRIDGEWATER. A loc. n., Somers.

BRIDLE. From Bridell; a loc. n., Pembroke. Or *Fl.* Breydel; a p.n.

BRIERLEY. A loc. n., Glost., Yorks

BRIGGS. From Bruges; a loc. n., Belgium. *N. bryggia*, a pier, gangway; *D.* Bricka, Brix; *S.* Brügge; *Dch.* Breek, Brigg; *Fl.* Bricke, Brixis, Bruges; *G.* Bricke, Brieck; *Fr.* Bricque; *D.B.* Bric, Brixi; p.n.

Brig and de Brug occur in Rot. Obl. et Fin., K. John.

BRIGHT. *D.* Bryti; *Dch.* Breithor; *G.* Breit; p.n.

BRIGHTING. Fam. n.; descendant of Bryti

BRIGNALL. A loc. n., Yorks

BRIGSTOCK. A loc. n., Northants

BRILEY. *See* Brierley

BRILL. A loc. n., Bucks. Or *D.* Brill; *Fl.* Brille; *Dch.* Briel; *G.* Briehl; a p.n.

BRIMBLE. From Bremble; a loc. n., Wilts

BRINE. *Fr.* Breyne; a p.n. *See* Brain

BRINKHURST. From Bringhurst; a loc. n., Leics.

BRINKLEY. From Brinklow; a loc. n., Warw.

BRINSLEY. A loc. n., Notts

BRISCOE. A loc. n., Yorks

BRISCOMBE. From Brinscombe; a loc. n., Somers.

BRISLEY. A loc. n., Norf.

BRISTOW. From Bristow, the ancient name of Bristol

BRITCHER. *Fl.* Brichard, Brichart; *D.B.* Brictuard; *G.* Brichta, Brieger; *Fr.* Briche; p.n.

BRITTON. *Fr.* Breton, Britton, le Breton; *D.* Bretton; *Fl.* Breting; *D.B.* Brito; p.n.

Breton in Roll of Battell Abbey. Brito, Briton, le Briton in Rot. Obl. et Fin., K. John.

BROAD. *See* Brady

BROADHURST. A loc. n., Lincs

BROADWAY. A loc. n., Dorset, Heref., Somers., Worcest.

BROADWOOD. A loc. n., Devon

BROCK. *N.* Broki; *S.* Brock; *D.*, *Dch.* Broch, Brock; *Fl.* Brockx; Bruch; *D.B.* Broc; p.n.

Robert le Broc and Ranulph de Broc in Rot. Obl. et Fin., K. John.

BROCKBANK. *See* Brocklebank

BROCKLEBANK. A loc. n., Cumb.

BROCKLEHURST. From Brockenhurst; a loc. n., Hants

BROCKLESBY. A loc. n., Lincs

BROCKLEY. A loc. n., Suff.

BROCKSOPP. From Brockthrop (?); a loc. n., Glost.

BROCKWELL. *Fl.* Brocolle; *G.* Brockel; p.n.

BRODICK. A loc. n., Bute

BRODIE. A loc. n., Nairn

BROGDEN. A loc. n., Yorks

BROMAGE. *See* Bromwich

BROMEDGE. *See* Bromwich

BROMLEY. A loc. n., Staffs.

BROMMELL. From Broomhill; a loc. n., Norf.

BROMWICH. A loc. n., Staffs.

BROOKE. A loc. n., Norf.

BROOKES, BROOKS. *Fl.* Broeckx; *G.* Brucks, Brucksch, Bruksch; *Dch.* Broeks; p.n.

BROOKHOUSE. A loc. n., Staff., Yorks

BROOM. From Broome; a loc. n., Norf. Or *D.* Brummer; *S.* Broms, Broomé; *Dch.* Brom, Bromet; *G.* Brumme; *D.B.* Brumar; p.n.

BROOMHALL. A loc. n., Worc.

BROOMHEAD. *See* Brummit

BROTHERHOOD. From Boughrood; a loc. n., Radnor (?)

BROTHERIDGE. From Brodrick; a loc. n. (?)

BROTHERS. *N.* Broddr; *Fl.* Broothaers; *Dch.* Broeders; p.n.

BROTHERSTON. *See* Brotherton

BROTHERTON. A loc. n., Yorks

BROUGHAM. A loc. n., Westmd.

BROWN. *N.* Bruni; *D.* Braun, Bruhn, Brun, Bruun; *D.B.* Brun; *F.* Brûno; *Dch.*, *Fl.* Bruin, Brun, Brune, Brown; *G.* Braun, Brun, Bruno; *Fr.* Brune, Bruné, Brunet; p.n.

Brun, Bruni, Brunus in Rot. Obl. et Fin., K. John.

BROWNING. *F.* Brûninga; *D.* Breuning, Bryning; *D.B.* Bruning; *Dch.* Bruining, Bruininga, Bruning; *Fl.* Brunin; *G.* Braunisch, Brünig, Brüning; p.n.

BROWNJOHN. From Brongwyn; a loc. n., Cardigan (?)

BROWNLOW. A loc. n., Ches., Lancs

BROWNRIGG. A loc. n., Cumb.

BROWS. *Fl.* Browaeys; *G.* Brause; *D.B.* de Braiose; *Fr.* Brousse; p.n. *See* Bruce

BROXHOLM. A loc. n., Lincs

BRUCE. *N.* Brúsi; *D.* Bruse, Bruus; *S.* Bruse, Bruze; *Fr.* Brousse, de Brouas; *Fl.* Broos, Brouez; *Dch.* Brus, Brusse; *G.* Brusch, Brysch; p.n.

D.B. Robertus de Bruis, a tenant in chief (Yorks). The founder of the family of Brus of Skelton, from whom the Kings of Scotland and the family of Bruce, Earl of Ailesbury, are descended. His seal is engraved in the *Registrum Honoris de Richmond.* Bruys in Roll of Battell Abbey (from Breux; loc. n., Normandy (?)). Giles de Brewse, Bishop of Hereford, 1200. Adam, Peter and William de Brus in Rot. Obl. et Fin., K. John.

BRUDENELL. *Fr.* De Bretignolles; a p.n.

BRUFF. From Brough; a loc. n., Yorks

BRUMBRIDGE. From Broomridge; a loc. n., Northbd.

BRUMBY. *See* Bromby

BRUMMELL. *See* Brommell

BRUMMIT. *Dch.* Bromet; a p.n. Or Bramwith; a loc. n., Yorks. *See* Broom

BRUNDSDEN. *See* Brunsdon

BRUNDSDON. From Brundon; a loc. n., Ess.

BRUNLEES. From Bronllys; a loc. n., Brecknock

BRUNT. From Brund; a loc. n., Staffs. Or *Dch.* Brunt; *D.* Brund; *Fl.* Brunard; *Fr.* Brunet; p.n.

BRUNTON. A loc. n., Fife

BRUNYEE. *N.* Bruni; *Fr.* Bruné; *D.B.* Brune; p.n. Or Bryn-y; a loc. n., Heref. (?)

BRUSH. *G.* Brusch; a p.n.

BRYANT. *Fr.* Briand, Briant; p.n.

BRYER. *D.* Breyer; *Dch.* Bruijer; *Fl.* Breyer, Briers; *G.* Breier, Breyer; *Fr.* Brière, Bruyère; p.n. *See* Brewer

BUBB. *D.* Bobe; *D.B.* Bubba; p.n.

BUBBINGS. *See* Bubb

Descendants of Bobe. Comp. Bobbinger, a loc. n., Ess.

BUBEAR. *See* Boobyer

BUCHANAN. A loc. n., Fife

BUCK. *S.*, *D.* Buck; a p.n.

Herlewin Buc in Rot. Obl. et Fin., K. John.

BUCKBY. A loc. n., Northants

BUCKENHAM. A loc. n., Norf.

BUCKETT. *Fr.* Bouquet, Buchet; p.n.

Richard Bucket in Rot. Obl. et Fin., K. John.

BUCKHURST. A loc. n., Ess., Lancs

BUCKINGHAM. The county town

BUCKLAND. A loc. n., Berks, Bucks, Devon, Hants, Herts, Kent, Surr., Wilts

Boc-land was copyhold land.

BUCKLE. *G.* Buchal, Buckol; p.n.

BUCKLEY. A loc. n., Bucks

BUCKNELL. A loc. n., Salop, Staffs.

BUCKTON. A loc. n., Yorks

BUCKWELL. *Fr.* Bouquerel; a p.n.

BUCKWORTH. A loc. n., Yorks

BUDD. *D.*, *Dch.* Budde; *G.* Bude; p.n.

Simon Bude in Rot. Obl. et Fin., K. John.

BUDDELL. *See* Buddle

BUDDEN. *Fr.* Boudain, Boudin; *G.* Budan; p.n.

BUDDERY. *Fr.* Butré; a p.n. *See* Butter

BUDDLE. A loc. n., Northbd.

BUDGEN. *Fl.* Bughin; a p.n.

BUDGETT. *Fl.* Bougaert; *Fr.* Bougeard, Bugat; p.n.

BUDICOMB. *See* Puddicombe

BUGG. *N.* Bui (Mod. Icl. Bogi); *S.* Bugge, Boije; *D.* Bugge, Boye; *F.* Boyo, Boye, Boy; *G.* Böger, Böck, Büge, Bugge, Buke, Bühr, Böer, Böhr, Boy; *Fr.* Bougy, Bugué; *Fl.* Boes, Boen, Bour, Bues; *Dch.* Boh, Boggia, Bowen, Boijenk, Boeg, Büger, Bugers, Buggers, Boeje, Buijs, Buys; p.n. Bougy; a loc. n., Normandy

Bushy on Roll of Battell Abbey. *D.B.* De Buci and Bugg, tenants in chief (Notts). Boi, Boia, Bou, Bu, Buge, Bugo, Saxon tenants. W. Bugge in Rot. Obl. et Fin., K. John.

BUGGINS. *Fl.* Buchin, Bughin, Buyghens; p.n. *See* Bugg

BULBECK, BULBICK. From Bolbec; a loc. n., Normandy

D.B. de Bolebec; a tenant in chief. In Rot. Obl. et Fin., K. John.

BULCRAIG. A loc. n., Cumb.

BULFORD. A loc. n., Wilts

BULKLEY. From Bulkeley; a loc. n., Ches.

BULL. *N.* Bolli; *F.* Bóle, Boele, Bólen; *D.B.* Bollo, Bolli, Boln, Bollers, Bole; *G.* Buhl, Bulla, Buller; *S.* Bolle, Bollin, Bolling; *Fl.* Bully, Buls, Bulens, Boel; *Dch.* Boll, Boel, Bull; *D.* Bull, Bollé, Boelle; p.n.

Richard Bole and Radulph Bule in Rot. Obl. et Fin., K. John.

BULLEN. *F.* Bólen; *S.* Bollin; *Fl.* Bulens; *Dch.* Boelen; p.n.

Bolling, the fam. or tribal name of Bolli.

BULLER. *See* Bulwer

Baldwin de Buller in Rot. Obl. et Fin., K. John.

BULLETT. *Fr.* Boullet; a p.n.

BULLIFANT. *See* Bullivant

BULLIMORE. From Bullmore; a loc. n., Wilts

BULLINGBROOK. From Bolingbroke; a loc. n., Lincs

BULLIVANT. *Dch.* Belinfante; a p.n.

BULLOCK. *G.* Bullok; p.n. *See* Bull

BULLWINKLE. *Dch.* Belwinkel; a p.n.

BULPIT. From Bullapit; a loc. n., Devon

BULSTRODE. A loc. n., Bucks

BULTITUDE. *Dch.* Boldoot; *Fr.* Bultot; p.n.

BULWER. From Bouloire; a loc. n., Normandy

D.B. Bulvi (?).

BUMPUS. *See* Bompas

BUNCE. *Dch.* Bunge; a p.n.

BUNGEY. From Bungay; a loc. n., Suff.

BUNKALL. *G.* Bunkale; a p.n.

BUNN. *See* Boon

BUNNETT. *Fr.* p.n.

BUNNEY. *See* Bunnet

BUNTER. *D.* Bunde; *Dch.* Bunte; p.n.

BUNTING. *Fl.* Buntinx; a p.n.

Unfrid Bunting in Rot. Obl. et Fin., K. John.

BUNYAN, BUNYON. *Fr.* Bonjean; or *Fl.* Bonichon, Bonnewyn, Bundgen; p.n.

BURBIDGE. From Burbage; a loc. n., Derbysh., Leics., Wilts

BURBRIDGE. *See* Burbidge

BURCH. *See* BURDGE

BURDEN. From Beaudéan or Beaudoin; loc. n., Normandy (?)

Burdon in Roll of Battell Abbey; *D.B.* Buerd (?); *Fr.* Bourdain, Bourdin, Bourdon; p.n. Bourdon in Rot. Obl. et Fin., K. John. *See* Bird

BURDETT. *Fr.* Bourdet; a p.n.

Burdet in Roll of Battell Abbey and in *D.B.* William Burdet in Rot. Obl. et Fin., K. John.

BURDGE. *D., G., Dch.* Berg; *D.B.* Burg; p.n.

Burc and de Burch, tenants in chief *D.B.*

BURFIELD. From Burghfield; a loc. n., Berks

BURFITT. *See* Barfoot

BURFOOT. *See* Barfoot

BURFORD. A loc. n., Salop, Wilts

BURGE. *See* Burdge

BURGESS. *Dch.* Burges, Burgess; p.n.

Burges is an old way of spelling Bruges.

BURGIS. *See* Burgess

BURGRAVE. A loc. n., Lincs

BURKET, BURKITT. *See* Borret

BURLEY. A loc. n., Hants, Rutl.

BURNABY. *See* Burnby

BURNBY. A loc. n., Yorks

BURNESS. *See* Burns

BURNHAM. A loc. n., Bucks, Ess., Lincs, Norf., Somers.

BURNINGHAM. From Briningham; a loc. n., Norf. or Birmingham

BURNS. *N.* Björn (a bear); *D.* Bjoern, Born; *S.* Björn, Berns; *Fl.* Burny; *D.B.* Barn, Burn, Bern; p.n.

BURNSIDE. A loc. n., Westmd.

BURR. From Burgh; a loc. n., Lincs, Norf.

BURRELL, BURRILL. From Burrell; a loc. n., Yorks. Or *Fr.* Burel; *G., Dch., Fr., D.B.* Borel; p.n.

BURRIDGE. A loc. n., Devon

BURROWS. A freq. loc. n.

BURSTALL. A loc. n., Suff.

BURT. *Fr.* Burette; a p.n.; or *see* Bird

BURTENSHAW. *See* Birkenshaw

BURTON. A freq. loc. n.

BURWASH. A loc. n., Suss.

BUSBY. A loc. n., Yorks

BUSCALL. From Buscel; a loc. n., Normandy; *D.B.* Buissell; a p.n.

BUSH. *S.* Busck; *D.*, *G.* Busch, Busk; p.n.

Bushy in Roll of Battell Abbey. De Bosch, tenant in chief, and Busch (Hertf.) a Saxon tenant in *D.B.* Robert de Buscy in Rot. Obl. et Fin., K. John. Paul Bushe, Bp. of Bristol, 1542.

BUSHBY. From Bushbury; a loc. n., Staffs.

BUSHELL. *See* Buscall

BUSKARD. *Dch.* Bosschaart; *Fr.* Boisard; *D.B.* de Boscroard (?); p.n.

BUSS. *D.*, *Dch.*, *Fl.* Bus; a p.n.

BUSSEY. *See* Boosey

BUSZARD. From Buzet; a loc. n. in Flanders. Or *Dch.* Boshart; *Fl.* Bossaert, Buysschaert; *Fr.* La Bussate; *D.B.* de Boscroard; p.n. *See* Buskard

BUTCHER. *N.* Buðker; *D.* Boedker; *G.* Boettcher; *Dch.* Boddekke; *Fl.* Buker, Buscher; *Fr.* Boucher, Bucher; p.n.

BUTLIN. *Fr.* Boutevillaine (?); a p.n.

BUTTANSHAW. *See* Birkenshaw

BUTTER. *N.* Buttr; *D.* Butho; *Dch.* Boot, Buter, Butti; *Fr.* Buteau; *G.* Buthy, Butte, Butter; *D.B.* Buter, Butor; p.n.

Roger But in Rot. Obl. et Fin., K. John.

BUTTERFIELD. From Butterfell; a loc. n., Cumb.

BUTTERICK. *See* Butterwick

BUTTERWICK. A loc. n., Lincs, Yorks

BUTTERWORTH. A loc. n., Lancs

BUTTEVANT. A loc. n., co. Cork

BUTTIFANT. *See* Buttevant

BUTTLE. *Fr.* Bouteille; a p.n.; or *see* Buddle

BUTTON. *Fr.* Boutin, Bouton, Butant; p.n.

BUTTRUM. *D.B.* de Bertram; a loc. n.

BUTTS. *Fl.* Budts, Buedts; p.n.

BUXTON. A loc. n., Derbysh., Norf.

BUZZARD. *See* Buszard

BYAS. From Biars; a loc. n., Normandy; *Fr.* Bias; a p.n.

BYE. A loc. n., Dorset. Or *D.* Bie, Bye; p.n.

BYERS. *See* Byas

BYFIELD. A loc. n., Northants

BYFORD. A loc. n., Heref.

BYGOTT. *Fr.* Bigot; *Dch.* Biko; p.n.

D.B. Bigot, a tenant in chief. Bigot in Roll of Battell Abbey.

BYGRAVE. A loc. n., Herts

BYLES. *G.* Beil; *Fl.* Byl, Buyl; *Dch.* Buijl; p.n.

BYNOE. *N.* Beinir; *D.* Beine; *F.* Baino; *Dch.* Beenhouwer; p.n. *See* Baines

BYRNE. From the Irish O'Broin; a p.n. *See* Burns

BYROM. From Byram; a loc. n., Yorks

BYRON. From Biron; a loc. n., Guienne, France

D.B. de Burun, tenant in chief. Robert de Burun in Rot. Obl. et Fin., K. John. Biroune in Roll of Battell Abbey.

BYRTH. From Berth; a loc. n., Heref. Or *Fl.* Berth; a p.n. Or *see* Byworth

BYWATER. *See* Byworth

BYWORTH. A loc. n. Suss.

C.

CABLE. *G.* Kabel; a p.n.

CABORN. *See* Cabourne

CABOURNE. A loc. n., Lincs

CACKETT. *Dch.* Cachet; a p.n.

CADBURY. A loc. n., Devon

CADDICK. From Catwick; a loc. n., Yorks

CADDIE. *See* Caddy

CADDY. *G.* Kade, Kathe, Kattey; *Fr.* Chaté; *S.* Kadier; *D.B.* Cadio (?); *D.* Kadow; p.n. Or *Fr.* Cadet; a Huguenot n.

CADE. *See* Caddy

CADEBY. A loc. n., Yorks

CADEY, CADY. *See* Caddy

CADGE. *See* Cage

CADWELL. *See* Caldwell

CAFFIN. *Fr.* Chaufin; a p.n.

CAFFREY. From the Irish O'Craffrey; a p.n.

CAGE. *N.* Kaggi, n.n.; *S.* Karge; *G.* Kage; *Dch.* Kagie, Keg; p.n.

CAIGER. *Dch.* Keja, Kagie; *Fl.*, *G.* Geger, Geiger; p.n.

CAIN. *See* Caine

CAINE. From Cahaignes; a loc. n., Normandy. *D.B.* de Cahainges. Or Irish O'Cathain; a p.n.
W. de Kaynes in Rot. Obl. et Fin., K. John.

CAIRNS. From the Irish O'Cairn; a p.n. (*Carn*, a heap, a little hill.)

CAISEY. *N.* Keis, n.n.; *Fl.* Casy; *G.* Kasig, Käse; p.n.

CAKE. *See* Keck

CAKEBREAD. *Fl.* Kaekelbeck or Cakelberg; p.n. Comp. *Dch.* Kechel; *G.* Kegel; *D.* Keck

CALCOTT. A loc. n., Wilts

CALCUTT. A loc. n., Warw.

CALDECOTE. A loc. n., Lincs, Monmouth, etc.

CALDECOURT. *See* Caldecot

CALDERBANK. A loc. n., Lanark

CALDERWOOD. A loc. n., East Kilbride, Scotl.

CALDWELL. A loc. n., Derbysh., Yorks, etc.

CALEY. *N.* Kali; *S.* Kall; *D.* Kall, Keil; *Fl.* Cail; *Fr.* Caillet; *G.* Calow, Callas, Kalis; *Dch.* Kaales, Kehl; p.n.

CALLIER. *See* Colyer

CALLIFORD. From Callford; a loc. n., Suff.

CALLOW. A loc. n., Worcest.

CALLOWAY. *Fl.* Callewaert; a p.n.; or *see* Galloway

CALSTOCK. A loc. n., Cornw.

CALTHORPE. A loc. n., Derbysh., Lincs, Norf.

CALTHROP. From Colthrop; a loc. n., Glos.

CALVER. *N.* Kálfr; *G.* Kalfar; *D.B.* Calvus; p.n. Or from Calver (*D.B.* Caluore); a loc. n., Derbysh.

CALVERLEY. A loc. n., Yorks

CALVERT. *Fl.* Callewaert; a p.n.

CAMERON. A loc. n., Fife

CAMFIELD. From Canfield; a loc. n., Ess.

CAMIDGE. From Gamaches; a loc. n., Normandy. *See* Gamage

CAMM. From Cam; a loc. n., Glos.

CAMMELL. *See* Gamble

CAMMIDGE. *See* Gammage

CAMP. *N.* Kampi, n.n.; *S.* Camp, Kemp; *D.*, *Dch.* Kemp; *G.* Kampe; *D.B.* Camp, Campa, Campo; p.n.

CAMPAIN. *D.*, *Dch.* Campagne, Campen; p.n.

CAMPBELL. *See* Gamble

CANE. *See* Caine

CANEY. *See* Caine

CANHAM. From Cainham; a loc. n., Salop

CANLER. From Cantley (?); a loc. n., Yorks

CANN. From Caen; a loc. n., Normandy. Or *N.* Kaun; *D* Kann; *Fl.* Cahn; *Fr.* Cahen; *G.* Kann; *Dch.* Canne, Kan; *D.B.* Cana, Cane, Cano, Canus; p.n.
W. de Kanne and Ric. de Can in Rot. Obl. et Fin., K. John.

CANNELL. From Canwell; a loc. n., Staffs. Or Canville; a loc. n., Normandy

CANNER. *Dch.* Canne; *S.* Kander; p.n. *See* Cann

CANNON. *Fr.* Canonne; a p.n.

CANNOT. *Fl.* Canoodt; *Fr.* Carnot; *N.* Knútr; *D.* Knud, Knuth; p.n. *See* Nutt

CANTER. *Fr.* p.n.

CANTERFORD. From Kentford; a loc. n., Suff.

CANTLOW. *Fr.* Cantillon; a p.n.

CANTRELL. *Fr.* Cantrel, Chantrell; p.n.
William Chanterell, *temp.* K. John.

CANTWELL. From Canwell; a loc. n., Staffs. (?)

CAPEL. A loc. n., Suff., N. Wales, S. Wales

CAPON. *Fl.* Capon, Capen; *Dch.* Capoen; p.n. *See* Capp

CAPPER. *See* Capps

CAPPS. *N.* Kappi; *S.* Kapo; *D.* and *Dch.* Kappers; *Fl.* Cap, Cappe; *G.* Kaps; p.n.
Capin, Capra, Capus, Cepe, Chepin, Copsi, under-tenants in *D.B.*

CAPSTICK. From Copestake; a loc. n.

CARD. *See* Cardin

CARDEW. *See* Carthew or Cordeaux

CARDIN. *Dch.* Cardon; *D.B.* Cardun; p.n.

CARDINAL. *Dch.* Cardinaal; *Fl.* Cardinael, Cardinal; p.n.

CARDWELL. *See* Caudwell

CARDY. *See* Cardin

CARELESS. *Fr.* Carliez; *Fl.* Carles; *Span.* Carlos; p.n. From Carolus

CAREW. A loc. n., Pembrokesh.

CARFRAE. A loc. n., Scotl.

CARGILL. A loc. n., Perth

CARLETON. A loc. n., Lancs, Yorks

CARLEY. *N.* Karli; *D.* Carli; *Dch.* Carlee; *D.B.* Carle; p.n.

CARLILL. From Carlisle

CARLINE. *N.* Kerling; *S.* Carling; p.n.

CARLYON. A loc. n., Cornw. Also Carlehon, Bretagne, France

CARMAN. *Fr.* Carmanne; a p.n.

CARMICHAEL. A loc. n., Lanark

CARNABY. A loc. n., Yorks

CARNE. From Carn; a loc. n., Cornw.

CARNEGIE. A loc. n., Forfar

CARNELLEY. From Carnalway; a loc. n., Kildare (?)

CARNSEW. *See* Carnzu

CARNZU. *Fl.* Carnseuw; a p.n.

CARPUE. *Fr.* Carpiaux; a p.n.

CARR. *N.* Kárr; *S.* Karr; *G.* Karo; *Fr.* Karré; *Dch.* Kar; p.n.
Cari, a Saxon tenant in *D.B.*

CARRATT, CARRITT, CAROTTE; *Fr.* Carette; a p.n.

CARRINGTON. A loc. n., Notts

CARROLL. From the Irish O'Cearbhoil; a p.n.

CARRUTHERS. A loc. n., Dumfries

CARRY. *Fr.* Karré; a p.n. *See* Carr

CARSBOULT. *See* Casebow

CARSLAKE. A loc. n., Somers.

CARSLEY. From Kersley or Cursley; a loc. n., Warw.

CARSTON. *F.* Karsten; *D.* Carsten; *G.* Kasten; *Dch.* Karsten; p.n. (from Christian)

CARSWELL. A loc. n., Berks

CARTER. *N.* Köttr (Kahtar), n.n.; *G.* Kathe, Katte, Kartte; *Dch.* Kater; *Fr.* Cartaud, Cartiaux, Cartier, Chartieau, Catoir, Catteau, Cattier; p.n.

CARTERLEY. From Chartley; *D.B.* Certelie; a loc. n., Staffs.

CARTHEW. A loc. n., Cornw. Or Catheux; a loc. n., Normandy

CARTHY. From the Irish Mac Carthaigh; a p.n. (*Carthac*, the founder of a city.)

CARTLEDGE. From Cartlett; a loc. n., Glos. (?)

CARTMELL. From Cartmel; a loc. n., Lancs

CARTWRIGHT. From Cauterêts; a loc. n., Normandy
Cateray in Roll of Battell Abbey. De Ceterith, a tenant in chief in *D.B.*

CARVER. *See* Calver

CARWARDINE. From Shrawardine; a loc. n., Salop

CASBOLT. *See* Casebow

CASBURN. A loc. n. *See* Chase

CASE. *N.* Kaas; *D.* Casse, Kasse; *Dch.* Kas, Käss, Caisse; *Fl.* Cas, Casse, Casy; p.n. *See* Cawse

CASEBOW. *Fr.* Cassabois; a p.n.

CASEMENT. *Fl.* Casman; a p.n.

CASHMORE. From Cashmoor; a loc. n., Dorset

CASSON. *F.* Kassen, from Christian; *i.e.*, Kristjan, Kersten, Karsten, Karsen, Kasjen, Kassen; *D.* Kasten; S. Cassen; *Dch.* Carsten; *Fl.* Kastan, Casen, Cason; *D.B.* Cassa; p.n.

CATCHPOLE. From Cageypole; a loc. n., Dorset. Or Caterpole, Suff.

CATCHPOOL. *See* Catchpole

CATCHSIDE. From Catcherside; a loc. n., Northumbd.

CATER. *N.* Köttr; *Dch.* Kater, Ketter; *G.* Katte; *Fr.* Chaté; p.n. *See* Catt and Carter

Walter Cater occurs in a deed A.D. 1076, Harl. MS. John de Catara, Beswick, Yorks, and Walter Catar his nephew in a deed 1 Steph. Chaitres in Roll of Battell Abbey (?).

CATESBY. A loc. n., Northants

CATFORD. A loc. n., Kent

CATHCART. A loc. n., Lanark

CATHEY. From Cathay; a loc. n., S. Wales; or *see* Caddy

CATLING. *Fl.* Catelin; p.n. *See* Catt

CATMORE. A loc. n., Berks

CATMUR. From Catmer; a loc. n., Ess.; or *see* Catmore

CATT. *N.* Köttr (a cat), n.n.; *D.* Kett; *Dch.* Cate, Kat; *G.* Kathe, Katte; *D.B.* Cedde (?); p.n.

CATTEE. *G.* Kathe, Kattey; *Fr.* Chaté; p.n.

CATTEN. *Dch.* Kattan, Ketting; *S.* Kaeding; p.n.

CATTERMOLE. *Dch.* Cattermolen; a p.n.

CATTLE. From Cattall; a loc. n., Yorks. Or *N.* Kaðall; *Fr.* Catel; p.n. *See* Ketel

CATTLEY. From Chatterley; a loc. n., Staffs.

CATTY. *See* Caddy

CAUDLE. *See* Cawdwell

CAULFIELD. From Chalfield; a loc. n., Wilts (?)

CAUNT. *See* Gaunt

CAUSTON. A loc. n., Warw.

CAUTLEY. From Caughley; a loc. n., Salop

CAUX. From Caux; a loc. n., France

CAVE. A loc. n., Yorks; or *see* Chafy

CAVELL. *See* Cavill

CAVENDISH. A loc. n. (a manor), Suff.

It was assumed by the Norman Knight, Gernon de Montfichet; *D.B.* Gernon.

CAVILL. From Cavill; a loc. n., Yorks

CAWDWELL. *See* Caldwell

CAWKER. *D.* Kalckar; *G.* Kalke; *Fl.* Caukens; *Dch.* Kalker; p.n.

CAWLEY. A contraction of Macaulay

CAWS. *See* Caux

CAWSE. *See* Caux

Robert Cause, Gilbert de Cause, John de Cauz in Rot. Obl. et Fin., K. John.

CAWSTON. A loc. n., Norf., Warw.

CAWTHORNE. A loc. n., Yorks

CAXTON. A loc. n., Camb.

CAYLESS. *See* Careless

CAYLEY. From Cailli; a loc. n., Normandy

Hugh de Cailly was Lord of Orby, Norf., *temp.* Edw. I.

CHACEMOOR. From Chackmore; a loc. n., Bucks

CHADD. From St. Chad; a loc. n., Salop and Staffs. *See* Catt

CHADWICK. A loc. n., Lancs

CHAFFE. *See* Chave

CHAFFER. *Fr.* Chavée. Or *Fl.* Schaffer; p.n.

CHAFFEY. *See* Chafy

CHAFY. From the Norman le Chauve (?)

Lewin Chava, a tenant in chief in *D.B.* *Fr.* Chavée; *Dch.* Keve; *G.* Kayfer (?); p.n. Cava, a Saxon tenant *temp.* K. Edw. Conf.

CHALCRAFT. *See* Calcraft

CHALK. A loc. n., Kent

CHALLACOMBE. A loc. n., Devon

CHALLICE, CHALLIS. *G.* Callas, Kallaus, Kallesse, Kalio, Kalisch; *Dch.* Kalis; *Fl.* Calis; *D.* Callisen; p.n.

CHAM. *See* Camp

CHAMBERLAIN. *Fr.* Chambellan; a p.n.

CHAMLEY. From Chamilly; a loc. n., Normandy

CHAMNEY. From Chamneis or Champneis, the ancient district of Champagne; *D.B.* Chemarnhee

CHAMPION. *Fr.* p.n.

CHANCE. *Dch.* Janse; a p.n. (?)

CHANNON. A loc. n., Devon

CHANTER. *See* Canter

CHARD. A loc. n., Somers.

CHARLEY. From Challey; a loc. n., Ess.

CHARLTON. A loc. n., Berks, Glos., Kent, Oxf., Salop, Somers., Suss.

CHARNLEY. A loc. n.

CHARRINGTON. From Charentonne; a loc. n., Normandy

CHASE. *D.* Jess; *Fl.* Jesse; *Dch.* Jes; *G.* Jesche; p.n.

CHASTEN. *See* below

CHASTENEY. *Fr.* Chesnais, Chesneau; p.n.

CHATBURN. A loc. n., Yorks

CHATFIELD. A loc. n., Suss.

CHATER. *See* Cater

CHATT. From Chatt-moss; a loc. n., Lancs. Or *Fr.* Chaté; a p.n.

CHATTAWAY. From Chitway; a loc. n., Wilts

CHATTERIS. A loc. n., Camb.

CHATTERLEY. A loc. n., Staffs.

CHATTERTON. From Chadderton; a loc. n., Lancs

CHATTIN. *See* Chatwin

CHATTO. *Fr.* Chateau; *Dch.* Katto; *Fl.* Katto; p.n.

CHATWIN. *See* Chetwynd

CHAYTOR. *See* Chater

CHECKLAND. *See* Checkley

CHECKLEY. A loc. n., Staffs.

CHEEK. *See* Chick

CHEESE. *Dch.* Chijs; a p.n.

CHEETHAM. From Chidham; a loc. n., Suss.

CHELL. A loc. n., Staffs.

CHENEY. Chênée, Chiny; loc. n., Flanders; Chaignes, Le Chesne; loc. n., France

Cheyne, Cheines, Cheyni in Roll of Battell Abbey. *D.B.* Chenisis; *Fr.* Chesnais, Chesnée; p.n. Robert de Chesney, Bishop of Lincoln, 1147; Richard Cheyney, Bishop of Lincoln, 1562. William de Chesne in Rot. Obl. et Fin., K. John, 1208. *See* Cheyne

CHERITON. A loc. n., Devon

CHERRY. *Fl.* Cherwy; a p.n.

CHESELDEN. From Chiseldon; a loc. n., Wilts

CHESLYN. From Chisledon; a loc. n., Wilts. *See* Cheselden

CHESSELL. *G.* Jessel; a p.n.

CHESSON. *See* Jesson

CHESTERTON. A loc. n., Camb.

CHESWRIGHT. From Chisworth; a loc. n., Derbysh. (?)

CHETEL. *N.* Ketel; *D.B.* Chetel; p.n.

CHETWYND. A loc. n., Salop

CHEVELEY. A loc. n., Camb.

CHEVERTON. From Chevington; a loc. n., Northbd., Worcest.

CHEW. From Chew; a loc. n., Somers.

CHEYNE. *Fl.* Cheyns, Kenne; *D.* Kinney; a p.n.

Chenna and Chenui, Saxon tenants in *D.B.* *See* Cheney

CHICK. From Chich; a loc. n., Ess.

CHICKALL. From Chicknall; a loc. n., Ess.

CHIDLEY. From Chudleigh; a loc. n., Devon

CHIETHAM. *See* Cheetham

CHILD. *N.* Skjöldr; *D.* Skjold; *D.B.* Cild, Cilt; *Fl.* Child; *G.* Schild; *Dch.* Schilt; p.n.

CHILDERS. *Dch.*, *Fl.* Schilders; a p.n. *See* Child

CHILDS. *See* Childers

CHILLCOTT. A loc. n., Somers.

CHILLEY. *N.* Gils, Gille; *Fr.* Gille, Gillet, Gilliet; a p.n.

Gilo, a tenant in chief, and Ghile, a Saxon tenant in *D.B.*

CHILLINGWORTH. From Chilworth; a loc. n., Hants

CHILLINTON. From Chillington; a loc. n., Somers.

CHILLYSTONE. From Chellaston; a loc. n., Derbysh.

CHILMAID. From Kilmeedy; a loc. n., Limerick (?)

CHILMAN. *G.* Killmann; *D.* Kielman; p.n.

CHILTON. A loc. n., Berks, Suff., Somers.

CHILVERS. A loc. n., Warw.

CHING. From Chinnock; a loc. n., Somers. (?)

CHIPCHACE. A loc. n., Northbd.

CHIPP. *D.* Kib (?); a p.n.

CHIPPENDALE. From Chipnall; a loc. n., Salop (?)

CHIPPERFIELD. A loc. n., Herts

CHISHOLM. A loc. n., Inverness

CHISNALL. *Fr.* Chesnel; a p.n.

CHISWELL. From Chishall; a loc. n., Ess.

CHITTAM. *See* Cheetham

CHITTENDEN. From Chittingstone; a loc. n., Kent

CHITTOCK. From Chideock; a loc. n., Dorset

CHITTY. From Chittoe; a loc. n. near Cheltenham. Comp. *Dch.* Chits; a p.n.

Chit, a Saxon tenant in *D.B.*

CHIVERS. *See* Chilvers

CHOAT. From Chute; a loc. n. in Wilts. Or *Fl.* Jot (?); a p.n.

CHOFFIN. *Fr.* Chauvin; a p.n.

CHOPE. *See* Jope

CHOULES. *Dch.* Jaulus; a p.n.

CHREES. From Chris, a dimin. of Christopher (?)

CHRISTIAN. *Fl.* Christaen; *Dch.* Christan; *S.* Christen; *G.* Christian; p.n.

CHRISTOPHERSON. *S.* Kristofferson; a p.n.

CHUBB. *Fr.* Chupé (?); p.n. *See* Jubb

CHUBBOCK. Dimin. of Chubb. Or *Dch.* Kubbe, Kuhbauch; *G.* Kubick; p.n.

CHUCK. *G.* Schuch; a p.n.

CHUDLEIGH. A loc. n., Devon

CHUGG. *G.* Schüge; a p.n.

CHURCHILL. *Fr.* de Curcelle; a p.n. From Courcelles; a loc. n., France. Or Churchill; a loc. n., Somers.

CHURTON. A loc. n., Ches.

CHUTTER. *G.* Chudy; a p.n.

CIVILL. *Fr.* Civiel; a p.n.

CLABOD. *Fl.* Clabots; a p.n. (?)

CLABON. *Fr.* Cléban; a p.n.

CLACK. *N.* Klöku; *Dch.* Kloek; p.n.

Clac, a Saxon tenant in *D.B.*

CLAMP. *D.* Klamer, Klamke; *G.* Klamm, Klammt; p.n.

Claman, a Saxon tenant in *D.B.*

CLAMPETT. From Clampitt; a loc. n., Cornw.

CLAPCOTT. A loc. n., Berks

CLAPP. *N.* Klápr; *D.* Klepsch; *S.* Klop; *Dch.* Klapp; p.n.

CLARABUT. *Fl.* Clairbaut, Clerebaut; p.n.

CLARE. A loc. n., Cornw., Suff.

CLARICOAT. From Clerewoodcott; a loc. n., Hants

CLARIDGE. From Clarach; a loc. n., Cardigan

CLARK. *D.* p.n.

CLATWORTHY. A loc. n., Somers.

CLAUGHTON. A loc. n., Lancs

CLAXTON. A loc. n., Leics., Norf.

CLAYDON. A loc. n., Suff.

CLAYE, CLAY. A loc. n., Normandy. Or *D.* Klee; a p.n.

CLAYPOLE. A loc. n., Lincs

CLAYTON. A loc. n., Lancs., Yorks

CLEAK. *Fr.* Cliquet; a p.n.

CLEARE. *See* Clare

CLEASBY. A loc. n., Yorks

CLEATHER. From Clitheroe; a loc. n., Lancs

CLEAVER. *G.* Kliewer; a p.n.

CLEEVE. A loc. n., Glos.

CLEGHORN. A loc. n. near Carstairs, Scotl.

CLEMENTS. *Fl.* Clement; *G.* Clemens; p.n.

Clement, a Prot. refugee n.

CLEMO. *Fr.* Clement; a p.n.

CLEMOW. *See* Clemo

CLENDINNING. *See* Glendinning

CLENT. A loc. n., Worcest.

CLERK. *Dch.* Clerk, Clercq; p.n.

CLEVELAND. A loc. n., Yorks

CLEVELEY. A loc. n., Lancs

CLEVERDON. From Clevedon; a loc. n., Somers. Or Cleverton, Wilts

CLEVERLEY. *See* Cleveley

CLEWER. A loc. n., Berks

CLEWORTH. From Clayworth; a loc. n., Notts, Somers.

CLIBRAN. *See* below

CLIBURN. A loc. n., Westmd.

CLIFF. A loc. n., Yorks

CLIFFORD. A loc. n., Glos., Heref., Yorks

CLIFT. *D.* Klifoth; a p.n.

CLIFTON. A loc. n., Beds, Derbysh., Lancs, Notts, Somers., Staffs., Warw., Yorks

CLINCKETT. *Dch.* Klinkert; a p.n.

CLINGO. *G.* Klinger; *S.* Klinga; p.n.

CLIPSTON. A loc. n., Northants, Notts

CLISBY. *See* Cleasby

CLIXBY. A loc. n., Lincs

CLOAKE. *See* Cloakie

CLOAKIE. *Fr.* Cloquet; a Huguenot p.n.

CLOD, CLODD. *D.* Kloth; *Dch.* Kloot; *G.* Clott; p.n.

CLOSE. From *Fl.* Claus, contraction of Niklaus, Prot. refugee n.; *Dch.* Kloos; *Fl.* Close; p.n. *See* Clowes

CLOSSON. *S.* Klason; *G.*, *Dch.* Clauson; p.n., from Nikolaus

CLOUDESLEY. A loc. n., Warw.

CLOUDSDALE. From Clydesdale; a loc. n., Lanark

CLOUT. *D.* Kloth; *Dch.* Kloot, Kluit; p.n.

CLOUTING. *D.* Kloth; *G.* Klatting; *Dch.* Cloetingh; *Fl.* Cloeten; p.n.

CLOVER. *N.* Klaufi; *Dch.* Kloover; *D.* Klüver; p.n.

CLOW. *See* Cluff

CLOWES. Dimin. of Niklaus; *Fr.* Klás; *D.* Kloos, Klose; *Fl.* Cloes, Close; *Dch.* Klous; *G.* Klaus, Klaas, Klaws, Klos, Klose; p.n.

CLUBB and CLUBBE. *N.* Klyppr (?), n.n.; *G.* Kloebb, Klobe, Klober, Klupsch; *Dch.* Clob, Klop; *Fl.* Clop; p.n.

CLUER. *See* Clewer

CLUES. *Dch.* Clüjs; a p.n.; or *see* Clowes

CLUFF. From Clough; a loc. n., Yorks

CLUNE. From Clun; a loc. n., Salop

CLUSE. *See* Clowes

CLUTTEN. *See* Clutton

CLUTTERBUCK. A Flemish refugee n.

Cloerterbooke was Sheriff of Glos. in 1586.

CLUTTON. A loc. n., Ches., Somers.

CLYNE. *D.*, *G.*, *Dch.* Klein; a p.n.

CLYST. A loc. n., Devon

COACHAFER. *Fl.* Cauchefer; a p.n.

COATES. A loc. n., Edinbgh., Yorks

COBB. *N.* Kobbi, dimin. of Jakob; *S.* Kobbs, Cobel; *Dch.* Kop; *G.* Kobe, Kober, Kobitz, Kopp, Kopper; p.n. *D.B.* Copsi

COBBETT, COBETT. Dimin. of Kobbi (Jakob); *Dch.* Cobet; *Fl.* Cobbaert; p.n. *See* Cobb

COBBLE, COBLE. *S.* Cobel; *Fl.* Copal; *G.* Kopple; p.n. *See* Cobb

COBBLEDICK. From Coppledyke or Coupledyke; a loc. n., Lincs. Or Koppeldijk; a *Dch.* loc. n.

COBBOLD. *S.* Cobel; *D.B.* Cubold; p.n.

COBLEY. A loc. n., Worcest.

COBON. From Coburn, a contraction of Cockburn

COCHRANE. A loc. n., Renfrew

COCK. *D.* Cock; *Fr.* Cocq; *Dch.* Kok; *G.* Koch; *S.* Kock; *D.B.* Coc; p.n.

COCKAYNE. From Cocking; a loc. n., Suss. Or *Fr.* Cocagne; a p.n.

COCKBURN. A loc. n., Scotl.

COCKER. *Fr.* Cocard, Coqueau; p.n.

COCKERELL. *Fr.* Cocquerel; a p.n. From Cocherel; a loc. n., Normandy, or Cockerhill, Ches.
Richard Cokerell in Rot. Obl. et Fin., K. John.

COCKERHAM. A loc. n., Lancs

COCKERTON. A loc. n., Dur.

COCKIE. *Fr.* Coché; a p.n.

COCKING. A loc. n., Suss.

COCKLE. From Cockhill; a loc. n., Somers.

COCKRAM. *See* Cockerham

COCKRILL. *See* Cockerell

COCKSEDGE. From Cockhedge; a loc. n., Lancs

COCKSHAW. *See* Cockshott

COCKSHOTT. A loc. n., Salop

CODD. *Dch.* Kode; a p.n.

CODE. *See* Codd.

CODEY, CODY. From Codhay; a loc. n., Devon; or *see* Codd

CODLING. A loc. n., Dur.

CODNER. From Codnor; a loc. n., Derbysh.

CODRINGTON. A loc. n., Glos.

COE. *Dch.* Coe, Koe; p.n.

COFIELD. *See* Coffield

COFFEE. *Fr.* Coffé; a p.n.

COFFEY. *See* Coffee

COFFIELD. From Cockfield; a loc. n., Dur., Suff.

COFFIN. *Fr.* Coffin; a p.n.

COGGAN. *Fl.* Coghen; a p.n.

COGGER. *N.* Kuggi; *Fl.* Cogen; *G.* Cogho; *Dch.* Kogghee; p.n.

COGGING. *See* Coggan

COGHILL. *See* Cargill

COGHLAN. From the Irish O'Cochlain; a p.n.

COGMAN. *N.* Kaggi; n.n. *G.* Coghs; *Dch.* Koghee; *Fl.* Coghen; p.n.

COGSWELL. From Coggeshall; a loc. n., Ess.

COKER. A loc. n., Somers.

COLBECK. A loc. n., Lincs. Or Coalbatch, Salop

COLBORNE. *N.* Kolbjörn; a p.n.
Colebern, a tenant in chief in *D.B.*

COLBRANT. *N.* Kolbrún; a p.n. *See* Colls

COLBY. From Coleby; a loc. n., Norf.

COLCLOUGH. A loc. n., Staffs.

COLCOMBE. From Challacombe; a loc. n., Devon. Or Chalcombe Northants

COLDHAM. A loc. n., Camb.

COLDWELL. A loc. n., Northbd.

COLE. *See* Colls
Richard Cole in Rot. Obl. et Fin., K. John.

COLEMORE. A loc. n., Hants

COLERIDGE. A loc. n., Devon

COLES. *Fl.* Cools; a p.n. *See* Colls

COLGATE. A loc. n., Suss.

COLGROVE. A loc. n., Herts

COLK. *N.* Kolka; n.n. *D.* Kalkar; *Dch.* Kolk, Kalker; *G.* Kalk; p.n.

COLLACOTT. A loc. n., Devon

COLLAMBELL. From Colomby; a loc. n., Normandy. *D.B.* de Columbels; *Fr.* Colombel; p.n.

COLLEGE. From Colwich; a loc. n., Staffs. Or *Fr.* Collige; a p.n.

COLLETT. *Fr.* Collette; a p.n.

COLLIE. *Fr.* Colleye; a p.n.

COLLIER. *See* Cullyer

COLLING. A loc. n., Yorks

COLLINGBOURNE. A loc. n., Wilts

COLLINGTON. A loc. n., Heref.

COLLINGWOOD. From Callingwood; a loc. n., Staffs.

COLLINS. *See* Colls

COLLISHAW. *See* Cowlishaw

COLLS. *N.* Kollr and Kolr; *S.* Kull; *D.* Koelle; *G.* Kolla, Koller, Kolley, Kohl, Kohler; *Dch.* Koll; *D.B.* Col, Cola, Colo, Cols; *Fl.* Colas, Colle, Colles, Culus; p.n.

COLLYNS. *See* Colling

COLMAN. *Dch.* Koelman; *G.* Kohlmann; p.n. *See* Colls

John Coleman in Rot. Obl. et Fin., K. John.

COLMER. *See* Colemore

COLOMB. From St. Colomb; a loc. n., Cornw.

COLPUS. *N.* Kálfr; *Fl.* Calphas; *G.* Kalbas; *D.B.* Calpus and Calvus; p.n.

Saxon Tenants *temp.* Edw. Conf., and under-tenants at Survey.

COLQUHOUN. A loc. n., Dumbarton

COLSON. *Fl.* p.n.

COLTON. A loc. n., Lancs, Staffs., Yorks

COLWELL. A loc. n., Northumbd.

COLYER. *See* Cullyer

COMAN. *Fl.* Coeman; a p.n.

COMBE. A loc. n., Glos.

COMERFORD. *See* Comfort

COMFORT. From Comberford; a loc. n., Staffs.

COMLEY. A loc. n., Salop

COMMERELL. From Comberwell; a loc. n., Wilts (?)

COMPTON. A loc. n., Dorset, Hants, Somers., Staffs., Wilts

CONDER. Norm. *Fr.* Condé; a loc. n. in Normandy; *D.B.* Conded

CONDY. From Condé; a loc. n., Normandy

CONE. *N.* Konr; *Dch.* Con; *Fl.* Coen; p.n.

CONGDON. A loc. n., Cornw.

CONGRAVE. *See* Congreve

CONGREVE. A loc. n., Staffs.

CONINGHAM. *See* Cunningham

CONINGSBY. A loc. n., Lincs

CONISBEE. *See* Coningsby

CONLEY. From Cononley; a loc. n., Yorks

CONNOR. From the Irish O'Conchobhair; a p.n. *N.* Konr (noble); a p.n., derived from the Celtic

CONNORTON. From Conderton; a loc. n., Glos. (?)

CONOLLY. From the Irish O'Conghaile; a p.n.

CONQUEST. From Conques or Conquet; loc. n., Normandy

CONWAY. A loc. n., N. Wales

COOCH. *N.* Kúgi; n.n. *G.* Kütsch; *Fl.* Couche, Gouche; p.n.

COOKSEY. A loc. n., Worcest.

COOMBE. A loc. n., Cornw., Devon, Hants, etc.

COOPER. From Cupar; a loc. n., Fife. Or *Fl.* Kupper; *Dch.* Cuyper; p.n.

COOPMAN. *Fl.* Coopman; a p.n.

COOTE. *Fl.* Coet; *Dch.* Koot; *G.* Kutt; p.n.

COPE. *See* Coppon

COPLAND, COPELAND. *See* Coupland

COPEMAN. *See* Coopman

COPESTICK. From Copestake; a loc. n.

COPLESTONE. A loc. n., Devon

COPPING. *See* Cobb

COPPINGER. *N.* Kaupungr; n.n. *D.* Koeppen; *S.* Koppang; *Dch.* Koppen; p.n. *See* Coppon

COPPON. *N.* Kaupungr, n.n. *D.* Kopp, Koeppen; *S.* Kopp, Koppang; *Dch.* Koppe, Koppen; a p.n.

COPSEY. *See* Cobb

CORAH. From Corrar; a loc. n., Salop

CORBYN.
Corbine in Roll of Battell Abbey, and Corbin among the under-tenants in *D.B.*

CORBY. A loc. n., Cumb., Lincs. Or Corbie, France

CORDINGLEY. From Cottingley; a loc. n., Yorks

CORDREY. *See* Cowderoy

CORDY. *Fr.* Cordeau; *Dch.* Cordes, Cordia; *G.* Korte; p.n.

CORFIELD *See* Cornfield

CORKE. *D.* Kork; *Dch.* Korck; p.n.

CORNELL. *Fl.* Cornehl; *G.* Cornely; from Cornelius; p.n.

CORNFIELD. *G.* Kornfeld; a p.n.

CORNFOOT. *See* Cornforth

CORNFORD. *See* Cornforth

CORNFORTH. A loc. n., Dur.

CORNWALL. The county

CORPE. *S.* Korp; *D.* Korrup; a loc. and p.n. (Korrthorp); *Dch.* Corper; p.n.

CORSBY. *See* Cosbey

CORSER. *G.* Korsawe; p.n.

CORY. *See* Currie, or *N.* Kári or Kori; *S.* Carré; *Dch.* Koring; p.n.
Cari, a Saxon tenant in *D.B.* *See* Carr.

COSBEY. From Cosby; a loc. n., Liecs.

COSGRAVE. A loc. n., Northants

COSGROVE. *See* Cosgrave

COSHAM. A loc. n., Hants

COSSEY. From Cossy; a loc. n., Norf.; or *N.* Kausi, n.n.; *D.* Koese; *G.* Kose, Kosig; *Dch.* Cossa; *Fl.* Cossé; p.n.

COSSHAM. A loc. n., Hants

COSSINGTON. A loc. n., Somers.

COSSINS. *See* Cozens

COSSTICK. *See* Copestick

COSTELLO. From Mac Ostello, descendants of Hostilio de Angulo, settled in Ireland *temp.* Hen. II. Or *G.* Gostelle; a p.n.

COSTERTON. A loc. n., Scotl.

COTES. A freq. loc. n.

COTESWORTH. From Cottesford; a loc. n., Oxf.

COTHAM. A loc. n., Glos., Yorks

COTHER. *See* Cotham

COTON. A loc. n., Staffs.

COTTAM. A loc. n., Lancs, Notts

COTTERELL, COTTERILL. From Cottlehill; a loc. n., Fife.

COTTEW. *Fr.* Cotteau; a p.n.

COTTINGHAM. A loc. n., Yorks

COTTLE. *Fr.* Coutelle; a p.n.

COTTON. A loc. n., Suff.

COTTY. *G.*, *Dch.* Kothe; a p.n.

COUCH. *See* Cooch

COULLING. *See* Cowling

COULSTON. A loc. n., Wilts

COULTHART. *D.* Coulthardt; *Fl.* Colleart; *Dch.* Collard; *D.B.* Couta; p.n.
Probably from the *N.* Kollottahart, a hart without horns.

COULTON. From Colton; a loc. n., Lancs

COUNSEL. *Fr.* Conseil; a p.n.

COUPLAND. A loc. n., Northumbd.

COURAGE. From Curridge; a loc. n., Berks

COURTEEN. *See* Curtain

COURTNAY. From Courtenay; a loc. n., France
William de Curtenay, *temp.* K. John. Rot. Obl. et Fin.

COUSENS. *See* Cozens

COVENTRY. A loc. n., Warw.

COVERDALE. From Cuerdale; a loc. n., Lancs (?)

COVERLEY. *Fr.* Coveliers; a p.n.

COVINGTON. A loc. n., Hunts.

COW. *Fr.* Cahu (?); a p.n.

COWARD. *Fl.* Couard; *Fr.* Chouard; a Huguenot n.

COWDEROY. From Cowdray; a loc. n., Suss. Or *Fr.* Coudeyre; a p.n.

COWDRY. *See* Cowderoy

COWELL. From the Irish Mac Cathmhoil; a p.n.

COWES. *D.* Koese; *Dch.* Koes, Coes; *Fl.* Couez; *Fr.* Caux (?); p.n.

Cowie. *Fr.* Couez (?); a p.n.

Cowland. A loc. n., Edinbgh.

Cowley. A loc. n., Bucks, Derbys., Middlsx., Oxf., Staffs.

Cowling. A loc. n., Suff., Yorks

Cowlishaw. From Cowlishall; a loc. n., Lancs

Cowls. *See* Colls

Cowperthwaite. A loc. n., Westmd.

Cox. *Fl.* Kockx; *Dch.* Koks, Kokx; p.n.

Cozens. From Couzon; a loc. n., France; or *Fr.* Cousin; *Dch.* Couzijn; a p.n.

Crab. *G.* Krappe; *Dch.* Krabb; *Fl.* Crab, Crabbe; p.n.

Crabtree. A loc. n., Devon

Crack. *D.* Krag; *Fl.* Crach; *Dch.* Kraak; p.n.

Crac, a Saxon tenant in *D.B.*

Crackenthorpe. A loc. n., Westmd.

Cracknall, Cracknell. From Craigneill; a loc. n., Edinbgh.

Craddock. A loc. n., Devon. Or Cradoc, S. Wales

Crafer. *G.* Kreifer; *Fl.* Creve, Creyf; p.n.

Craft. *D.* Kraft; *Dch.*, *G.* Kraft, Kroft; p.n.

Cragg. A loc. n., Yorks. Or *D.* Krag; a p.n.

Craig. A loc. n., Forfar.

Craigie. A loc. n., Ayrshire

Craik. A loc. n., Sutherland

Craike. A loc. n., Dur., Yorks

Crake. A loc. n., Norf., Yorks

Crampton. From Crompton; a loc. n., Lancs

Cranage. A loc. n., Ches.; or from Cranwich; a loc. n., Norf.

Cranbrook. A loc. n., Kent

Crane. *D.* Krener; *G.* Kren; *Fl.* Craen; p.n.

Crang. *See* Cranke

Crank. A loc. n., Lancs; or *D.* Kranker, Crenker; *Fl.* Craninck; *G.* Krancke; p.n.

Crankshaw. *See* Cronshaw

Cranmer. A loc. n., Devon. Comp. Cranmore, Camb.

Crannis. *G.* Krannisch, Krentsch; a p.n. *See* Crane

Cranston. A loc. n., Edinbgh.

Cranwell. A loc. n., Lincs

Crapp. *Fl.* Crabbe, Craps; p.n.

Craske. *G.* Kraske; p.n. Dimin. of *D.*, *Fl.*, and *Dch.* Crass

Craven. A loc. n., Yorks

Crawford. A loc. n., Dorset, Lanark, Lancs

Crawhall. From Crakehall (*D.B.* Cracele); a loc. n., Yorks. Or Croxall, Derbysh. and Staffs.

Crawley. A loc. n., Bucks, Hants, Suss.

Crawshaw. A loc. n., Lancs

Craze. *Fr.* Crez; *Dch.* Kress; a p.n.

Creagh. *See* Creak

Creak. From Creake; a loc. n., Norf. Or *N.* Kráka; n.n. (a crow). Comp. Corn-crake; *G.* Kreks; *S.* Kraak, Krok; *D.* Krack, Krok; *Fl.* Crack; *Dch.* Kriek, Crick; *D.B.* Crac, Croc; p.n.

Saxon tenants, or the Celtic Crug (Creege), Scotl., Craig.

Cream. *See* Gream

Creamer. *Fl.* Cremer, Crimmers; *G.* Kremer; *Dch.* Cramer, Cremer; p.n.

Crease. *N.* Gris; *Fr.* Criez; p.n.

Creasey. *See* Cresey

Creed. A loc. n., Cornw.

Creedy. A loc. n., Devon

Creeke. *See* Creak

Creighton. A loc. n., Staffs.

Cresey. From Crécy; a loc. n. in Normandy. Or Cressing; a loc. n., Essex

Cressy is on the Roll of Battell Abbey, and Norman Crasus is a tenant in chief in *D.B.*

Cresswell. A loc. n., Northbd., Staffs.

Crewdson. *Fl.* Crusen, Crutzen; *D.* Kruse; *S.* Creutz; *Dch.* Crouse; *G.* Krutsch; p.n.

CREW. *Fr.* Croux; a p.n.; or *see* Crewe

CREWE. A loc. n., Ches.

CREYKE. From Crayke; a loc. n., Yorks

CRICHTON. A loc. n., Edinbgh.

CRICK. A loc. n., Northants; or *see* Creak

CRIPPS. *G.* Krips; a p.n.

CRISELL. *Dch.* Kressel or Kristel; a p.n.

CRISP. *See* Crispin

CRISPIN. From St. Crispin; a Norman-French loc. n.

Milo Crispin, a tenant in chief in *D.B.*

CRITCHLEY. From Crickley; a loc. n., Glos.

CRITTENDEN. *See* Cruttenden

CROAGER. *See* Crocker

CROAKER. *See* Crocker

CROASDALE. From Croixdal; a loc. n., Normandy

CROCKER. *N.* Kráka, n.n.; *S.* Krok; *D.* Krogh; *G.* Kroker; *Dch.* Krook; *Fl.* Crockaert; p.n.

Croc, a tenant in chief, and Crac and Croc, Saxon tenants in *D.B.*

CROCKETT. *Fl.* Crockaert; *Fr.* Croquet; p.n.

CROCKFORD. A loc. n., Kircudbright

CROCKITT. *See* Crockett

CROCOMBE. From Crowcombe; a loc. n., Somers.

CROFT. A loc. n., Glos., Heref., Yorks; or *Dch.* Kroft; a p.n. *See* Craft

CROMIE. *Fr.* Crombez; a p.n.

CROMWELL. A loc. n., Notts

CRONK. *G.* Krancke; p.n. *See* Cranke

CRONSHAW. From Cranshaws; a loc. n., Berwick

CROOK. A loc. n., Westmd.

CROOKENDEN. From Crookdean; a loc. n., Northbd.

CROOKES. A loc. n., Yorks

CROOMBE. From Croome; a loc. n., Worcest., York

CROOTE. *N.* Krydd; *A.S.* Krud; *G.* Krutsch, Krutge; *Dch.* Kroode; p.n.

Grud, Grut, Grutt, Saxon tenants in *D.B.*

CROPPER. *N.* Kroppr; n.n. *S.* Cropps; *Dch.* Krop; *G.* Kropp, Kroppe; p.n.

CROSBY. A loc. n., Cumb., Lancs, Lincs, Westmd.

CROSHER. *See* Crawshaw

CROSLAND. A loc. n., Yorks

CROSSINGHAM. From Cressingham; a loc. n., Norf.

CROSSLEY. From Crosslee; Renfrew

CROSSTHWAITE. A loc. n., Cumb.

CROSTON. A loc. n., Lancs

CROUCH. *Fr.* Croux; *G.* Krüsch; p.n.

CROUDACE. *See* Carruthers

CROUGHTON. A loc. n., Northants

CROWDER. *Dch.* Kroode; a p.n.

CROWDSON. *See* Crewdson

CROWDY. *See* Crowder

CROWHURST. A loc. n., Surr.

CROWLEY. *See* Crawley

CROWSHAW. *See* Crawshaw

CROWSHAY. *See* Crawshaw

CROWSON. *S.* Kruhs; *D.* Kruse; *Dch.* Kroese, Kruijs; *G.* Krause, Krusche; *Fl.* Crousse, Croze, Crusens, Crutzen; p.n.

CROWTHER. *See* Crowder

CROYDEN. *See* Croydon

CROYDON. A loc. n., Surr.

CROYSDALE. *See* Croasdale

CRUDGE. *G.*, *Dch.* Kruge; a p.n.

CRUDGINTON. A loc. n., Salop

CRUMMEY. *Fr.* Crombez; a p.n. (?)

CRUMPTON. *See* Crompton

CRUNDALL. From Crundale; a loc. n., Kent

CRUSE. *S.*, *D.* Kruse; *G.* Krusch; *Dch.* Kruse; *Fl.* Cruys; p.n. Or from Cruwys Morchard; a loc. n., Devon

CRUSO. *Fr.* Creuseau (Huguenot n.)

CRUTCHER. *G.* Krutsche; a p.n.

CRUTHE. *See* Croote

CRUTTENDEN. A loc. n., Kent

CRUTWELL. From Crudwell; a loc. n., Wilts

CRYER. *G.* Kreyher; *Dch.* Kreije; p.n.

CUDBAR. *See* Cutts

CUDBY. *See* Cutts

CUDDEFORD. From Cuttiford; a loc. n., Cornw.

CUDDEN. *D.* Gude; *N.* Gude, Gudde; a p.n. Gudden, a fam. n.

Cudhen and Gudhen, under-tenants in *D.B.*; *Fl.* Guttin; a p.n.

CUDDING. *See* Cudden

CUDDON. *See* Cudden

CUFFE. *See* Coffee

CUISHEN. *See* Cozens

CULHAM. A loc. n., Berks

CULL. *G.* Kulla; a p.n.

CULLEN. A loc. n., Banffs.; or from the Irish O'Coilean; a p.n. (*coilean*, a young warrior).

CULLEY. From Couillet; a loc. n., Flanders

Cuilly in Roll of Battell Abbey. Hugo de Cuilly in Rot. Obl. et Fin., K. John.

CULLINGFORD. *See* Cullingworth

CULLINGWORTH. A loc. n., Yorks

CULLY. *See* Culley

CULLYER. *Fr.* Coulier; a p.n. *See* Culley

CULMER. *See* Culmore

CULMORE. From Cullamore; a loc. n., Staffs.

CULPECK, CULPICK. From Kilpeck; a loc. n., Heref. Or *Fl.* Callepeck; a p.n.

CULPIN. From *N.* Kolbeinn; *D.B.* Colben; p.n.

CULPIT. *Fl.* Calepet; a p.n.

CULY. *See* Culley

CUMBERBATCH. From Comberbach; a loc. n., Ches.

CUMBERLEGE. From Cumberlow; a loc. n., Herts

CUMBERPATCH. *See* Cumberbatch

CUMBY. *N.* Kumbi; n.n.; *Fl.* Combe; *Fr.* Combet; *G.* Kumberg (?); p.n.

CUNDY. *G.* Kunde; a p.n.

CUNLIFFE. From Concliffe or Cunliff; a loc. n., Lancs

CUNNINGHAM. A loc. n., Ayrshire

CUPISS. *Dch.* Cuipers; a p.n. (?)

CUPPAGE. From Kippax; a loc. n., Yorks

CUPPER. *See* Cooper

CURD. *G.* Kurde; a p.n.

CURE. *G.* Kuhr; *D.* Kure; p.n.

CURL. *D.* Curjel; *S.* Correll; *Dch.* Kurrell; p.n.

CURLING. *N.* Karl, Kerling; *G.* Kerling; p.n. *See* Curl

CURLY. A loc. n., Normandy (?). *See* Curling

John de Curly in Warwickshire. Rot. Obl. et Fin., K. John.

CURNOCK. From Carnock; a loc. n., Fife

CURNOW. *Fr.* du Cournau; or *G.* Kuhnow; p.n.

CURREY. *See* Currie

CURRIE. A loc. n., Edinbgh.

CURSHAM. From Corsham; a loc. n., Wilts

CURSON, CURZON.

Curson in Roll of Battell Abbey. De Curcan in *D.B.*

CURTIS. *D.* Curdts; *Dch.* Koerdes; *Fr.* Courtois; p.n.

CURTLER. From Curtley; a loc. n., Northants. Or *G.* Gertler; a p.n.

CUSHING. *See* Cozens

CUSHION, CUSHON. *See* Cozens

CUSS. *G.* Kuss; a p.n.

CUSTANCE. From Coutance; a loc. n., Normandy

CUTBARTH. *See* Cuthbert

CUTCHER. *G.* Kutscher; *Fl.* Cutsaert; p.n.; or *see* Gudger, Goodyear

CUTHBERT. A loc. n., Beds; *D.B.* Cutbert; p.n. *See* Gotobed

CUTLER. *Fl.* Cotteleer; a p.n.
Gaufrid de Cuteler in Rot. Obl. et Fin., K. John.

CUTMORE. *See* Catmur

CUTTER. *Fr.* Couteaux, Cuttier; p.n.

CUTTING. Fam. n. *See* Cutts

CUTTLE or CUTHILL. A loc. n., Haddington

CUTTS. *G.* Kutt, Kutter, Kuttig; *Fl.* Couthy, Coutier; p.n. Or dimin. of Cuthbert

CYPHER. *See* Sypher

D.

DABBS. *G.* Dabisch; a p.n.

DACK. *G.* Dach; *Fl.* Dache; *Dch.* Dake; p.n.

DADE. *N.* Dadi or Dodi; *F.* Datter, Dede, Dodo; *G.* Duda, Dudy; *Fl.* Dodd, Dudart, Duthoit; *D.* Dodt; *Dch.* Dood; p.n.
Dode, Dodin, Dodesone, Dodo, Dodeman, Dott, Duttel, in *D.B.*

DADY. *See* Dade

DAGG. *G.* Dach; *Dch.* Dake; p.n.

DAGGET. *D.B.* Dagobert (?); or *D.* Daugaard, Doggert; *Fl.* Degard, De Geyt; p.n.

DAGLEY. *Fr.* Dachelet; a p.n. (?)

DAGNALL. From Dagnell; a loc. n., Worcest.

DAGWORTHY. From Dagworth; a loc. n., Norf.

DAINES. *See* Dane

DAINTREE. From Daventry; a loc. n., Northants

DAINTY. *S.* Dente; *Fr.* Dantée; p.n.

DAISLEY. From Disley; a loc. n., Ches.

DAKING. *Dch.* Dekking; p.n. *See* Dack and Deck

DALBY. A loc. n., Lincs, Yorks

DALE. *S.* Dahl; *D.* Dall; *Fr.* Dailly, Daly; p.n.

DALLAS. A loc. n., Moray

DALLEY. *See* Dale

DALLINGER. *N.* Dellingr; *G.* Döllinger; *Dch.* Dallings, Dallinghaus; p.n.

DALRYMPLE. A loc. n., Ayrshire

DALTON. A loc. n., Dumfries, Devon, Dur., Lancs, Yorks

DALZELL. *See* Dalziel

DALZIEL. A loc. n., Lanark.

DAMANT. *Dch.* and *G.* Diamant; p.n.

DAMS. *D.* and *S.* Damm; *G.* Dammas, Dammer, Damis, Dams; *Dch.* Dam, Dammers; *Fl.* Dams; p.n.

DANBROOK. From Danbury; a loc. n., Ess. (?)

DANBY. A loc. n., Yorks

DANCE. *G.* Dance; *S.* Dann; *D.* Dan; *Fl.* Danse; *D.B.* Dain, Dainz; p.n.

DANCER. *Fl.* Dansaert; a p.n.

DANDRIDGE. From Danebridge; a loc. n., Ches.

DANDY. *Fr.* Dandoy; a p.n.

DANE. *N.* Danir; *S.* Dann; *D.* Dehn, Dein; *G.* Denia, Deny; *D.B.* Dane, Dinni, Dene, Dena; p.n.

DANGAR. *D.* Dankert; *G.* Danger; a p.n.

DANGERFIELD. *Fr.* Dandville; a p.n. (?)

DANIEL. *Fr.*; p.n. A Huguenot n.

DANSIE. *See* Dance

DANSON. *D.* Dan; *S.* Dann; *Fl.* Danne; *G.* Dann; p.n. *See* Dean

DAPLIN. *S.* Döbelin (Dahbelin); a p.n.

DARBEY. From Derby; a loc. n.

DARBY. From Derby; loc. n.
Dyrbye is a loc. and p. n. in Denmark.

DARCY. From de Ardreci, D'Arcie.
A tenant in chief, *D.B.* (Lincs).

DARKIN. *See* Dorking

DARLOW. From Darly; a loc. n., Derbysh.

DARNTON. *See* Darrington

DARRINGTON. A loc. n., Yorks

DARROCH. From Darragh; a loc. n., Isle of Man

DARTNALL. From Darnhall; a loc. n., Ches.

DARYALL, DARWALL. *See* Darvell

DARVELL. A loc. n., Ayrshire. Or *Fr.* Darteville; a p.n.

DARWEN. A loc. n., Lancs. From the British Darwenydd, Derguint (Derwent)

DASENT. *Fr.* Dessaint; a p.n.

DASH. *Fr.* D'Assche; a p.n.
Roger De Asc in Rot. Obl. et Fin., K. John.

DATE. *Fr.* Dethy; a p.n.

DAUBENY. *N.-Fr.* D'Albini; a p.n. D'Albini in *D.B.*

DAUNTON. *See* Darnton

DAVAGE. *Fr.* Duverger; a p.n.

DAVID. *Fr.*, *D.*, *Dch.*, *G.*; p.n.

DAVIE. *See* Davy

DAVIS. *Fr.* Devis; a p.n.

DAVITT. *Dch.* Dawit, Davijt; p.n.

DAVY. *Fr.* Dévé; a p.n.

DAW. *D.* Daue; *F.* Dauewes, Douwes; *G.* Thou, Dohse; p.n.
Dore, a Saxon tenant in *D.B.*

DAWBARN. *See* Dawbin

DAWBIN. *Fr.* Daubin; a p.n.

DAWBORN. *See* Dawbin

DAWBRY. A loc. n., Derbysh.

DAWDY. *See* Dade

DAWDRY. *See* Dordry

DAWES. *See* Daw

DAY. *N.* Dagr; *S.* Daug; *G.* Dege; *Fl.* Day, Daye; p.n.

DAYNES. *See* Dane

DEACLE. From Diggle; a loc. n., Yorks

DEACON. *See* Dicks

DEADMAN. *N.* Þjoðmar; *D.* Dettmer; *Dch.* Dettman; *G.* Dittmann, Dittmer, Tiedemann; *D.B.* Dodeman, Dudeman

DEAN. A loc. n., Hants, Yorks

DEANE, DENE. *See* Dean

DEARDEN. A loc. n., Lancs

DEARING. *Dch.* Dieren; *S.* Dyring; *D.B.* Dering; p.n. *See* Deary

DEARSLEY. From Dursley; a loc. n., Glost. (?)

DEARTON. From Dearden; a loc. n., Lancs

DEASON. *D.* Dyresen; *S.* Dyrssen; *Dch.* Diesen; p.n.

DEATH. *Fr.* D'Aeth; a p.n. Aeth; a loc. n., Flanders

DEAVES. *Fr.* Devis; a p.n.
Dives, a loc. n. in Normandy. Devise in Roll of Battell Abey. *D.B.* de Dive.

DEAVIN. *Fr.* Devins; a Huguenot n.

DEBENHAM. A loc. n., Suff.

DECENT. *See* Dasent

DECK. *G.* Deck, Decke, Decker; *Dch.* Dekker; p.n.

DEDMAN. *See* Deadman

DEEDES. *Fl.*, *G.* Dietz; p.n.

DEEKER. *Dch.* Dieker; p.n. *See* Dicks

DEEKES. *See* Dicks

DEEVES. *See* Deaves

DEIGHTON. A loc. n., Yorks

DELLAR. *G.* Della; *Fr.* Delot; p.n.

DELVE. *Fr.* Delvaux; a p.n.

DEMER. *Fr.* De Meur; a p.n.

DENCH. *Fl.* Dengis; a p.n. *See* Ding

DENHAM. A loc. n., Beds, Suff.

DENNENT. *Fr.* Denin; p.n.

DENNETT. *Fr.* Denet; a p.n.

DENNEY. A loc. n., Stirling. Or *N.* Daini; n.n. Or *Fl.* Denis, Denie, Deny; *G.* Dann, Deny; *D.B.* Dena, Dene, Dane, Dinni, Dennis; p.n.

DENNINGTON. A loc. n., Norf., Suff., Yorks

DENNIS. *Fr.* Denis; p.n.

DENNISON. *See* Dennis

DENNISTON. From Denerdiston; a loc. n., Suff.; or Denston, Staffs.

DENNY. *See* Denney

DENT. A loc. n., Yorks

DENTON. A loc. n., Lincs, Norf., Lancs, Northants, Northbd., etc. (16 places)

DERHAM. *See* Deerham or Durham

DERLYN. *Fr.* Deliens; a p.n.

DERRICK. *Fr.* Deryck, D'Eryc or D'Heriche; p.n.

D.B. Derch (?).

DESBOROUGH. A loc. n., Northants

DEVERELL. From Deverill; a loc. n., Wilts

DEVILLE. *Fr.* D'Eville; a p.n.

Devile and Doiville are on the Roll of Battell Abbey. Devle is in *D.B.*

DEWDNEY. *See* Dudeney

DEWESBURY. From Dewsbury; a loc. n., Yorks

DEWFALL. *Fr.* Duval; a p.n.

DEYNE. *D.* Dehn, Dein; *S.* Dann; *Dch.* Deen, Deene; *G.* Dane, Diehne; *Fl.* Daens; p.n.

Dana, Dena, Dene, Saxon tenants in *D.B.*

DEYNES. *See* above

DIAPER. *Dch.* Diepe; *Fr.* D'Eppe; p.n.

DIBALL. *See* Double

DIBBEN. *D.* Dibbern; a p.n.

DIBBLE. *See* Dipple

DIBBS. *G.* Dibus; a p.n.

DIBDIN. From Dibden; a loc. n., Hants

DIBOLL. *See* Double

DICKENS. *See* Dix

DICKMAN. *See* Dix

DICKS. *F.* Dîko, Dyko, fam. n., Dîken, Dyken, Dikena; *G.* Dix, Dieck, Dicke; *Dch.* Diek, Dieker, Dikkers, Dikken; p.n.

DIDSBURY. A loc. n., Lancs

DIDWELL. A loc. n. Or *G.* Dittel, Dittfeld; p.n.

Tedwald in *D.B.* (?).

DIFFEY. *Fr.* Divé; a p.n.

DIGBY. A loc. n., Lincs

DIGGENS. *D.* Dige; *Dch.* Dikken; p.n. *See* Dicks

DIGGES. *See* Diggins

DIGGON. *See* Deeks

DILLON. From the Irish O'Dilmhain; a p.n.

DILWORTH. A loc. n., Lancs. *Fl.* Dielwart; a p.n.

DIMBLEBY. From Thimbleby; a loc. n., Lincs

DIMMER. *See* Dimon

DIMMOCK. From Dymock; a loc. n., Glost.

DIMON. *Fr.* Diman; a p.n. Or *see* Dimond

DIMOND. *D.* Demandt; *Dch.* Dieman, Diamant; *G.* Demand, Demant, Diamant; *Fl.* Deman; p.n.

DIMPLE. A loc. n., Derbysh., Lancs

DIMSDALE. From Dinsdale; a loc. n., Dur.

DING. *N.* Dengir; cogn. *G.* Dinger; *Dch.* Denike, Dinger; *Fl.* Dengis; p.n.

DINGLEY. A loc. n., Northants

DINGWALL. A loc. n., Scotl.

DINHAM. A loc. n., Monmth.

DINNER. *Fr.* Diner, Dineur; *Fl.* Dinear; p.n.

DINSDALE. A loc. n., Dur.

DINSMORE. From Dinmore; a loc. n., Heref.

DINWOODIE, DUNWOODIE. A loc. n., Dnmfries

DIPPLE. A loc. n., Devon

DISBROWE. From Desborough; a loc. n., Northants

DITCHFIELD. *G.* Dickfeld; a p.n.

DITCHLEY. A loc. n., Oxf.

DIVE. *Fr.* Dive, Divé; a p.n.

DIVER. *Fr.* Divoire; a p.n. (?)

DIX. *See* Dicks

DIXIE. *D.* Dich; *F.* Diko or Dyko (fam. n., Diken), dimin. Dikje; *Dch.* Dieke; *G.* Dicke, Dix; p.n.

DOBBIE. *N.* Dapi; *G.* Daber, Dabin, Dabisch, Dober, Dobers; *Dch.* Dobben; p.n.

DOBBIN. *Dch.* Dobben; *G.* Dobin; p.n.

Hugo Dobin in Rot. Obl. et Fin., K. John.

DOBBS. *See* Dobbie

DOBELL. *D.* Dobel; a p.n.

DOCKER. *Fr.* Docquet; a p.n. Or *see* Dockwra

DOCKRAY. From Dockwray; a loc. n., Cumb.

DOCKWRA. *See* Dockray

DOD, DODD. *N.* Dadi; *D.* Dodt; *F.* Dodde; *D.B.* Dode; *Fl.* Dod, Dodd; p.n.

DODDERIDGE. A loc. n., Devon

DODDING. *D.B.* Dodin; a p.n. *See* Dodd

William Dodin (Worc.) *temp.* K. John.

DODINGTON. A loc. n., Kent, Lincs, Northants, Northbd.

DODSON. *D.B.* Dodesune; a p.n. *See* Dodd

DODSWORTH. *See* Dodworth

DODWELL. A loc. n., Hants, Warw.

DODWORTH. A loc. n., Yorks

DOE. *D.* Dau, Dawe; *Dch.* Douw; p.n. *See* Daw

DOGGETT. *See* Dagget

Or from Dowgate, one of the ancient gateways of London (?).

DOGOOD. *See* Toogood

DOLAMORE. *See* Dolleymore

DOLEMAN. *D.* Dohlmann; a p.n.

DOLL. *Dch.*, *G.* Doll; a p.n.

DOLLAR. A loc. n., Clackmannan

DOLLEYMORE. From Delamere; a loc. n., Derbysh.

DOLLING. *G.* Dollen; a p.n.

DOLPHIN. *Fl.* Dolphin; *Dch.* Dolhein; p.n.

Dolfin, a tenant in chief in *D.B.*

DOMINY. *G.* Domina; a p.n.

DOMONEY. *See* Dominy

DONISTHORPE. A loc. n., Derbysh.

DONITHORNE. From Dinnethorn; a loc. n., Devon

DONKIN. *See* Dunkin

DONNE. A loc. n., Perth

DONNITHORNE. *See* Donithorne

DORDERY. *See* Dordry

DORDRY. From St. Audrey (?); or *Dch.* Dordregter, Dordrecht (?)

DORE. *Fr.* Doré; *Dch.* Dórr, Dorre; *D.B.* Dore. Or Dore, a loc. n., Derbysh.

DORKING. A loc. n., Surr.

DORMAN. *Dch.* Doorman; a p.n.

DORR. *See* Dore

DORRELL. *Fr.* Durell; a Huguenot n.

DORRINGTON. A loc. n., Lincs

DOTTRIDGE. *See* Dodderidge

DOUBLE. *N.* Djúp-ðalr; *D.* Dybdal, Diebel, Dibel, Dybbel; *Dch.* Dubbel, Dubbeld; *Fl.* Duballe; *G.* Dubiel; *Fl.* Debil, Debolle, Dubal; p.n. Debdale, a loc. n., Notts

DOUBLEDAY. *Fr.* Doublet; a p.n. (?)

DOUGHTY. *G.* Daute; *Dch.* Dothée, Daudeij; *Fr.* Daudé; *Fl.* Dotheij; *D.B.* Dodid, Doth, Dot; p.n.

DOUGLAS. A loc. n., Lanark

DOULTON. From Dolton; a loc. n., Devon

DOUSE. *D.* Dous, Duus, Duusen; p.n.

DOUTHWAITE. A loc. n., Cumb., Yorks

DOVE. *N.* Dufan; *S.* Dufva; *D.* Duvier; *Fl.* Dufey; *Dch.* Douwe; *G.* Dove; p.n.

DOW. *See* Doe

DOWDNEY. *See* Dudeney

DOWE. *See* Doe

DOWLEY. From Dowlais; a loc. n., S. Wales

DOWNING. A loc. n., Worc.

DOWNTON. A loc. n., Hants, Wilts

DOWNWARD. From Downhead; a loc. n. in Somerset

DOWSING. *See* Douse

DOWTELL. *Fl.* Dautel; a p.n.

DOY. *Fl.*, *Fr.* Doy, from Douy and Douai; loc. n.

DRAKE. *D.* Dræger, Dracke; *S.* Draghi, Drake; *Dch.* Drager; *Fl.* Draecke; p.n.

DRANE. *N.* Þráin; *D.* Trane; *S.* Trana; *G.* Trenner; p.n.

DRAPER. *Fr.* Drapier; *Dch.* Draper; p.n.

DRAYTON. A loc. n., Heref.

DREDGE. *Dch.* Dröge; a p.n. (?)

DREW. From Dreux; a loc. n., Normandy. *See* Druse

DRIFFIELD. A loc. n., Yorks

DRING. From Tring; a loc. n., Herts

DRINKALL. From Trinkeld; a loc. n., Lancs. Or Dringhow, Yorks

DRIVER. *Dch.* Druyve, Drijver; a p.n.

DROUGHT. *G.* Drath; a p.n.

DROZIER. *Fr.* Deruisser; a p.n.

DRUCE. *See* Druse

DRUMMOND. A loc. n., Ross, Scotl.

DRUSE. *D.* Drews; *G.* Drusche; *Dch.* Dros; *D.B.* De Dreuues; p.n.

DRY. *Fr.* Draye; a p.n.

DRYDEN. A loc. n., Lasswade

DRYSDALE. A loc. n., Dumfries

DUBBLE. *See* Double

DUBBLEDICK. From Doubledykes, Stonehouse, Lanark

DUCE. *See* Douse

DUCK. *Dch.*, *Fl.* Duc; *G.* Duch; *S.* Ducke; p.n.

DUCKER. *N.* Doka (?); *S.* Ducke, Dücker; *Dch.* Duker; *Fl.* Duck; *G.* Duch; *D.B.* Tochi, Toco; p.n.

DUCKHAM. A loc. n., Devon

DUCKWORTH. From Dikewid; a loc. n., Cardigan. Or *D.* Duchwärder; a p.n.

The name was anciently written Dykewarde.

DUDDERIDGE. *See* Dodderidge

DUDDING. From Dudden; a loc. n., Ches.

DUDENEY. *Fr.* Dieudonné; a p.n.

DUDGEON. *See* Dodgson

In the north of England Dodgson is frequently so pronounced.

DUERDON. *Fr.* Dourdoigne; a p.n.

DUFF. *N.* Dufan; a p.n. adapted from the Gaelic in the tenth century. *See* Dove

DUFFETT. *Fr.* Duffaut; a p.n.

DUFFIELD. A loc. n., Derbysh.

DUFFILL. *See* Duffield

DUGDALE. A loc. n., Staffs.

DUKINFIELD. From Dunkinfield; a loc. n., Ches.

DULLEY. From the *Fr.* D'Ully; a Huguenot n.

DUMBLETON. A loc. n., Glost.

DUNBAR. A loc. n., Haddingtonshire

DUNCE. From Dunse; a loc. n., Berwick

DUNCOMBE. From Duncomb; a loc. n., Dur.

DUNCUM. *See* Duncombe

DUNDAS. A loc. n., Dalmeny, Scotl.

DUNDONALD. A loc. n., Ayr

DUNFORD. A loc. n., Yorks

DUNGER. *Dch.* Duncker; a p.n. From Dunckhart

DUNGEY. From Dengie; a loc. n. in Essex; or Dangu, a loc. n. in Normandy

DUNHAM. A loc. n., Norf., Notts

DUNHILL. A loc. n., Waterford

DUNKIN. From Dunnichen; a loc. n., Forfar (?)

DUNKLEY. From Dinkley; a loc. n., Lancs

DUNLOP. A loc. n., Ayr

DUNN. From Dun; a loc. n., Forfar. Or *N.* Tunni (?); *S.* Duner; *Dch.* Dun; *G.* Donner; *D.B.* Dun, Dune; p.n.

DUNNETT. *Fr.* Donnet. *See* Dunn

DUNNICLIFF. *See* Tunnicliffe

DUNNING. A loc. n., Perth

DUNSTALL. A loc. n., Staffs.

DUNSTAN. A loc. n., Northbd.

DUNTHORN. From Dunterton; a loc. n., Devon

DUNTHORPE. A loc. n., Oxf.

DURBRIDGE. From Dwrbach; a loc. n., Pembroke

DURDEN, DURDON. From Dourdan; a loc. n., France

DURNFORD. A loc. n., Wilts

DURRANT. *D.* Durandin; *Fr.* Durand, Durant; p.n.
Durand in Roll of Battell Abbey. *D.B.* Durand.

DURRELL. *Fr.* Duril; a p.n.
Darell in Roll of Battell Abbey.

DURST. *See* Durston

DURSTON. A loc. n., Somers.

DURY. From Durie; a loc. n., Fife. Or *Fr.* Duray, Duré; p.n.

DUTHY. *Fr.* Du Thais; p.n. Or *see* Doughty

DUTT. *See* Dade

DUTTON. A loc. n., Ches., Lancs

DWIGHT. *See* Thwaite

DYAS. *See* Dyce

DYBALL. *See* Double

DYBBELL. *See* Double

DYCE. A loc. n., Aberdeen. Or *Dch.* Deis, Duijs; *Fl.* Duys; p.n.

DYE. *G.* Thei; p.n. *See* Tye

DYER. *N.* Dyri; *D.* Dyhr; *S.* Dyr; *G.* Dier; *D.B.* Dering; p.n.

DYKES. *See* Dix

DYMOCK. A loc. n., Glost.

DYMOKE. *See* Dymock

DYMOTT. *Fr.* Demotte; a p.n.

DYOTT. *Fl.* Deyaert; a p.n.

E.

EACHER. *D.* Egger; *Dch.* Eger; p.n.

EACOTT. *D.* Eckert, Eigaard; *G.* Eckardt; *Fl.* Eekhout; p.n.

EADE. *N.* Eiðr; *F.* Edde; *S.* Ed; *G.* Eder; *Dch.* Ede, Edie, Ide; *Fl.* Ide; *Fr.* Ede; *D.B.* Eddid, Edret; p.n.

EAGLE. A loc. n., Lincs; *D.B.* Aycle

EAGLETON. A loc. n., Rutland

EAGLING. *N.* Egill; *S.* Egelin; *Dch.* Eggeling; p.n.

EALY. From Ely; a loc. n., Camb. Or *D.* Ihle; *Dch.* Elie; p.n.

EARDLEY. From Eardisley; a loc. n., Heref. Or Eardlew, Staffs.

EARL. *N.* Erli, dimin. of Erlingr; *S.* Erling; *G.* Erle, Erler; *D.B.* Erleching, Erluin, Erlenc; p.n.

EARNSHAW. A loc. n., Lancs. Or Ernsheugh, Berwick

EARP. From Erpe; a loc. n., Belgium. Or *N.* Erpr; *Dch.* Erp, Herpe; *G.* Erpff; *Fr.* Herpin; p.n.

EARWAKER. *N.* Eireker; *D.B.* Eureuuacre, Euroac, Euuacre; *G.* Ehrich; *D.* Eyrich; p.n.

EARWICKER. *See* Earwaker

EASLEE. From Eastling; a loc. n., Kent. Or Eastlee, Hants

EASTALL. From Eastwell; a loc. n., Kent

EASTER. A loc. n., Ess.

EASTERBROOK. A loc. n., Devon

EASTHAUGH. *See* Easter

EASTO, EASTOE. *See* Easter

EASTON. A loc. n., Ess., Herts, Northants, Yorks

EASTWOOD. A loc. n., Ess., Notts, Renfrew, Yorks

EASTY. *See* Easter

EASY, EASEY. From Easby (?); a loc. n. Yorks

EATWELL. From Etwall; a loc. n., Derbysh.

EAVES. A loc. n., Lancs, Staffs., and other counties. Or *F.* Eve; *D.* Ivers; *Dch.*, *Fl.* Evers, Ivers

EAVIS. *See* Eaves

EBBAGE. From Abridge; a loc. n., Ess.

EBBLETHWAITE. *See* Ablewhite

EBBS. *F.* Ebbe; *D.* Eber; *Dch.* Ebers; *S.* Ebbes; p.n.

EBBUTT. *See* Hebbert

EBDEN. From Hebden; a loc. n., Yorks

EBRIDGE. From Abridge; a loc. n., Ess.

EBSWORTH. From Ibsworth; a loc. n., Hants

ECCLES. A loc. n., Lancs

ECKERSLEY. *See* Exley

EDDINGTON. A loc. n., Berks, Somers.

EDDLESTON. A loc. n., Peebles

EDDY. From Aidie; a loc. n., Normandy. Or *see* Eade

EDEN. *See* Eade

EDEY. *See* Eade

EDGAR. *S.* Edgard; *D.B.* Edgar; a p.n.

EDGCUMBE. A loc. n., Devon

EDGE. A loc. n., Yorks

EDGELL. From Edgehill; a loc. n., Somers. Or *N.* Egil; a p.n.

EDGELOW. A loc. n. *See* Edgerley

EDGERLEY. A loc. n., Ches., Salop

EDGINTON. *See* Egginton

EDGLEY. A loc. n., Salop

EDGWORTH. A loc. n., Glost., Lancs

EDINTON. A loc. n., Somers., Wilts

EDLESTON. From Egliston; a loc. n., Dorset

EDMASTON. From Edmonstone; a loc. n., Edinbgh.

EDMUNDS. *N.* Játmundr; *S.* Edman; *D.B.* Ædmund, Edmund; *Fr.* Edmond; p.n.

EDRIDGE. *See* Etridge

EDWARDS. *N.* Játvarðr; *D.* Edvard, Edwards; *Fr.* Edouard; *D.B.* Eduard, Eduuard; p.n.

EELS. *G.* Ilse; a p.n.

EGARR. *N.* Heggr; *F.* Egge, Eggen; *S.* Eger, Eggers; *Dch.* Eggers; *G.* Eger, Eggert, Eggart; *D.B.* Egbert, Eghebrand; p.n.

EGERTON. A loc. n., Kent, Lancs

EGGETT. *G.* Eggert; a p.n. *See* Egarr

EGGINTON. A loc. n., Derbysh.

EGGLETON. A loc. n., Heref.

EGGS. *Dch.* Eggers; a p.n. *See* Egarr

EGLETON. A loc. n., Rutland

EGLINGTON. From Eggleton (?); a loc. n., Heref.

EGREMONT. A loc. n., Cumb.

EKE. *D.* Ek; *N.* Eik; *Dch.* Eik; p.n.

EKINS. *See* Eykins

ELAND. A loc. n., Northbd. Or *Dch.* Elandt; a p.n.

ELBOROUGH. A loc. n., Somers.

ELBROW. *See* Elborough

ELBURY. *See* Elborough

ELCOAT. From Elcot; a loc. n., Berks, Wilts

ELDERSHAW. *See* Oldershaw

ELDERTON. A loc. n., Ross. Or Alderton, Northants

ELDRID. *See* Aldred

ELDRIDGE. From Eldrig; a loc. n., Wigton. Or *see* Aldridge

ELENGER. *N.* Erlinger; a p.n. *See* Earl

ELGAR. *S.* Elg; *D.* Helge; *G.* Elga, Elger; *Dch.* Elgers; p.n.; *D.B.* Elgar, Elfgar, Elget, Algar. *See* Algar

ELGOOD. *D.* Ellegaard; *D.B.* Elgert; p.n.

ELKINGTON. A loc. n., Lincs

ELLABY. From Ellerby; a loc. n., Yorks. Or *D.* Elleby; a loc. and p.n.

ELLACOMBE. A loc. n., Devon

ELLAM. From Elham; a loc. n., Kent

ELLAND. A loc. n., Yorks

ELLER. *D.* Eller; a p.n. *See* Aylward and Elliot

ELLERAY. A loc. n., Westmd.

ELLERBECK. A loc. n., Yorks

ELLERD. *See* Aylward

ELLERSHAW. From Elishaw; a loc. n., Northbd.

ELLERTON. A loc. n., Salop, Yorks

ELLICOMBE. *See* Ellacombe

ELLICOT. From the Irish Mac Elligott; a p.n.; *Scot.* Mac Leod; or *see* Elcoat

ELLINGHAM. A loc. n., Norf.

ELLINGTON. A loc. n., Hunts

ELLINGWORTH. *See* Illingworth

ELLIOT. *F.* Elle, Eilert; *D.B.* Ailward, Ailuert, Ailiet, Eli, Eliard, Eliert, Eliet; *Fr.* Eliot; p.n. *See* Aylward

ELLWICK. From Eldwick; a loc. n., Yorks

ELLWOOD. *Dch.* Elewoud; *Fl.* Elewaut; p.n. *See* Aylward

ELLYARD. *D.B.* Elward, Ailward. *See* Aylward

ELMAR. *N.* Hjálmr; *F.* Helmer; *S.* Hjelm; *Dch.* Helmer; *G.* Elmers

D.B. Elmar, as tenant in chief and under-tenants.

ELMHIRST. A loc. n., Staffs.

ELMY. From Elmley; a loc. n., Kent. *See* Elmer

ELNAUGH. From Ellenhall; a loc. n., Staffs.

ELNEY. *See* Elnaugh

ELPHIC. *N.* Álfsrekkr; *D.B.* Ælfric, Ælfec, Alfeg; p.n.

ELPHINSTONE. A loc. n., Haddington

ELSLEY. From Allesley; a loc. n., Warw.

ELSMERE. From Ellesmere; a loc. n., Salop

ELSTON. A loc. n., Devon, Yorks

ELSWORTH. A loc. n., Camb.

ELTON. A loc. n., Lancs

ELVEY. From Elveden; a loc. n., Suff.

ELVIN. *N.* Álfarin; *S.* Elfwin; *A.S.* Ælfing; *Dch.* Elven; *D.B.* Elving, Elwi, Eluenc, Alfwin, Elfin; p.n.

ELVIS. *S.* Elvers; *D.* Elvius; p.n.

ELWELL. A loc. n., Dorset

ELWES. *See* Elvis

ELWYN. *Dch.* Elven; a p.n. *See* Elvin

ELY. A loc. n., Camb.

EMBLETON. A loc. n., Northbd.

EMBURY. From Emborough; a loc. n., Somers.

EMERIDGE. A loc. n., Devon

EMERSON. *See* Emms

EMERTON. A loc. n., Devon

EMERY. *Dch.* Emmerie; *Fl.* Emery. From Emmerich; a loc. n.

EMES. *See* Emms

EMLY. From Elmley; a loc. n., Kent. Or *G.* Emler; *Dch.* Emelar, Emigli; p.n.

EMMS. *N.* Heimir; *F.* Emme, Emmo, Emminga, Emmins; *D.* Emme; *S.* Hemmet, Hemming; *G.* Emmes; *Dch.* Emous; p.n. *See* Ames

EMSDEN. From Elmstone; a loc. n., Kent

ENDACOTT. A loc. n., Devon

ENDERBY. A loc. n., Leics.

ENDERWICK. *See* Inderwick

ENDICOTT. A loc. n., Devon

ENEFER, ENNEFER. From Henfynyw; a loc. n.

ENGLAND. *D.* Engelund; *S.* Englund; p.n.

ENGLEDOW. *See* Ingledew

ENGLEFIELD. A loc. n., Berks

ENNIONS. *See* Onions

ENNIS. From Enys; a loc. n., Cornw.

ENSBY. From Ensbury; a loc. n., Dorset

ENSELL. From Hensall; a loc. n., Yorks

ENSOLL. *See* Ensell

ENSOR. From Edensor; a loc. n., Derbysh.
ENTECOTT. *See* Endicott
ENTWISTLE. A loc. n., Lancs
EPTON. From Heppington; a loc. n., Kent
ERLAM. From Earlham; a loc. n., Suss.
ERRINGTON. From Erringden; a loc. n., Yorks
ERSKINE. A loc. n., Renfrew
ERT. *See* Hart
ESAM. From East Ham; a loc. n., Ess.
ESCOTT. A loc. n., Devon
ESDAILE. From Eskdale; a loc. n., Camb.
ESHELBY. From Exilby; a loc. n., Yorks
ESLER. *See* Easlee
ESLING. *S.* Esselin; a p.n. *See* Ess and Easlee
ESPIE. *D.*, *G.* Espe; a p.n.
ESS. *N.* Asi; *F.* Eisse, Aisse; *G.*, *D.*, *Fl.* Esser; *S.* Esselin, Essen; *Dch.* Es; p.n.
Asa, Asi, Saxon tenants in *D.B.*
ESSINGTON. A loc. n., Staffs.
ESTCOURT. *See* Estcott
ESTWICK. A loc. n., Herts
ETCHES. *D.*, *Dch.* Eggers; *G.* Egers; p.n.
ETHERIDGE. From Etterick; a loc. n., Selkirk (?)
ETHERINGTON. From Atherington; a loc. n., Devon
ETRIDGE. *See* Etheridge
ETTLES. From Etal; a loc. n., Northbd.
EVANS. *Fl.* Evens; a p.n. *See* Eve
EVE. *F.* Eve; a p.n.
EVELEIGH. From Everley; a loc. n., Wilts
EVELY. From Everley; a loc. n., Wilts
EVELYN. *Dch.* Evelein; a p.n.
EVENS. *See* Ivens
EVERARD. *Fl.*, *Dch.* Everard; *Fr.* Evrard; *S.*, *D.* Evert; *G.* Eberhardt; p.n.
Ebrard, a tenant in chief in *D.B.*
EVERED. *See* Everard
EVERETT. *See* Everard
EVERINGHAM. A loc. n., Yorks
EVERITT. *See* Everard
EVERSHED. From Evershot; a loc. n., Dorset (?)
EVERSON. *N.* Evarr; *F.* Eve; *S.*, *Fl.* Evers; *D.*, *Dch.* Eversen; *D.B.* Eve; p.n.
EVERTON. A loc. n., Beds
EVILL. From Yville; a loc. n., Normandy
EVINGTON. A loc. n., Glost., Leics.
EVISON. *See* Everson
EWAN, EWEN. *N.* Eyvindr; *Dch.* Euwen; *G.* Euen; *D.B.* Ewen; p.n.
EWBANK. From Yewbank; a loc. n., Cumb.
EXELL. A loc. n., Belgium. Or from Exwell; a loc. n., Rutland
EXLEY. A loc. n., Yorks
EXON. The ancient name of Exeter
EXTON. A loc. n., Devon, Rutland, Somers.
EYES. *Fl.* Eyers; a p.n. (?)
EYKIN. From Iken; a loc. n., Suff. Or *F.* Eke, Eike; *D.* Eiche, Eicken, Eken; *A.S.* Ecca; *Dch.* Eck, Eik, Eijken; p.n.
EYKINS. *Fl.* Eykens; a p.n. *See* Eykin
EYLES. *F.*, *Dch.* Eijlerts; a p.n.
EYRE. *See* Ayre
EYTON. A loc. n., Heref., Salop

F.

FABB. *D.*, *Dch.*, *Fl.*, *G.* Faber; *Fr.* Fabri, Fabry; p.n.

Faber and Fabri, under tenants in *D.B.*

FACER. *N.* Fasi; *D.* Fase; *Dch.* Feesse; *G.* Fesser; p.n.

FACHNEY. From Fakenham; a loc. n., Norf.

FACON. *Fr.* Facon; a p.n.

FAGAN. From St. Fagan; a loc. n., Glamorgan

FAGE. *Fl.* Feyke; *Fr.* Facq; *F.* Fekke, Feyke; *Dch.* Feeker, Fack; *G.* Fach; *D.B.* Fech, Feg; p.n.

FAGG. *See* Fage

FAIERS. *See* Fayers

FAIL. *N.* Veili; *Fl.* Vael; *D.* Feill; p.n.

FAILES. *Dch.* Fels, Velse; *Fr.* Fèliers (?); p.n. *See* Fail

FAIRALL, FAIRHALL. From Fairhaugh; a loc. n., Northbd.

FAIRBAIRN. From Fairburn; a loc. n., Yorks

FAIRBROTHER. From *Fl.* Verbrugghe; a p.n.

FAIRCHILD. *Fl.* Verschilde; a p.n.

FAIRCLOTH. *See* Fairclough

FAIRCLOUGH. A loc. n.

FAIRFOOT. From Fairford; a loc. n., Glos.

FAIRHEAD. *Fl.* Verheide; a p.n.

FAIRHURST. From Fairest; a loc. n., Yorks (?)

FAIRLEY. *Dch.* Verlee; *Fl.* Verlegh, Verley; p.n. Or *see* Fairlie

FAIRLIE. From Fairlee; a loc. n., Hants. Or Fairlie, Ayrshire

FAIRMAN. *See* Fearman

FAIRS, FAIRES. *See* Fayers

FAIRWAY. From Farway; a loc. n., Devon

FAIRWEATHER. From Fairwater; a loc. n., Glamorgan

FAIRY. *Fr.* Ferry, Féré; p.n.

FAITH. *S.* Feith; *D.* Faith; *G.* Veith; p.n.

FAKES. *D.* Fack; *D.B.* Fech; *Fl.* Feykens; p.n.

FALCONER. *See* Faulke

FALKLAND. A loc. n., Scotl.

FALLE. *Fl.* Vale; a p.n.

FALLICK. *Fl.* Falck; *G.* Falk; p.n.

FALLON, FALLOON. *Fl.* Falon; a p.n.

FALLOWS. From Falaise; a loc. n., Normandy. Also Fallais, in Flanders; *Fl.* Falise, Falloise; p.n.; *D.B.* de Faleise; p.n.

William de Faleis in Rot. Obl. et Fin., K. John.

FALLS. *D.* Falz; a p.n.

FALLSHAW. From Fullshaw; a loc. n., Ches.

FALVEY. *Fr.* Faluet; a p.n.

FAMIN. *Fl.* Vermin; a p.n.

FANCOURT. From Falencourt; a loc. n., Normandy

FANE. From Fains; a loc. n., Normandy (?); *D.B.* Fenise (?); *F.* Feyen; *Dch.* Feen; *Fr.* Faine; *Fl.* Fayen, Feyen; p.n.

Thomas de Vein held lands in Glost. *temp.* K. John. A.D. 1207. Rot. Obl. et Fin. Sir Francis Fane of Fulbeck, Lincs, and Aston, Yorks, third son of Francis, first Earl of Westmd., made K.B. at coronation of Charles I., Feb. 1, 1625.

FANN. *Fl.* Vane; a p.n.

FANNER. *Dch.* Fano; a p.n. (?)

FANNING. *Fl.* p.n.

FANSHAWE. A loc. n., Derbysh.

FARADAY. *Dch.* Ferwerda (?); a p.n.

FARDELL. A loc. n., Devon

For some time the residence of Sir Walter Raleigh.

FARE. *See* Phair

FAREY. *See* Fairy

FARGER. *N.* Fagr, n.n.; *S.* Fager; *Dch.* Fages; p.n.

FARIS. *G.*; p.n.
FARISH. *G.* Faris; a p.n.
FARJON. *Dch.*; p.n.
FARLER. *See* Farley
FARLEY. A loc. n., Hants, Salop, Staffs., Surr., Wilts
FARLOW. A loc. n., Salop
FARMAN. *See* Fearman
FARMER. *See* Fearman. Or *Fr.* Fermier; *Dch.* Vahrmeijer; p.n.
FARNBOROUGH. A loc. n., Berks, Hants
FARNFIELD. From Farnsfield; a loc. n., Notts
FARNHAM. A loc. n., Ess., Hants, Surr., Yorks
FARNINGTON. From Farmington; a loc. n., Glost.
FARNLEY. A loc. n., Yorks
FARR. A loc. n., Sutherland. Or *G.* Farr; *Fr.* Varé; p.n.
FARRALL. *D.* Ferrall; *G.* Forell; p.n.
FARRANCE. *See* Farrant
FARRANT. *Fr.* Farrand; a p.n.
FARRAR. *See* Farrer
FARRELL. *See* Farrall
FARREN. *Fl.* Farin; a p.n.
FARRER. *D.* Farrer; a p.n.
FARRINGTON. A loc. n., Dorset, Somers., Yorks
FARROW. *Dch.* Faro; a p.n.
FARTHING. *D.* Warding; *G.* Wardein; *Dch.* Fardon, Vaarting; *Fl.* Verdeyen; *D.B.* Fardan, Fardein (Saxon tenants); p.n. *See* Varden
FARWIG. A loc. n. in Kent
FASHAM. From Faversham; a loc. n., Kent (?)
FASSETT. *Fl.* Fassaert, Vassart; p.n.
FATHERS. *N.* Fjöder, Vaði (?); *Dch.* Vader; *D.*, *G.* Vater; *D.B.* Fader; p.n.
FATLING. *Fr.* Vaudelin; a p.n. (?)
FAUCIT. *See* Fawcett
FAUCUS. *See* Vaux
FAUGHT. *S.* Vought, Fought; *G.* Fauth; p.n.
FAULCONBRIDGE. From Fauquembergues; a loc. n., Normandy
FAULKE. *N.* Falki; *F.* Fôlerk, Fôke, Fauke; *S.* Falck, Falk; *D.* Falck; *Dch.* Folkers, Valk, Fok, Vokke; *Fl.* Volck, Fockx; *G.* Falk, Forcke, Fox; p.n.; *D.B.* Fulcher, Fulk, Fulco, Fulcui, etc.

Fouke and Fitz Fouk are in the Roll of Battell Abbey. Fulche, Fulc, Fulco, tenants in chief in *D.B.*

FAULKNER. *Fr.* Fauconnier; a p.n. *See* Faulke
FAUX. *See* Vaux
FAWCETT. From Forcett; a loc. n., Yorks. Or Farcet, Hunts
FAWELL. *See* Fowell and Vowell
FAWN. *See* Vaughan
FAY. *D.* Faye, Feigh; *G.* Fay, Fei; p.n.
FAYERMAN. *See* Fairman
FAYERS. *S.*, *D.* Fehr; *G.* Fuhr; *Fl.* Feer; *Dch.* Fehrs; p.n.
FAZACKERLEY. A loc. n., Lancs
FEA. *Fr.*, *Fl.* Fey; a p.n.
FEAKS. *See* Feek
FEAR. *See* Fayers
FEAREY. *See* Fairy
FEARMAN. *S.* Fehrman; *G.* Fuhrmann; *D.B.* Farman, Ferme; p.n. *See* Fayers
FEARNCOMBE. From Farncombe, a loc. n., Surr.
FEARNE. A loc. n., Ross
FEARNHEAD. A loc. n., Lancs
FEARNLEY. From Fernilee; a loc. n., Derbysh.
FEARNSIDE. From Fenside; a loc. n., Lincs (?)
FEARON. From Fearn; a loc. n., Forfar. Or *Dch.* Ferron; *S.* Féron; p.n.
FEASEY. *See* Veasey
FEAST. *Fr.* Fisette; a p.n.
FEATES. *Dch.* Viet; *Fl.* Vieth, Vits; *G.* Fietz; p.n. *D.B.* Fitheus (?)
FEATHERSTONE. A loc. n. in Yorks

FEAVERYEAR. *Fr.* Febvrier, Février; *G.* Fiebiger, Fieweger; p.n.
Richard Feverer in Rot. Obl. et Fin., K. John.

FEAVIOUR. *See* Feaveryear

FEAVYER. *See* Feaveryear

FEEK. *S.*, *D.* Fick; *Dch.* Ficke; *F.* Feyke, Fekke; *G.* Fieg, Ficus; *Fl.* Fige; *D.B.* Fyach, Feg, Feche; p.n.

FEEN. *See* Fane

FEETHAM, FEETUM. From Feetham; a loc. n., Yorks

FELCE. *Dch.* Velse; *G.* Felsch; p.n.

FELDWICK. *Dch.* Veldwijk; a loc. and p. n.

FELL. A loc. n. from *N. fell*, a wild hill (*fjall*, pl., is a range of hills); *D.* Fjel; *Dch.* Fels, Fellinger, Vel, Velde, Veldt, Wel; *G.* Feldt, Feller; *Fl.*, *Fr.* Velle; p.n.
Richard-de-la-Felda occurs in Rot. Obl. et Fin., K. John, A.D. 1201 (Yorks).

FELLOWES. *Fr.* Féliers; a p.n. Or *see* Fallows

FELTHAM. A loc. n., Middlx., Dorset

FELTON. A loc. n., Northbd., Somers.

FELTWELL. A loc. n., Norf.

FENDER. *G.*; p.n.

FENN. *See* Fane

FENNER. *See* Venner

FENNIMORE. From Fennemere; a loc. n., Salop. Or Fenemere or Finmere, Oxon
Gilbert de Finemere held lands there in Oxon, A.D. 1208.

FENTON. A loc. n., Cornw., Lincs, Notts, Yorks

FENWICK. A loc. n., Ayrshire, Yorks. Or *Dch.* Vennick; p.n.

FENWRICK. *D.* Wendrick; *G.* Fenrich; *Dch.* Vendrik; *D.B.* Wenric; p.n.

FEREDAY. *See* Faraday

FERGUS. From St. Fergus; a loc. n., Banff

FERGUSON. *See* Fergus

FERNIE. *Fr.* Vernie; a p.n. From Vernet; a loc. n., France

FERNIHOUGH. From Fernihalgh; a loc. n., Lancs

FERNLEY. *See* Farnley

FERRABY. From Ferriby; a loc. n., Lincs, Yorks

FERREBO. *See* Ferraby

FERRETT. *Fl.* Feraert; *Fr.* Ferrett; *G.* Fereth; p.n.

FERRIE. *See* Fairy

FERRIER. *Fl.* Ferier; a p.n.

FERRIES. *Fl.* Verraes; a p.n.

FERRIS. *See* Ferries

FERRY. *See* Fairy

FERTEL. *G.* Virtel; a p.n.

FESSEY. *See* Veasey

FETCH. *G.* Vietsch, Fitza; *D.* Fitzer; *N.-Fr.* Fitz; p.n.

FEWKES. *G.* Fuchs; a p.n. Or *see* Faulke

FEWSTER. *Fl.* Deveuster and Devuyster; p.n.
William Fuster in Rot. Obl. et Fin., K. John.

FFOLKES. *See* Faulke

FFOOKS. *See* Fewkes

FICKLING. *Dch.* Fikkelie; a p.n. *See* Feek

FIDDAMAN. *See* Fiddyman

FIDDEMAN. *See* Fiddyman

FIDDES. *See* Fiddy

FIDDY. *N.* Viðarr; *D.* Wiede; *D.B.* Wider, Wido; *G.* Wiedig; p.n.

FIDDYMAN. *D.*, *G.* Wiedemann; *S.*, *Dch.* Wideman; *Fl.* Widmer, Wydeman; p.n.

FIDDYMONT. *See* Fiddyman

FIDGEON. *N.* Fiðr or Viðarr; *Dch.* Viegen; *Fl.* Vigen; p.n. (dimin.)

FIDGETT. From *Fr.* Fichet,
Which is in the Roll of Battell Abbey. Perhaps from the loc. n. Figeac in Normandy.

FIDLER. *G.* Fiedler; a p.n. *See* Vidler

FIDOE. *N.* Fiðr; a p.n. Or *see* Fiddy

FIELD. *D.* Fjelde; a p.n. *See* Fell

FIELDING. *S.* Felldin; *Dch.* Velden; p.n.

FIEN. *See* Fane

FIENNES. *Fl.* Feyens; a p.n. *See* Fane

FIFETT. *Fr.* Fivet; a p.n.

FIFIELD. A loc. n., Ess., Hants, Wilts

FIFOOT. *See* Fifett

FIGGINS. *D.* Wiegand; *Dch.* Viegen; *Fl.* Vigen; p.n.

FIGGIS. *Fl.* Figeys; a p.n. *See* Feek

FIGURES. *Fl.* Figeys (?); a p.n. Or *see* Vigers, Vigors

FILBERT. From St. Philbert; a loc. n., France. Or *D.* Filbert; a p.n.

FILL. *G.* Filla, or *Fr.* Ville; a p.n. Or dimin. of Philip (?)

FILLINGER. *N.* Veljungr; *D.* Felling; *Dch.* Fellinger; *D.B.* Felaga; p.n.

FILLINGHAM. A loc. n., Lincs

FILLISTON. *Dch.* Vilsteren; a p.n. (?)

FILLMORE. *See* Phillemore

FILMER. *See* Phillemore

FILMORE. *See* Phillimore

FINBOW. From Finborough; a loc. n., Suff. Or *S.* Finnborg; *N.* Finnbogi; p.n.

FINCH. *Fl.* Finch; *G.*, *Dch.* Finke; p.n.

FINCHAM. A loc. n., Norf.

FINDLATER. A loc. n., Banff.

FINIGAN. From the Irish O'Finnegan; a p.n.

FINKELL. *Dch.* Finkel, Vinkel; *D.B.* Fenchel; p.n.

FINLAY. From Finningley; a loc. n., Notts

FINNEMORE. *See* Fenimore

FINNEY. *N.* Finni; *D.* Finne; *Fl.* Finné; *S.* Finn; *D.B.* Fin; p.n.

FINNIS. *D.* Finne; *N.* Finni; p.n. Ulf Finisc; a p.n. in *D.B.*

FIRMAN. *Dch.* Ferman; a p.n. *See* Fairman

FIRMIN. *Fl.* Vermin; a p.n. *See* Firman

FIRMINGER. *Fl.* Verminger; a p.n.

FIRTH. *Dch.* Fürth; a p.n.

FISH. *D.*, *S.* Fisch; a p.n.

FISHBOURNE. A loc. n., Dur., Suss.

FISHLOCK. From Fishlake; a loc. n., Yorks

FISHPOOL. A loc. n., Lancs, Notts

FISKE. *S.* Fiske; *D.* Fisker; *G.* Fisch; *Fl.* Fisco; *D.B.* Fisc; p.n.

FITCH. *Fl.* Vits; a p.n. Or *see* Fetch

FITCHEW. Fitz Hugh (?)

FITHIAN. *See* Vythian

FITT. *Fr.* Viette; *Dch.* Vieth; p.n. *See* Fiddy

FITZPATRICK. *See* Gilpatric

FIVASH. *See* Vivish

FIX. *D.*, *Fr.*; p.n.

FLACK. *See* Flagg

FLAGG. *G.* Flach, Flack; *Dch.* Vlak; p.n. *See* Flegg

FLAMANK. *Fl.* Flamand, Flament, Vleminck; p.n.

FLAMSTEAD. A loc. n., Herts

FLANDERS. *G.* Flanter; *D.B.* Flandren; p.n.

FLATHER. *G.* Flauder, Flatau; p.n.

FLATMAN. *D.B.* Floteman; *Dch.* Flotman; *G.* Flottmann; p.n.

FLATT. *G.* Flatt; a p.n.

FLAXMAN. *Dch.* Vlasman; a p.n.

FLECK. *G.* Fleck; a p.n.

FLEECE. *Dch.* Vlies; *G.* Fleege; p.n.

FLEET. A loc n., Lincs. Or *Dch.* Vliet; a p.n.

FLEETWOOD. A loc. n., Lancs

FLEGG. *N.* Flegg; *D.* Vlak, Fleck; *Dch.* Vleck; *G.* Fleck, Fleger; p.n.

G. and W. Flegg are hundreds in Norf.

FLEMING. *S.* Flemming; *Dch.* Vlaming; *Fl.* Vleminck; *G.* Flemming; *D.B.* Flamand, Flandren; p.n.

William le Fleming received the Manor of Aldingham, Lancs, from the Conqueror.

FLETCHER. *Fl.* Vleeschauwhr; *Fr.* Fléchard; *G.*, *Dch.* Fleischer; p.n.

FLEURY. *Fr.* Fleury; p.n.

FLEWELLEN. *See* Llewellyn

FLEY. *Dch.* Vlie; *D.* Flye; p.n.

FLICK. *Dch.* Flick; *D.* Flig, Flycht; *Fr.* Flèche (?); p.n.

FLIGHT. *Dch.* Vliet; a p.n.

FLIN. *See* Flynn

FLINDERS. *See* Flanders

FLINT. *D.* Flindt, Flint; p.n.

FLITT. From Fleet; a loc. n., Hants, Lincs; *Dch.* Vliet; a p.n.

FLITTEN. *See* Flitton

FLITTON. A loc. n., Beds

FLOOD. *S.* Flod; *D.* Flott; *G.* Flöte, Fluder; p.n.

FLOOK. *D.* Floecke; a p.n.

FLOOKS. *See* Flux

FLORY. *Fl.* Flory; p.n. *See* Flowers

FLOWERDAY. *See* Flowerdew

FLOWERDEW. *Fr.* Fleureau; a Huguenot n.

FLOWERS. From Fleurus; a loc. n., Flanders. Or Flers; a loc. n., Normandy. Or *S.* Flor; *D.* Floor; *G.* Flohr; *Fl.* Flore, Floris, Vloors; *Dch.* Floor, Florus; p.n.

Elyas Flur in Rot. Obl. et Fin., K. John.

FLOYD. *See* Lloyd

FLUCK. *See* Flook

FLUDE. *G.* Fluder; a p.n.

FLURRY. *Fr.* Floris; a p.n.

FLUTTER. *G.* Fluder; *Fr.* Floutier; p.n.

FLUX. *G.*; p.n.

FLY. *See* Fley

FLYNN. *N.* Fleinn; a p.n.

FOALE. *See* Foll

FOGG. *See* Foggo

FOGGIN. *Dch.* Focken, Vogin; p.n.

FOGGO. *N.* Foka; *F.* Fokko; *G.* Fökke, Vocke; *S.* Fock; *D.* Fog; p.n.

FOGWELL. From Vogwell; a loc. n., Devon

FOISTER. *See* Fewster

FOL. *Dch.* Fol; *Fl.* Fol; *Fr.* Folie, Follett; p.n.

FOLEY. *Dch.* Fol; *Fr.* Folie; *D.B.* Folet; p.n.

Folet in Rot. Obl. et Fin., K. John.

FOLKARD. *Fr.* Volckaert; *G.* Folkert; p.n.

FOLLETT. *Fr.*; p.n. *See* Foley

FOLLIOTT. *Fr.* Foliot; a p.n.

In Roll of Battell Abbey and Rot. Obl. et Fin., K. John.

FOLLOWES. *F.* Fôlers; a p.n. Or *see* Fallows

FOLLY. *See* Follett

FOLTROP. From Felthorpe; a loc. n., Norf.

FOOKS. *See* Fewkes

FOOT. *N.* Vöttr; *Dch.* Wout; *G.* Wuthe; *S.* Futy; *D.B.* Fot; p.n.

FOOTER. *Dch.* Wouter; a p.n. *See* Foot

FOOTMAN. *Dch.* Woutman; a p.n. *See* Foot

FOOTTIT. *Dch.* Affourtit; a p.n. (?)

FORBES. A loc. n., Aberdeensh.

FORD. A loc. n., Dur., Salop, Staffs.

FORDER. *See* Fordham

FORDHAM. A loc. n., Ess.

FORDOM. *See* Fordham

FORDYCE. A loc. n., Banff

FORFEITT. *Fl.* Forfert; a p.n.

FORGAN. A loc. n., Fife

FORGE. *Fr.*; p.n.

FORKES. *See* Faulke

FORMAN. *D.* Formann; *Dch.* Foreman; *Fr.* Formont; p.n.

FORMBY. A loc. n., Lancs

FORMON. *See* Forman

FORREST. A loc. n., Cornw., Salop

FORSAITH. *See* Forcett

FORSBREY. *See* Fosbery

FORSBROOK. A loc. n., Staffs.; *D.B.* Fotesbroc

Osbert de Focebroc was living 3 John, A.D. 1201. Pipe Roll, under Staffordshire.

FORSCUTT. A loc. n., Somers. Or *see* Foscote

FORSDICK. *See* Fosdyke

FORSGATE. From Forscott; a loc. n., Somers. (?)

FORSHAM. From Fosham; a loc. n., Yorks

FORSHAW. *D.* Fourschou; a p.n. From *N.* Fagriskógr (Fairwood); a loc. n. Or *Fr.* Faucheur, Fauchois; p.n.

FORSYTH. *See* Forsaith

FORT. *Dch.* Voort; a p.n. Or *see* Fought

FORTY. *Fr.* Fortie; a p.n.

FORWARD. *See* Forwood

FORWOOD. A loc. n., Glost.

FOSBERRY. *See* Fosbery

FOSBERY. From Fosbury; a loc. n., Berks, Wilts

FOSBROOKE. *See* Forsbrook

FOSCOTE. A loc. n., Bucks

FOSDYKE. A loc. n., Lincs

FOSSETT. *See* Fawcett

FOSTER. *Dch.* Forster; *Fl.* Fostier; *D.B.* Forst; p.n.

FOTHERBY. A loc. n., Lincs

FOTHERINGHAM. A loc. n., Inverarity, Scotl.

FOULE. *See* Foley

FOULGER. From Fulgent; a loc. n., France

FOULIS. A loc. n., Perthsh.

FOULSHAM. A loc. n., Norf.

FOUNTAIN. *Fr.* Fontaine; a Huguenot n.

FOURACRE. *See* Foweraker

FOVARGUE. *Fr.* Fouache (?)

FOWELL. *Fr.* Fauvel, Vauvelle; p.n.

FOWERAKER. From Fouracre; a loc. n., Devon. Or *Fl.* Fleuracker, Voordecker; p.n.

FOWLE. *See* Fowler

FOWLER. *Fr.* Fouiller; a p.n.

FOX. *N.* Foka; *F.* Fokke, Fauke; *Fl.* Fockx; *S.* Fock; p.n. *See* Faux

FOXALL. *See* Foxhall

FOXHALL. A loc. n., Suff.

FOXLEY. A loc. n., Hants, Norf., Staff.

FOXTON. A loc. n., Camb.

FOXWELL. *See* Foxhall

FOY. From Foye; a loc. n., Heref.

FOYSON. *See* Fyson

FOYSTER. *See* Fewster

FRADGLEY. From Fradley; a loc. n., Staff.

FRAME. *Dch.* Vreem; *D.* Frahm; p.n.

FRAMPTON. A loc. n., Dorset, Lincs

FRANKLAND. A loc. n., Devon

FRANKLANDS. A loc. n., Cumb.

FRAREY. *See* Freer

FRASER. *Fr.* Fraiseur; a p.n.

FREARSON. *N.* Freyer; *S.* Fria; *G.* Freier; *Fl.* Frey; p.n.

FRECKLETON. A loc. n., Yorks

FREEBORN. *G.* Frieben (?); a p.n.

FREEKE. *Fr.* Friche; *Fl.* Frick; *D.* Frich, Fricke; p.n.

FREEMAN. *D.* Frieman; *S.* Friman; *G.* Friedemann; *Fl.* Freyman; *Fr.* Frémont; p.n.

FREER. *See* Frere

FRENCH. *Fl.* Frentz; *Dch.* Fransche, Franse; p.n.

FRERE. *N.*, *S.*, *D.*, *Dch.* Freyr; *G.* Freier; *Fr.* Frère; a p.n. *See* Freer

FRESHFIELD. A loc. n., Lancs

FRESHWATER. A loc. n., I. of Wight

FRESTON. A loc. n., Lincs, Suff.

FRETWELL. From Fredville; a loc. n., Kent (?)

FREUER. *See* Freer

FREWER. *See* Freer

FRICKER. *G.* Frick, Fricke; *Fr.* Friche, Fricot; p.n.

FRIGGENS. *G.* Frigge; a p.n.

FRIGHT. *S.* Freit; *G.* Freiheit; p.n.
FRISBY. A loc. n., Leics
FRISWELL. From Freshwell; a loc. n., Ess.
FRITCHLEY. A loc. n., Derbysh.
FRITH. *D.* Fryd; a p.n.
FRODSHAM. A loc. n., Ches.
FROHAWK. *See* Frohock
FROHOCK. From Frowick; a loc. n., Ess.
FROMANT. *See* Fromow
FROMOW. *N.*, *D.*, *S.* From, Fröman; *Dch.* Fromme; *G.* Frommer; *Fl.* Fromont; *Fr.* Froment; *D.B.* Frumond; p.n.
FROOM. From Frome; a loc. n., Somers.
FROSDICK. From Fosdyke; a loc. n., Lincs; *D.B.* Frodo (?). Comp. Frodsley, Frodsham
FROST. A loc. n., Devon. Or *D.*, *G.*, *Dch.* p.n.
FROSTICK. *See* Forsdyke
FROUDE. *N.* Fróði; *D.* Froede; *S.* Frode; p.n.
D.B. Fradre, Frodo, Saxon tenants. Frodo also a tenant in chief.
FROWDE. *See* Froude
FRUSHER. *Fl.* Fruchart; *Dch.* Froschart; *D.B.* Froissart; p.n.
FRY. From Fry; a loc. n., Normandy. Or Icelandic Frey; a fam. n.; *N.* Freyer, Frayr; *S.* Fria, Freja, Freijer; *Fl.* Frey; *D.* Frey, Freij, Frie; *D.B.* Vruoi (?); *G.* Frei, Freier, Frey, Freyer; *A.S.* Freâ; *Dch.* Frey, Freij, Frie; p.n.
FRYER. *N.*, *S.*, *D.*, *G.* Freyer; a p.n. *See* Frere
FUDGE. From Fuidge; a loc. n., Devon
FUDGER. *See* Fudge
FUGGLE. *N.*, *D.* Fugl; *S.* Fogel; *Fl.*, *Dch.*, *G.* Vogel; *Fr.* Figille (?); *D.B.* Fuglo; p.n.
FUGILL. *See* Fuggle
FULCHER. *See* Fullagar
FULFORD. A loc. n., Devon, Yorks
FULLAGAR. *G.* Fulge; a p.n.
FULLALOVE. From *Dch.* Vollenhove; a p.n. (?)
FULLARTON. A loc. n., Ayr, Hants
FULLBROOK. From Fullerbrook; a loc. n., Devon
FULLER. *See* Fowler
FULLERTON. *See* Fullarton
FULLMER. A loc. n., Bucks
FULLWOOD. A loc. n., Lancs, Notts, Yorks
FULSHAW. *See* Fullagar or Falshaw
FULTON. *See* Fullerton
FUNGE. *D.*, *G.*, *S.*, *Fl.*, *Dch.* Funck, Funke; a p.n.
FUNNELL. From Fundenhall; a loc. n., Norf. Or *Fr.* Forneville (?)
FURBER. From *Fr.* Foubert, a Huguenot n.
FURBY. From Firby; a loc. n., Kent, Yorks
FURLEY. A loc. n., Devon
FURLONG. A loc. n., Devon
FURNER. From *Fr.* Fournier; a Huguenot n.
FURNESS. A loc. n., Ess., N. Lancs, Flanders
FURNISH. *See* Furness
FURNISS. *See* Furness
FURSDON. A loc. n., Cornw., Devon
FURSE. *Fr.* Fourez (?); a p.n.; *D.B.* Fursa
Forz in Roll of Battell Abbey.
FUSEDALE. A loc. n., Westmd.
FUSSEY. *D.* Fussing; *G.* Fusseck; *Fl.* Fussen; p.n.
FUSSLE. *D.*, *G.* Füssel; a p.n.
FUSTLING. *D.* Füsterling; a p.n.
FUTCHER. *G.* Füger; a p.n.
FUTLER. *See* Footer
FYFFE. From Fife, a county in Scotland
FYLER. *G.* Feiler; a p.n.
FYNES. *See* Feyn and Fenn
FYSON. *N.* Fusi (dimin. of Vigfús); *G.* Fuhs, Fuss; *Fl.* Fussen; p.n.

G.

GABB, GABE. *D.* Gabe ; a p.n.
GABBETT. *Fr.* Gabet ; a p.n.
GABY. *See* Gabb
GACHES. *Fr.* Gauchez ; a p.n.
GADD. *D.* Gad, Gade ; *G.* Gade ; p.n.
GADNEY. From Gedney ; a loc. n., Lincs
GADSBY. From Gaddesby ; a loc. n., Leics.
GADSDEN, GADSDUN. From Gaddesden ; a loc. n., Herts
GADSWORTHY. From Godsworthy ; a loc. n., Devon
GAFF. *Fr.* Gaffé ; a p.n.
GAFFER. *See* Gaff
GAGE. *S.* Gagge ; *Fl.* Gegers ; a p.n. *See* Cage
GAGEN. *See* Geoghegan
GAIGER. *Fl.* Gegers, Geiger ; p.n.
GAINSFORD. From Gainford ; a loc. n., Dur., Yorks
GAISFORD. *See* Gainsford
GAITSKELL. From Gaitsgill ; a loc. n., Cumb.
GALE. A loc. n., Devon, Lancs. Or Gayle, Yorks
GALILEE. *N.* Galli, Gallŏr ; n.n. *Dch.* Gallé, Gallee, Galjee ; *Fl.* Gali ; *Fr.* Gailly, Gailliet, Gailliez, Gaillait ; *G.* Galley ; p.n.
GALL. *D.* Gall ; *Fr.* Galle ; *Fl.* Gal ; p.n.
GALLAGHER. From Gellygaer ; a loc. n., S. Wales
GALLAND. *Fr.* Gaillande ; *Fl.* Galland ; *G.* Gallant ; *D.* Galen ; p.n.
GALLANT. *See* Galland
GALLICK. *G.* Galeiske, Galisch ; p.n.
GALLING. *Dch.* Galen ; p.n. *See* Gall
GALLEY. *Fr.* Gallais, Gallait, Gallay, Gallet, Gally ; p.n.
GALLOP. *Fr.* Galopin ; a p.n.
GALLOWAY. A loc. n., Scotl.
GALLYON. *Fr.* Gaillon ; a p.n.
GALT. *Fl.* Gallet ; a p.n.
GALTON. A loc. n., Somers.
GAMBLE. *N.* Gamli ; *D.* Gamel ; *G.* Kammell ; *D.B.* Game, Gamel, Gam ; p.n.
GAMBLING. *Fr.* Gamblin ; a p.n. *See* Gamble
GAME. *See* Gamble
GAMES. *D.* Gemz, Gjems ; *G.* Gems ; *Dch.* Gemke, Gemmeker ; *Fl.* Geemers, Gemers ; p.n.
GAMMAGE. From Gamaches ; a loc. n., Normandy

Gamages in Roll of Battell Abbey. Gamas in *D.B.* ; p.n.

GAMMON. *See* Gamon
GAMON. *N.* Geir-mundr ; *F.* Gërman ; *G.* Gehrmann ; *D.* Garman, Germund ; *Fr.* Gamain, Germain ; *Fl.* Germon ; *D.B.* Garmund, German, Germund ; p.n.
GANDY. *G.* GANDE ; a p.n.
GANE. *Dch.* Geen ; a p.n.
GANLY. From Ganilly ; a loc. n., Scilly Isles
GANNAWAY. *See* Janeway
GANT. *Fr.* Gand ; *Dch.* Gant ; p.n.

De Gand, tenant in chief in *D.B.* From Ghent ; a loc. n. in Flanders.

GANTREY. *Fr.* Gantier ; p.n. *See* Gant
GAPP. *See* Gabb
GARD. *See* Garth
GARDEN. A loc. n., Kirkcudbright
GARFIT. From Garforth ; a loc. n., Yorks
GARFORD. A loc. n., Berks
GARFORTH. A loc. n., Yorks
GARLAND. A loc. n., Devon. Or *see* Galland
GARLICK. *G.* Gawlick ; a p.n. Or *see* Gallick

GARMAN. *See* Gamon

GARNER. *D.* Gartner; Gerner; *Fr.* Garnier; *D.B.* Garner; p.n.

GARRARD. *See* Garrod

GARRETT. *See* Garrod

GARRICK. From Gerrick; a loc. n., Yorks. Or *Fr.* Garrigues; a p.n.

GARROD. *N.* Geirröðr; *Dch.* Gerhard, Gerardts, Geraets; *Fl.* Gheeraerts, Geeraerts, Geerts; *G.* Gerhard, Gerhardt; *Fr.* Garet, Garot, Gérard; *D.B.* Gerard, Girard; p.n.

GARSIDE. A loc. n., Yorks

GARTH. *N.* Garðr; *S.* Gardt; *Fl.* Gard; *G.* Görth; *D.B.* Guerd, Guert, Gurt; p.n. A loc. n., S. Wales

GARTHWAITE. From Gawthwaite; a loc. n., Lancs

GARTLEY. A loc. n., Aberdeensh.

GARTON. A loc. n., Yorks

GARWOOD. From Garswood; a loc. n., Lancs

GASCOIN. *See* Gaskin

GASCOYNE. *See* Gaskin

GASELEE. *See* Gazeley

GASKARTH. From Geitaskarth; a loc. n. in Iceland

GASKELL. From Gaisgill; a loc. n., Westmd.

GASKIN. *Fr.* Gascon; p.n.

GASS. *G.* Gasse; *Dch.* Gase; *Fr.* Gassé; p.n.

GASTON. *Fl.* Gasten; *Fr.* Gaston; p.n.

GATEHOUSE. A loc. n., Kirkcudbright

GATES. *Fl.* Gets; a p.n.

GATH. *D.*; a p.n.

GATLAND. From Garthland; a loc. n., Renfrew

GAULT. *N.* Galti; *Fr.* Gualtier; p.n.

GAUNT. *See* Gant

GAWMAN. *See* Gamon

GAWTHORPE. A loc. n., Yorks

GAY. *Fr.*, *Dch.* Gay; *G.* Gey; p.n.

GAYFER. *See* Gayford

GAYFORD. From Gateford; a loc. n., Notts

GAYLEARD. *Fl.* Gellaert; a p.n.

GAYTHORPE. From Garthorpe; a loc. n., Lincs

GAYTON. A loc. n., Lincs, Norf., Staffs.

GAZE. From Gays; a loc. n., Devon. Or *Fr.* Gazet; a p.n.

GAZELEY. A loc. n., Suff. Or *Fr.* Gasly; a p.n.

GEARY. *N.* Geiri; *Fr.* Géry; *D.* Gier, Gjeraae; *Fl.* Giers; *G.* Geyer, Gierig; *D.B.* Gheri; p.n.

GEATER. *D.* Giede; *D.B.* Gida; p.n.

GEDDES. A loc. n., Nairn

GEDGE. *See* Geddes

GEE. *Fr.* Ghys; *G.* Gey; *Dch.* Gee; p.n.

GEEN. *See* Ginn

GELL. *Fr.*, *Fl.* Geill; *Dch.* Geel; p.n.

GELSTHORPE. A loc. n., Notts. *D.* Gjelstrup; *Dch.* Geldorp; loc. and p. n.

GELSTON. From Geldeston; a loc. n., Norf.

GEMLEY. From Gembling; a loc. n., Yorks

GENGE. *Fr.* Gence; a p.n. Or *see* Ginger

GENN. *See* Ginn

GENT. *Dch.* Gendt; a p.n. *See* Gant

GENTLE. *Fr.* Gentil; *D.* Genkle; p.n.

GENTRY. *Fr.* Genty; *G.* Gendreck (?); p.n. Or *see* Gantrey

GEOGHEGAN or MACGEOGHAGAN. From the Irish MacEachagain or MacEoghagain

The MacGeoghagans were hereditary marshalls of Meath.

GERLING. *Dch.* Gerling; *D.B.* Girling; p.n.

GERMAN. *See* Gamon

GERY. *See* Gearey

GETHING. From Geddiug; a loc. n., Suff. Or *Fl.* Goetinck; a p.n.

GETTEN. *See* Gething

GETTING. *See* Gething

GIBBENS. *See* Gibbings

GIBBINGS. *F.* Jibbo, Jibben; *Fl.* Giebens, Gibbs; *S.* Jippson; *D.* Gieb; *Dch.* Gebbing; p.n.

GIBERNE. *See* Gibbings

GIBLET. *Fr.* dimin. *See* Gibbs

GIDDENS, GIDDINGS. From Gidding; a loc. n., Hunts. Or *D.* Giede; a p.n.

GIDLEY. From Gidleigh; a loc. n., Devon

GIDNEY. From Gedney; a loc. n., Lincs

GIEN. *See* Ginn

GIFFEN. A loc. n., Ayrsh.

GIFFORD. *Fr.* Giffard; a p.n. Or Gifford, a loc. n., Haddington

Giffard in Roll of Battell Abbey. Gifard, a tenant in chief in *D.B.*

GILBERT. *N.* Gisli-bjártr; *Fl.* Gillebaert; *Fr.* Gibert, Gilbert; *D.B.* Chilbert, Ghilebrid, Giselbert; p.n.

GILBEY. From Gilby; a loc. n., Lincs

GILCHRIST. *S.* Gillqvist; a p.n. Or from the Irish Giolla Chriosd

GILDEN. *Dch.*; p.n.

GILDERSLEEVES. From Geldersleeuw; a loc. n., Holland

GILES. *Fl.* Gilis; *Fr.* Gilles; *D.* Giles; p.n.

GILHAM. From Gillingham; a loc. n., Dorset, Kent. Or *S.* Gilljam; *Fr.* Gillaume; p.n.

GILL. *N.* Gils; *G.* Gilla; *Fr.* Gille; *S.* Gihl; *D.* Gille; *D.B.* Gilo, Gile, Ghil; p.n.

GILLAM. *See* Gilham

GILLESPIE. From Gillesbie; a loc. n., Dumfries

GILLETT. *Fr.*; p.n. *See* Gill

GILLIBRAND. From Gillyburn; a loc. n., Perth

GILLINGHAM. A loc. n., Somers.

GILLINGS. *S.* Gillen; *Dch.* Gilling; *Fl.* Gillain; p.n.

GILLOT. *Fr.* Huguenot n.

GILMORE. A loc. n., Yorks. Or from the Irish Mac Giolla Muire; a p.n.

GILMOUR. *See* Gilmore

GILPATRICK or KILPATRICK. From the Irish Giolla Padraig; a p.n. (devoted to St. Patrick)

GILPIN. *See* Kilpin

GILSON. *Fl.*; p.n. *See* Gill

GILYARD. *Fr.* Gilliard; a Huguenot n.

GIMLETT. *Fr.* Gimlette; a Huguenot n.

GINDER. *Fl.* Gindra (?); a p.n.

GINGEL. *G.* Ginschel; a p.n.

GINGER. *Dch.* Genger; a p.n.

GINN. *Fr.* Gynn; *D.* Gihn; *Dch.* Gijn; *G.* Gins; p.n.

GIPPS. *Dch.* Gips; a p.n.

GIRDLER. *See* Curtler

GIRLING. *See* Gerling

GISBOURNE. From Gisburne; a loc. n., Yorks

GISCARD. *Fl.* Gischard; a p.n.

GISSING. A loc. n., Norf.

GISSON. *See* Gissing

GITTENS. *See* Giddings

GITTINGS. *See* Giddings

GITTUS. From Gits; a loc. n., Flanders. Or *Dch.* Gidts; a p.n. *See* Geater

GIVEEN, GIVEN. *See* Giffen

GLADDING. *D.* Glad; *G.* Glade; *A.S.* Gladwin; p.n.

GLADSTONE. From Glaston; a loc. n., Rutland; *D.B.* Gladestone. *See* Gledstanes

GLADWYN. *N.* Glædir, a f. p.n.; *D.* Glad, p.n.; *N.* Vinr, a friend—a gladsome friend; *D.B.* Gladewin, Gladuin, Gleuuin, Gledwin (Leics.); p.n.

GLAISHER. *D.* Glæser; *G.* Gläser; *Fl.* Glaser; p.n.

GLASS. *S.* Glas; *D.* Glase, Glass; *G.* Glass, Gless; *Dch.* Glas; *Fr.* Glace; p.n.

GLASSCOCK. *D.* Glass; a p.n.; Cock, dimin. Or Glascote; a loc. n., Staffs.

GLASSINGTON. From Glasserton; a loc. n., Wigtonshire

GLASSON. A loc. n., Lancs

GLASSPOLE. A loc. n. *B. glâs*, grey; *pwll*, a pool. Or *D.* Glas; a p.n., and pollr, pool

GLASSPOOL. *See* Glasspole

GLASSUP. *See* Glossop

GLATWORTHY. *See* Clapworthy

GLAZEBROOK. A loc. n., Lancs

GLAZIN. *D.* Glass, Glazener; *Fr.* Glaçon; p.n. Glasen or Glassing, a fam. n.

GLAZZARD. From Glasoed; a loc. n., Monmouth

GLEAD. *See* Gleed

GLEADAH. *See* Gleadowe

GLEADOWE. From Gleadhow; a loc. n., Yorks

GLEASON. From Gleaston; a loc. n., Lancs

GLEDSTANES. A loc. n. *See* Gladding

GLEED. *N.* Glædir; *D.* Glad; *G.* Glied; p.n.

GLENDINNING. A loc. n., Dumfries

GLENHAM. From Glentham; a loc. n., Lincs

GLENNIE. From the Celtic Gleannau, a little upland glen. Or *see* Glynne

GLEW. *D.* Gleu; *G.* Glauer; *Dch.* Glewink; *D.B.* Gleu, Gleuuin; p.n.

GLISTER. *D.* Glistrup; a loc. and p. n.

GLOAG. *See* Cloake

GLOSSOP. A loc. n., Derbysh.

GLYDE. *See* Gleed

GLYNNE. A loc. n., Cornw. Or *N.* Glenna, n.n.; *S.* Glenne; *D.* Glyhn; *Fr.* Glin; *Dch.* Glindt; p.n.

GOAD. *N.* Goddi (dimin. of comp. names, as Guð-run, etc.); *S.* Godha, Gohde; *G.* Göde; *D.* Goth; *Fl.* Gody, Gœdde; *Fr.* Godde, Goudé, Got; *Dch.* Goede, Götte; *D.B.* Code, Godde, Gote, Goda, Goti, Gouti; p.n.

Walter Gode occurs in Rot. Obl. et Fin., K. John.

GOADBY. A loc. n., Leics.

GOATE. *See* Goad

GOATLEY. From Godeley; a loc. n., Ches.

GOBBETT. From Gobit; a loc. n., Worcest. Or *F.* Garbert; *G.* Göbert; *Fl.* Gobert, Gobbet; *Dch.* Gobits; *D.B.* Godvert, Goisbert, Gausbert, Gosbert; p.n.

GOBBY. *See* Gobbett

GOBLE. *G.* Göbel; a p.n.

GODBEER. *G.* Gutbier; a p.n.

GODBOLD. *N.* Goðbaldr; *D.B.* Godebold; p.n.

GODBOLT. *See* Godbold

GODBY. *See* Goadby

GODDARD. *N.* Guð-ödr; *Fl.* Godart, Godet; *Dch.* Goddard; *D.*, *G.* Gotthard; *Fr.* Godard; *D.B.* Godet, Godard, Godred, Godrid; p.n.

GODFREY. *N.* Guðfriðr; *D.* Godfred; *D.B.* Godefrid; *Fr.* Godefroy; p.n.

GODING. *Dch.*, *Fl.* Godding; a p.n. *See* Goodwin

GODLEE. *See* Godley

GODLEY. A loc. n., Ches.

GODSON. From Godstone; a loc. n., Staffs. Or *see* Goad, Goodson

GOE. From Goé; a loc. n., Belgium

GOFF. *N.* Gjafvaldr (?); *Fl.* Goffart, Goffe; *G.* Göffi, Gaffert, Gaffarth, Geffarth; *D.B.* Geoffrey; p.n.

GOFFEN, GOFFIN. *G.* Göffwein; a p.n.

GOFT. *See* Goff

GOGGS. *D.B.* Gogan; *Dch.* Gog, Gokkes; p.n. *See* Gage

GOLD. *D.* Gold; *G.* Golde; p.n.

GOLDBY. From Coleby; a loc. n., Kent, Lincs

GOLDING. *G.* Golding; a p.n.

GOLDINGHAM. From Coldingham; a loc. n., Berwick

GOLDRIDGE. From Coleridge; a loc. n., Devon

GOLDRING. A *G.* p.n.
GOLDSBURY. From Goldsborough; a loc. n., Yorks
GOLDSWORTHY. A loc. n., Devon
GOLDTHORPE. A loc. n., Yorks
GOLDUP. *See* Goldthorpe
GOLDY. *G.* Golde; a p.n.
GOLIGHTLY. From Gellatly; a loc. n.
GOLL, GOLLE. *G.* Golla, Golli; p.n.
GOLLEDGE. *See* College
GOLLOP. *G.* Gollob; a p.n. *See* Gallop
GOMM. *G.;* p.n.
GONNER. *D.B.* Gonhard, Gonnar, Gonni, Gonuerd; p.n. *See* Gunn
GOOBY. *See* Goadby
GOOCH. *Dch.* Gootjes; a p.n. *See* Goodyer
GOODA. *Fr.* Goudeau; a p.n. *See* Goad
GOODACRE. From Goatacre; a loc. n., Wilts
GOODAY. *D.* Goday; *Fr.* Godet, Goudé; *D.B.* Goda; p.n. *See* Goad
GOODBAN. *N.* Guðbrandr; a p.n.
GOODBODY. *See* Gotobed
GOODCHAP. From Goodcheap; a loc. n., Kent
GOODCHILD. From Goodchill; a loc. n., Westmd. Or *G.* Gudschal; a p.n. (?)
GOODDY. *See* Goodday
GOODE. *See* Goad
GOODENOUGH. *Fr.* Godineau; a p.n.
GOODEY. *See* Goodday
GOODFELLOW. *Fr.* Goudaillier (?); a p.n.
GOODGER. *See* Goodyer
GOODHART. *See* Goddard
GOODING. *See* Gooda and Goad, or Goodwin
GOODLAD. A *Dch.* p.n.
GOODLIFFE. *N.* Guð-leif; p.n.
GOODMAN. *N.* Guðmundr; *S.* Gudmund; *D.* Gudmann; *F.* Goddeman, Goodman; *G.* Guttmann; *D.B.* Godman, Godmund, Gudmund; p.n.
GOODRICH. A loc. n., Heref.
GOODRICK. *N.* Guðrikr; *D.B.* Godric; p.n. *See* Goodrich
GOODRUM. *N* Guð-ormr; *A.S.* Guthrum; *G.* Gundrum; *Dch.* Gottmer; p.n.
GOODSON. A loc. n., Norf.
GOODWILL. From Goderville; a loc. n., Normandy
GOODWIN. *N.* Guð-vinr (good friend); *D.B.* Godwin; *Fl.* Goddyn, Goetinck, Goetvinck, Guttin; *Fr.* Goudinne, Godefin; *G.* Guttwein; p.n.

Goduin, a tenant in chief; *D.B.* Godinc, Goding, Goduin, Gotwin, under-tenants at time of Survey. Goding, Goduin, Saxon tenants, Edw. Conf. For varieties of spelling *see* Introduction.

GOODY. *Fr.* Goudé; a p.n. *See* Goad
GOODYER. *Fr.* Goudier; a p.n. Or *see* Goyder
GOOSE. *D.*, *Dch.* Goos; *Fl.* Gous; *Fr.* Gosse, Gouis; *S.* Gooes; *D.B.* Gos; p.n.
GOOSEY. *See* Goozee
GOOZEE. *Fr.* Guizy; a p.n.
GOPP. A loc. n., Flint
GORDON. A loc. n., Berwick
GORE. *N.* Gorr; *Dch.* Goor; a p.n.
GORING. A loc. n., Oxf., Suss.
GORMAN. *Dch.* Gortman; *Fl.* Gouman; *Fr.* Gourmont; p.n.
GORNALL. From Gortnell; a loc. n., Somers.
GORRILL. *D.* Gorell; *G.* Gorille; p.n.
GORTON. A loc. n., Lancs
GOSLING. *Dch.* Goseling; *Fr.* Gosselin; p.n. *See* Goss
GOSS. *S.* Gooes; *G.* Gosse, Gossel; *Dch.* Goos, Goes, Goseling; *Fl.* Gosselin, Gosse, Gossy, Goossens; *D.B.* Gos, Gozer, Gozlin, Goscelin, Godzelin; p.n.
GOSTELLOW. *See* Costello
GOTHORP. *See* Gawthorpe

GOTLEY. From Godley; a loc. n., Ches.

GOTLING. *See* Gooda and Goad

GOTOBED. *N.* Guðbjártr; *A.S.* Cuthbert; *D.B.* Gutbert; a p.n.

GOTSON. *See* Goodson

GOTTO. *See* Goad

GOTTS. *See* Goad

GOUK. *See* Gowk

GOULBURN. From Goulborn; a loc. n., Ches., Lancs

GOULD. *See* Gold

GOULDER. *N.* Gull-thorir (?); *S.* Gulda; *G.* Goldert; *D.B.* Goel, Golde, Golderon, Goldus; p.n.

GOUNDRY. *Fr.*, *Fl.* Gondry; a p.n.

GOW. *Dch.* Gouw; a p.n.

GOWEN. *Dch.* Goijen; *Fl.* Goens; p.n. *See* Gow

GOWER. A loc. n., S. Wales. Also a *G.* p.n.

GOWERS. *Dch.* Govers; *Fl.* Govaerts

Gower in Roll of Battell Abbey.

GOWING. *See* Gowen

GOWK. *N.* Gaukr; *G.* Gauck; *Fr.* Gouche; p.n.

GOWLAND. *See* Garland

GOWTHORPE. A loc. n., Yorks

GOWTHWAITE. A loc. n., Yorks

GOWTRIDGE. *See* Gutteridge

GOY. *Fl.* Goye; *Dch.* Goey; *Fr.* Gouy; p.n. *See* Joy. Gouy; a loc. n., Normandy

GOYDER. From Gwydyr or Gwydre; a loc. n., S. Wales. Or *G.* Geuther; *Dch.* Goede; p.n. *See* Goad

GOYMER. *See* Guymer

GOZZARD. *Fr.* Gozet, Gosset; p.n.

GRACEY, GRACIE. *Fr.* Gresy; p.n. From Graçay; a loc. n., France

GRADDON. *See* Gratton

GRADWELL. A loc. n.

GRAFHAM. A loc. n., Hunts

GRAFTON. A loc. n., Warw., Wilts, Yorks

GRAHAM. From Graham; a loc. n. near Kesteven, Lincs. Or *D.* Gram; a p.n.

William de Graham settled in Scotland in the twelfth century.

GRAIN. A loc. n., Kent. Or *Fr.* Graine; a p.n. *See* Green

GRAND. *Fr.* Grand; *D.B.* Grand; p.n.

GRANDISON. *Fr.* Grandjean (?); a p.n.

GRANGER. *Fr.* Grangé; a p.n.

GRANT. *See* Grand

GRANTHAM. A loc. n., Lincs

GRANTLEY. A loc. n., Yorks

GRAPES. *N.* Greipr; *S.* Grape; *G.* Gräber; *Dch.* Graap; *Fl.* Greps; p.n.

GRASBY. A loc. n., Lincs

GRATTAN. *See* Gratton

GRATTON. A loc. n., Devon

GRATTRIDGE. *See* Greatrex

GRAVATT. *Fl.* Grauwet; *Fr.* Gravet, Gravot; p.n.

GRAVE. *S.* Grave; *Dch.* Greeve, Greive; *G.* Gräve, Gräfe; *D.B.* Greve; p.n.

GRAVENER. *Fl.* Greven; p.n. *See* Greef

GRAVER. *Dch.* Greve; *Fr.* Gravé; p.n. *See* Greef

GRAVES. *D.*, *S.* Grave; *Dch.*, *G.* Gräve, Greeve; *Fl.* Gravis; *D.B.* Greve; p.n.

GRAVESTON. A loc. n. *See* Graves

GRAY. *Fr.* Grey; *G.* Graye; *D.B.* De Grai; p.n.

De Gray or Grai in Rot. Obl. et Fin., K. John.

GREAM. *D.*, *Dch.* Grim; a p.n. *See* Grimm

GREATHEAD. From Graithwaite; a loc. n., Lancs

GREATOREX. From Great Rocks; a hamlet, Tideswell, Derbysh. (?)

GREBBY. *Fr.* Grebert; *Dch.* Grebe; p.n.

GREEDAY. *Dch.* Greede; a p.n.

GREEF. *D.* Greiff; *Dch.* Griev, Greve; *Fl.* Greven; *G.* Grief; *D.B.* Griffin; p.n.
GREEN. *D.* Grün; *Dch.* Groen; *D.B.* Greno, Grino; p.n.
GREENAWAY. A loc. n., Devon. Or *N.* Gronveg; *Dch.* Groeneweg; loc. and p. n.
GREENHALGH. A loc. n., Lancs
GREENHOW. A loc. n., Yorks
GREENLEAF. *D.B.* Grunulf (?). Perhaps a corruption of the *N.* Grímólf
GREENSLADE. A loc. n., Devon
GREENSTREET. From Greenstead; a loc. n., Ess.
GREENWAY. A loc. n., Devon
GREENWELL. A loc. n., Yorks; or from Greenwill, a loc. n., Devon
GREER, GREIR. *Dch.* Greijr, Greier; a p.n.
GREET. A loc. n., Glost., Salop
GREETHAM. A loc. n., Rutland
GREEVES. *See* Grave
GREGG. From Gréges; a loc. n., France, Graig, Monmouth. Or *N.* Greager, Grieg; *D.* Greger; *G.* Gregor, Grieger, Kreck, Krex; *Fl.* Greck; *Fr.* Grégoire; p.n. *See* Grigg
GREIG. *See* Gregg
GRENHAM. From Greenham; a loc. n., Berks
GRENTO. *See* Grint
GRESLEY. A loc. n., Leics., Notts
Nigel, second son of Nigel de Toigni (afterwards de Stafford), took the name of de Gresley from his lordship of Gresley, Leics. De Grisele in Rot. Obl. et Fin., K. John.
GRESSWELL. *See* Cresswell
GRETTON. A loc. n., Glost., Northants, Salop
GREW. *Fr.* Grieu, Grout; *D.B.* Greue; *N.* Gro; *S.*, *D.* Groh; p.n.
GREX. *G.* Krex; p.n. *See* Gregg
GREY. *See* Gray
GRIBBLE. A loc. n., Devon
GRICE. *N.* Gris; *D.* Greis; *G.* Gries, Greis; *Fl.* Gries; p.n.
GRICKS. *See* Grix
GRIEF. *See* Greef
GRIGG. *Dch.* Griek, Kriek; p.n.
GRIGGS. A loc. n., Cornw. Or *see* Grix
GRIGSON. *See* Grigg
GRIMBLE. *Fr.* Grimoult; a p.n.
GRIMDITCH. A loc. n.
GRIME. *See* Gream
GRIMER. *See* Grimmer
GRIMES. *See* Grimmer
GRIMLEY. A loc. n., Worcest.
GRIMMER. *N.* Grimr; *D.*, *S.*, *Dch.*, *G.* Grimm, Grimmer; *D.B.* Grim, Grimbert; *Fr.* Grimont; p.n.
GRIMMETT. *Fr.* dimin. of Grim
GRIMMOND. *N.* Grimmundr; *Dch.* Grimmon; p.n.
GRIMOLDBY. A loc. n., Lincs
GRIMSDALE. From Grinsdale; a loc. n., Cumb.
GRIMSEY. From Grimsby; a loc. n., Lincs
GRIMSHAW. A loc. n., Yorks
GRIMSON. *See* Grimston
GRIMSTON. A loc. n., Leics., Norf., Yorks
GRIMTHORPE. A loc. n., Yorks
GRIMWADE. *See* Grimwood
GRIMWOOD. A loc. n., Suff.
GRINDLEY. A loc. n., Staffs.
GRINLING. *See* Grint
GRINSTED. From Grinstead; a loc. n., Kent, Suss.
GRINT. *S.* Gren; *Dch.* Grin, Groen; *Fl.* Grinaert; *G.* Grünert, Grün; p.n.
GRINTER. *Fr.* Grintel (?); a p.n.
GRISKS. *G.* Grischke; a p.n. *See* Grice
GRISS. *N.* Gríss; *N.*, *Fr.* Grisy; p.n. *See* Grice
GRISTOCK. From Greystock; a loc. n., Cumb.
GRISTON. A loc. n., Norf.
GRITTON, GRITTEN. *See* Gretton
GRIX. *Fl.* Krickx; *Dch.* Kriek; a p.n. *See* Grigg
GRIZEDALE. A loc. n., Yorks, Lancs

GROCOTT, GROWCUTT. *See* Groocock

GROGAN. A loc. n., Queen's Co., Ireland

GROMIT. *See* Groom

GROOCOCK. *G.* Groche; a p.n.

GROOM. *D.* Grum; *Dch.* Grummer; *Fr.* Grummeau; *G.* Crumm, Grummich; p.n.

GROSS. *D.* Gross; *Fl.* Groos, Gros; *Fr.* Grosse; *Dch.* Grosz; *D.B.* Grossus; p.n.

GROUND. *S.*, *G.* Grund; a p.n. Or *see* Grand

GROUT. *N.* Graut; *G.* Grutz, Kraut; *Dch.* Groot; *Fl.* Groeters, Groutars; *D.* Grude; p.n. *D.B.* Grutt, Grud. *See* Croote

GROVES. *D.* Grove; a p.n.

GROWSE. *Dch.* Graus; a p.n.

GRUBB. *D.* Grubb; *G.* Grube; *Dch.* Grob; p.n. Grube; a loc. n., Holstein

GRUEL. *D.* Groule; *S.*, *Dch.* Grewell; *Fr.* Gruelle; *G.* Greul, Grüel; *D.B.* Cruel; p.n.

Griuel in Roll of Battell Abbey.

GRUGGEN. From the Irish Grogan; a p.n.

GRUNDY. *D.* Gruntvig; *S.* Grundin; *G.* Grundey, Grundig; p.n.

GRYLLS. *S.* Grill; *G.* Griehl; *Fr.* Grille; p.n.

GUBBINS. *Fl.*; p.n.

GUBBY. *G.* Gubig; a p.n.

GUDGE. *Fr.* Gouge; a p.n.

GUDGEON. *Fl.*; a p.n. *See* Gudgin

GUDGIN. *D.* Gude; a p.n. Dimin. Gudchen. *See* Gooda

GUERIN. From Gueron; a loc. n. in Normandy

Gurry in Roll of Battell Abbey. Gerin, a tenant in chief in *D.B.*

GUEST. *Fr.* Guest; *Dch.* Gest; a p.n.

GUINNESS or MACGUINNESS. From the Irish Aongusa

Ancient lords of Iveagh, co. Down.

GUIVER. *Fr.* Guibert, Quivy (?); *D.B.* Guibert; p.n.

GULL. *D.* Goll; *G.* Gühl; p.n.

GULLIFORD. A loc. n., Devon

GULLY. *Fr.* Gully; *G.* Gülle, Gülich; p.n.

GUMBLETON. From Gomeldon; a loc. n., Wilts

GUMLEY. A loc. n., Leics.

GUMMER. *N.* Guð-ormr; *D.* Gummer; *D.B.* Gummar; a p.n.

GUNBY. A loc. n., Yorks

GUNDRY. *See* Goundry

GUNN. *N.* Gunnarr; *S.* Gunner; *Fl.* Guns; *D.B.* Gunnr, Gunse, Gunnine; p.n.

GUNNELL. *D.B.* Gunnild, Gun nulf; p.n *See* Gunn

GUNNER. *See* Gunn

GUNNERY. *See* Gunn

GUNNS. *See* Gunn

GUNSON. *S.* Gunnarson; *D.* Gunarson; p.n. *See* Gunn

GUNTON. A loc. n., Norf., Suff.

GUPPY. *Fl.* Goupy; a p.n.

GURLING. *See* Gerling

GURNER. *D.* Gerner; *Fl.* Gernet; p.n.

GURNEY. From Gournai; a loc. n., Normandy

Hugo de Gurnai, tenant in chief in *D.B.* (Essex).

GURRIN. *See* Guerin

GUSCOTTE. From Goscote; a loc. n., Staffs.

GUSH. *Fr.* Gouche; a p.n.

GUTHRIE. A loc. n., Forfar

GUTTERIDGE. *See* Goodrich

GUYMER. *Fl.* Ghémer or Guillemare (?); p.n. *See* Gamon

GWATKIN. The Welsh form of Watkin

GWILLYAM. *Fr.* Guillaume; p.n. Or the Welsh form of William

GYE. *Dch.* Guye; *G.* Goy; *Fr.* Gay; p.n.

GYFORD. *See* Gifford

GYTON. *See* Gayton

H.

HACKER. *N.* Hákr; *S.* Hake; *D.* Hackhe; *D.*, *G.* Hacke; *Fl.* Hacker; *D.B.* Hache; *Dch.* Hakker, p.n.

HACKETT. *Dch.* Hackert, Hakkert; *Fl.* Acket; p.n. *See* Hatchett

HACKNEY. A loc. n., Devon, Middlx.

HACKSHAW. *See* Hawkshaw

HACKWELL. A loc. n., Devon

HACKWILL. *See* Hackwell

HACKWOOD. A loc n., Devon

HACKWORTH. *See* Ackworth

HACON. *N.* Hákon; *F.* Hagen, Heiko, Heiken; *G.* Hache, Hake; *S.* Hake; *Fl.* Haaken; *Fr.* Hacquin; *D.B.* Hacon, Haco, Hago, Hache; p.n.

HADDAH. *D.* Hader; *Dch.* Ader; *S.* Hadders; *G.* Hader; p.n.

HADDAWAY. *See* Hathaway

HADDEN. *See* Haddon

HADDER. *See* Haddah

HADDESLEY. A loc. n., Yorks

HADDOCK. *See* Adcock

HADDON. A loc. n., Beds, Derbysh., Middlx., Northants

HADFIELD. A loc. n., Derbysh.

HADLEY. A loc. n., Herts, Middlx., Staffs.

HADLINGTON. *See* Adlington

HADOW, HADDOW. *F.* Haddo; *G.* Hader; p.n. *See* Haddah

HADWIN. *N.* Auðun (?); *F.* Adde; *D.B.* Hadewi, Haduuin; p.n.

HAGG. *See* Aggs

HAGGARD. *N.* Hagbarðr; *D.* Aaggaard; *S.* Hagert; *Dch.* Hageraats, Hakkert, Hagers, Hagoort, Hagt; *G.* Hoeger; *Fl.* Hager; *D.B.* Hago, Aghete (Lincs), Hagebert; p.n.

HAGGER. *See* Haggard

HAGGIE. *F.* Agge; *N.* Ögurr; *D.* Agier; *Fl.* Hager; p.n. *See* Aggs

HAGGIS. *See* Aggs

HAGGIT. *See* Haggard

HAGON. *See* Hacon

HAGRAM. From Hargham (?); a loc. n., Norf.

HAGREEN. *S.* Haggren, Hagren; p.n.

HAGUE. *Fl.* Huyghe; *Fr.* Hague; p.n.

HAILL. *See* Hale. Or *Fl.* Heyl; a p.n.

HAILSTONE. From Aylestone; a loc. n., Leics.

HAINES. *See* Haynes. Or *N.* Hein; *F.* Hein, Heini; *G.* Hein, Hain, Heine; *Dch.* Hens; *Fl.* Hennes; p.n.

HAKE. *Dch.* Heck; *Fl.* Haeck; p.n.

HAKEN. *See* Hacon

HALCRO. *N.* Hjallkárr (?); a p.n.

HALDANE. From Halden; a loc. n., Kent. Or *N.* Halfdan; a p.n.

HALE. A loc. n., Ches., Cornw., Hants, Lincs, Somers., Staffs., Yorks

HALES. A loc. n., Norf. Or *Dch.* Hales; *D.* Hallas, Halse, Hels; p.n.

HALESTRAP. *D.* Alstrup; a loc. and p. n.

HALFACRE. A loc. n., Devon. Or *N.* Hálfrekkr; a p.n.

HALFNIGHT. *G.* Elvenich (?); a p.n.

HALFORD. A loc. n., Devon, Warw.

HALFPENNY. *Dch.* Alphenaar; a p.n. *See* Alphen

HALFYARD. *N.* Álf-jótr; a p.n.

HALKET. From Halcote; a loc. n., Northants

HALL. *N.* Hallr; *D.*, *Dch.*, *S.* Hall; *Fl.* Hal; p.n.

HALLACK. *See* Hollick

HALLETT. *N.* Hallaðr; *Fr.* Hallett; p.n.
HALLIDAY. *S.* Helleday; a p.n.
HALLIFAX. From Halifax; a loc. n., Yorks
HALLIWELL. A loc. n., Lancs
HALLOCK. *See* Hall
HALLSTEAD. From Halstead; a loc. n., Ess., Kent, Leics.; *D.* Alsteed; *S.* Hallstedt; loc. and p. n. From *N.* Háls-staðr (Hall's Stead)
HALLUM. From Hallam; a loc. n., Derbysh., Notts, Yorks
HALLWARD. *N.* Hallvarðr; *S.* Hallbahr; *G.* Halfar; *D.* Halvor; *Fl.* Hallart; *Dch.* Haller; *D.B.* Alward, Aluert; p.n.
HALLYBONE. *See* Allbone
HALTON. A loc. n., Bucks
HAM. A loc. n., Dorset, Glost., Hants, Somers., Wilts. Or *S.*, *Dch.* Ham; a p.n.
HAMAWAY. From Hammerwick; a loc. n., Staffs. Or *Dch.* Hamwijk; a p.n.
HAMBLETON. Leics., Lincs, Surr., Yorks
HAMBLETT. *N.* Ambloði (Hamlet); a p.n.
HAMBLIN. *Dch.* Hamerling; a p.n.
HAMBY. From Hanby; a loc. n., Yorks. Or *D.* Hampe; *G.* Hempe; p.n.
HAMER. A loc. n., Lancs. Or *N.* Heimir (name of a Jarl); *F.* Heimo; *Fl.* Haemer; *D.B.* Haemer, Haimer; p.n.
HAMERTON. *See* Hammerton
HAMEY. *Fr.* Ameye, Hamiet; p.n.
HAMILTON. A loc. n., Scotl. Or Hambleton, Lincs; Hamelton, Yorks
HAMMACK. *Fl.* Hamecher; *Dch.* Hamacker; p.n.
HAMMANT. *See* Hammond
HAMMERSLEY. *D.* Hammerlev; *S.* Hammarlöw; *Dch.* Hamerslag; loc. and p. n.
HAMMERTON. A loc. n., Yorks
HAMMON. *See* Hammond
HAMMOND. *N.* Hámundr; *D.* Hamann; *G.* Hammann; *D.B.* Hame, Hamon, Hamine, Amund; p.n.
HAMPSON. *D.* Hampe; a p.n.
HAMPTON. A loc. n., Middlx., Warw., Worcest.
HAMSHAW. *See* Hamshire
HAMSHIRE. From Hampshire, the county
HANBURY. A loc. n., Staffs., Worcest.
HANCER. From Handsworth; a loc. n., Yorks (?)
HANCHETT. *Fl.* Hannecart, Hansett; p.n.
HAND. *G.* Hander; a p.n.
HANDFIELD. From Hanningfield; a loc. n., Ess.
HANDFORD. A loc. n., Staffs.
HANDLEY. A loc. n., Derbysh., Staffs.
HANDOVER. From Andover; a loc. n., Hants
HANEY. *See* Heney
HANFORD. A loc. n., Dorset, Staffs.
HANINGTON. A loc. n., Hants, Wilts
HANKEY. *Fl.* Hancke; a p.n. *See* Hanks
HANKINSON. *See* Hanks
HANKS. *F.* Anke; *Dch.* Hanke; *Fl.* Hancke, Hancq; *G.* Hanke, Hanko; p.n.
HANNAFORD. *See* Hanford
HANNAH. *N.* Hani, n.n.; *D.* Henne; *S.* Hane, Hanner; *Fl.* Hannart; *Fr.* Hany, Hannay; *G.* Hanner, Hannert; p.n.
HANNAM. From Harnham; a loc. n., Wilts (?)
HANNANT. *See* Heney and Hennant
HANNATH. From Hanworth; a loc. n., Suff.
HANNAY. *See* Hannah
HANNER. *S.* Hanner; a p.n. Or *see* Hannah and Heney

HANSELL. *S.* Hansell; a p.n. *See* Heney

HANSOM. *Fr.* Anceaume; a p.n.

HANSON. *D.* Hansen; *S.* Hanson; p.n. *See* Heney

HANWELL. A loc. n., Middlx.

HARBARD. *N.* Há-bjártr; a p.n.

HARBORD. *Dch.* Harbord; a p.n. *See* Harbard

HARBOTTLE. A loc. n., Northbd.

HARBOUR. *See* Harbard

HARBUTT. *See* Harbard

HARCOURT. A loc. n., Normandy
Harecourt in Roll of Battell Abbey.

HARCUM. From Harcomb; a loc. n., Devon

HARDACRE. *G.* Hardtke; a p.n. (?)

HARDAWAY. From Hardway; a loc. n., Hants, Somers.

HARDBOARD. *Dch.* Harbord; a p.n.

HARDCASTLE. From Hardencastle; Roxburghshire (?)

HARDEN. *See* Horden or Arden

HARDIMENT. *N.* Hjörtmundr; *D.*, *Fl.* Hardman, Hartman; *Dch.* Hardeman; *G.* Hartman; p.n.

HARDING. *N.* Haddingr; *D.* Harding; *S.* Hardin; p.n.
Harding, a tenant in chief in *D.B.*, held lands which he had occupied *temp.* Edw. Conf. in Glost., Somers., Wilts.

HARDMEAT. From Hardmead; a loc. n., Oxf.

HARDWICKE. A loc. n., Camb., Derbysh., Norf., Northants, Staffs., Warw., Worcest., Yorks

HARDY. *Fr.*; p.n. *See* Harding

HARE. *N.* Hár; *F.* Hére; *D.*, *G.* Herr; *Dch.* Haar; *Fl.* Hery; *D.B.* Her, Har; p.n.

HARFORD. A loc. n., Devon, Somers.

HARGRAVE. A loc. n., Northants, Suff.

HARGREAVES. A loc. n., Lancs

HARKAN. *See* Hacon

HARKER. A loc. n., Cumb.

HARKNESS. From Hackness; a loc. n., Yorks

HARKORT. *See* Harcourt

HARLAND. A loc. n., Caithness

HARLE. *N.* Erli; *F.* Harl; *G.* Erle, Erler; *S.* Harling, Ahrling, Erling, Ahl; *Dch.* Harlaar; *D.* Erleuin, Herlin; *D.B.* Herluin, Herling; p.n. *See* Earl

HARLEY. A loc. n., Salop. Or *Fr.* Harlé; a p.n.

HARLOCK. A loc. n., Lancs

HARMAN. *See* Hammond

HARMER. *See* Armes

HARNESS. *G.* Harnisch; a p.n.

HARPER. *N.* Erpr; *D.* Arp; *S.* Arpi, Hjerpe; *Dch.* Arp; *D.B.* Erp, Hapra; p.n.

HARPHAM. A loc. n., Yorks

HARPLEY. A loc. n., Norf. and Worcest.

HARRADEN. From Harrowden; a loc. n., Northants

HARRADINE. *See* Harrowden

HARRALD. *N.* Haraldr; *Dch.* Herold; p.n. Harrald; a loc. n., Beds

HARRINGTON. A loc. n., Cumb., Northants

HARRISON. *N.* Harri, dimin. of Harald; *D.B.* Har; p.n.

HARRIS. *N.* Harri; *Dch.* Harries; *Fl.* Hariche; p.n.

HARROD. *See* Harwood or Howard

HARROP. From Harehope; a loc. n., Northbd.

HARSAM. *See* Hearsum

HARSANT. *D.* Herschend; *Fl.* Herssen; p.n.

HARSTON. A loc. n., Camb., Leics.

HART. *N.* Hjörtr; *S.* Hjerta; *D.* Harth; *Dch.* Hart; *G.* Hart, Herte; *D.B.* Artor, Hard; p.n.

HARTCUP. *G.* Hartkopf; p.n. *See* Hart

HARTLEY. A loc. n., Kent, Northbd. Or Hardley, Norf.

HARTOPP. From Hartoft; a loc. n., Yorks

HARTSHORNE. A loc. n., Derbysh.

HARTWELL. A loc. n., Bucks

HARVARD. *N.* Hávarðr; *S.* Herouard; *Dch.* Herwaarde, Huart; *Fl.* Heywaert; Houward, Huaert; *G.* Hofert, Hoffarth; *D.B.* Hauuard, Hereward, Huard; *Fr.* Houard, Huard; p.n.

HARVEY. *N.* Hávarr (?); *D.* Hartvig; *Fl.* Harvig; *Fr.* Hervé; p.n.

William Hervei in Rot. Obl. et Fin., K. John.

HARWOOD. A loc. n., Lancs and Yorks. Or *see* Howard

HASE. *G.* Hase; p.n.

HASELDINE. From Hazledine; a loc. n., Worcest.

HASELL. From Hasle; a loc. n., Yorks. Or *see* Hazle

HASLAM. From Asheldham; a loc. n., Ess. Or Hasland (?); a loc. n., Derbysh., Devon

HASLEDEN. *See* Haseldine

HASLEHAM. *See* Haslam

HASLEWOOD. A loc. n., Yorks

HASLOCK. *See* Hasluck

HASLOP. *See* Heslop

HASLUCK. *D.* Hasselfluck (?); a p.n.

HASLUP. *See* Heslop

HASSALL. A loc. n., Ches.

HASSARD. *D.* Hassert; *Fl.* Hasaert; p.n. *See* Hazzard

HASTED. From Ashstead; a loc. n., Surr. Or Hawstead, Suff.

HASTING. From an island off the coast of Normandy

In Roll of Battell Abbey. De Hasting in Rot. Obl. et Fin., K. John.

HASTINGS. A loc. n., Suss.

HASTWELL. *See* Haswell

HASWELL. A loc. n., Dur.

HATCH. A loc. n., Beds, Kent, Somers.

HATCHAM. A loc. n., Middlx.

HATCHER. *G.* Hatscher; a p.n. Or *see* Hatchett

HATCHETT. *N.* Haki; a mythical p.n. (a hook). *S.* Hake; *D.* Haak; *G.* Hake, Hatscher; *Fl.* Hack, Hacker; *Fr.* Hachez, Hache, Hachette; *Dch.* Hackert; *D.B.* Achi, Hache; p.n. *See* Hacket

Achard and Haket in Rot. Obl. et Fin., K. John.

HATE. *Fl.* Het; a p.n.

HATFIELD. A loc. n., Ess., Herts, Worcest., Yorks

HATHAWAY. *See* Ottaway

HATHERLEY. From Hatherleigh; a loc. n., Devon

HATT. *N.* Höttr; *D.* Hatte; *F.* Hatto; *D.B.* Hato; p.n.

HATTEN. *See* Hatting or Hatton

HATTERLEY. A loc. n., Ches.

HATTERSLEY. *See* Haddesley

HATTING. *D.*; p.n.

HATTON. A loc. n., Middlx., Staffs.

HAUGHTON. A loc. n., Dur., Staffs.

HAVELL, HAVILL. *See* Hovel

HAVERS. *N.* Hávarr; *Dch.* Havers; p.n. Or Hever; a loc. n., Kent

HAVILAND. *G.* Haveland; a p.n. Or Haverland; a loc. n., Norf.

HAWARD. *See* Harvard

HAWKES. From Hawkers; a loc. n., Northbd. Or *see* Auker

HAWKINS. From Hawking; a loc. n., Kent

Osbert de Hawking, *temp.* Henry II.

HAWKRIGG. A loc. n., Westmd.

HAWKSHAW. A loc. n., Lancs

HAWKSLEY. A loc. n., Somers. Or Hauxley; Northbd.

HAWKSWORTH. A loc. n., Yorks

HAWORTH. A loc. n., Yorks

HAWS. From Hawes; a loc. n., Yorks

HAWTHORN. A loc. n., Lincs

HAXALL. *See* Haxell

HAXELL. From Exwell; a loc. n., Rutl. Hackensall, Lancs

HAY. A loc. n., Staffs. *See* Heyhoe

HAYCOCK. A hill in Cumb. Or *Dch.* Haeij-Koch; a p.n.
HAYCROFT. A loc. n., Dorset
HAYES. A loc. n., Salop. Also *Dch.* Hees; a p.n.
HAYGREEN. A loc. n., Yorks
HAYLES. A freq. loc. n. *See* Hales
HAYLEY. From Haylie; a loc. n., Largs, Scotl.
HAYNES. A loc. n., Beds, Devon. *See* Haines
HAYTER. *See* Haytor
HAYTOR. A loc. n., Derbysh.
HAYWARD. *See* Harvard
HAZARD. *See* Hassard
HAZELRIGG. A loc. n., Northbd.
HAZLE. *S.* Hasle; *D.* Hassel; *Dch.* Hazel; *G.* Hessell; *D.B.* Hezelin; p.n.
HAZZARD. From Hazard; a loc. n., Devon. *See* Hassard
HEACOCK. *See* Haycock
HEAD. *N.* Heidr; *D.* Heede, Heide; *G.* Heder, Hede; p.n.
HEADIN. *S.* Hedin; *Dch.* Hedden; *G.* Hedin; p.n. *See* Head
HEADLAM. A loc. n., Dur.
HEADLEY. A loc. n., Hants, Surr., Worcest.
HEAGREEN. *See* Haygreen
HEAL. A loc. n., Surr.
HEALEY. A loc. n., Northbd., Yorks
HEANEY. *See* Heney
HEAP. *F.* Ippe; *G.* Hippe; *Dch.* Hiep; p.n.
HEARNE. A loc. n., Kent, Surr.
HEARSUM. From Hersham; a loc. n., Surr.
HEASELL. *See* Hasell and Hazle
HEATH. A loc. n., Derbysh., Yorks, etc.
HEATHCOTE. A loc. n., Derbysh.
HEATHER. A loc. n., Leics.
HEATLEY. A loc. n., Staffs.
HEATON. A loc. n., Ches., Lancs, Staffs.
HEAVEN. *See* Evan
HEAVENS. *See* Evans
HEAVER. *Fl.* Heyvaert; a p.n.
HEBB. *Fl.* Hebbe; *F.* Ebbe; p.n.
HEBBERT. *Dch.* Ebert; a p.n. *See* Hibbert
HEBBLETHWAITE. *See* Ablewhite
HEBGIN. *F.* Ebo, Ebbo, Ebbe, Ebken; *S.* Hebbe; *G.* Ebbeke, Heppe; p.n.
HECKFORD. From Hackforth; a loc. n., Yorks; *D.B.* Acheford
HEDACH or HEADECH. *N.* Heidrekr; a p.n.; *D.B.* Ederic, Edic; *D.* Heyderick; *Fl.* Heiderih; *G.* Heydrick, Heyduck, Hedicke; p.n. *See* Hettich
HEDDERLEY. *See* Adderley
HEDDERWICK. From Hedrick; a loc. n., Dur. (?)
HEDGE. *Dch.*, *G.* Heege; a p.n.
HEDGECOCK. *G.* Hedtke (?); a p.n.
HEDGELAND. *D.* Hegeland, Hegge-lund; *S.* Hägglund; loc. and p. n.
HEDGES. *See* Etches
HEEPS. *See* Heap
HEFFER. *N.* Evarr; *F.* Eve; *G.* Heffe; p.n.
HEFFILL. *S.* Hedvil; a p.n.
HEFFORD. *D.* Heerfordt; a p.n.
HEGGS. *D.*, *Dch.* Eggers; a p.n. *See* Eggs
HELLERAY. *See* Elleray
HELLING. *F.* Elle, Ellen; *S.* Helin, Helling; *Fl.* Hellin, Hellings; *D.B.* Eluine; p.n.
HELM. *N.* Hjálmr; *S.* Helmer, Hjelm; *Fl.*, *G.* Helm; *D.B.* Elmar, Elmer; p.n.
HELMORE. From Elmore; a loc. n., Glost. Or *N.* Hjalmr; *S.*, *Fl.* Helmer; *D.B.* Elmer; p.n.
HELMSLEY. A loc. n., Yorks
HELSHAM. From Hailsham; a loc. n., Suss.
HELY. *See* Healey
HEMANS. *See* Hemmans
HEMERY. *Fl.* Hemeryck; *Dch.* Emmerich; a loc. and p. n.

HEMINGWAY. From Hemingby; a loc. n., Lincs

HEMMANS. *N.* Hemingr; a p.n. *Dch.* Hemminga; *F.* Emmen; *Fl.* Heman; *G.* Hemens, Heymann; *S.* Hemming; p.n.

HEMMANT. *See* Hammond

HEMMENT. *See* Hammond

HEMMINGTON. From Hemington; a loc. n., Leics.

HEMS. *See* Ames

HEMSTEAD, HEMSTED. From Hempstead; a loc. n., Ess., Glost.

HEMSWORTH. A loc. n., Yorks

HEMUS. *See* Ames

HENCHMAN. *G.* Heinzmann; a p.n.

HENDERSON. *See* Hendry

HENDRA, HENDREY, HENDRY. *N.* Endriði; *F.* Hinderk; *G.* Henry, Hendric; *Dch.* Hendrik; *D.B.* Henric; p.n.

HENEY. *See* Henny

HENGULF. *See* Ingle

HENN. *D.* Henne; *Fl.* Hen; p.n.

HENNANT. *Dch.* Hent; a p.n.

HENNELL. From Henlle; a loc. n., Salop

HENNESY. From the Irish O'h Aengusa; a p.n.

HENNY. A loc. n., Ess.

HENSHAW. A loc. n., Northbd.

HEPBURN. A loc. n., Northbd.

HEPHER. *See* Heffer

HEPPLEWHITE. *See* Ablewhite

HEPTONSTALL. A loc. n., Lancs

HEPWORTH. A loc. n., Suff., Yorks

Stephen de Hepworth, Chancellor of Cambridge University A.D. 1257-99. Adam de Heppeworth, Yorks (formerly de Belmont) assumed the name with the manor A.D. 1303.

HERBAGE. *G.* Herbich, Herbig; *Dch.* Herberich; *Fl.* Herbecq; p.n.

HERRICK. *Fr.* de Héricher; a p.n.

HERRING. *D.* Herring; *S.* Herrling; *Fl.* Herinckx; *Fr.* Herinne; *G.* Häring; p.n. From *N.* Hjörr

HERSUM. *See* Hearsum

HESELTINE. *See* Haseldine

HESKETH. A loc. n., Lancs

HESLAM. *See* Haslam

HESLOP. A loc. n., Derbysh.

HETHERINGTON. A loc. n., Cumb.

HETTICH. *See* Headach

HEUGH. *See* Hughes

HEUSTICE. *See* Eustace

HEWES. *See* Hughes

HEWETT. *Fr.* Huet, Huett; a Huguenot n.

HEWISH. From Huish; a loc. n., Devon, Somers. Or *Dch.* Huis, Huysse; *Fr.* Huez; p.n.

HEWITT. *See* Hewett

HEWKE. *See* Hook

HEXTALL. *See* Hextell

HEXTELL. A loc. n., Staffs.

HEY. From Hay; a loc. n., Staffs.

HEYCOCK. *See* Haycock

HEYGATE. *D.* Hoegaard; *Fl.* Heegaerts; *G.* Heygütte; *Dch.* Hegt; *S.* Hegart; p.n.

HEYHOE. *F.* Hayo, Heie, Hei, *S.* Ey; *Dch.* Heij; *G.* Hey, Heyer; p.n.

HIBBINS. *F.* Ibo, Ibe, fam. n., Ibben; p.n.

HIBBIT. *See* Hibbert

HIBBLE. *Dch.* Hibbel; *G.* Hiebel; p.n.

HIBGANE. *See* Hebgin

HIBLING. *Dch.* Hibelen

HICHENS. *S.*; p.n.

HICK. *F.* Iko, Ike, Iken; *Dch.* Hikke; *Fl.* Ickx; p.n.

HICKEY. *Dch.* Hikke; a p.n.

HICKLING. A loc. n., Notts

HICKMAN. *Dch.* Heckman, Hekman; p.n. *See* Hick

HICKS. *See* Hick

HICKSON. *See* Hick

HIDDELSTON. *See* Huddleston

HIDE. From Hyde; a loc. n., Middlx. Or *N.* Heidr; *D.*, *G.*, *Dch.* Heide, Heyde; p.n.

HIGGIN. *F.* Iggs, Iggen; p.n.

HIGH. From Haigh; a loc. n., Lancs

HIGHAM. A loc. n., Kent, Lancs, Leics., Northants

HIGMAN. *Dch.* Eggeman; a p.n.

HILARD. *See* Hildyard

HILDERSLEY. From Yeldersley; a loc. n., Derbysh.

HILDYARD. *D.* Hilleraad; *G.* Hilger; p.n.

HILES. *D.* Heil; *Dch.* Heillers; *Fl.* Heilaerts; p.n.

HILEY. From Highley; a loc. n., Salop

HILL. A loc. n., Hants, etc. Or *D.*, G. Hille; *Fl.* Hil; p.n.

HILLEARY. *See* Elleray

HILLEN. A *Dch.* p.n. *See* Hill

HILLIARD. *See* Hildyard

HILLYARD. *See* Hildyard

HILLYER. *See* Hildyard

HILTON. A loc. n., Derbysh., Dorset, Lancs, Staffs.

HIMUS. *See* Ames

HINCHLIFFE. A loc. n., Yorks

HINDE. *G.* Heinz; a p.n.

HINDLE. *Dch.* Hindael; a p.n.

HINDLEY. A loc. n., Lancs

HINDRIE. *See* Hendry

HINDSON. *S.* Hinderson; a p.n.

HINE. *D.* Hein; *G.* Heine; p.n.

HINER. *G.* Heine; a p.n.

HINGE. *D.* Hingé; *G.* Hinze; *Dch.* Hinse; p.n.

HINNEL. *See* Hennell

HIPKIN. *See* Hipper

HIPPER. *F.* Hibbo, Hibbe; *G.* Hippe, Hipper, Ibich; *Dch.* Hipken; *Fl.* Hippert; *D.B.* Ibi; p.n.

HIPPERSON. *See* Hipper

HIPSLEY. From Ipsley; a loc. n., Warw., Worcest.

HIRD. *D.* Herth; *S.* Hierta; *Fl.* Herdies; *Dch.* Heerde; *G.* Hirt; p.n.

HISBENT. *D.* Isbrand; a p.n.

HISCOX. *See* Hitch

HITCH. *Fl.* Hittecher; a p.n.

HITCHCOCK. *See* Hitch

HIVES. St. IVES; a loc. n., Cornw., Hunts

HOADLEY. From Hoathley; a loc. n., Suss.

HOARE. From Oare; a loc. n., Kent. Or Ore, Suss.

HOBART. *See* Hubbard

HOBBES, HOBBS. *See* Hobbis

HOBBINS. *Dch.* Obbens; *Fl.* Hobin, Hoeben; p.n.

HOBBIS. From Hobbies; a loc. n., Norf. Or *Dch.* Obbes; a p.n.

HOBBLE. *D.* Hobolth; *Dch.* Hobbel; *Fl.* Houbel; p.n.

HOBEN. *G.* Hoben; *Dch.* Hobben; p.n.

HOBHOUSE. *See* Hobbis

HOBKIRK. A loc. n., Roxburghsh.

HOBLYN. *Fr.* Houblinne, Oblin; p.n.

HOBOURN. From Holborn; a loc. n., Middlx.

HOBSON. *D.* Obbe; a p.n.

Leuric Hobbesune, a Saxon tenant in *D.B.* (Suff.).

HOCKLEY. A loc. n., Derbysh., Ess.

HODDS. *See* Hoddy

HODDY. *N.* Oddi; *F.* Ode, Oddo; *D.* Odde, Odder, Otzen; *Fl.* Hody; *Dch.* Hoddes; *D.B.* Ode, Oda, Oddard, Odesune; p.n.

HODGERS. *See* Odgers

HODGSON. *N.* Odd-geirr; *D.B.* Oger; p.n.

HODSKINSON. *See* Hoddy

HOFF. *S.*, *D.*, *Fl.*, *Dch.*, *G.* Hoff; a p.n.

HOGAN. From the Irish O'h-Ogain; a p.n. Or *Dch.*, *Fl.* Hoogen; a p.n.

HOGARTH. *See* Hoggarth

HOGBEN. *S.* Hagerbonn; *D.B.* Haghebern; p.n. Or *see* Ogben

HOGG. *Dch.* Hoog; *Fl.* Hogger; *D.B.* Hoga, Hock; *G.* Hoch, Hocher; p.n. *See* Haggard and Ogg

HOGGARTH. *N.* Hofgarðr; *Fl.* Hogger; Hoogaerts; *D.* Hofgaard; *D.B.* Hofward, Hoga; *Fr.* Hocquart; p.n.

HOGGER. *Fl.*; p.n. *See* Hoggarth
HOGGETT. *See* Hoggarth
HOLBECHE. From Holbeach; a loc. n., Lincs. Or *D.* Holbech; a loc. and p. n.
HOLBECK. A loc. n., Notts
HOLBROOK. A loc. n., Derbysh., Yorks
HOLCOMBE. A loc. n., Devon, Somers.
HOLCROFT. A loc. n., Lancs
HOLDAM. From Oldham; a loc. n., Lancs
HOLDAWAY. From Holdawit; a loc. n., Cornw.
HOLDEN. A loc. n., Yorks. Or *S.* Hollden; *D.* Holten; p.n.
HOLDERNESS. A loc. n., Yorks
HOLDITCH. A loc. n., Devon, Dorset
HOLDOM. *See* Holdam
HOLDON. *See* Holden
HOLDRON. *See* Oldring
HOLDSWORTH. A loc. n., Yorks
HOLE. A loc. n., Cornw.
HOLEYMAN. *Dch., Fl.* Hollemann; a p.n.
HOLGATE. A loc. n., Lancs, Yorks
HOLKER. A loc. n., Lancs
HOLKHAM. A loc. n., Norf.
HOLL. *N.* Halli; *S.* Hall; *G.* Hall, Haller; *Dch.* Holl, Holk; *D.B.* Ala; p.n.
HOLLAND. From Hulland (*D.B.* Holund); a loc. n., Derbysh. Or *Dch., Fl.* Holland; a p.n.
HOLLEY. *Fl.* Holle; a p.n.
HOLLICK. *D.* Holck; *Dch.* Hollak; *G.* Hallisch, Holleck; p.n.
HOLLIDAY. *See* Halliday
HOLLINGHAM. From Holdingham; a loc. n., Lincs
HOLLINGSHEAD. From Hollingsend; a loc. n., Yorks. Or Hollinswood; a loc. n., Salop (?)
HOLLINGSWORTH. *See* Hollingworth
HOLLINGWORTH. A loc. n., Lancs
HOLLOMON. *See* Hollyman
HOLLOWAY. A loc. n., Warw.
HOLLYMAN. *Dch., Fl.* Holleman; *G.* Ohlmann; *S.* Ollman; *D.* Hollman; p.n.
HOLMES. A loc. n., Lancs. Or *D., S., Dch., G.* Holm; *Fl.* Holms; *D.B.* Holmo; p.n. From *N.* Holm, an islet in a lake or river
HOLROYD. From Holyrood; a loc. n., Lancs
HOLTBY. A loc. n., Yorks
HOLTHUM. From Haltham; a loc. n., Lincs. Or *D.* Holtum; a loc. and p. n.
HOLTOM. *See* Holthum
HOMBERSLEY. From Ombersley; a loc. n., Worcest.
HOMFRAY. *N.* Holmfriðr; *G.* Humpfer, Humphrey; p.n.
HOLT. A loc. n., Norf. Or *Dch.* Holt; *S.* Holter; *D.* Holte, Holde; *G.* Holdt; p.n.
HOLYOAKE. A loc. n., Staffs.
HONEYCHURCH. A loc. n., Devon
HONSLOWE. From Hounslow; a loc. n., Middlx. Or *see* Onslow
HONYWILL. From Honeywell; a loc. n., Devon
HOOD. *N.* Udi; *F.* Udo, Ude; *D.* Hude; *G.* Hudy; *Dch.* Ouda; *D.B.* Udi, Eudo; p.n.
HOOK. A loc. n., Hants. Or *N.* Húkr; *F.* Uko, Uke; *G.* Hücke, Hucke, Huck; *S.* Huch; *Dch.* Hoek; *Fr.* Hucq; *D.B.* Hueche, Hoch; p.n.
HOOKER. *See* Hook
HOOKWAY. A loc. n., Devon
HOOLE. A loc. n., Lancs
HOOPER. A loc. n., Cornw.
HOOPPELL. From Upwell (Camb.) or Uphill (Kent)
HOPE. A loc. n., Derbysh., Heref., Salop, N. Wales, Yorks. Or *Dch.* Hoop, Hop; p.n.
HOPKING. *Dch.* Hoppe, Hop, Höpken; p.n.
HOPKINS. *See* Hopking
HOPKIRK. *See* Hobkirk

HOPPER. *D.*, *Dch.* Hoppe, Hopper; *G.* Hoppe; *D.B.* Hapra; p.n.

HOPSON. *See* Hopking and Hobson

HOPTON. A loc. n., Yorks

HOPWOOD. A loc. n., Lancs

HORN. *N.* Hjörn or Örn; *D.*, *S.*, *Dch.*, *G.* Horn; *D.B.* Horne; p.n.

HORNBLOW. From Hornblotton; a loc. n., Somers. (?). Or Horninglow, Derbysh.

HORNBLOWER. *See* Hornblow

HORNBY. A loc. n., Lancs, Yorks

HORNER. *S.* Horner; a p.n. *See* Horn

HORNEY. *S.* Horney; a p.n. *See* Horn

HORNINGHOLD. A loc. n., Rutl.

HORNSBY. *See* Ormsby

HORNSEY. A loc. n., Middlx.

HOROBIN. *N.* Örrabeinn; a n.n. (scar-leg)

HORREX. *N.* Orækja or Há-rekr; *Dch.*, *Fl.* Horrickx; p.n. Or Orrek; n.n.

HORSEBURGH. A loc. n., Tweeddale

HORSELL. A loc. n., Surr. Or *Fr.* Oursel; a p.n.

HORSENAIL. *Fr.* D'Arsenel (?); a p.n.

HORSEPOLE. From Herspool; a loc. n., Cornw.

HORSEY. A loc. n., Ess., Norf.

HORSFIELD. From Horfield; a loc. n., Glost.

HORSFORD. A loc. n., Norf.

HORSHAM. A loc. n., Norf., Suss.

HORSINGTON. A loc. n., Lincs, Somers.

HORSLEY. A loc. n., Camb., Surr., Yorks

HORSWELL. *See* Horsell

HORTH. From Horwath or Hoath; a loc. n., Kent. Or *see* Hart

HORTON. A loc. n., Kent, Surr., Yorks

HORYAN. *Fr.* Horion; a p.n.

HOSGOOD. *N.* Ásgautr; *D.B.* Auesgot, Osgot, Osgod; p.n.

Tenant in chief in *D.B.* Richard Ausgod in Rot. Obl. et Fin., K. John.

HOSKINS, HOSKYNS. *Dch.* Huskens; a p.n.

HOTCHKIN. *See* Hodgkin

HOTINE. *Fr.* Autin; a p.n.

HOTSON. From Hoddesdon; a loc. n., Herts. Or *see* Hoddy

HOUCHEN. *See* Huggin

HOUGHTON. A loc. n., Beds, Dur., Lancs, Norf., Northants

HOULGRAVE. From Youlgreave; a loc. n., Derbysh.

HOULTON. *See* Hulton

HOUSEHOLD. *G.* Hauschild; a p.n. Or Howsell; a loc. n., Worcest.

HOUSTON. *Fl.* Houstonn; a p.n. Or *see* Owston

HOVELL. *Dch.* Hoevel; *D.* Howalt; p.n.

HOW. *See* Howe

HOWARD. *See* Harvard

HOWARTH. *See* Horth

HOWE. A loc. n., Norf., Yorks. From *N.* *haugr*; a cairn over one dead. Or *D.* Hau, Hou; p.n.

HOWELL. A loc. n., Lincs

HOWES. *Dch.* House; a p.n. *See* Howe

HOWGHIN. *See* Huggin

HOWITT. *D.* Howitz; *Dch.* Hoet; *Fl.* Hauwaert, Houwaert, Huart; p.n. *See* Howard

HOWLETT. *See* Hullett

HOWSTON. *See* Owston

HOY. *See* Heyho

HUARTSON. *See* Huard

HUBBARD. *N.* Ubbi; *F.* Ubbo, Ubbe; *D.B.* Hubert, Hubi, Hubb, Hubald; *G.* Huber, Hüba, Hubert; *Fl.* Houba, Houbard; *Fr.* Houbart; *Dch.* Huber; p.n.

HUBBLE. *Fl.* Houbel; *G.* Hübel; *D.B.* Hubald, Hubold; p.n.

HUBERT. *See* Hubbard

HUBY. *See* Hubbard

HUCKER. *See* Hook

HUCKLE. From Ughill; a loc. n., Yorks

HUCKLEBRIDGE. *Fl.* Hucklenbroich; a p.n.

HUDBUD. *See* Hubbard

HUDD. *See* Hood

HUDDEN. *Dch.* Uden; *Fl.* Utten; p.n.

HUDDLESTONE. From Huddleston; a loc. n., Yorks

Nigel de Hudelston was Provost of the Archbishop of York, A.D. 1110. Sir Richard de Hodelston was living at his manor house of Huddleston in 1262.

HUDGELL. *See* Hugill

HUDSON. *N.* Udr; *D.* Hude; *S.* Udden; *F.* Udo, Ude; *Dch.* Uden, Udsen; *Fl.* Hudson, Hudsyn; *D.B.* Udi; p.n.

HUFF. From Hough; a loc. n., Yorks

HUGGARD. *See* Hoggarth

HUGGETT. From Huggate; a loc. n., Yorks

HUGGINS. *N.* Hugi or Uggi; *F.* Uko, Uke, Uken; *Dch.* Hoogen, Huygens; *G.* Huge, Hugo; *Fl.* Hugens; *D.B.* Hugh, Hugo, Hugolin; p.n.

HUGHES. *N.* Hugi; *D.* Huhs; *Dch.* Hugues; *D.B.* Hugo; p.n.

HUGILL. A loc. n., Westmd.

HUGMAM. *N.* Ögmundr; *Fl.* Houman; *Dch.* Haagman, Homan, Human; *D.* Hageman; *Fl.* Haakman; *D.B.* Agemund; p.n.

HUKE. *See* Hook

HULKE. *G.* Ulke; a p.n.

HULLAH. From the Irish O'h-Oiliolla; a p.n.

HULLETT. *Fr.* Houllet, Hulet; *D.* Uhlott; *Dch.* Uloth; p.n.

HULLEY. *Fr.* Hulet; a p.n.

HULTON. A loc. n., Lancs

Bleythen de Hulton was lord of the manor *temp.* Hen. II. Jorvet de Hulton in Rot. Obl. et Fin., K. John, A.D. 1199.

HULVER. *See* Hildyard

HUMAN. *See* Hugman

HUMBY. A loc. n., Lincs

HUMBLE. *D.* Humble, Hummel; *Fr.* Humblet; p.n.

HUME. A loc. n., Berwick

HUMM. *G.*, *Dch.* Humme; p.n. From Humme; a loc. n. in Hesse Cassel

HUMMERSTON. From Humberstone; a loc. n., Leics., Lincs

HUMPHREY. *See* Homfray

HUNN. *N.* Unnr; *G.* Huhn; p.n.

HUNNIBELL. *D.* Hannibal; *Fl.* Hungerbuhler (?); a p.n.

HUNNYBUN. From Honeybourne; a loc. n., Worcest.

HUNT. *N.* Hundi; *G.* Hund, Hundt, Hunder; *Dch.* Hunt, Hunter; *D.B.* Hunta; p.n.

HUNTER. *See* Hunt

HUNTINGDON. County town, Hunts

HUNTLY. A loc. n., Aberdeensh., Staffs.

HUPTON. From Upton; a loc. n., Devon, Norf., etc.

HURLESTONE. A loc. n., Ches.

HURLOCK. From Harlock; a loc. n., Lancs

HURLY. From Hurley; a loc. n., Berks

HURN. *See* Hearn and Horn

HURNARD. *N.* Arnodd; *Fl.* Hernadain, Arnoeyd; *Fr.* Arnaud; p.n.

HURNDALL. *See* Arundel

HURRAN. *See* Uren

HURRELL. *Fr.* Hurel; a p.n. *See* Orrell

HURRING. *See* Herring

HURSAM. *See* Hearsum

HURST. A freq. loc. n.

HURY. A loc. n., Yorks. Or from Urray; a loc. n., Ross. Or *Fr.* Huré, Huret, Hurey; p.n.

HUSBAND. From Husborne (?); a loc. n., Beds

Simon Huseband in Rot. Obl. et Fin., K. John.

HUSE. *See* Hughes

HUSKISSON. *See* Hodgkinson

HUSON. *See* Hughes
HUSSEY. *Fr.* Houssaye; from *N.-Fr.* de Hossé or de Heuzé; a p.n.
HUSTHWAITE. A loc. n., Yorks
HUSTWAIT. *See* Husthwaite
HUSTWITT. *See* Husthwaite
HUTCHINGS. *Fl.* Huygens; a p.n. *See* Huggins
HUTCHINSON. *See* Hutchins
HUTH. *D.* Huth; *Fl.* Hutt; a p.n.
HUTHWAITE. A loc. n., Cumb.
HUTT. *D.*, *Dch.* Huth; a p.n. *See* Huth
HUTTON. A loc. n., Somers., Westmd., Yorks
HUXFORD. A loc. n., Devon
HUXHAM. A loc. n., Devon
HUXLEY. A loc. n., Ches.
HYAM. From Eyam; a loc. n., Derbysh. Or *see* Higham
HYATT. From Ayott; a loc. n., Herts. Or *Fl.* Hyart; a p.n.
HYE. *Dch.* Heije; a p.n. *See* Heyho
HYLTON. From Hilton; a loc. n., Staffs. and Suff. Or *S.* Hylten; a p.n.
HYMERS. *See* Emmes
HYMUS. *See* Emmes
HYNE. From the Irish O'h-Eidhin; a p.n. Also Heyne

I.

I'ANSON. *See* Johnson
IBBERSON. *F.* Ibo, Hibbo; *D.* Ibsen; p.n. Or Ibstone; a loc. n., Oxf. (?)
IBBOTSON. *See* Hibbert
ICELY. From Isley; a loc. n., Leics. Or Islip; Northants, Oxf.
ICKE. *Dch.* Icke; *F.* Ikke; p.n.
IDDON. *N.* Iðunn; *S.* Idun; *F.* Hiddo, Ide, Hidden, Iden; p.n. Iden; a loc. n., Suss.
IDE. A loc. n., Devon. Or *F.*, *D.*, *Dch.*; p.n.
IDLE. A loc. n., Yorks
IFE. *See* Ivatt and Ives
IGGLESDEN. *See* Iggulden
IGGULDEN. From Ickleton; a loc. n., Camb. Or Hickleton, Yorks
ILBERRY. From Hilbury; a loc. n., Ches. Or Hilborough, Norf.
ILDERTON. A loc. n., Northbd.
ILETT. *Fl.* Heylaert; *G.* Heilert; *N.* Egilharð; *F.* Eilert, Eilt
Æluert, a tenant in chief in *D.B.*
ILIFF. *See* Ayliffe
ILLING. *G.* Illing; *Fl.* Hillen; a p.n.
ILLINGWORTH. A loc. n., Yorks
ILOTT. *See* Aylott
ILSLEY. A loc. n., Berks. Or Hillsley, Glost.
IMAGE. *G.* Immich, Immig; a p.n.
IMLAY. From Himley; a loc. n., Staffs.
INCE. A loc. n., Lancs. Or *see* Innes
INCLEDON. From Ingleton; a loc. n., Dur., Yorks
IND. *See* Hinde
INDERWICK. From Innerwick; a loc. n., Haddington
INESON. *F.* Ino, Ine, Inke; *S.* Hinnerson; *Fl.* Hinnsen; *D.* Ingverson; *Dch.* Ingwarsen; p.n. *See* Innocent
ING. *N.* Ingi, a contraction of compounds in Ing, as Ingimundr, etc.
INGALL. *See* Ingle
INGAMELLS. From Ingoldmels; a loc. n., Lincs
INGATE. *Fr.* Hincourt (?); a p.n.
INGELOW. From Inchigeelagh; a loc. n., Cork. Or *S.* Engellau; a p.n.

INGERSOL. From Inkersall; a loc. n., Derbysh.

INGLE. *N.* Ingolfr; *Fl.* Inghels; *S.* Ingelsson; *Dch.* Ingelse, Inckel; p.n.

Ingulf, a tenant in chief; and Ingelric, Ingolf, Ingulf, Saxon tenants in *D.B.*

INGLEDEW. *N.* Íngjaldr; *D.B.* Engeler; p.n.

INGLET. *See* Ingle

INGLETON. A loc. n., Yorks

INGOLDBY. From Ingoldsby; a loc. n., Lincs

INGPEN. *See* Inkpen

INGRAM. A loc. n., Northbd.

INGREY. From Ingrave; a loc. n., Herts

INKER. *F.* Ino, Ine, Inke; p.n. *See* Hinks

INKPEN. From Inkpen; a loc. n., Bucks

INKSON. *D.* Ingverson; a p.n. *See* Ineson

INKSTER. From Ingestre; a loc. n., Staffs.

INMAN. *N.* Ingi-mundr; *S.* Ingman; *D.* Ingemann; *Dch.* Ingerman; *Fl.* Indeman; *D.B.* Ingemund; p.n.

INNES, INNIS. *See* Guinness

INNOCENT. *Fr.* Innocent; *D.B.* Enisan, Enisant; p.n. *See* Inerson

Enisant in Rot. Obl. et Fin., K. John.

INSKIP. A loc. n., Lancs

INSLEY. *See* Hingeley

INSOLE. *See* Ensell

ION. *N.* Jón; *D.* Johan, Johne, John; *Dch.* Jans, Joon; *F.* Jan; *G.* John; *Fr.* Jonné; p.n.

IRBY. A loc. n., Lincs. Or Ireby, Cumb.

IREDALE. From Airedale; a loc. n., Yorks

IRELAND. *Fl.* Irlen (?); a p.n.

IREMONGER. *D.* Irminger; a p.n.

IRONMONGER. *See* Iremonger

IRTON or IRETON. From Ireton; a loc. n., Derbysh. *D.B.* Hiretune, Iretune

IRVIN. From Irvine; a loc. n., Ayr

IRVING. *See* Irvin

IRWIN. *See* Irvin

ISHERWOOD. From Ishlawrcoed or Ushlawrcoed; a loc. n., Monmouth

ISLIP. A loc. n., Northants, Oxf.

ISOM. From Isham; a loc. n., Northants

ISON. *See* Izon

ISSITT. *See* Izzard

IVATT. *Fl.* Heyvaert; p.n.

IVERS. From Iver; a loc. n., Bucks (?)

IVES. From St. Ives; a loc. n., Hunts

IVETT. *See* Ivatt

IVORY. From Ivry; a loc. n., Normandy

IVY. *See* Ivatt

IXER. From Ixworth; a loc. n., Suff.

IZON. *F.* Eisse, Eissen; *D.*, *S.* Eisen; p.n.

IZZARD. *Fl.* Izouard; *D.B.* Ise uuard; p.n.

J.

JACKMAN. *G.* Jachmann; *Fl.* Jacqmain; a p.n.

JACKSON. *D.* Jacobsen; *S.* Jacobson; *F.* Jak, Jäkchen; a p.n.

JACQUES. *Fr.* Jacques; a p.n.

JAFFRAY. *See* Geoffry

JAGGARD. *F.* Jak; *Fr.* Jacquart; *G.* Jagode, Jache, Jach; *Dch.* Jager, Jagt, Jacot; *D.B.* Jagelin; *Fl.* Jacquet; p.n.

JAGGERS. *See* Jaggard

JAGGS. *See* Jaggard

JAKES. *See* Jacques

JAKYLL. *See* Jekyll

JALMAN. *N.* Hjálmarr; *S.* Hjelman; *G.* Hallmann; *Fl.* Jaman; p.n.

JAMES. *D.* Gjems; *G.* Gems; *D.B.* James; p.n.

JAMIE, JAMY. *F.* Jimme, Jimmen; a p. and fam. n. *Fr.* Gimai; p.n.

JANE. *Fl.* Jegn; *Fr.* Janet; Jean, Jeanne; p.n.

JANES. *D.* Jans, Jenson; *Dch.* Janse; *G.* Jensch; *Fl.* Jennes, Jeyens; p.n.

JANNINGS. *S.* Jahn; *F.* Jan; *D.* Janniche; *Dch.* Janning; *D.B.* Junain (?); a p.n.

JARDINE. *Fr.* Jardin

Jarden in Roll of Battell Abbey.

JARMAIN. *N.* Geirmundr; *Fl.* Germain, Germon; *D.* Garman; *G.* Gehrmann; *F.* Gërman; a p.n. *See* Guymer

JARMAN. *See* Jarmain

JARRED. *N.* Geir-raðr; *F.* Gerd, Gerhard; *G.* Jerathe; *Dch.* Gerhardt, Gererts; *D.B.* Girard Gerard; p.n.

JARROLD. *F.* Garrelt, Gerrelt; *N.* Geirhildr; p.n. *See* Jarred

JARVIS. *Fr.* Gervais; a p.n.

JARY. *N.* Geiri (?); *F.* Djure; *G.* Jury, Jurei; *Fl.* Jarry; *D.B.* Iwar, Ivri; p.n.

JASPER. *Dch.* Jasper, Jaspers; *G.* Gaspary; *Fl.* Gaspard, Gaspar, Jaspar; p.n.

JAY. A loc. n., Heref. Or *F.* Gayo; *Dch.* Jay, Jehee; *Fl.* Jeyens; p.n.

Jay is in the Roll of Battell Abbey.

JEAFFRESON. *See* Geoffrey

JEAKES. *See* Jacques

JEALOUS. *Dch.* Jaulus; *G.* Gelse, Jelsch; p.n.

JEARY. *See* Jary

JECKELL. *See* Jekyll

JECKS. *See* Jacques

JEFFCOCK. *See* Jeffery

JEFFERY, JEFFREY. *Fr.* Geoffroy; *N.* Guðriðr; *D.B.* Godefrid; a p.n. *See* Guthrie

JEFFS. *See* Geoffrey

JEKYLL. *N.* Jökull; *D.* Jœkel; *A.S.* Gicel; *G.* Jäckel, Jähkel, Jäkel, Jagel; *Dch.* Jeekel; *Fl.* Jacklé; p.n.

Iuichel or Iuikel, a Presbyter (Norf.), is among the tenants in chief in *D.B.* Jukel, King of Westmorland, was one of the eight vassal kings summoned by Edgar to Chester, A.D. 973.

JELF. *N.* Jólfr; *D.B.* Jalf; a p.n. *See* Yule

JELLETT. *See* Gillett

JELLICOE. Dimin. of *F.* Jelle; a p.n. Or *Dch.* Gellecum; a p.n.

JELLY. *F.* Jelle, Jellen; *G.* Jellin; *Fl.* Jelley; p.n.

JEMPSON. *See* Jamy

JENEWAY. *Fr.* Genvier; a p.n. *See* Jenner

JENKIN, JENKINS. *Dch.* Jenck, Jenk, Jenkens; *G.* Jenke; a p.n.

JENNER. *G.* Jenner; *Fl.* Jenar, Jenart; *Dch.* Jener; *Fr.* Genvier; p.n.

JENNERY. *See* Jeneway

JENNEY. *Fl.* Genis; a p.n. *See* Jenner

JENNINGS. *Dch.* Janning, Jenting; p.n. *See* Jenkin and Jannings

JENNIS. *Fl.* Jennes; *G.* Jensch; p.n.

JENNYNS. *Fl.* Genin; a p.n. *See* Jenkins

JEPHSON. *D.* Jeppesen, Jepsen; *S.* Jepson, Jippson; a p.n.

JERAM. *Fr.* Jerome; a p.n.

JERMY and JERMEY. *See* Jarmain

JERMYN. *See* Jarmain

JERRETT. *See* Jarred

JERROLD. *See* Jarrold

JESSON. *D.*, *N.*, *Dch.*, *Fl.* Jess, Jessen; p.n. *See* Chase

JESSOP. *D.* Jess; a p.n. Jesshope; a loc. n.

JESTY. *Fr.* Jestin (?); a p.n.

JEWELL. *D.* Hjul, Juell, Juuel, Juul; p.n. *See* Yule

JEWKES. *See* Jukes

JEWSBURY. *See* Dewsbury

JEWSON. *F.* Juist; *Dch.* Joosten; *Fl.* Jossen; *D.* Justesen; *D.B.* Justan, Justin (?); p.n.

JEX. *See* Jacques

JICKLING. *See* Hick

JIGGENS. *Fr.* Gigniez; *Fl.* Jiegers; *G.* Gigas; p.n.

JIGGLE. *Fl.* Gigault; a p.n.

JILBERT. *See* Gilbert

JILLINGS. A loc. n., Yorks. Or *Dch.* Gilling; *Fl.* Ghilain, Gielen, Gilin, Gillain; p.n.

JOBLIN. From Jublains; a loc. n., France

JOCKEL. *See* Jekyll

JODDRELL. *S.* Jordell (?); a p.n.

JOHN. *N.* Jón, Jóhann, Jóan; *D.* Johann, John, Jon, Jahn, Johne; *Dch.* Johan; *S.* Johnn; *D.B.* Johannes; p.n.

JOHNS. *N.* Jón; *F.* Jan; *G.*, *Fl.*, *Dch.*, *D.* Jan, Jans, Jahn, Jahns, Jen, Johan, Johans, John, Johne, Johns, Jons, Jones; *Fr.* Jean, Jouan, Jouen; p.n. *Lat.* Johannes. *See* Jonas

JOHNSON. *D.* Johannsen, Johanson, Johnssen, Johnson; *S.* Jansen, Johnsson, Johnson; *Dch.* Jannissen, Jansen, Johannissen, Johanson; p.n.

JOLLY. *N.* Jólfr; *G.* Jolles, Jolly; *Dch.* Jolle; *Fl.*, *Fr.* Joly; p.n. *See* Yule

JONAS. *D.*, *Dch.*, *G.*, *S.*: p.n.

JONES. *See* Johns and Jonas

JOPE. *D.* Job, Jopp; *Dch.* Job, Joppe; *Fl.* Job, Jobin; *Fr.* Chopin; p.n.

JOPLING. *See* Joblin

JORDAN. *D.*, *G.*, *Dch.* Jordan; *Fl.* Jordaen; p.n.

JOSH. *G.* Josch; a p.n.

JOSSELYN. *See* Goss

JOUEL. *N.* Jólfr; *D.B.* Jalf, Jaul; *D.* Juell, Juhl; *S.* Juel; *Fr.* Juhel; *Dch.* Jolle, Jolly, Joly; *G.* Jouly, Jolles, Jolly, Johl; p.n.

JOY. *Fr.* Joet; *Fl.* Goye; *Dch.* Goey; p.n. Or *see* Joyce

JOYCE. From Joyeuse; a loc. n., Normandy

Johais in *D.B.* François de Joyeuse was Abbot of Mont-Saint-Michel in 1594.

JOYES. *See* Joyce

JUBB. *G.* Jube; a p.n. *See* Jupp

JUBY, JUBEY. *F.* Jabbe, Jabe; *G.* Jube, Juppe, Jupe; *Fl.* Jubin; *D.* Juby; p.n.

JUDD. *F.* Udo, Ude; *Dch.* Joode; *Fl.* Jude; *D.* Jud; *D.B.* Udi, Judichel, Judhell; p.n.

JUDGE. *Fr.* Juge; *G.* Chutsch; p.n. Or *see* Judds

JUDKINS. *See* Judd

JUDSON. *See* Judd

JUGG. *D.* Joeg; *Fl.* Juge; p.n.

JUGGINS. *D.* Jürgens (?); a p.n. *See* Jugg

JUKES. *Fr.* Joux (?); a p.n.

JULER. *N.* Jólfr; *G.* Julich, Jouly; *D.* Juhler; *Fr.* Julez; p.n. *See* Yule

JULIAN. *Fr.* Julien; a p.n.

JULIER. *Fr.* Juliard; a p.n.
JULIET. *Fr.*; Huguenot n.
JULNES. *See* Joll and Yule
JUMP. A loc. n., Devon, Yorks
JUNGUIS. *N.* Ingvi; *F.* Inguis; *G.* Jung, Junghaus, Jungnitsch; *Fl.* Junges; p.n.
JUNIPER. *Dch.* Jongeboer (?); a p.n.
JUPP. *G.* Jupp; *Fr.* Chupé; p.n. *See* Jubb
JURY. *See* Jary
JUST. *D.* Just; *G.* Just; *Dch.* Juist; *Fl.* Juste; p.n.

K.

KAIL. *D.* Keil; *Dch.* Kehl; *G.* Keyl; p.n.
KAINE. *See* Caine
KARSLAKE. *See* Carslake
KAVANAGH. From the Irish O'Caomhanach; a p.n.
KAY. *D.* Kai; *S.* Key; *Fl.* Kai, Key; *Dch.* Kea; p.n.
KAYNES. *See* Keynes
KEABLE. *See* Keble
KEAL. *See* Keel
KEAN. *See* Keen
KEATS. From Kitts; a loc. n., Devon. Or *G.* Kietz; a p.n.
KEBLE. *Fr.* Quibel; *G.* Kiebel; p.n.
KECK. *N.* Kekkja; n.n. *D.* Keck; *Dch.* Koek; *Fl.* Koecke; *D.B.* Cec; p.n.
KEDGE. *See* Gedge
KEDGLEY. *See* Keighley
KEED. *See* Kidd
KEEFE. *D.* Kieffer; a p.n.
KEEL. From Keele; a loc. n., Staffs.
KEELER. *See* Kieley
KEELEY. *See* Kieley
KEELING. From Killing or Keeling (*D.B.* Chellinge); a loc. n., Yorks
KEEN. *D.* Kiehn; *Fl.* Kien; p.n.
KEEP. *Dch.* Kiepe, Kip; p.n.
KEEPING. *See* Kippen
KEER. *Fl.* Kiere; *G.* Kiera; a p.n.
KEETLEY. *See* Keightley
KEEVIL. A loc. n., Wilts
KEFFORD. *Fr.* Quifut (?); a p.n.
KEHOE. *Fr.* Cahot, Cahut, Cayeux; p.n. Or *see* Keogh
W. de Keheu in Rot. Obl. et Fin., K. John.
KEIGHLEY. A loc. n., Lancs, Yorks
KEIGHTLEY. A loc. n., Yorks
KEINCH. *S.*, *D.* Kinch; *Fl.* Kints; *G.* Kensche; p.n.
KEKEWICH. From Kekwick; a loc. n., Ches.
KELF. *N.* Kálfr; *Dch.* Kalff, Kalf, Kelfkins; p.n.
KELK. A loc. n., Yorks
KELLAWAY. A loc. n., Wilts
KELLEWAY. *See* Kellaway
KELLETT. A loc. n., Lancs
KELLIE. A loc. n., Fife
KELLY. A loc. n., Renfrew. Or Irish O'Ceallach; a p.n.
KELSEY. From Kelsale; a loc. n., Suff.
KEMBLE. A loc. n., Wilts
KEMP. *N.* Kembir or Kampi; *G.* Kämp, Kämpe; *Dch.* Kamp, Kemp; *D.B.* Camp; p.n. *See* Camp
KEMPSON. From Kempston; a loc. n., Beds
KEMPSTER. From Kempston; a loc. n., Norf.
KEMPTHORNE. A loc. n., Devon
KEMPTON. From Kemberton; a loc. n., Salop. Or *see* Kimpton
KEMSHEAD. From Kempshott; a loc. n., Hants
KEMSLEY. A loc. n., Kent
KEMSTEAD. *See* Kemshead

KEN, KENN. A loc. n., Somers.
John and Richard de Ken in Rot. Obl. et Fin., K. John.

KENDRICK. From Kenwrick; a loc. n., Salop

KENISTON. From Kenstone; a loc. n., Salop

KENNARD. From Kennarth; a loc. n., S. Wales

KENNEDY. From the Irish O'Ceann-fhada or O'Cinnidh; p.n.
Cineadh, a nation.

KENNEWAY. From Kennoway; a loc. n., Fife

KENNEY. *Fr.* Kenis, Kennis; p.n.

KENNION. *See* Kenyon

KENT, KENTISH. The county

KENYON. A loc. n., Lancs

KEOGH. From the Irish Mac-Eochaidh; a p.n.

KERBY. *See* Kirkby

KERR. *Dch.* Karr, Kers; *Fl.* Kersse; *D.B.* Cari. *See* Carr

KERSHAW. From Cirshay (?); a loc. n., Dorset. Or *Fl.* Kersse, or *G.* Korsawe; p.n. *See* Corser

KERSWELL. A loc. n., Devon

KESSANLY. From Kessingland; a loc. n., Norf.

KESTERTON. From Casterton; a loc. n., Westmd.

KESTEVEN. A loc. n., Lincs

KETLEY. A loc. n., Salop

KETT. *See* Catt

KETTERIDGE. From Catterick; a loc. n., Yorks

KETTERING. A loc. n., Northants

KETTLEWELL. A loc. n., Yorks

KEY. From Quy; a loc. n., Camb. Or *D.*, *Fl.* Kai; *S.* Key; *G.* Kay; *Dch.* Kea, Keij; *D.B.* Kee; p.n.

KEYLOCK. From Killough; a loc. n., co. Down, Ireland

KEYMER. A loc. n., Ess.
Symon de Kyma in Rot. Obl. et Fin., K. John.

KEYNES. *D.* Kiens; a p.n. Or *see* Caine

KEYWORTH. A loc. n., Notts

KIBBLE. *See* Keable

KIDALL. From Kiddall; a loc. n., Yorks

KIDD. *D.* Kidde; *Dch.* Kidd; p.n.
R. Kide in Rot. Obl. et Fin., K. John.

KIDDELL, KIDDLE. *See* Kidall

KIDGELL. *G.* Kitschelt; a p.n.

KIDGER. *Dch.* Kigge; *G.* Kitscher; p.n.

KIELEY. From the Irish O'Caolidh; a p.n. Or *Dch.* Kiella; *G.* Kieler, Kille; p.n.

KIGHTLY. *See* Keightley

KILBOURN. From Kilburn; a loc. n., Middlx.

KILBY. A loc. n., Leics., Lincs

KILL. *G.* Kille; a p.n.

KILLICE. From Killisk; a loc. n., Wexford

KILLICK. *See* Kilwick

KILMINSTER. A loc. n., Caithness

KILNER. A loc. n., Somers.

KILPACK. From Kilpeck; a loc. n., Heref.

KILVINGTON. A loc. n., Yorks

KILWICK. From Kildwick; a loc. n., Yorks

KIMBELL. *See* Kimble

KIMBERLEY. A loc. n., Notts

KIMBLE. A loc. n., Bucks. Or *G.* Kimbel; *Dch.* Kimpel; *Fl.* Quimbel; p.n.

KIMM. From Kyme; a loc. n., Lincs

KIMPTON. A loc. n., Hants

KINCHIN. *Fl.* Kinkin; *G.* Kinsing; p.n.

KINCHLEY. *See* Kingerley

KINDRED. *Fl.* Kindt (?); *D.* Kin-derin; p.n.

KING. *D.* Kinck, Kink; p.n.

KINGDOM. From Kingham; a loc. n., Oxf. Or *see* Kingdon

KINGDON. A loc. n., Devon

KINGERLEY. From Kingley; a loc. n., Warw. Or Kinsley, Yorks

KINGSBURY. A loc. n., Warw.

KINGSFORD. A loc. n., Devon, Worcest.

KINGSLEY. A loc. n., Hants, Staffs.

KINGSMILL. A loc. n., Hants

KINIPPLE. *Fr.* Kinable; a p.n.

KINSEY. *D.* Kinzi; a p.n.
Kynsy, Bishop of Lichfield, A.D. 960.

KIPLING. From Kiplin; a loc. n., Yorks. *D.B.* Chipeling

KIPPEN. A loc. n., Stirling

KIRBY. *See* Kirkby

KIRKALDY. A loc. n., Scotl.

KIRKBY. A freq. loc. n.
One family of this name lived for eighteen generations at the Old Hall, Kirkby in Furness, Lancs.

KIRKLAND. A loc. n., Cumb., Fife, Lancs, Westmd.

KIRKPATRICK. A loc. n., Dumfries

KIRKUP. From Kirkthorpe; a loc. n., Yorks

KIRKWOOD. A loc. n., Dumfries, Lanark

KIRSHAW. *See* Kershaw

KIRTLAND. *See* Kirkland

KIRTLEY. From Kirtling; a loc. n., Camb.

KIRTON. A loc. n., Lincs, Suff.

KISBEE. From Kisby; a loc. n., Hunts

KISSACK. *Fr.* Queyssac; a p.n.

KISSICK. *See* Keswick

KITCAT. From Kitcott; a loc. n., Devon

KITCHEN. *N.* Kikini; n.n. *D.* Ketjen; *S.* Kitzing; *Dch.* Ketjen; *Fl.* Kicken, Kitson, Kitzen; p.n.

KITCHIN. *See* Kitchen

KITCHINGMAN. *G.* Kitschmann; a p.n.

KITLEY. A loc. n., Devon

KITT. Dimin. of Christopher. *D.B.* Chit; *G.* Kitt; *Dch.* Kits, Chits; p.n.

KITTERIDGE. *See* Ketteridge

KITTLE. *See* Kiddle

KNAPP. *N.* Knappi; *G.* Knappe; *D.* Knaap, Knappick; *Fl.* Knapp; p.n. Knaby*; a loc. n., Sweden

KNAPPIT. *See* Knapp

KNAPTON. A loc. n., Leics., Norf.

KNEE. *G.* Knie; a p.n.

KNEEBONE. *D.* Nyebo; a p.n. *See* Neebe

KNEEBORN. *See* Kneebone

KNEWSTUBB. From Knostrop; a loc. n., Yorks

KNIBB. *Dch.* Knibbe; a p.n.

KNIFTON. From Kniveton; a loc. n., Derbysh.

KNIGHT. *A.S.* Kniucht; *Dch.* Knegt; *G.* Knecht (a servant); p.n.

KNILL. From Knylle or Knill; a loc. n., Heref.
Sir John de Braose received the Manor of Knille, *temp.* K. John.

KNIPE. *N.* Kneif; n.n. *Dch.* Knip; *D.*, *G.* Kniep; p.n.

KNOCK. *N.* Knjúkr; *G.* Knoch; *Dch.* Knoek; *D.* Knock; p.n.

KNOTT. *N.* Knöttr; *D.* Knodt; *G.* Knoth; a p.n.

KYBIRD. *Dch.* Kiberd; a p.n.

KYFFIN. *Welsh* Cyffin; a p.n.

KYLE. *G.* Keil; *Fl.* Kuyle; p.n.

KYNASTON. A loc. n., Salop, Staffs.

KYTE. *Dch.* Kuyt; *Fl.* Kayaert; p.n.

L.

LACHOHEE. *D.* Lackje; a p.n.
LACK. *See* Lake
LADBROKE. From Ladbrook; a loc. n., Warw.
LADBROOKE. *See* above
LADBURY. From Ledbury; a loc. n., Heref.
LADD. *Dch.* Laddé; a p.n.
LADLER. *See* Laidlaw
LADLY. *See* Laidlaw
LAFFEATY, LAFFERTY. *See* Laverty
LAIDLAW. A loc. n., Selkirk. Comp. Ludlow
LAIDLAY. *See* Laidlaw
LAITY. A loc. n., Cornw.
LAKE. A loc. n., Devon, Hunts, Salop, Wilts. Or *Dch.* Lek; a p.n.
LAKIN. *Dch.* Ley, Leyking; p.n.
LAMB. *N.* Lambi; *S.* Lamby, Lamm; *Dch.* Lam; *Fl.* Lamme; *D.B.* Lambe; p.n.
LAMBERT. From St. Lambert; a loc. n., France. *Fr.* Lambard, Lambert, Lambret; *D.* Lamberth; *Dch.* Lambert, Lambrecht, Lammers, Lammerts; *G.* Lambart; *D.B.* Lambert, tenant in chief; p.n.
Gen. Lambert, Governor of York, A.D. 1531.
LAMBERTH. *See* Lambeth
LAMBETH. A loc. n., Surr.
LAMBOURNE, LAMBURN. From Lamborne; a loc. n., Berks, Cornw.
LAMBSON. From Lambston; a loc. n., S. Wales
LAMBTON. A loc. n., Dur.
LAMERTON. A loc. n., Devon
LAMPARD. *Fl.* Lampaert; *G.*, *Dch.* Lampert; p.n.
LAMPLUGH. A loc. n., Cumb.
LAMPSON. *See* Lambson
LANCASTER. The county town
LANCE. *Dch.*, *G.* Lanz; a p.n. Dimin. of Lancelot or Laurence
LAND, LANT. *See* Lound
LANDER. *D.*, *Dch.*, *G.*; p.n.
LANDFEAR. *Dch.* Landweer; a p.n. Or *see* Lanfear
LANE. *D.* Lehn; *Fl.* Leyn; *Dch.* Leijn; p.n.
In Roll of Battell Abbey.
LANEY. *Fr.* Lainé; a p.n.
LANFEAR. From Llanfair; a loc. n., N. Wales
LANGDALE. A loc. n., Cumb.
LANGFORD. A loc. n., Devon, Notts, Somers., Wilts
LANGHORNE. *D.* Langhorn; *Dch.* Lankhoorn; p.n.
LANGLEY. A loc. n., Derbysh., and other counties
LANGMAID. *See* Langmead
LANGMEAD. A loc. n., Devon
LANGMORE. From Langmere; a loc. n., Norf.
LANGRIDGE. A loc. n., Devon, Somers.
LANGSHAW. A loc. n., Dumfries
LANGSTON. A loc. n., Devon
LANGTON. A loc. n., Devon, Leics., Somers.
LANGTREE. A loc. n., Devon
LANGTRY. *See* Langtree
LANGWORTHY. A loc. n., Devon
LANKESTER. *See* Lancaster
LANSDELL. *See* Lonsdale
LANSDOWNE. A loc. n., Somers.
LANYON. A loc. n., Brittany and Cornw.
LAPPER. *Fr.* Lapièrre, Lappé; *D.* Lappé; p.n.
LAPSLEY. From Lapley; a loc. n., Staffs.
LAPTHORNE. A loc. n., Devon
LAPWORTH. A loc. n., Warw.
LARCHIN. *See* Larkin
LARCOMBE. A loc. n., Devon
LARGE. *G.* Larisch; a p.n.

LARK, LARKE. *S.* Larka; *G.* Lerch, Lorke; *D.* Larcher; *Fl.* Levacq, Larock; *D.B.* Lorch; p.n.
LARLHAM. From Laleham; a loc. n., Middlx.
LARTER. *Fr.* Latour; *Fl.* Latteur; p.n. *See* Latter
LASHAM. A loc. n., Hants
LASHMAR. *See* Latchmore
LAST. *Dch.*; p.n.
LATCHFORD. A loc. n., Ches.
LATCHMORE. From Letchmore; a loc. n., Herts
LATHAM. From Letham; a loc. n., Fife; Lathom, Lancs; or Laytham, Yorks
LATHBRIDGE, LETHBRIDGE. *See* Lathbury
LATHBURY. A loc. n., Bucks
LATTA. *See* Larter and Latter
LATTER. *Fr.* Latour; *Fl.* Latteur; p.n.
LAUGHLAND. From Lawkland; a loc. n., Yorks
LAUGHTON. A loc. n., Lincs, Yorks
LAURENCE. *Fr.*; p.n.
LAURIE. A contraction of Laurence. Or *see* Lowry
LAVENDER. From Lavendon; a loc. n., Bucks
LAVER. *Dch.* Lever; *Fr.* Leva; p.n.
LAVERTON. A loc. n., Somers., Yorks
LAVERTY. From the Irish O'Labhradha; a p.n.
LAVIES. *Fl.* Lavie and Lavies; Protestant refugee n.
LAVIN. *Fr.* Lavigne; a p.n.
LAVINGTON. A loc. n., Wilts
LAW. A loc. n., Lanark
LAWFORD. A loc. n., Warw.
LAWLESS. From Loulas; a loc. n., S. Wales
LAWLEY. A loc. n., Salop
LAWN. *See* Lound
LAWS. *Fl.* Lauwers; *S.* Lohse; *D.B.* Lorz; p.n.
LAWTON. A loc. n., Salop
LAXTON. A loc. n., Northants, Notts, Yorks
LAY. *N.* Leggr; *G.* Lege, Lija, Lies; *D.* Leigh; *Dch.* Lee; *S.* Leja; Mod. *N.* Lia, Lie; p.n.
LAYBORN. From Labourn; a loc. n., Surr. Or Leybourne, Kent
LAYBOURN. *See* Layborn
LAYCOCK. From Laycock; a loc. n., Wilts, Yorks. *D.B.* Lacoc; or *Fr.* Lecocq; a p.n.
LAYLAND. A loc. n., Cornw., Lancs, Somers.
LAYMAN. *Fl.* Leman; a p.n. *See* Lemon
LAYT. *D.B.* Leit. *See* Lay
LAYTON. A loc. n., Ess. *See* Lay
LAZEL. *Fr.* Lasalle; a p.n.
LAZENBY. A loc. n., Yorks. Comp. Lazonby, Cumb.
LEA. A freq. loc. n. *See* Lee and Lay
LEACH. *G.* Liche; a p.n.
LEACROFT. A loc. n., Staffs.
LEADER. *G.* Lieder; a p.n.
LEAF. *See* Leefe
LEAGE. From Liege; a loc. n., Belgium. Or *see* Leach
LEAK. From Leak; a loc. n., Lincs, Staffs. *D.B.* Leche. Comp. Leek, Staffs.
LEAKEY. *G.* Lichey; a p.n.
LEAN. *Dch.* Lien; a p.n.
LEAPMAN. *D.*, *Dch.* Lipman; *G.* Lipman, Liebermann; p.n.
LEAR. *G.* Liehr; *Dch.*, *D.* Lier; p.n.
LEARNER. *Fr.* Lernoud; a p.n. Or *see* Leonard
LEARY. *See* Laurie
LEATHERDALE. From Leverdale; a loc. n., Staffs. (?)
LEATHLEY. A loc. n., Yorks
LEATHWAITE. *See* Lewthwaite
LEAVER, LEVER. *Dch.* Liever; a p.n.
LECK. A loc. n., Yorks
LECKY. *See* Leakey
LEDGER. *Fl.* Leger; a p.n.
LEE. A loc. n., Ess., Kent, etc.

LEEFE. From Liff; a loc. n., Forfar (?)

LEEMING. A loc. n., Yorks

LEES. A loc. n., Lancs

LEESON. *G.* Lieson; *Fl.* Liessens; p.n.

LEETE. *Dch.* Liet; a p.n.

LEETHAM. From Leatham; a loc. n., Yorks

LEEVERS. A loc. n., Lincs. Or *Dch.* Lievers; a p.n.

LEFGOOD. *Dch.* Lievegoed; a p.n.

LEFTWICH. A loc. n., Ches.

LE GRICE. *Fr.* Legris; a p.n.

LEIGH. A loc. n., Lancs. Or *D.* Leigh; a p.n. *See* Lay

LEIST. *G.*; p.n.

LEMAN. *N.* Ljoðmundr; *G.* Lehmann; *D.* Lejman; *Fl.* Leman, Lemmen; *S.* Lemon, Leman; *D.B.* Ledman, Leodmar, Leomar, Lemar; p.n.

LEMMON. *See* Leman

LENDRUM. A loc. n., Aberdeen

LENTHALL. From Leinthall; a loc. n., Heref. Or *G.* Leinethall; a loc. and p. n.

LEPPARD. *G.* Liepert; a p.n.

LEPPER. *Fr.* Lepère; a p.n.

LESLIE. A loc. n., Aberdeen, Stirling

LESSELS. *See* Lazel

LESSEY. *D.* Lesse; *G.* Lesse, Lessig; *Fl.* Lesy; *D.B.* Lefsi, Levesin; p.n.

LESTER. From Leicester; a loc. n.

LETCHWORTH. A loc. n., Herts

LETT. *Dch.* Leth; *Fl.* Lette; p.n.

LETTIS. *G.* Lettig; a p.n.

Lettice is also a contraction of Letitia, a fem. p. n.

LETTS. *G.* Letsch; a p.n.

LETTY. *Fl.* Lette; a p.n. *See* Lettis

LEUTY. *Dch.* Loeté; a p.n.

LEVENSTON. *See* Livingstone

LEVER. A loc. n., Lancs

LEVERETT. *Dch.* Levert; a p.n. (?)

LEVERMORE. *See* Livermore

LEVERS. *See* Leevers

LEVERSON. From Lewson; a loc. n., Heref.

LEVERTON. *See* Laverton

LEWTHWAITE. From Lowthwaite or Lothwaite; a loc. n., Cumb.

LEY. *See* Lee and Lay

LIBBIS. *Fl.* Libois; *G.* Libas, Liebes; p.n.

LIBBY. *See* Libbis

LIBERTY. A loc. n., Fife. Or *D.* Libbert, Lippert; a p.n.

LICENCE. *Fl.* Liessens, Lissens; *Dch.* Leyssens; p.n.

LICKFOLD. A loc. n., Suss.

LICKORISH. From Lickerigg; a loc. n., Galway

LIDDARD, LIDDIARD, LIDIARD, LIDYARD. From Lydiard; a loc. n., Wilts

LIDDICOTT. From Lidcott; a loc. n., Cornw.

LIDDON. From Lidden; a loc. n., Kent

LIDGEY. From Lidsey; a loc. n., Suss.

LIDSTONE. A loc. n., Oxf.

LIELL. *Fr.* Lille. *See* Lyall

LIGERTWOOD. *See* Lightfoot

LIGHTBAND. From Lightbounds; a loc. n., Lancs

LIGHTBOWN. *See* Lightband

LIGHTFOOT. *Dch.* Ligtvoet; a p.n.

LIGHTWOOD. *See* Lightfoot

LILLINGTON. A loc. n., Dorset

LILWALL. A loc. n., Heref.

LILY. From Lilley; a loc. n., Berks, Yorks. Or *D.* Lillie; *G.* Lilie; *Fr.*, *Fl.* Lille; *S.* Lilje; *Dch.* Lelie, Lelij; p.n.

LILYWHITE. From Liliethwaite; a loc. n.

LIMBY. *See* Limbeer

LIMEBEER. From Limber; a loc. n., Lincs

LIMMER. *N.-Fr.* Limers; *G.* Limer; *Fl.* Lemaire; p.n.

Limers in Roll of Battell Abbey; and Leimar, a tenant in *D.B.* at the Survey.

LINDOW. A loc. n., Ches. Or *G.* Lindau, Lindow; *S.* Linder, Lindau; *Fl.* Linters; *Fr.* Lintot; p.n.

LINDSAY. A loc. n., Ess.

LINE, LINES, LYNES. From Luynes; a loc. n., Normandy

LINFOOT. *See* Linford

LINFORD. From Lynford; a loc. n., Norf.

LINFORTH. *See* Linford

LING. A loc. n. in Norf.

LINGARD. *D.* Lyngaard; a p.n.

LINGFER. *See* Lingford

LINGFORD. From Linford; a loc. n., Bucks, Leics.

LINGHAM. A loc. n., Ches.

LINNIKER. From Lenacre; a loc. n., Yorks

LINSDELL. From Linsdale; a loc. n., Westmd.

LINSELL. From Lindsell; a loc. n., Ess. Or *Fl.* Linseele; a p.n.

LINSEY. From Lindsey; a loc. n., Norf.

LINSTEAD. A loc. n., Kent

LINTHWAITE. A loc. n., Yorks

LINTON. A loc. n., Camb., Derbysh., Devon, Haddington, Heref., Kent, Peebles, Roxburgh, Yorks

LINTOTT. From Lintot; a loc. n., Normandy

LIPTON. *See* Lupton

LIQUORISH. *See* Lickorish

L'ISLE. A loc. n., Vaucluse, France

LISTER. *See* Lester

LISTON. A loc. n., Ess.

LITHERLAND. A loc. n., Lancs

LITTLEBOY. *Fr.* Lillebois (little wood); a loc. n.

LITTLEDALE. A loc. n., Lancs. Or from Liddeldale; a loc. n., Roxburgh

LITTLEJOHN. From Littlejoy; a loc. n., Devon (?)

LITTLEMORE. A loc. n., Oxf.

LITTLEPROUD. From Littleport; a loc. n., Camb.

LITTLER. *See* Laidlaw

LITTLETON. A loc. n., Derbysh., Glost., Hampsh., Middlx., Somers., Surr., Suss., Wilts, Worcest.

LITTLEWOOD. A loc. n., Lancs

LIVERMORE. From Livermere; a loc. n., Suff.

LIVERSAGE, LIVERSIDGE. From Liversedge; a loc. n., Yorks

LIVESEY. A loc. n., Lancs

LIVING. *N. Leifr*, a p.n. *ing*, descendants; *Fl.* Livain; *D.B.* Living, Leving. Or Leaven; a loc. n., Yorks

LIVINGSTONE. A loc. n. near Linlithgow

LIVOCK. *Fl.* Levacq; *Fr.* Levaque; p.n.

LLOYD. From Llwyd; a loc. n., Denbigh. A river in Montgomerysh.

LOADER, LODER. *N.* Ljótr (?); *G.* Lode; *D.B.* Lodi; *Dch.* Lodder; p.n.

LOADES. *Fl.* Lodens; a p.n. *See* Loader

LOAKE. *G.* Loch; p.n.

LOANE. *Dch.* Loon; a p.n.

LOASBY. From Lowesby; a loc. n., Leics.

LOBB. A loc. n., Devon, Oxf. Or *Dch.* Lobbe; *G.* Lobe; p.n.

LOBBETT. *G.* Lobbrecht (?); a p.n.

LOBLEY. *Fr.* Lobleaux; a p.n. (?)

LOCH, LOCK. A loc. n., Cornw. Or *N.* Loki; *D.B.* Lochi; p.n.

LOCKER. *G.* Locker; *Dch.* Lokker; a p.n. *See* Lock

LOCKETT. *Fr.* Locquet; a p.n. *See* Lock

LOCKWOOD. A loc. n., Yorks

LOCKYER. *See* Looker

LOCOCK. *See* Luccock

LODBROOK. From Ludbrook; a loc. n., Devon

LODGE. *Fr.* Logé; a p.n.

LOE. *Dch.* Louw; *Fr.* de Lo; *G.* Lohe; p.n.

LOFTE. *See* Lovett

LOFTHOUSE. A loc. n., Yorks. *D.B.* Lofthus

LOFTS. *See* Lofthouse

LOFTUS. *See* Lofthouse

LOGAN. From the Irish O'Leochain; a p.n.

LOMAS. *Dch.* Lommerse; a p.n.

LOMAX. *See* Lomas

LONGBOTTOM. From Longbeddom; a loc. n., Dumfries

LONGCAKE. From Longacre; a loc. n., Somers. Or Lankaker; a loc. n., Westmd.

LONGDEN. A loc. n., Staffs., Worcest.

LONGFELLOW. From Longueville; a town of Seine, France

LONGFORD. A loc. n., Derbysh., Glost., Salop, Wilts

LONGHURST. A loc. n., Northbd.

LONGLEY. A loc. n., Yorks

LONGMAID. *See* Langmead

LONGMAN. A loc. n., Banff

LONGMIRE. A loc. n., Westmd.

LONGMORE. *See* Longmire

LONGRIDGE. A loc. n., Lancs

LONGSHANKS. From Longchamps; a loc. n., Normandy

It was a n.n. of Edward I.

LONGSTAFF. From Longstow; a loc. n., Camb. Or Longstock, Hants

LONGSTON. A loc. n., Staffs.

LONGTON. A loc. n., Lancs, Staffs.

LONSDALE. A loc. n., Lancs and Westmd.

LOOKER. *Fr.* Locquet; a p.n.

LOOMES. *Fl.* Loomans (?); a p.n.

LOOSE. A loc. n., Kent. Or *Dch.* Loose, Loos; *Fl.* Loze; p.n.

Luse in Roll of Battell Abbey. Lewes in *D.B.* (?).

LORKIN. *See* Larkin

LOTHERINGTON. From Lotherton; a loc. n., Yorks

LOTT. *G.* Lott; *Fl.* Lotte; p.n.

LOUDON. A loc. n., Ayrsh.

LOUGHTON. A loc. n., Salop

LOUND. *N.* Lundi; *D.* Lundt, Launy, Landt; *S.* Lund; *G.* Launer, Launhardt; *Dch.* Lund, Loen, Lonte, Lantz; *D.B.* Lant, Landri; p.n.

LOUTTID. *Fr.* Leautard (?); a p.n.

LOVE. *Fl.* Loef; a p.n.

LOVEDAY. *Fl.* Lovatty (?); a p.n.

LOVELACE, LOVELESS. *See* Lawless

LOVELL. *Fl.* Louvel; *Fr.* Lovel; p.n.

In Roll of Battell Abbey. Luvel in Rot. Obl. et Fin., K. John.

LOVER. *Fr.* Lovau; a p.n.

LOVERIDGE. From Loughrigg; a loc. n., Westmd.

LOVETT. *Fl.* Lowet; a p.n.

Luvet in Rot. Obl. et Fin., K. John.

LOVEWELL. *See* Lovell

LOW. *Fl.* Louw; a p.n. Or *see* Law

LOWDEN. *See* Loudon

LOWE. A loc. n., Salop

LOWELL. *See* Lovell

LOWLESS. *See* Lawless

LOWMAN. *G.* Lohmann; a p.n.

LOWNDES, LOWNES. From Lounds; a loc. n., Lincs

LOWRY. From Loury; a loc. n., France

LOWTHER. A loc. n., Cumb.

LOWTHIAN. From Lothian, Scotl.

LOXLEY. A loc. n., Staffs., Warw., Yorks

LOYDELL. *See* Lydal

LUBBOCK. *F.* Lübbo; *G.* Löbe, Löbbecke; *Dch.* Lub, Lubke; *Fl.* Lubcké; p.n.

LUCAS. *Fr.*; p.n.

LUCCOCK. *Fr.* Le Coq, or Lucq; *G.* Lücke; p.n. Dimin. of Lucas

LUCK. *Fl.* Luc, Lucq; p.n.

LUCKETT. A loc. n., Cornw.

LUCKEY, LUCKIE. *N.* Loki; n.n. *Fr.* Lucké; *G.* Lücke; *D.B.* Lochi; p.n.

LUCKHURST. *Fl.* Luckhaus; a p.n.

LUCKING. *Dch.*; p.n.

LUCRAFT. *See* Leacroft

LUCY. *Fr.* Louiset; a p.n.
LUDBROOK. A loc. n., Devon
LUDFORD. A loc. n., Salop
LUDLOW. A loc. n., Salop
LUFF. *N.* Lúfa; *D.*, *Dch.* Luf; *S.* Löf; p.n.
LUGG. *G.* Luge; *Dch.* Lugt; *Fl.* Luig; p.n.
LULHAM. *See* Larlham
LUMB. A loc. n., Lancs, Yorks
LUMBARD. *Dch.* Lombart; *Fl.* Lombaert; p.n.
LUMBY. A loc. n., Yorks
LUMLEY. A loc. n., Dur.
LUMMIS. *See* Lomas
LUMSDEN. A loc. n., Aberdeen, Berwick
LUND. A loc. n., Yorks. *See* Lound
LUNN. *See* Lund
LUNNON. From London
LUNT. A loc. n., Lancs. *D.B.* Lont. *See* Lund
LUPSON. *See* Lubb
LUPTON. A loc. n., Westmd.
LUSCOMBE. A loc. n., Devon
LUSH. *G.* Lösch; a p.n.
LUSHER. *Dch.* Lösher; *G.* Löschau; p.n.
LUSK. A loc. n., Dublin
LUSON. *See* Lusson
LUSTY. *Fl.* Lust; *G.* Lustig; p.n.
LUTLEY. A loc. n., Staffs.
LUTRIDGE. From Lutheridge; a loc. n., Glost.
LUTTRELL. *Fr.* Latreille (?); a p.n.
Lutterell in Rot. Obl. et Fin., K. John.
LUXON. A loc. n., Devon
LUXTON. *See* Luxon
LYCETT. A loc. n., Staffs.
LYDAL. *Fl.* Liedel; a p.n.
LYDLE. *See* Lydal
LYE. A loc. n., Devon, Worcest.
LYNCH. A loc. n., Devon, Somers., Suss.
LYNDALL. A freq. loc. n., Lancs, Sweden, etc.
LYNES, LINES. From Luynes; a loc. n., Normandy
LYNN. A loc. n., Norf., Staffs.
LYON. *Fr.* Lion, Lyon; a p.n.
LYSACHT. From the Irish MacGiolla Josacht; a p.n.
LYSONS. *See* Licence
LYTTON. From Litton; a loc. n., Yorks
LYWOOD. From Leawood; a loc. n., Devon. Or Lythwood, Salop

M.

MABB. From Mabe; a loc. n., Cornw. Or *Fl.* Mabbe, Mobers; *D.B.* Maban; p.n. *See* Mabbutt
MABBOTT. *See* Mabbutt
MABBUTT. *N.* Mód-bjartr; *D.B.* Modbert, Motbert; *Fl.* Mabeyt; *Fr.* Maubert; p.n.
MABER. *See* Mabb
MABSON. *Fl.* Mabesoone; *D.B.* Mappeson; p.n.
MACAULAY. From the Irish MacAmhailgaidh; a fam. n. Also MacAuley, MacAwley, MacAuliffe, Macgawley
MACCHEYNE. Irish MacShane; a p.n., Jackson, Johnson
MACCLOSKEY. From the Irish MacBlosgaidh; a p.n.
MACCULLAGH. From the Irish MacCeallach; a p.n.
MACDERMOTT. From the Irish MacDiarmada; a p.n.
MACDONALD, MACDONNELL. From the Irish MacDomhnaill; a p.n.
MACDUFF. *See* Duff
MACE. *N.* Mási; n.n. *F.* Mês or Mewes (contraction of Bartolomæus); *G.* Mais, Mese; *Dch.* Mes, Muis, Moes, Mees; *Fl.* Maas, Maes, Mees, Moys, Muys; *D.* Maes, Mess; p.n.

MACER. *G.* Meser; a p.n. *See* Mace

MACHELL. *F.* Machelt; *S.* Mæchel; *Fl.* Machiels; *Dch.* Mäschel, Machielse; *G.* Machol; *D.B.* Machel; p.n.

Machel held lands at Crackenthorpe, Westmd., *temp.* Edw. Conf. William Mauchel was living *temp.* K. John, A.D. 1201.

MACK. *N.* Magr; *D.B.* Machus, Macus Machar; *Gaelic* Mac; *G.* Mache, Machon, Mack; *D.* Maak; *Dch.* Mack; p.n.

MACKAREL. *Dch.* Makkreel; a p.n.

Makerell in Rot. Obl. et Fin., K. John.

MACKARETH. From the Irish MacCraith, Macgrath, Magrath; Scot. Macreath; p.n. (*craith*, to weave, the son of a weaver). Or *N.* Mágröðr (*mágr* or *mögr*, a boy, youth, son and Rauðr; a p.n.); *G.* Mackrodt; *Fl.* Mackaert; *D.B.* Machar; p.n.

MACKARNESS. *See* Magness and Guinness

MACKLEY. Scotch, MacLae or MacLeay; p.n.

McCLEVERTY. *See* Laverty

MACKROFF. *See* Mackworth

MACKWORTH. A loc. n., Derbysh.

MACRAE. *See* Mackareth

MACY. *See* Maisey

MADDEN. From the Irish O'Madadhain; *Dch.* Mattern; a p.n. Madden, a loc. n., Armagh; Maddern, a loc. n., Cornw.

MADDER. *G.* Mader; a p.n. *See* Maddy

MADDICK. *See* Maddox

MADDIN. *See* Madden

MADDISON. *D.* Madsen; p.n. *See* Maddy

MADDLE. *Fl.* Madyol; *Fr.* Madoulé; p.n.

MADDOCK. *See* Maddox

MADDY, MADDEY. *D.* Madie; *Dch.* Maade, Made; *G.* Mader; *Fr.* Madou; p.n.

MADELL. *See* Maddle

MADEWELL. From Maidenwell; a loc. n., Dorset, Lincs

MADGE. *Fr.* Maggi; a p.n.

MADGETT. *Fr.* Magits; a p.n.

MADGIN. *D.* Magens; *Fl.* Maguin; *Fr.* Magin; p.n.

MADOCKS. *See* Maddox

MADOX, MADDOX. From Maddocks; a loc. n., Devon. Or *Fr.* Madoux; a p.n.

MAGEE. From the Irish O'Maolgaoithe; a p.n.

Chief of Muintir Maolgaoithe (*gaoth*, wind; pronounced 'ghee').

MAGGS. *See* Magness

MAGINNES. *See* Guinness

MAGNAC. A loc. n., Upper Vienne, France

MAGNAY. *Fr.* Magny, Magnée; p.n.

MAGNESS. *N.* Magnús; *D.B.* Magne, Maigno; *G.* Magnus; *Fr.* Magniers, Magniez; p.n. Or *see* Guinness

MAGNIAC. *See* Magnac

MAGRATH. *See* Mackareth

MAGUIRE or MACGUIRE. From the Irish of MacUibhir or Maguibhir, chief of Fermanagh. Also MacIvir, MacIvor

MAHON, MAHONY, MACMAHON. From the Irish MacMathghamhna; a p.n. Mehun; a loc. n., France

MAIDWELL. *See* Madewell

MAINWARING. From the *Fr.* Mesnilwarin

In Roll of Battell Abbey.

MAISEY. A loc. n., Wilts

MAITLAND. *Dch.*; p.n.

MAJOR. *Fr.* Major, Mége; p.n.

MAJORIBANKS.

The barony of Ratho formed the marriage portion of Marjorie, only daughter of Robert Bruce. It was called Terra-de-Marjorie-Banks (Lower).

MALE. *Dch.* Mell; *Fl.* Mail; *Fr.* Maillé; a p. and Huguenot n.

MALET. *N.*, *Fr.*
The Conqueror, after the battle of Hastings, committed the body of Harold to W. Malet to see it buried. His son Robert was a tenant in chief in *D.B.* (Surr.). He founded the Monastery of Eye. Malet held lands *temp.* K. John.

MALINS. *Fl.* Maelens, Melens; p.n.

MALLET. *See* Malet

MALLORY. *Fr.* Mellery; a p.n.

MALLOWS. *See* Marlow

MALPAS. A loc. n., Ches., Cornw.

MALT. *N.* Moldi; n.n. *Dch.* Molt; a p.n.

MALTBY. A loc. n., Lincs and Yorks

MALTON. A loc. n., Yorks

MANBY. A loc. n., Lincs

MANCLARKE. *Fr.* Mauclerc; a p.n., *temp.* K. John, 1208

MANDER. *Dch.* Mandere; *Fr.* Mandre; p.n.

MANGAN. From Mannacan; a loc. n., Cornw. Or *Fr.* Mangin, Mangon; p.n.

MANGER. *Fr.* Mangez; a p.n.

MANHILL. *Fr.* Manneville; a p.n. From Mandeville; a loc. n. in Normandy
Maundeville or Meneville in Roll of Battell Abbey. Manneville or Mannville a tenant in chief in *D.B.*

MANISTRY. *D.* Mannstead; a loc. and p. n.

MANLEY. A loc. n., Devon

MANLOVE. *See* Menlove

MANN. *N.* Manni; *F.* Manne, Manno; *G.* Mann; *D.B.* Man, Manna, Manne, Manus; *D.* Mann; *Dch.* Mahn, Man; p.n.

MANNERING. *See* Mainwaring

MANNERS. *Fl.* Mannaers, Mannaerts; p.n.

MANNING. *Dch.* Manen, Mening; p.n. *See* Mann

MANSELL. A loc. n., Heref. Or *Fr.* Mancel; a p.n.
Robert Le Mansel held lands in Leics., *temp.* K. John.

MANSER. *D.* Mansa; a p.n. Or Mansergh

MANSERGH. A loc. n., Westmd.
Thomas de Mansergh occurs 12 Edw. II. (1319). John de M. represented Westmd. in Parliament 7 Ric. II. (1384).

MANSFIELD. A loc. n., Notts

MANSON. From Manston; a loc. n., Devon, Yorks. Or *Dch.* Manson; a p.n.

MANT. *D.* Manthey; *G.* Manth; *Dch.* Mandt, Mante; p.n. Or from Mantes; a town of Seine and Oise, France

MANTELL, MANTLE. *Fr.* Mantel; a p.n.

MANTHORPE. A loc. n., Lincs

MANTON. A loc. n., Lincs, Notts, Wilts

MANWARING. *See* Mainwaring

MANWELL. *Fr.* Manville, Manderville; p.n.

MAPLE. From Mepal; a loc. n., Camb. Or *see* Maypole

MAPLESTON. From Mapleton; a loc. n., Derbysh.

MAPLEY. From Mapperley; a loc. n., Derbysh.

MAPP. *See* Mabb

MARCH. A loc. n., Camb.

MARCON. *Dch.* Marken; a p.n.

MARDEL, MARDLE. *See* Maddle

MARDEN, MARDON. A loc. n., Heref., Suss., Wilts

MARE. *See* Marr or Meyer

MAREHAM. A loc. n., Lincs

MARGETTS. *Fl.* Magits; a p.n.

MARGRIE. *Fr.* Marguerie; *Dch.* Magerey; p.n.

MARIS, MARRIS. *Fr.* Mariess, Maris; p.n.

MARJORAM. From Margam; a loc. n., Glamorgansh.

MARKETT. *Fl.* Merkaert; *Fr.* Marquet; p.n.

MARKHAM. A loc. n., Notts

MARKIN. *See* Marcon

MARKWELL. A loc. n., Cornw.

MARLOW. A loc. n., Herts

Marple. A loc. n., Ches.

Marr. A loc. n., Yorks. Or *N.* Már; *S.* Mars; *Dch.* Mar; *Fl.* Maere; *D.B.* Mere; p.n.

Marrack. *Fr.* Marique; a p.n.

Marriage. A loc. n., Devon. Or *Fr.* Mariage; *D.* Mariager; p.n.

Marrifield. From Merrifield; a freq. loc. n.

Marriott. From Merriott; a loc. n., Somers. Or *Fr.* Marriette; a p.n. Or *see* Marryat

Marritt. *See* Marriott

Marryat. A loc. n., Yorks

Marsden. A loc. n., Lancs, Yorks

Marsh. A loc. n., Lancs. *See* March

Marshall. *Fl.* Marchal; *Fr.* Maréchal; p.n.

Marshallsay. From Marshallsea (near Crewkerne); a loc. n., Wilts

Marsland. A loc. n., Cornw.

Marston. A loc. n., Ches., Heref., Lincs, Staffs., Warw., Yorks

Marter. *Fr.* Marteau; a p.n.

Martindale. A loc. n., Lincs

Martineau. *Fr.* Martiny, Martinais, Martinant, Martinet; p.n. From Martigne; a loc. n. of Ille and Vilaine, France

Martyr. *See* Marter

Marvin. *D.B.* Maruuen; a p.n.

Marwood. A loc. n., Devon, Dorset, Dur.

Mase. *See* Mace

Mash. *Fr.* Masse; a p.n.

Masham. A loc. n., Yorks

Masheder. *See* Mashiter

Mashiter. *G.* Meschter; *Fl.* Mestdagh; p.n.

Maskall, Maskell. *See* Maskelyne

Maskelyne. *Fr.* Masquelin; a p.n.

Maskew. *G.* Maschke; *Fr.* Mascot; p.n.

Maslen, Maslin. *Fr.* Masselin; a p.n.

Mason. *Fl.* Meessen; *Fr.* Maçon, Masson; p.n.

Massey. From Massay; a loc. n., France. Or Massey, Wilts

Massingberd. *G.* Massenberg; a loc. and p. n.

Massinger. *See* Massingham. Comp. Messenger

Massingham. A loc. n., Norf.

Masters. *See* Musters

Masterton. From Mastertown; a loc. n., Fife

Matcham. From Masham; a loc. n., Yorks

Matchett. *Fr.* Machotte; a p.n.

Mate. *Dch.*, *Fl* Met; *Fr.* Mette; p.n.

Mather. *D.* Mathe, Mather, Mathow; *Fr.* Mathieu; p.n. From Mathew

Mathews. *Dch.* Matthes, Matthies; *Fl.* Mathys; p.n.

Matsell. From Mattishall; a loc. n., Norf.

Mattison. *D.* Matteson, Mathiessen; *Dch.* Mathiesen; a p.n.

Mattix. *See* Maddocks

Mattocks. *See* Maddox

Maude. A loc. n., Aberdeensh. Or *D.* Madie; *Dch.* Made; p.n.
John Maud was living *temp.* K. John.

Maudsley. A loc. n., Lancs

Maugham. A loc. n., Monmouth

Maughan. From Mawgan; Cornw. Or *see* Maugham

Maule. A loc. n., France

Maulkin. *See* Mole

Maun. *See* Mann

Maunder. *See* Mander

Maw. From Mawr; a loc. n., Glamorgan. Or *Fl.* Mauw; *D.* Mau; *Dch.* Mouw; *G.* Mauwe; p.n.

Mawbery. *See* Mowbray

Mawby. From Moorby; a loc. n., Lincs. Or Mautby, Norf.

Mawdesley. A loc. n., Lancs

Maxell. *See* Maxwell

Maxse. From Maxey; a loc. n., Northants

MAXWELL. A loc. n., Roxburgh
MAY. *Dch.* Maij, Mee, Mei; *Fl.* Mahy, May; *D.*, *G.*, *S.* May; p.n. Mays; a loc. n., France
MAYBERRY. From Mayborough; a loc. n.
MAYCOCK. *F.* Maike; *G.* Mäcke; p.n.
MAYDEW. From Meadow; a loc. n., Surr.
MAYGER. *Fr.* Mégard; a p.n.
MAYHEW. *Fr.* Mahieu, Mayeux; p.n.
MAYNARD. *D.* Meinert; *Dch.* Meijnhardt; *Fl.* Meynaert; *D.B.* Mainard; *Fr.* Ménard; p.n.
Maniard in Roll of Battell Abbey.
MAYNE. From Mayenne; a town in France. Or St. Meen; loc. n., Ille and Vilaine, France
MAYPOLE. From Maybole; a loc. n., Ayrsh.
MAYS. *See* Mace
MAYSENT. *See* Mason
MACKREATH. *See* Mackareth
MEACHAM. From Mitcham; a loc. n., Surr.
MEACHEN, MEAKIN, MEEKIN. *Dch.* Meegen, Meeken; *G.* Michan; p.n. Dimin. of Mee
MEAD. A loc. n., Somers.
MEADOWS. A loc. n., Surr.
MEADWAY, MEDWAY. A river, Kent
MEADWELL. From Meadenwell; a loc. n., Cornw.
MEALL. *N.* Mjöll; *D.B.* Mule; *G.* Mielay, Mylius; *D.* Moyell; *Fl.* Mylle; *Fr.* Mille; p.n.
MEAN. *See* Meen
MEANS. *Fl.* Minnens; a p.n. *See* Meen
MEAR. *See* Meer
MEARS. *See* Meers
MEASE. *See* Mace
MEAUX. A loc. n., Yorks. Or *Fr.* Mieux; a p.n.
MECK. *See* Meek
MECRATE. *See* Mackereth
MEDCALF. *See* Metcalf
MEDE. *See* Mead
MEDEX. *G.* Meder; *Fl.* Medaets. Or *Fr.* Madoux; p.n.
MEDHURST. From Midhurst; a loc. n., Suss.
MEDLEY. A loc. n., Oxon
MEDLICOTT. A loc. n., Salop
MEDLOCK. A loc. n., Lancs
MEDWELL. *See* Meadwell
MEDWIN. *See* Methven
MEDWORTH. *Dch.* Medevoort; a loc. and p. n.
MEE. *Dch.* Mee; a p.n. *See* May
MEECH. *See* Meek
MEEK. *N.* Mikill; *D.* Micha; *Fr.*, *Dch.* Miche; *G.* Micke; a p.n.
MEEKING. *See* Meachen
MEEN. *F.* Meino, Menne; *D.B.* Moine; *G.* Miny, Minner; *Dch.* Minne, Mijn; *Fl.* Mine, Minne, Min; p.n.
MEER. A loc. n., Wilts
MEERS. A loc. n., Worcest.
MEFFEN. *Fl.* Meeuwens; a p.n.
MEGGS. *See* Maggs
MEGGINS. *See* Maginns
MEINS. *See* Meen
MELBOURNE. A loc. n., Derbysh., Herts
MELDRUM. A loc. n., Aberdeensh.
MELLER. *See* Mellor
MELLERSH. *See* Mellis
MELLIS. A loc. n., Suff.
MELLISH. *See* Mellis
MELLOR. A loc. n., Derbysh., Lancs
MELLOWS. *Fl.* Mellaerts; *Fr.* Mellisse; p.n.
MELLUISH. *See* Mellish
MELVILLE. From Malleville; a loc. n., Normandy
MENHINNICK. From Menhynnet; a loc. n., Cornw.
MENLOVE. From Menlough; a loc. n., Galway
MENZIES. *Fr.* Mengus (?); a p.n.
MERCER. *See* Merser
MEREDITH. From Mirridith; a loc. n., Heref.
MEREST. *Fr.* Merresse (?); a p.n.

MERRELLS. *See* Morell
MERRICK. From Marrick; a loc. n., Yorks. Or *see* Meyrick
MERRIDEW. *See* Meredith
MERRINGTON. A loc. n., Dur., Salop
MERRISHAW. *Fr.* Maréchal or Marescot; p.n.
MERRISON. *Dch.* Merisson; a p.n.
MERRITT. *Fr.* Méret; a p.n.
MERRY. *Fr.* Méret, Merre, Mery; p.n.
MERRYFIELD. A loc. n., Devon
MERRYDEW. *See* Meredith
MERSER. *Fl.* Meerschaert; a p.n.
MESS. From Meese; a loc. n., Staffs. Or *D.* Mess; a p.n.
MESSENGER. From Messingham; a loc. n., Lincs
MESSETER. *See* Mashiter
METCALF. *S.*, *D.* Meth; *Dch.* Met, and Kalf; both p.n.
METCHIM. *See* Meacham
METFORD. *See* Mitford
METHVEN. A loc. n., Perthsh.
MEW. *Dch.* Mewe; *Fr.* Mieux; p.n.
MEYER. *G.*; p.n.
MEYRICK. *D.* Meyring; *Dch.* Meijrink; p.n. Or *see* Marrack
MIALL. *Dch.* Meijll; *D.* Meil; p.n.
MICKLESON. *S.* Michaelson; *Dch.* Michelsen; *D.* Mikelsen; p.n.
MICKLETHWAITE. A loc. n., Yorks
MIDDLEMASS. From Middlemarsh; a loc. n., Lincs
MIDDLEMISS. *See* Middlemass
MIDDLEMORE. A loc. n., Worcest.
MIDDLETON. A loc. n., Derbysh., Dur., Lancs, Norf., Northants, Yorks
MIDDLEWEEK. From Middlewich; a loc. n., Ches.
MIDGLEY. A loc. n., Yorks
MIDWINTER. From Middlewinterbourne; a loc. n., Wilts (?)
MIELL. *See* Miall
MIGEON. *Fr.* Migeon; a p.n.
MIGHT. *Fr.* Miette, Myte; p.n.
MILBORROW. From Millbrook; a loc. n., Cornw., Hants
MILBOURN, MILBURN. From Milborne; a loc. n., Dorset, Wilts
MILDMAY. *Fr.* Mildmé; a p.n.
MILEHAM. A loc. n., Norf.
MILES. *Dch.* Meijlis; *Fl.* Miles, Milis; p.n.
MILESON. From Milson; a loc. n., Salop. Or *Fr.* Milsan; a p.n.
MILESTONE. *G.* Milostan; a p.n.
MILFORD. A loc. n., Devon, Hants, Salop, Staffs., Surr., S. Wales
MILICAN. *Dch.* Milikan; *Fl.* Milecan; p.n.
MILK. *G.* Milich, Milke; *D.B.* Melc; p.n. *See* Mills
MILL. *See* Miall
MILLETT. *Fr.*; p.n., dimin. *See* Miall
MILLIGAN. *Dch.* Milligen; a p.n.
MILLIKIN. *See* Milican
MILLINGER. *See* Mullinger
MILLINGTON. A loc. n., Ches., Yorks
MILLS. *Dch.* Mills; *Fl.* Miles, Millis; *G.* Milisch; *D.B.* Milo, Miles; p.n.
MILNE. *See* Miall
MILSON. *See* Mileson
MILTON. A loc. n., Devon, Dorset, Fife, Hants, Kent, Northants, Oxf., Westmd., Yorks. etc.
MILWARD. *D.* Moellgaard; *Fr.* Milliard; p.n.
MIMMS. A loc. n., Herts and Middlx.
MINCHIN. *See* Minnikin
MINES. *See* Meen
MINETT. *Fl.* Minnaert; *G.* Minuth; *Fr.* Minet; p.n.
MINGAY. *Fr.* Minquet; a p.n.
MINNIKIN. *F.* Menken; *G.* Mennicke; *Fl.* Minique; *Dch.* Mennecken; p.n.
MINNS. *See* Meen
MINSHULL. A loc. n., Ches.
MINTER. *G.* Minte; *Fr.* Minder; p.n.
MINTERN. A loc. n., Dorset

MINTEY. *See* Minter

MINTING. A loc. n., Lincs

MINTON. A loc. n., Salop. Or *Fl.* Minten; a p.n.

MISSEN. *Fl.* Misson; a p.n. Or Misson; a loc. n., Staffs.

MIST. *Dch.* Misset; a p.n.

MITCHAM. A loc. n., Surr.

MITCHELL. *See* Michel

MITCHINSON. *See* Meachen

MITFORD. A loc. n., Northbd.

MITTON. A loc. n., Staffs., Yorks. *D.B.* Mutone

MOBBS. *Fl.* Mobers; p.n. *See* Mabb

MOBERLEY. From Mobberley; a loc. n., Ches., Staffs.

MOCKLER. *Fr.* Mauclere; a Huguenot n.

MODGERIDGE, MODGRIDGE. *See* Modridge

MODRIDGE. From Modrydd; a loc. n., Brecon

MOELLEDON. From Moel-y-don; Menai Straits, N. Wales

MOGER. *N.* Mágr; *D.* Maag; *Fr.* Mauger; p.n. *See* Mogg

MOGG. *N.* Mágr; *D.* Maag; *Dch.* Mock, Mok; *Fl.* Moke; *G.* Moch; p.n.

MOGGS. *See* Magness and Mogg

MOLD. A loc. n., Flint

MOLDEN. From Malden; a loc. n., Surr. Or Maldon, Ess.

MOLE. *G.* Mohl; *Fr.* Molé; p.n. *See* Moll

MOLESWORTH. A loc. n., Hunts

MOLINEUX. From Moulineaux; a loc. n., Normandy

MOLL. *Dch.*, *Fl.*, *G.* Moll; p.n.

MOLLET. *Fr.* Mollet; *Fl.* Moulaert; *G.* Mulitz; p.n.

MONCKTON. A loc. n., Devon, Dorset, Kent, S. Wales, Wilts, Yorks

MONCRIEFF. A hill in Perthsh.

MONGER. *Fr.* Moncheur, Mongars; *G.* Monicke; p.n.

MONK. *N.* Munki; n.n. *D.* Munck; *Dch.* Monch, Monk, Munk; *Fr.* Moncq; p.n.

MONKHOUSE. A loc. n., Northbd.

MONNINGTON. A loc. n., Heref.

MONSER. *See* Mountseer

MONSEY. *See* Mountseer or Mounsey

MONTAGUE. From Montaigu; a loc. n., France and Holland

MONTEITH. A loc. n., Perth

MONTFORD. A loc. n., Salop

MONTGOMERY. A loc. n., Normandy. Occurs in *D.B.*

MONUMENT. *Fr.* Mahimont or Morimont; p.n.

MONEY. *Fr.* Monnaye, Muny; p.n. Mauny, Monnaie; loc. n., France

MOODY. *G.* Mude; *D.* Muthe; p.n.

MOON. From Moyon or Mohun; a loc. n., Normandy. Or *Dch.* Moen; *G.* Mohn; *Fl.* Moine; p.n.

MOONEY. *See* Money

MOOR. *N.* Már; *Dch.* Moor; *Fl.* Morre; *G.* Mohr; p.n.

MOORHOUSE. From Muirhouse; a loc. n., Forfarsh.

MOPPET. *Fr.* Moppert; a p.n. *See* Mabbut

MORBEY. *See* Mawby

MORCOM. *Fr.* Marcomb; a Huguenot n.

MORELAND. A loc. n., Westmd.

MORELL, MORRELL. *Fr.* Morel; *D.B.* Morel; a p.n. A loc. n., Normandy

In Roll of Battell Abbey. Philip de Morel in Rot. Obl. et Fin., K. John. Also a Huguenot n.

MOREWOOD. From Moorwood; a loc. n., Yorks

MORGAN. From the Irish O'Muiregain; a p.n.

MORLEY. A loc. n., Derbysh., Yorks

MORRALL. *See* Morell.

MORRISS. *Fr.* Maurice, Morisse; p.n.
Morreis in Roll of Battell Abbey.

MORSE. A loc. n., Glost. Or *Dch.* Mors; a p.n.

MORTER. *Fr.* Mortiaux, Mortier, Mortoire; p.n. Morteaux; a loc. n., Normandy

MORTIMER. From Mortemer; a loc. n., Normandy. *D.B.* De Mortemer; a p.n.
In Roll of Battell Abbey, and Rot. Obl. et Fin., K. John.

MORTLOCK. From Mortlach; a loc. n., Banff. Or Mortlake, Surr.

MORTON. A loc. n., Derbysh., Dumfries, Lincs, Yorks

MOSEDALE. A loc. n., Cumb. Also *D.* Mosdal; a loc. and p.n.

MOSER. *D.* Mose; *G.*, *Fl.*, *Dch.* Moser; *Fr.* Moussier; p.n.

MOSSOP. *Dch.* Masdorp, Massop; p.n.

MOSTYN. A loc. n., N. Wales

MOTHERSIL. *See* Mothersole

MOTHERSOLE. From Mottishall; a loc. n., Suff. (?)

MOTION. *See* Motton

MOTT. *Fr.* Motte and De la Motte; *D.* Mothe; p.n. From Motte; a town of Cotes du Nord, France

MOTTON. *See* Mutton
Sir William Moton, Knight, was living at Peckleton, Leics., A.D. 1174. Sir Robert Moton was killed at the battle of Evesham, A.D. 1265.

MOTUM. From Mottingham; a loc. n., Ess.

MOUEL. *See* Mole

MOULD. Moult; a loc. n., Normandy. *See* Mold

MOULES. *See* Mole

MOUNSEY. From *N.* Manarsey, the I. of Man; *Dch.* Monsee; *Fr.* Montoisy (?); a p.n. Or *see* Mountseer

MOUNSHER. *See* Mountseer

MOUNTAIN. *Fr.* Montaigne; a p.n.

MOUNTSEER. *Fr.* Monseur; a p.n.

MOUSE. *D.* Muus; *G.*, *Dch.*, *Fl.* Maus, Mus; *D.B.* Musard, Musla; p.n.

MOUSER, MOUSIR. *Fr.* Moussier; a p.n.

MOWBRAY. From Moutbray; a loc. n., Normandy, or Maubray in Flanders
Moribray and Mowbray in Roll of Battell Abbey. William de Mowbray held lands in Notts. Rot. Obl. et Fin., K. John, A.D. 1205.

MOWLE. *See* Mole

MOXON. *D.* Mogensen; *Dch.* Mock, Mok; p.n.

MOY. *D.*; p.n.

MOYSE, MOYSEY. *Fr.* Moisy; a Huguenot p.n.

MOZLEY. From Moseley; a loc. n., Staffs.

MUCKALL. *N.* Mikill; *D.* Michael, Muxoll; *S.* Michal; *Fl.* Michils; p.n. Mucholls; a loc. n., Kincardine

MUCKLESTON. A loc. n., Salop, Staffs.

MUCKLOW. From Mucklagh; a loc. n., Kerry, Ireland. Or *see* Mockler

MUDD. *Dch.* Mudde; a p.n.

MUDDLE. From Muthill; a loc. n., Perthsh. (?)

MUDGE. *Fr.* Mouche; a p.n.

MUDIE. *See* Moody

MUELUISH. *See* Mellish

MUFFET. *Fl.* Muffat; a p.n.

MUGFORD. From Mogford; a loc. n., Devon

MUGGERIDGE. *See* Modridge

MUGGLESTON. From Muclestone; a loc. n., Staffs.

MUGGLETON. From Muckleton; a loc. n., Salop

MUGGS. *See* Moggs

MUGLISTON. *See* Muckleston

MUGRIDGE. *See* Modridge

MUIR. A loc. n., Scotl. *See* Moor

MULHOLLAND. From the Irish O'Maolchallain; a p.n.

MULINGER. *Fr.* Moulinier (?); a Huguenot n.

MULLEN. *Fr.* Moulin; *Dch.* Mullen; *G.* Mühlan; p.n.

MULLEY. *Fr.* Mullie; a p.n.

MULLINER. *See* Molineux

MULLINS. From Moulins; a loc. n., Normandy

MULLIS. *G.* Mulitz; a p.n.

MUMBY. A loc. n., Lincs

MUMFORD. From Mundford; a loc. n., Suff.

MUMMERY. *Fr.* Momerie; p.n.

MUNCASTER. A loc. n., Cumb.

MUNCH. *G.* Münch, Münich; *D.* Munnich; p.n. Or *see* Monk

MUNCY. *See* Mounsey

MUNDY. *N.* Mundi (abbrev. of names ending in mundr); *G.* Mund, Munder, Mundri; *Dch.* Munne; p.n.

MUNGY. From Montjoye; a loc. n., France. Or *N.* Mangi; a pet n. for Magnus

MUNN. *Dch.* Munne; a p.n. Or *see* Moon

MUNNING. *See* Munn

MUNT. *S.* Munthe; *G.* Mund; p.n.

MUNTING. From Munden; a loc. n., Herts

MURCHISON. From Merchiston; a loc. n., Edinburghsh.

MURCOTT. A loc. n., Wilts

MURE. *See* Moor

MURIEL. *See* Morell

MURLEY. From Moorly; a loc. n., Wilts

MURNANE. From Minane; a loc. n., Cork

MURPHY. From the Irish MacMurchada; a p.n. MacMorrow, MacMurrogh

MURRAY. From Moray; a loc. n., Scotl. Or Irish O'Muiredhaigh; a p.n.

MURRELL. *See* Morell

MURROW. A loc. n., Camb. Or *D.* Murer; *Fr.* Moreau; *Dch.* Morreau; a p.n. Or *see* Murphy

MURTHWAITE. A loc. n., Westmd.

MUSCHAMP. From Muskham; a loc. n., Notts

MUSGRAVE. A loc. n., Cumb.

MUSGROVE. *See* Musgrave

MUSK. *Dch.*, *Fl.* Musch; *G.* Muske; p.n., dimin. of Mus (?). Comp. Muskau; a loc. n., Prussia, and Muskham (*D.B.* Muscham), Notts

MUSKETT. *Fl.* Musschaert, Musschot; *G.* Muskat; p.n.

MUSSETT. *Fr.* Moussett, Musset; *Dch.* Most, Mussert; p.n.

Musett in Roll of Battell Abbey.

MUSSON. From Mousson; a loc. n., Normandy. Or Muston, Leics., Yorks

MUST. *See* Mussett

MUSTERS. *Fr.* Mustière; a p.n.

Robert de Mosters, a tenant in chief in *D.B.* Gaufrid de Musters *temp.* K. John, Rot. Obl. et Fin.

MUTIMER. *See* Mortimer

MUTTITT. *Fr.* Mottet; *D.* Muthe; *Fl.* Muth; p.n.

MUTTON. *Fr.* Mouton; a p.n. Or *see* Mitton and Motton

Hugo de Mutton *temp.* K. John, Rot. Obl. et Fin.

MYERS. *D.*, *S.* Meyer; *Dch.* Meier; *G.* Mayer, Meyer; *Fl.* Meyers, Miers; *D.B.* Mere; p.n.

MYERSCOUGH. A loc. n., Lancs

MYHILL. *See* Miall

MYNOTT. *See* Maynard

N.

NAGLER. *N.* Nagli; *Fr.* Naglée; p.n.

NAILER. *See* Neal

NAISH. *See* Nash

NANGLE. From Angle, near Milford Haven

Gilbert de Angulo, baron of Angle, 1172 (Lower).

NANKIVEL. From Nanckivel; a loc. n., Cornw.

NAPIER.

The officer of the King's Household who had charge of the napery or table linen.

NAPLETON. A loc. n., Worcest.

NAPP. *N.* Knappi; n.n. *D.*, *Fl.*, *Dch.* Knapp; *G.* Knapp, Knabe, Knappe, Knaps, Knop, Knopping; p.n.

NAPPER. From Nappa; a loc. n., Yorks. Or *see* Napp

NAPTHEN. From Napton; a loc. n., in Warwicksh.

NASH. A loc. n., Heref., Kent

NASLEN. *See* Nesling

NASSAN. *Dch.* Nussen; a p.n.

NATERS. *See* Nattrass

NATT. *Dch.* Nat; *G.* Nath; p.n. From Nathaniel (?)

NATTRASS. *Fl.* Nateris, Natris; p.n.

NAUGHTON. A loc. n., Suff., Nawton, Yorks

NEACH. *G.* Nietz, Nietch, Nische; a p.n.

NEAGLE. *D.* Nagel; *G.* Niegel; p.n. *See* Neale

NEALE. *N.* Njáll; *S.* Nihl; *D.*, *Dch.* Niel; *G.* Niegel; *D.B.* Nigel; *Fl.* Niels, Nille; *Fr.* Neel; p.n.

Neile in Roll of Battell Abbey; and Nigel, a tenant in chief in *D.B.*

NECK. *Dch.*; p.n.

NEEBE. From Newby; a freq. loc. n. Or *see* Neighbour

NEECH. *See* Neach

NEEDELL. *D.* Nedahl; *G.* Niedel; *Fr.* Nidoul; p.n.

NEEDHAM. A loc. n., Norf.

NEEP. *N.* Kneipr; n.n. *G.* Kneip; *Dch.*, *Fl.* Knip; *D.B.* Nepos; p.n.

NEGUS. *G.* Niegisch, Nikish; *Fr.* Nicaise; p.n.

NEIGHBOUR. *D.* Nyeboe; *G.* Neubauer, Neuber, Niebour, Niebuhr; *S.* Neijber, Nieber; *Dch.* Nieubuur, Nueboer; p.n.

NELSON. *D.* Neilson, Nielsen; *S.* Nelson, Nelzon; *Dch.* Nelson, Nielsen; p.n. *See* Neale

NEOBARD. *Fr.* Néaubert; a p.n.

NERTIGAN. *Fl.* Neutgens; *Dch.* Neutegem; p.n.

NESBET. A loc. n., Dur., Northbd.

NESLEN, NESLIN. *See* Nesling

NESLING. *D.* Ness; *Dch.* Nes, Nesselaar; *Fl.* Nees, Nessen; *G.* Niesel, Nessel; p.n.

NESS. *D.*, *S.*; p.n. Also a loc. n., Ches., Salop, Yorks

NETHERCLIFT. From Nethercleugh; a loc. n., Dumfries

NETHERCOTT. A loc. n., Devon, Somers.

NETHERSOLE. From Netherseal; a loc. n., Leics.

NETTLE. *Fr.* Niatel; a p.n.

NETTLEFOLD. From Netherfold; a loc. n., Yorks

NETTLETON. A loc. n., Lincs, Wilts

NEVARD. *Fr.* Nivard; a p.n.

NEVE. *Dch.* Neef; *Fr.* Nève and le Nève; p.n.

NEVELL. *See* Neville

NEVILLE. From Néville; a loc. n., Normandy. *D.B.* Neuille; p.n.

Nevill in Rot. Obl. et Fin., K. John.

NEVISON. *N.* Nefja; n.n. *D.* Neve; *Dch.* Neef, Neeve, Neff; *Fl.* Neefs, Neave; *Fr.* Nève; p.n.
NEWALL. From Newhall; a loc. n., Ches.
NEWARK. A loc. n., Notts
NEWBEGIN. *See* Newbiggin
NEWBERRY. From Newbury; a loc. n., Berks
NEWBIGGIN. A loc. n., Camb.
NEWBOLT. *See* Newbould
NEWBOULD. From Newbold; a loc. n., Leics., Yorks
NEWBY. A loc. n., Yorks, etc.
NEWDICK. From Newdigate; a loc. n., Surr.
NEWDIGATE. A loc. n., Surr.
NEWELL. *See* Neville
NEWHAM. A freq. loc. n.
NEWITT. *Fl.* Neute; a p.n. *See* Newt
NEWMAN. *G.* Neumann; *Dch.* Nieman, Numan; *S.*, *D.* Nyman; p.n.
NEWNES. A loc. n., Salop
NEWNHAM. A loc. n., Glost., Hants, Salop, Warw., Worcest.
NEWNUM. *See* Newnham
NEWPORT. A loc. n., Bucks, Glost., Hants, Montgy., Salop, Somers., S. Wales
NEWSAM. *See* Newsome
NEWSOME. A loc. n., Lincs, Yorks
NEWSON. *Dch.* Nussen, Nijssen; p.n.
NEWSTEAD. A loc. n., Lincs, Notts, Staffs.
NEWT. *See* Nutt and Nute
NEWTH. *See* Nutt
NEWTON. A freq. loc. n.
NIBBS. *G.* Nibisch; a p.n.
NIBLET. From Nibley; a loc. n., Glost.
NICE. *D.* Niss; *Fl.* Neys, Nys; *Dch.* Nies; *G.* Kneis; p.n.
NICHOLAS. *See* Nicker
NICHOLLS. *D.* Nickels; *S.* Niekels; p.n. *See* Nicker
NICHOLS. *See* Nicholls
NICHOLSON. *S.* Nicolausson; *D.* Nikelsen; p.n. *See* Nicker
NICKER. *N.* Nikolás; *D.B.* Nicolaus, Nicol; *G.* Nick, Nicke, Nickel; *Fl.* Nicole; *D.* Nickels; p.n.
NICKERSON. *See* Nicker
NICKLESS. *See* Nicker
NICKOLS. *See* Nicholls
NICOL. *N.* Nikolás; *D.B.* Nicol; p.n.
NIEL. *See* Neale
NIGHTINGALE. *G.* Nachtigall; *Dch.* Nagtegaal; *Fl.* Nachtergael; p.n.
NIKER. *See* Nicker
NIMMO. *Dch.* Nimmo, Niemer, Nieman; *G.* Niemann; p.n.
NINCE. *G.* Nintz; a p.n.
NIPPER. *Fl.* Nepper; a p.n.
NISBET. A loc. n., Berwick, Haddingtonsh., Roxburgh
NIX. *See* Nicker
NIXON. *See* Nicker
NOAKES, NOAKS. *N.* Hnaki; *D.* Knoak; *Dch.* Noack; *G.* Knoch; p.n. Noke; a loc. n. Oxf.
NOBBS. *N.* Knappi; n.n. *G.* Nabe; *Fl.*, *D.* Knop; *Dch.* Knobbe, Noppe; p.n.
NOBES. *Fr.* Nobis; a p.n. *See* Nobbs
NOBLE. *D.*, *Dch.* Nobel; *Fl.* Nobels; p.n.
NOCK. *N.* Hnaki; *D.* Knock; *G.* Knoch; p.n.
NOCKALL. *See* Nockolds
NOCKLES. *See* Nockolds
NOCKOLDS. *D.B.* Nogiold; *Fl.* Nockels; p.n. *See* Noakes
NODDER. *Fr.* Nodé; a p.n.
NOEL. From Noailles; a loc. n., Normandy
NOKES. *See* Noakes
NOLLOTH. *D.* Nolleroth; *Fr.* Nolleau, Nollett; *G.* Nolte; p.n.
NOLAN. From the Irish O'Nuallain; a p.n.
NOON. *See* Nunn
NOOTT. *See* Nute
NOPS. *Dch.* Noppe; a p.n.

NORBURY. A loc. n., Ches., Derbysh., Salop, Staffs.

NORDEN. *D.* Norden; *Dch.* Noorden; p.n.

NORFOR. *N.* Narfi; *G.* Nafe, Nave, Naveau; *D.B.* Novi; *Fl.* Noeve; p.n.

NORKETT. *See* Northcote

NORMAN. *S.* Nordman; *G.* Nordmann; *D.* Norman; *Dch.* Normant; *D.B.* Norman; p.n.

NORMINGTON. From Normanton; Derbysh., Leics., Lincs, Wilts, Yorks

NORRINGTON. A loc. n., Wilts

NORRIS. *Fr.* Noris; a p.n.
Norice in Roll of Battell Abbey.

NORTHCOTE. From Northcott; a loc. n., Somers.

NORTON. A freq. loc. n.

NOSWORTHY. From Knaworthy; a loc. n., Devon

NOTCUTT. *See* Northcote

NOTLEY. A loc. n., Ess.

NOTSON. *Fl.* Knudsen; a p.n. *See* Nott and Nute

NOTT. *Fr.* Notte; a p.n.
Richard Not in Rot. Obl. et Fin., K. John.

NOTTAGE. A loc. n., S. Wales. Or *Fl.* Notez; *G.* Nöthig; p.n.

NOTTIDGE. *See* Nottage

NOURSE. *See* Nowers

NOWELL. *See* Noel

NOWERS. From Noyers; a loc. n., France
De Noiers, de Noies, de Nouners, occur among the tenants at the time of the Survey of *D.B.* Noers is on the Roll of Battell Abbey. Simon de Noers in Rot. Obl. et Fin., K. John.

NOY. *Dch.* Noy; a p.n.

NOYCE. *G.* Neuss; a loc. and p. n.

NOYES. *See* Nowers and Noyce

NUDD. *N.* Knútr; *D.B.* Cnud, Cnut; *D.* Knud; *G.* Knuth; *Fl.* Cnudde; *Dch.* Knuijt, Noot, Nutte; p.n. *See* Nute
Canud, a Saxon tenant in *D.B.*

NUDDS. *See* Nudd

NUELL. *See* Noel

NUGENT. From Nogent; a loc. n., Normandy

NUNN. *F.* Nanno, Nanne; *G.* Nunn; p.n.

NUNNELEY. From Noneley; a loc. n., Salop

NURSE. *See* Nourse

NURSERY. *See* Nowers

NURSEY. *See* Nourse and Nowers

NUTBEAM. *G.*, *Dch.* Nussbaum; a p.n.

NUTBEAN. *See* Nutbeam

NUTCHER. *G.* Knutsche; p.n.

NUTE. *N.* Knútr; *D.* Knudt; *Dch.* Noot, Nut, Knuijt; *G.* Knuth; *Fl.* Cnudde; p.n.
Canud, a Saxon tenant in *D.B.*

NUTH. *See* Nutt

NUTMAN. *Dch.* Nootman; a p.n. *See* Nute

NUTT. *See* Nute

NUTTAL. From Nuttall; a loc. n., Notts. *D.B.* Notele

NUTTER. *See* Nuthall and Nute

NUTTING. *See* Nute

NUTTY. *Fr.* Notez; a p.n.

NYE. *Dch.* Nije, Nuy; p.n.

O.

OAFS. *G.* Offhaus; *Dch.* Hofhuis (?); p.n.
OAK. A loc. n., Somers.
OAKDEN. *See* Ogden
OAKES. A loc. n., Derbysh., Lancs. Or *N.* Oxi; *Dch.* Ochs; *G.* Ocke; *F.* Okko; p.n.
OAKEY. *Fr.* Ocket; *Fl.* Ogy; *G.* Ocke; p.n.
OAKHAM. A loc. n., Notts, Rutland, Warw.
OAKLEY. A loc. n., Beds, Berks, Bucks, Ess., Hants, Staffs., Suff., Worcest., etc.
OAKSHETTE. *See* Oakshott
OAKSHOTT. From Oxshott; a loc. n., Surr.
OATES. *Fl.* Ots; a p.n.
OATLEY. *See* Ottley
OBBARD. *See* Hobart
OBEE. From Oadby; a loc. n., Leics. Or *Fr.* Aupée; a p.n.
OBORNE. A loc. n., Dorset
OCLEE. From Ockley; a loc. n. in Surr. Or Oakley, Ess.
ODAMS. *Dch.* Odems; a p.n.
ODDIN. *Dch.* Oddinck; a p.n. *See* Oddy
ODDY. *N.* Oddi; *F.* Ode, Odo; *D.* Odde; *Dch.*, *Fl.* Otte, Hody; *Fr.* Aude; *G.* Otho, Other, Ott, Otte, Otto; *D.B.* Oda, Ode, Otha, Odo, Odard; p.n.
ODEL. *N.* Oddkell or Ottkel; *D.B.* Odel, Oudchell, Ouetel; *G.* Hodel; p.n. Or *see* Odell
ODELL. A loc. n., Bucks
ODGER. *N.* Oddgeir; *Fl.* Oger; p.n.
O'DONOGHUE. From the Iris' O'Donchada or O'Donchu; p.n.
OFFIN. From Ofton; a loc. n., Suff.
OFFLEY. A loc. n., Herts
OFFORD. A loc. n., Hunts
OGBEN. *See* Ogbourne
OGBOURNE. A loc. n., Wilts
OGDEN. A loc. n., Lancs
OGG. *N.* Ögurr; *D.* Ager, Haag; *Dch.* Hog; *D.B.* Oghe; *Fl.* Hogge; p.n.
OKES. A loc. n., Lancs. *See* Oakes
OLCOTT. From Holcott; a loc. n., Northants
OLD. *Dch.*, *S.* Olde; a p.n.
OLDACRE. From Aldecar; a loc. n., Derbysh.
OLDERNESS. From Holderness; a loc. n., Yorks
OLDERSHAW. From Aldersholes; a loc. n., Yorks
OLDFIELD. A loc. n., Worcest.
OLDHAM. A loc. n., Lancs
OLDING. *D.* Olden; a p.n. *See* Old
OLDMAN. *G.* Ohlmann; *S.* Ollman; p.n.
OLDRIDGE. A loc. n., Devon
OLDRING. *Dch.* Olderen; a p.n. *See* Old
OLDROYDE. *Fl.* Oldrade; a p.n. *See* Holroyd
OLET, OLLETT. *Fr.* Oliette; a p.n. *See* Olyott
OLIFFE. *See* Oliver
OLIPHANT. *Dch.* Ollefen; *A.S.* Olfend (?); *D.B.* Elfain; p.n.
David de Oliphard, Scotl., 1142. Chaucer has 'Sire Oliphaunt.'
OLIVER. *N.* Óláfr or Óleifr; *S.* O[illegible]; *Dch.* Olfers; *Fl.* Oleff; [illegible]. Olivier; *D.B.* Oliv, Olviet; p.n.
OLLAY. *See* Olley
OLLE. *See* Olley
OLLEY. *N.* Oli; *D.* Olling; *G.* Oley, Eule, Ohle; *Dch.* Olie, Olij; *D.B.* de Ole, de Olgi, Oiley, de Oilli; p.n.
OLLIFFE. *See* Oliver
OLNEY. A loc. n., Bucks

OLYOTT. *Fl.* Holliette, Holler; *D.B.* Oilard, Oualet; p.n. *See* Olley

OMANT. *Fr.* Omont; a p.n.

OMASH. *Fr.* D'Ormasse; a Huguenot n.

OMER. A loc. n., Devon

OMMANEY. A loc. n., Hants

ONES. *Dch.* Onasse; p.n. Or Onehouse; a loc. n., Suff.

ONG. *N.* Ungi (?); *F.* Onke, dimin. of Onno; *G.* Unger; *Fl.* Ongers; p.n. Ongar; a loc. n., Ess.

ONGLEY. *See* Onley

O'NIELL. *See* Neale

ONIONS. From Angiens (?); a loc. n., Normandy. Or Aniange, France

ONLEY. A loc. n., Northants, Staffs.

ONSLOW. *See* Honslowe

OPENSHAW. A loc. n., Lincs

OPIE. *See* Obee

ORAM. From Owram; a loc. n., Yorks

ORCHARD. A loc. n., Somers.

ORD. A loc. n., Northbd. Or *Dch.* Oort, Ort; p.n.

ORFEUR. From Orvaux (?); a loc. n., Normandy

ORFORD. A loc. n., Lancs, Lincs, Norf., Suff.

ORGAN. *See* Hogan

ORGILL. A loc. n., Cumb.

ORGLES. *See* Argles

ORLEBAR. From Orlingbury; a loc. n., Northants (?). Or *Dch.* Haleber; a p.n. (?)

ORMAN. *See* Ormandy

ORMANDY. *N.* Há-mundr; *D.*, *S.* Amund; *Dch.* Ormondt; *G.* Hamman; *Fr.* Aumont; *D.B.* Amun; p.n.

ORMEROD. A loc. n., Lancs

ORMISTON. A loc. n., Edinbgh.

ORMOND. *See* Ormandy

ORMS. Contraction of Ormson, from *N.* Ormr; a p.n.

ORMSBY. A loc. n., Lincs, Norf., Yorks

ORR. *N.* Orri and Ör; n.n. *D.* Orr; *Dch.* Orri; *Fl.* Ories, Orys; *G.* Oehr; *D.B.* Ori; p.n.

ORRELL. A loc. n., Lancs

ORRIDGE. From Horridge; a loc. n., Devon

ORRIS. *N.* Orri; *D.* Orr; *Dch.* Orri; *Fl.* Oreys, Ories; p.n.

ORTH. *D.* Orth; *D.B.* Orthi; a p.n.

ORTHORPE. From Authorpe; a loc. n., Lincs

ORTON. A loc. n., Cumb., Hunts, Leics., Staffs., Westmd.

ORVIS. *Dch.* Avis; *Fr.* Avice, Avisse; p.n.

OSBALDESTONE. A loc. n., Lancs

OSBASTON. A loc. n., Salop

OSBORNE. *N.* Ás-Björn; *D.* Osborn; *D.B.* Osbern, Osba; p.n.

OSLAR, OSLER. *Fl.* Hosseley, Hostelet; a p.n.

OSMAN. *G.* Ossmann; a p.n. *See* Osmund

OSMENT. *See* Osmund

OSMOTHERLEY. A loc. n., Lancs, Yorks

OSMUND. *N.* Ásmundr; *D.B.* Assemann, Osmund; *D.*, *Fl.* Osmund; *Dch.* Osseman; *Fr.* Osmont; p.n.

OSSINGTON. A loc. n., Notts

OSTICK. *Dch.*, *Fl.* Oosterwijk; p.n. Also a loc. n. in Flanders

OSWALD. *N.* Ásvaldr; *Fl.*, *D.*, *G.* Oswald; p.n.

OTTAWAY. *G.* Ottawa; *Fl.* Ottevaere; p.n.

OTTLEY. A loc. n., Salop, Suff., Yorks

OTTY. *See* Oddy

OTTYWILL. From Outwell; a loc. n., Norf.

OTWAY. *See* Ottaway

OULTON. A loc. n., Cumb., Norf., Yorks

OUNSTEAD. From Houndstreet; a loc. n., Somers. (?)

OURY. *Fr.* Oury; a p.n.

OUSELEY. A loc. n., Northants
OUSEY. *See* Hussey
OUTHWAITE. *See* Huthwaite
OUTLAW. From Oathlaw; a loc. n., Forfar. Or *N.* Oddlaugr; *Dch.* Otterloo; p.n.
OUTON. *Dch.* Ouden; *Fr.* Othon; p.n. Or *see* Houghton
OUTTAN. *See* Outon
OVENS. *S.* Ovens; *Fl.* Ovyn; *Dch.* Oven; p.n.
OVENSTONE. A loc. n., Fife
OVER. A loc. n., Camb.
OVERBURY. A loc. n., Suff., Worcest.
OVEREND. A loc. n., Worcest.
OVERMAN. *Dch.* Overman; a p.n.
OVERTON. A loc. n., Ches., Derbysh., Hants, Lancs, Staffs., Wilts, Yorks
OVERY. A loc. n., Oxf. Or *Fr.* Ouvry; a p.n.
OVINGTON. A loc. n., Ess., Norf.
OWEN. British p.n. Also *D.* Owen; *Fr.* Ouin; p.n.
Ouen is a tenant in *D.B.*, *temp.* Ed. Con.
OWERS. A loc. n., Hants
OWGAN. *See* Hogan
OWLES. A loc. n., Suff.
OWSTON. A loc. n., Leics., Lincs
OWTHWAITE. *See* Huthwaite
OXBORROW. A loc. n., Norf.
OXENHAM. From Oxnam; a loc. n., Roxburghsh.
OXER. From Oxhall; a loc. n., Dur.
OXIER. *See* Oxer
OXLADE. From Oxlode; a loc. n., Camb.
OXLEY. A loc. n., Staffs.
OXX. *N.* Oxi; *Dch.* Ox; p.n.
OYLER. *G.* Eule; a p.n.

P.

PACE, PACEY. *Fr.* Pays, Peys; *Dch.* Pees; p.n.
PACKE. *Dch.* Pak; *Fl.* Paké; *G.* Pache; p.n.
PACKER. *Fl.* Paké; *G.* Pache, Pachur; p.n.
PACKHAM. A loc. n., Devon
PACKMAN. *Fl.* Packman; *G.* Pachmann; a p.n.
PADBURY. A loc. n., Oxf.
PADDAY. *D.*, *G.* Pade; a p.n.
PADDON. From Patton; a loc. n., Yorks (*D.B.* Patun). Or *Dch.* Paddinge; a p.n.
PADFIELD. A loc. n., Derbysh.
PADGET. *See* Paget
PADLEY. A loc. n., Derbysh.
PADMORE. From Pedmore; a loc. n., Worcest.
PAFFEY. *See* Pavett
PAGE. From the *Fr.* Page; a Huguenot n.
PAGET. *D.* Pagh; *Dch.* Pagez; *Fl.* Page, Pagis; a p.n. Pagett, the dimin. of Page
PAICE. *See* Pace
PAINE. *N.* Peini; n.n. *D.B.* Pinel, Pin; *G.* Pein, Penert, Pinn; *Fr.* Pain, Peigné, Pineau; *Fl.* Payen, Pien; *Dch.* Pen, Penn; p.n.
Wm. Paen *temp.* K. John.
PAINTER. *D.* Penter; *Fl.* Pinter; p.n.
PAKE. *Dch.* Peek, Pek; p.n. *See* Peake
PALETHORPE. From Pallathorp; a loc. n., Yorks. Or Perlethorpe, Notts
PALEY. *Fr.* Pelay, Pelet, Pelez; p.n.
PALGRAVE. A loc. n., Norf., Suff.
PALK. A loc. n., Devon
PALLETT. From Paillette; a loc. n., France

PALMER. *Fl.* Palmaert; *Dch.* Pallme; *G.* Palmer; p.n.
Richard Palmer held lands in Worcest. *temp.* K. John.

PANCHEN. From Paunchin; a loc. n., Devon. Or *S.* Panchéen; *Fr.* Panquin; p.n.

PANGBOURNE. A loc. n., Berks

PANK. *D.*, *S.* Pang; *G.* Pancke; p.n.

PANKHURST. A loc. n., Suss.

PANKS. *See* Pank

PANNELL. *Fl.* Pannell; *Fr.* Panel; p.n.

PANTER, PANTHER. *Fr.* Pante, Panthou; *Dch.* Pante; *G.* Panter; p.n.

PANTIN. *Fr.*; p.n.

PANTRY. From Penterry; a loc. n., Monmth.

PAPE. *Fr.* Pepe; a p.n. *See* Poppy

PAPWORTH. A loc. n., Camb.

PARADISE. *Fl.*, *Fr.* Paradis; a p.n.

PARAMAN. *See* Pearmain

PARAMORE. From Paramé; a loc. n., Normandy (?)

PARCELL. *Fr.* Parisel; a p.n.

PARCHMENT. *G.* Pergament; a p.n.

PARDOE. *Fr.* Pardieu; *Dch.* Pardo; *D.* Pardi; p.n.

PARDON. *Fr.* Pardant, Pardon; *Fl.* Pardaen; *G.* Pardon; p.n.

PARFITT. *Fr.* Parfait; a p.n.

PARISH. *See* Parritch

PARK, PARKE. A freq. loc. n. Or *Dch.* Park; *Fr.* Parc; p.n.
Richard de Parco held lands in Lincs., *temp.* K. John.

PARKER. *G.* Parke; a p.n.

PARKHOUSE. A loc. n., Northbd.

PARKHURST. A loc. n., I. of Wight

PARKINS. *Fl.* Parcyns; a p.n.

PARKINSON. *See* Parkins

PARLET. *See* Pallett

PARLOUR. *G.* Parlow; a p.n.

PARMETER. *See* Parminter

PARMINTER. *Fr.* Parmentier; a p.n.

PARNELL. *Fl.* Panneel; *Fr.* Panel, Purnelle; p.n.

PARR. A loc. n. in Lancs. Or *Dch.* Parre, Paare; *Fl.* Paré; p.n. *D.B.* Pur (?)

PARRINGTON. A loc. n., Ess.

PARRIS. *Fr.* Parez, Paresse, Paris, Parys; p.n.

PARRITCH. From Parwich; a loc. n., Derbysh.

PARROT. *See* Perrott

PARRY. *Fr.* Parré; a p.n. *See* Parr

PARSLEE. *See* Purslow

PARSLEY. *See* Purslow

PARSLOW. *See* Purslow

PARSON. *Dch.* Parson, Passen, Passon, Passens; *D.* Pass, Passen; p.n.

PARSONSON. *See* Parson

PART. *G.* Pathe; a p.n.

PARTINGTON. A loc. n., Ches.

PARTON. A loc. n., Camb.

PARTRIDGE. From Pettridge; a loc. n., Kent

PASCOE. *Fr.* Pasque; a p.n.

PASH, PAISH. *Dch.* Pashe; *G.* Pasch; p.n.

PASK, PASKE. *Dch.* Pasché; *Fr.* Pasque; *G.* Pasch, Paschke; p.n.

PASKELL. *Fr.* Pascal; a p.n.

PASS. *D.* Pass; *Fl.* Pas; *S.* Passy; *Dch.*, *G.* Pas, Pass, Passe; p.n.

PASSMORE. From Peasemore; a loc. n., Berks

PATCH. *G.* Patsch; a p.n. *See* Pate

PATCHITT. *See* Paget

PATCHING. A loc. n., Suss.

PATE. *N.* Pétr, Petarr; *D.B.* Pade, Pata, Peter, Petrus; *Fl.* Patte, Peet, Piette; *Dch.* Pet, Peet, Piet; p.n.

PATEMAN. *See* Pate

PATERNOSTER. *Dch.*, *Fl.*; p.n.

PATMAN. *G.* Patermann; a p.n.

PATON. *See* Peyton

PATRICK. *Lat.* Patricius; *N.* Patrekr; a p.n.

PATTEN, PATTON. A loc. n., Salop, Yorks
PATTERSON. *See* Pate
PATTISON. *D.* Pade; *Fl.* Patte, Patesson; *Dch.* Padt, Patte, Patzer; *G.* Pade; *D.B.* Padda; Pata, Pat; p.n.
PATTLE. From Pathull or Pattishall; a loc. n., Staffs.
PAUL. *N.* Páll; *D.* Poul, Pauli, Paulin; *Fl.* Pauwels, Pauly, Poel, Pol, Polet, Poly, Polyn, Spoel; *Dch.* Pool, Pouwels, Spall, Spoel; *G.* Pohl, Pohler, Pollack, Poli, Pohlit, Pollok, Paul; *D.B.* Paulin, Pauli, Pawel; p.n.
PAULETT. *Fr.* Polet; a p.n. *See* Paull
PAUSE. *G.* Pause; a p.n.
PAUSEY. *See* Pause
PAVETT. *Fr.* Pavot; *Fl.* Pevaert; p.n.
PAVEY. *Fr.* Pavie, Peyveye; p.n
PAVIS. *Dch.* Pavias, Paviers; p.n.
PAWLETT. A loc. n., Somers. Or *Fr.* Poulet; a p.n.
PAWLEY. *Fr.* Pauly; *D.* Pauli; p.n.
PAWSEY. *Fr.* Poussier; a p.n. Or *see* Pause
PAXTON. A loc. n., Berwick
PAYNE. *See* Paine
PAYTON, PEYTON. From Paythorne; a loc. n., Yorks
PEABODY. *See* Peberdy
PEACE, PEASE. *Dch.* Piesche, Pees; p.n. *See* Pace
PEACHE. *G.* Pietsch; a p.n. *See* Peak
PEACHEY. *G.* Piecha; a p.n. *See* Peak
PEACOCK. From Peakirk; a loc. n., Northants. Or *G.* Piechocki; a p.n. *See* Peak
PEAD. *D.* Pied; *Fl.* Piette; p.n.
PEAK. *N.* Pík; *Dch.* Pieck, Piek; *G.* Pick; *D.* Picker; p.n.
PEALL. *See* Peel
PEAR. *Dch.* Peer; *Fr.* Pièrre; p.n.
PEARD. *Fr.* Pirard; a p.n.
PEARL. *D.* Perle; *G.* Perl, Pirle; *Dch.* Perlee; *Fl.* Perlau; p.n. Perlo in *D.B.*
PEARMAIN. *D.* Permin; *S.* Perman; *Fl.* Pierman; p.n.
PEARMAN. *See* Pearmain
PEARSE. *Fl.* Piers; *Dch.* Peere, Pierse; *D.* Pers; p.n.
PEARSON. *Dch.*, *Fl.* Pierson; *D.* Persson; *G.* Person; *Fr.* Pierresenné; p.n.
PEASCOD. Welsh Pyscoed; *D.* Piscordi; a p.n. From Dinbych-y-Pys-god; the ancient name of Tenby
PEASE. *Dch.* Pees; a p.n.
PEASLEY. A loc. n., Lancs
PEBERDY. *See* Pepperday
PECKHAM. A loc. n., Surr.
PECHEY. *See* Peachey
PECK. *See* Pake and Peake
PECKETT. *Fr.* Pécuchet; *G.* Pickert; p.n. *See* Peake
PECKOVER. A loc. n.
PEDDER. *N.* Petarr or Pettarr (Peter); *S.*, *D.* Peder; *Fl.* Pètte; p.n.

This name is seldom found before the twelfth and thirteenth centuries.

PEDDIE. *Fr.* Pède; a p.n.
PEDDLE. From Pedwell; a loc. n., Somers.
PEDLAR, PEDLEY. *See* Padley
PEEBLES. A loc. n., Scotl.
PEED. *See* Pead
PEEK. *See* Peak
PEEL. A loc. n., Lancs. Or *S.* Piehl, Pihl; *G.* Piel; *Dch.* Piël; *D.* Pihl, Piell, Püi, Pille; p.n.
PEEN. *Fr.* Pin; a p.n. *See* Paine
PEENY. *See* Paine
PEEPS. *See* Pape
PEERLESS. *G.* Pieles (?); a p.n.
PEET. *See* Pead and Peter
PEGG. *Dch.* Peck, Pek; p.n.
PEGLAR. *S.* Pegelow; a p.n.
PEILL. *See* Peel
PEIRSON. *See* Pearson
PELGRAM. *Fl.* Pelgrim; a p.n.

PELHAM. A loc. n., Herts

PELL. *G.* Pell; *Fl.* Pelle; *Dch.* Pel; p.n.

PELLEW. *See* Bellew

PELLING. From Pelyn; a loc. n., Cornw.

PELLY. *Fr.* Pelay, Pelet; a p.n.

PEMBER. From Pembury; a loc. n., Kent, S. Wales

PEMBERTON. A loc. n., Lancs

PEMBURY. A loc. n., Kent

PENDERED. *Dch.* Pendraat; a p.n.

PENDERGAST. *See* Prendergast

PENDLEBURY. A loc. n., Lancs

PENDLETON. A loc. n., Lancs

PENFOLD. From Panfield; a loc. n., Ess.

D.B. Pancevold, a tenant in chief; and Pancefolt, under-tenant at time of Survey.

PENGELLY. A loc. n., Cornw.

PENGLAZE. A loc. n., Cornw.

PENLEY. From Pendley; a loc. n., Herts

PENMAN, PENMAIN. From Penmain; a loc. n., Monm. Or Penmaen, S. Wales

PENN. A loc. n., Bucks, Staffs. Or *see* Paine

PENNEFEATHER. From Pontfathew; a loc. n., Merioneth

PENNINGTON. A loc. n., Lancs

PENNISTON. From Penistone; a loc. n., Yorks

PENNY. *N.* Peini; n.n. *D.* Peine; *Fl.* Penet; *Dch.* Pen, Penha; *Fr.* Peigné, Penna; p.n. *See* Paine

PENNYCOOK. *See* Pennycuick

PENNYCUICK. From Penicuick; a loc. n., Scotl.

PENRHYN. A loc. n., Cornw., N. Wales

PENRICE. A loc. n., S. Wales

PENROSE. A loc. n., Cornw.

PENSTONE. *See* Penniston

PENTECOST.

Roger Pentecost occurs on the Rot. Obl. et Fin., *temp.* K. John.

PENTELOW. From Pentlow; a loc. n., Ess.

PENTON. A loc. n., Hants

PENTREATH. From Pentraeth; a loc. n., N. Wales

PENWARNE. A loc. n., Cornw.

PEPLAR. *See* Peplow

PEPLER. *See* Peplow

PEPLOE. *See* Peplow

PEPLOW. A loc. n., Lincs, Salop

PEPPER. *Dch.* Peper, Pieper; *Fl.* Pepet, Piepers; *S.* Piper; *G.*, *D.* Pieper, Piper; *D.B.* Pipe, Piperell; p.n.

Pepard in Roll of Battell Abbey.

PEPPERCORN. *Dch.* Peperkoorn; a p.n.

PEPPERDAY. From Pepperdon; a loc. n., Devon

PEPPERELL. From Pepperhill; a loc. n., Salop. Or *Fr.* Piperelle; *D.B.* Piperel; a p.n. Comp. Peverel

PERCY. From Percy; a loc. n., Normandy

PERFECT. *See* Parfitt

PERFETT. *See* Parfitt

PERFITT. *See* Parfitt

PERKINS. *D.* Perch; *Dch.*, *G.* Perk; *Fl.* Perkins; p.n.

PERKIS. *See* Perkins

PERNIE. A loc. n., France

PEROWNE. *Fr.* Peronny; a p.n. From Perronne; a loc. n., France. Or Péronne, Belgium

PERREN, PERRIN, PERRING. *Fr.* Perin; *G.* Piering; *Dch.* Perrin; p.n.

PERROTT. A loc. n., Wilts. Or *Fr.* Perot; a p.n.

PERRY. *Fr.* Perrée; *Dch.*, *D.* Perry; p.n.

Pery on the Roll of Battell Abbey; and Peret, a tenant in chief in *D.B.*

PERT. *Fr.* Pieret, Pirot; *D.B.* Pirot; p.n.

PERTWEE. From Pertuis; a loc. n. in France

PESCOD. *See* Peascod

PESKETT. *See* Peascod

PESTALL. *See* Pestell

PESTELL. *Fr.*, *S.*, *Dch.* Pestel; *G.* Pessel; p.n.

PETCH. *G.* Petsch; a p.n.

PETCHELL. *Fr.* Pechell; p.n. *See* Peake

PETEL. *Fr.* Petel, Pettell; p.n.

PETERS. *D.*, *G.* Peters; *Dch.* Peters, Peeters; *Fl.* Peeters; p.n.

PETERSON. *S.* Pedersen; p.n. *See* Pate

PETHERBRIDGE. From Pethybridge; a loc. n., Devon

PETHERHAM. From Petham; a loc. n., Kent

PETHERICK. A loc. n., Cornw.

PETHERIDGE. *See* Partridge

PETHICK. *See* Petherick

PETO. *Fr.* Piteaux, Pitot; p.n.

PETRE. *See* Pate

PETT. A loc. n., Suss. Or *Dch.* Pet; a p.n. *See* Pate

PETTAR. From Pettaugh; a loc. n., Suff. Or *see* Pate

PETTENGILL. From Portingal; an old name for a Portuguese (Lower)

PETTER. *Fr.* Petteau; a p.n. *See* Pate

PETTIGREW. From Pettigoe; a loc. n., Fermanagh

PETTIT. *Fr.* Petit; a p.n.

PETTY. A loc. n., Inverness. *Fr.* Peté; a p.n. Or *see* Pettit

PEW. *D.* Pugh; a p.n.

PEXTON. *See* Paxton

PEYTON. A loc. n., Ess. *See* Pate

PHAIR. *Gaelic*; p.n.

PHANTAM. *Fl.* Vandam; a p.n.

PHARE. *See* Phair

PHARO. *See* Farrow

PHAROAH. *See* Farrow

PHAYRE. *Fl.* Feyaerts; a p.n. *See* Phair

PHEAR. *See* Phair

PHEASANT. *Fr.* Paysan; a p.n.

PHELPS. *See* Phillips

PHIBBS. *See* Phillips

PHILBRICK. *G.* Phillipeck; a p.n.

PHILCOX. Dimin. of Philip

PHILLIMORE. From Fullamore; a loc. n., Devon

Wm. Fylymore, of Dursley, 1460, will proved 1491. The will of Henry Fylymore, of Wickwar, dated 1546, and proved at Glost., 1562, is endorsed Henry Fynymore. In the registers of Cam, Glost., from 1640 to 1680, Phillimore and Phinimore are used interchangeably.

PHILLIPS. *N.* Philippus; *Dch.* Philipps, Philipsen; *Fl.* Phlups; *S.* Philp; p.n.

PHILO. *G.* Philler; a p.n.

PHILPOTT. Dimin. of Phillip

PHIPPS. *See* Phillips

PHIPSON. *See* Phillips

PHIZACKERLEY. *See* Fasacklea

PHYSICK. *G.* Piescheck, Fietzek; p.n.

PICARD. *Fr.* Picard; *Dch.* Piekart; p.n.

PICKEL. *G.* Pickel; a p.n. Or from Pickhill; a loc. n., Yorks. *See* Peake

PICKEN. *See* Peake

PICKERING. A loc. n., Yorks

PICKESS. *See* Peake

PICKETT. *Fr.* Piquet; *Fl.* Pickert; p.n. *See* Peake

PICKFORD. *See* Pitchford

PICKFORTH. From Pickworth; a loc. n., Lincs, Rutld.

PICKUP. A loc. n., Lancs

PICKWICK. A loc. n., Wilts

PICTHALL. *N.* Peita (Pyetah), Poictiers; *N.-Fr.* Poictou

De Pictavensis, tenant in chief in *D.B.*

PICTHORN. A loc. n., Salop

PICTON. A loc. n., Flint, Yorks

PIDCOCK. From Pittcott (?); a loc. n., Somers.

PIDDING. *A.S.* fam. n. From Peada; *D.* Pied; p.n.

PIDDINGTON. A loc. n., Northants

PIDGEON. *Fr.* Pigeon; a p.n. Dimin. of Pik (Pikchen). *See* Piggin and Peake

PIERSON. *See* Pearson

PIGG. *See* Peake

PIGGIN. *See* Pigony or Pidgeon

PIGONY. From Picquigny; a loc. n., near Amiens, France. *Fr.* Pichonnier, Pigné, Pigny; p.n.

PIGOTT. *Fr.* Pegeaud, Pegot, Pichot, Picot; *G.* Pigotta; *D.B.* Picot, Pecoe; p.n. *See* Peake

Reginald Pigot held lands in Norf. *temp.* K. John.

PIKE. *See* Peake

PIKESLEY. From Pickersleigh; a loc. n., Worcest. Or Pigsley, Devon

PILBOROUGH. From Pulborough; a loc. n., Surr.

PILCH. *S.* Piltz; *Dch.* Pilger; *G.* Pils, Pilz; p.n.

PILE. *See* Peel

PILGRIM. *See* Pelgram

PILKINGTON. A loc. n., Lancs

PILL. A loc. n., Cornw., Glost., Somers. Or *see* Peel

PILLANS. *See* Peel

PILLOW. From Pilhough; a loc. n., Derbysh. Or *S.* Pilau, Pilo; p.n.

PILSON. *S.* Pylsson; a p.n. *See* Peel

PILTON. A loc. n., Devon, Northants, Rutland, Somers.

PIM. *G.* Pimmer; a p.n.

PINCH. *Fr.* Pinchart; *Fl.* Pinchaert; *Dch.* Pink, Pinks, Pinkse; *G.* Pinger, Pintsch, Pintzger

Pinchard is in the Roll of Battell Abbey.

PINCHBACK. *See* Pinchbeck

PINCHBECK. A loc. n., Lincs

PINCHEN. *Fl.* Pingeon, Pinson; *Fr.* Pinçon; *D.B.* Pinstan, Pinc'ū'n, Pinchengi; p.n. Dimin. of Peine. *See* Paine

PINCHES. *G.* Pincus, Pinkas; p.n. *See* Pinch

PINCHING. *See* Pinchen

PINCOMBE. From Pinnacombe; a loc. n., Devon

PINDAR. *See* Pinder

PINDER. *G.* Pinder; *Fl.* Pinter; p.n. Or *see* Pinner

PINE. *G.* Pein; a p.n. *See* Payne

PINK. *See* Pinnock

PINKERTON. From Punchardon or Pincherdon; a loc. n., Normandy (?)

PINKHAM. *See* Pincombe

PINKNEY. A loc. n., Wilts

PINN. *Fr.* Pin; *G.* Pinn; *D.B.* Pin; p.n. *See* Payne

PINNEGAR. *G.* Pinger; *Fr.* Pinguet; p.n.

PINNER. A loc. n., Middlx. Or *Fr.* Pineau; a p.n. *See* Paine

PINNION. From Pignan; a loc. n. in France. *Fl.* Pingeon, Pinon; p.n.

PINNOCK. A loc. n., Glost.

PINSENT. *See* Pinsun

PINSUN. *Fl.* Pinson; a p.n. *See* Pinchen

PIPE. A loc. n., Heref., Staffs. Or *Fr.* Pipe; a p.n.

PIPER. *S.* Piper; a p.n. *See* Pepper

PIPPET. *Fl.* Pipart; a p.n.

PITCHER. *Fr.* Pichard, Pichot; *G.* Picha, Piecha; p.n. *See* Peake

PITCHES. *See* Peache

PITCHFORD. A loc. n., Salop

PITE. *See* Pitt and Pyatt

PITFIELD. From Pitfold; a loc. n., Surr.

PITKIN. Dimin. of Peterkin

PITMAN. *Dch.* Piderman; or *G.* Pitschmann; p.n.

PITT. A loc. n., Cornw., Devon. Or *Dch.* Piet, Pitt; *Fr.* Piette, Pitte; p.n.

PITTOCK. *See* Pidcock

PIXEL. From Pickshill; a loc. n., Somers.

PIXLEY. A loc. n., Heref.

PIZEY. *G.* Peysey; a p.n. Or *see* Poysey

PIZZEY. *See* Poysey

PLACE, PLAICE. *D.* Plees; *G.* Pless; *Fl.* Pleis; *Dch.* Ples; *Fr.* Place; p.n.

PLAMPIN. *Fl.* Blampain; p.n.

PLANE. *N.* Bleingr; *G.* Plener; *D.B.* Pleines; *Dch.* Blanes; p.n.

PLANK. *D.* Planck; *Dch.*, *Fl.* Plank; *Fr.* Planche, Planque; p.n.

PLANT. *D.* Plant; a p.n.

PLANTIN. *Dch.* Planten; a p.n.

PLASTOW. From Plaistow; a loc. n., Derbysh., Ess., Kent, Suss.

PLATT. *G.* Platt; *D.*, *S.* Plaate; *Dch.* Platte; p.n.

PLATTEN. *D.*, *S.* Platen; *Fl.* Plétain, Plettinck; p.n.

PLAW. *See* Plow

PLAYER. *Fr.* Plehiers; a p.n.

PLAYFAIR. *G.* Plewa; a p.n.

PLAYFORD. A loc. n., Suff.

PLAYLE. *G.* Pleul; p.n.

PLEASANCE. *Fr.* Plaisance; a p.n.

PLEASANTS. *See* Pleasance

PLEDGER. *Dch.* Plieger, Ploeger; *G.* Pletteschke; p.n.

PLENTY. *G.* Plantier; a p.n.

PLEWS. *Fl.* Pluys; p.n. *See* Plow

PLIMPTON. From Plympton; a loc. n., Devon

PLIMSAUL, PLIMSOLL. From Plemstall or Plemonstall; a loc. n., Ches.

PLOW. *D.* Plógr and Ploug; *G.* Plew, Pluge, Plohs; *Dch.* Ploos; *Fl.* Pluys; p.n.

PLOWDEN. A loc. n., Salop

PLOWMAN. *S.* Ploman; p.n.

PLOWRIGHT. From Plougouvert; a loc. n., Normandy (?)

PLUCKROSE. *D.* Plockross; a p.n.

PLUM. *D.*, *Fl.* Plum; p.n.

PLUMB. *See* Plum

PLUMBRIDGE. A loc. n., Kent

PLUME. *See* Plum

PLUMMER. *Fr.* Plumard, Plumet, Plumier; p.n.

PLUMSTEAD. A loc. n., Norf.

PLUMTRE. A loc. n., Notts

PLUNKETT. From the Irish O'Pluingceid; a p.n. (*planc*, to strike severely; *cead*, first). Or from Plangenoit; a loc. n. in Brabant (?)

PLYMSELL. *See* Plimsaul

POATE. *Dch.*, *Fl.* Poot; a p.n.

POCHIN. *Fr.* Pouchin; a p.n.

POCKETT. *Fr.* Pochet; a p.n.

POCKLINGTON. A loc. n., Yorks

POCOCK. *D.* Pock; *G.* Pocha; p.n. *See* Pook and Peacock

PODD. *See* Paddy

PODGER. *Fr.* Pochez; *D.*, *Dch.* Pogge, or Welsh Ap Odger; p.n.

PODMORE. A loc. n., Staffs.

POINTER. *Fr.* Pointier; a p.n. *See* Poynter

POINTIN. *See* Poynton

POINTS. From Pontoise; a loc. n., Normandy (?)

Nicholas Puintz held land in Glost. *temp.* K. John.

POLDEN. A loc. n., Somers.

POLES. *See* Paull

POLEY. *D.* Pol, Poli; *Fr.* Pollet; p.n. *See* Paull

POLGLAZE. A loc. n., Cornw.

POLHILL. A loc. n.

POLKINGHORNE. From Polkinhorne; a loc. n., Cornw.

POLL, POLE. *See* Paul

POLLARD. *Fl.* Pollaert; *Fr.* Pollard; p.n. *See* Paull

Gaufrid Pollard on Rot. Obl. et Fin., *temp.* K. John.

POLLITT. *Fr.* Polet, Pollet; *Fl.* Pollaert; *Dch.* Politz; p.n. *See* Paul

POLLOCK. *Dch.* Polak; a p.n. *See* Paul

POLLY. *Fr.* Pollet; *Fl.* Polly; *D.* Poli; p.n. *See* Paull

POLLYN. *See* Paul

POLSUE. Cornish p.n.

POLWARTH. A loc. n., Berwick

POLWHELE. A loc. n., Cornw. *D.B.* Polhel

POMFREY. A loc. corruption of Pontefract; a loc. n., Yorks

Pond. From Pont; a loc. n., Cornw. Or *Dch.* Pont; a p.n.

Ponder. *Fr.* Ponteau; *D.B.* Ponther; *G.* Punde; p.n.

Ponsford. A loc. n., Devon. Or Pontesford, Salop

Ponsonby. A loc. n., Cumb.

Pont. *Dch.*; p.n. Or *see* Pond

Pontifex. *D.* Pontavice; a p.n.

Ponting. *S.* Pontin; a p.n.

Ponton. A loc. n., Lincs

Pook. *N.* Púki; *G.* Puche; *S.* Puke; p.n.

Poole. A freq. loc. n., Dorset, Yorks, etc. From *N. Pollr; B. pwl;* a pool. Or *see* Paul

Poore. *G.* Pur; *D.B.* Pur; *Fr.* Poirre; p.n.

John le Poer held lands in Yorks, *temp.* K. John, 1201.

Poos. *Fl.* Pues; a p.n.

Pope. *N.* Papar; *F.* Poppe; *D.* Pop; *S.* Pape; *Fl.* Papy, Poppin; *Dch.* Paap, Pop; *G.* Pape, Papke, Poppe, Poper; *D.B.* Papald; p.n.

Poppe was the name of a Duke of Friesland slain in battle by Charles Martel, A.D. 734.

Popham. A loc. n., Hants

Popjoy. *Fl.* Papegaey; a p.n.

Popkin. *See* Pope

Pople, Popple. *Dch.* Poppel; a p.n. *See* Pope

Poppleton. A loc. n., Yorks

Poppy. *See* Pope

Porcher. *Fr.*; p.n.

Porley. *Fr.* Poulet; a p.n. Or *see* Paull

Port. *Fr.*, *G.* Port; *Dch.* Porth, Porte; p.n.

Portal. *Fr.*; p.n.

Porteous. From Portways; a loc. n., Oxf. (?)

Porter. *Dch.* Port, Poort, Poorter; *G.* Port; *Fr.* Portier; p.n.

Portlock. From Porlock; a loc. n., Somers.

Portway. A loc. n., Worcest.

Portwine. *Fr.* Potvin; or *Dch.* Portheine; p.n.

Postel. *Fr.*; p.n.

Postle. *See* Postel

Postlethwaite. A loc. n. *D.* Poselt; *Fl.* Postel; p.n.

Poston. A loc. n., Heref., Salop

Pothecary. From Apothecary; the occupation

Laurencius Ypotecarius occurs among the tenants of Ipswich Priory in the thirteenth century.

Pott. *Fl.*, *Dch.* Pot; *S.* Pott; p.n.

Pottage. *Fr.* Potiez; a p.n.

Potter. *Dch.* Potter, Potters; *Fr.* Poteau, Pottier; p.n.

Pottinger. *Dch.* Pottinga; a p.n.

Potton. From Potterne; a loc. n., Wilts

Pottow. *Fr.* Poteau, Pottaux; p.n.

Potts. *Dch.*; p.n.

Poulter. *G.* Polte; *Fr.* Poultier; p.n.

Poulton. A loc. n., Glost., Kent, Lancs

Pounceby. *See* Ponsonby

Pound. A loc. n., Devon

Pountney. A loc. n., Suff.

Powell. *Fr.* Puel; a p.n. *See* Paul

Power. *Fr.* Pouyer; a p.n. *See* Poore

Powley. *See* Paul

Pownall. A loc. n., Ches.

Poynter. *See* Pointer

Poynton. A loc. n., Lincs

Poyser. *G.* Peiser, Peuser; *Fl.* Pizar; *Dch.* Peyser; p.n.

Poysey. From Poissy; a loc. n., Normandy

Prahl. *D.*, *G.*, *Dch.*; p.n.

Praill. *Dch.* Prell; a p.n.

Prall. *G.*; p.n.

Pratt. *Fr.* Prat; *Fl.* Praet; *G.* Pratsch; p.n.

Precious. *Dch.* Preussiche; a p.n. (?)

Predam. *Fr.* Predhom; a p.n.

Preddy. *See* Priddy

Preedy. *See* Priddy

PREESE. A loc. n., Lancs. Or *Fr.* Pris; a p.n.
PRENDERGAST. A loc. n., Pembroke
PRESCOTT. A loc. n., Devon, Lancs, Salop
PRESENT. *Fr.* Présent; a p.n.
PRESLAND. *Dch.*; loc. and p. n.
PRESOW. *Fr.* Preseau; a Huguenot p.n. Or Presall; a loc. n., Lancs
PRESS. *G.*; p.n.
PRESSEY. *Fr.* Presseau; a p.n.
PREST. *See* Priest
PRESTIGE. From Prestwich; a loc. n., Lancs
PRESTON. A loc. n., Kent, Lancs, etc.
PRETTY. *See* Priddy
PRETYMAN. *G.* Brettmann; a p.n.
PREVOST. *Dch.* Prevost; *Fr.* Prévost; p.n. A Prot. refugee n.
PRICE. From Prise; a loc. n., Yorks. Preece, Denbigh; or Welsh, Ap Rice; *D.* Preis, Price; p.n.
Roger Preise on Rot. Obl. et Fin., *temp.* K. John.
PRICKETT. *See* Prichard. Or dimin. of Prick
PRIDDEN. From Priding; a loc. n., Glost. Welsh, Pryddyn (?)
PRIDDY. A loc. n., Somers.
PRIDHAM. *See* Predham
PRIDMORE. *D.* Bredmore; a p.n.
PRIEST. *N.* Prestr; *Fl.* Prist; a p.n.
PRIESTLEY. From Priestcliffe; a loc. n., Derbysh.
PRIGG. *Fl.* Prick; a p.n.
PRIGGENS. *Dch.* Pricken; a p.n.
PRIKE. *See* Prigg
PRIM, PRIME. *Dch.* Priem; *D.* Prime; p.n.
PRIMROSE. A loc. n., Fife
PRINCE. *Fr.*, *Fl.* Prins; *Dch.* Prince, Prins; *G.* Prinz; p.n.
PRING. *G.* Bring; *Dch.* Brink; p.n.
PRINGLE. *Fl.* Pringiels; a p.n.
PRINSEP. From Brinsop; a loc. n., Heref. Or Princethorpe; a loc. n., Devon
PRIOR, PRYER. *Fl.* Preier; *Fr.* Prier; *D.* Prior; p.n.
PRITCHARD. Welsh, Ap-Richard
PRITTY. *N.* Pruði; a p.n. Or *see* Priddy
PROBART, PROBERT. Welsh, Ap-Robert; a p.n.
PROBY. *See* Probart
PROBYN. Welsh, Ap-Robin
PROCTER. *Lat.* Procurator, an Apparitor; *Fr.* Procureur; a p.n.
PRODHAM. *Fr.* Prodhomme; a p.n.
PROFFITT. *G.* Proft, Prophet; *Fr.* Profit; p.n.
PROPERT. *See* Probert
PROSSER. *G.* Preusser; a p.n.
PROTHEROE. From Prudhoe; a loc. n., Northbd.
PROUD. *Fr.* Praud; a p.n.
PROUDFOOT. *N.* Pruði-fotr; a n.n.
PROUDHAM. *See* Prudhome
PROUT. *G.* Prawit; a p.n. Or *see* Proud
PROWSE. A loc. n., Devon. Or *G.* Praus; *Dch.* Prousse; p.n.
PRUDAMES. *See* Prudhom
PRUDENCE. *Fr.* Prudans; a p.n.
PRUDHOE. A loc. n., Dur.
PRUE. *Fr.* Preux; a p.n.
PRUEN. *Dch.* Preün, Prooije, Prooijen; p.n.
PRUST. *Fl.* Proust; a p.n.
PRY. *Dch.* Pruis; a p.n.
PRYKE. *See* Prigg
PUCKETT. *G.* Puchat; a p.n. *See* Pook
PUCKEY. *See* Pook
PUCKLE. *G.* Puchelt; *Fl.* Puckle; p.n.
PUCKRIDGE. A loc. n., Herts
PUDDEFOOT. *See* Puddephatt
PUDDEPHATT. From Puddephats; a loc. n., Herts
PUDDICOMBE. From Pudcombe; a loc. n., Devon
PUDNEY. *See* Putney

PUGSLEY. From Puxley; a loc. n., Northants

PULESTON. A loc. n., Heref.

PULFORD. From Pulsford; a loc. n., Devon

PULHAM. A loc. n., Norf.

PULL. *See* Paul

PULLBROOK. From Polebrook; a loc. n., Northants

PULLEIN. *Fr.* Poullain; a p.n. *See* Paul

PULLEY. From Pullay; a loc. n., Normandy. Or *Fr.* Poullet; a p.n.

PULLUM. *See* Pulham

PULLYN. *See* Paull

PULYER. *See* Bulwer

PUMPHREY. From the Welsh Ap-Humphrey (?). Or *see* Pomfrey

PUNCHARD. *Fr.* Ponchaut; a p.n.

PUNG. *Dch.* Puncke; a p.n.

PUNNETT. *G.* Pundt; a p.n.

PUNSHON. *Fr.* Ponchon; a p.n.

PUNT. *G.* Pundt; a p.n.

PUNTER. *G.* Punte; a p.n.

PURBROOK. A loc. n., Hants

PURCELL. *Fr.* Pirsoul (?); a p.n.
Radulph Purcel held land in Bucks, *temp.* K. John.

PURCHAS. *Fr.* Pourchez; a p.n.
Andreas Purchaz held land in Kent, *temp.* K. John.

PURDAY, PURDEY, PURDIE. *See* Purdue

PURDON. From Purton; a loc. n., Glost., Wilts. Or Pirton; Herts, Staffs., Worcest.

PURDUE. *Fr.* Pardieu; a p.n.

PURDY. *See* Purdue

PURFITT. *See* Perfitt

PURITAN. From Puriton; a loc. n., Somers.

PURKHAM. From Purcombe; a loc. n., Devon

PURKIS. *See* Purchas

PURR. *G.* Pur; a p.n. *See* Poore

PURRIER. *Fr.* Perrier; a p.n.

PURSER. *Fr.* Perseau; a p.n.

PURSLEY. *See* Purslow

PURSLOW. A loc. n., Salop

PURSS. *G.* Pursche; a p.n.

PURTON. A loc. n., Glost.

PURVES. A loc n., Berwick

PURVIS. *See* Purves

PUTLEY. From Putloe; a loc. n., Glost.

PUTNAM. From Puttenham; a loc. n., Herts, Surr.

PUTNEY. A loc. n., Surr.

PUTT. *G.* Puth; *Dch.* Put; p.n.

PUTTERILL. *Fr.* Poutrel; a p.n.

PUTTOCK. *G.* Puttke; a p.n.

PUXON. From Puxton; a loc. n., Somers., Worcest.

PYATT. *See* Pyett

PYBUS. *Dch.* Pijpers; a p.n.

PYE. *D.* Pii; *Fl.* Peys, Pye; *G.* Poyer; p.n.

PYEMONT. *Fr.* Pimont; a p.n.

PYETT. *Fl.* Piette; a p.n.

PYGALL. *G.* Biegal; *Dch.* Biegel; p.n.

PYKE. *Fl.* Pycke; a p.n. *See* Peak

PYLE. *See* Peel

PYMAN. *See* Pyemont

PYMAR. *G.* Pimmer; *S.* Pemmer; p.n. *See* Pymer

PYMER. From Pyemoor; a loc. n., Camb.

PYNE. *See* Paine

PYTCHES. *See* Peake

PYWELL. From Bywell; a loc. n., Northbd. Or *Fr.* Puel; a p.n.

Q.

QUADLING, QUODLING. Dimin. of *D.* Quaade; a p.n. Or *Fr.* Quoilin (?); a p.n. Comp. Quadring, Lincs

QUAIE. *Fr.*; p.n.

QUAIL. *G.* Quiel; *D.* Quehl; p.n.

QUAIN. *Fr.* Quenne; *Dch.* Quien; p.n.

QUAINTANCE. *Fl.* Quintins; a p.n.

QUANT. *Dch.* Kwant; *G.* Quandt; p.n.

QUANTOCK. A loc. n., Somers.

QUANTRELL. *See* Cantrell

QUARMAN, QUARMANE. *Fr.* Querment; a p.n.

QUARMBY. A loc. n., Yorks

QUARRELLE. *Dch.* Querelle; a p.n.

QUARRINGTON. A loc. n., Dur., Lincs

QUARRY. *Fr.* Quarré; a p.n. Or Scotch, McQuarrie

QUARTERMAIN. *Fr.* Quatremains; a p.n.
In Oxon, *temp.* K. John.

QUARTLEY. A loc. n., Devon

QUAY. From Quy; a loc. n., Camb.

QUAYLE. *D.* Quehl; a p.n.

QUECKETT. *G.* Quickert; a p.n.

QUELCH. *See* Welch

QUENBY. A loc. n., Leics.

QUESTED. From Quenstadt; a *G.* loc. and p. n.

QUICK. A loc. n., Yorks. Or *Fl.* Kwick; *S.* Qvick; *Dch.* Kuijk; *G.* Quicker; p.n.

QUIGLEY. From Quedgeley; a loc. n., Glost.

QUINCEY. *D.B.* Chinesi; a p.n.
Quinci in Roll of Battell Abbey. De Quency in Leics., *temp.* K. John.

QUINN. A loc. n., Killaloe, Ireland. Or *Dch.* Quien; a p.n.

QUINNEY. From Queney; a loc. n., Camb.

QUINTOCK. *See* Quantock

QUINTON. A loc. n., Glost., Northants, Warw., Worcest.

QUIRK. From the Irish McQuirke; a p.n.

QUIXLEY. *See* Quigley

R.

RABAN. *Fr.* Raban, Raband; *Dch.* Rabanus; p.n.

RABBETH, RABETT. *G.* Rabat; a p.n.

RABBIDGE. *G.* Rabisch; a p.n.

RABBITS. *D.* Rabitz; a p.n.

RABEY, RABY. From Raby; a loc. n., Ches.

RABLEY. A loc. n., Herts

RACE. *Dch.* Rees; a p.n.

RACKHAM. A loc. n., Suss.

RACKSTRAW. *D.* Rockstroh; a p.n.

RADFORD. A loc. n., Notts

RADLEY. A loc. n., Notts, Staffs.

RADMALL. From Rathmell; a loc. n., Yorks

RADMORE. From Rathmore; a loc. n., Killarney. Or Redmire, Yorks

RADNALL. From Rednal; a loc. n., Worcest.

RAE. *See* Ray

RAEBURN. A loc. n., Dumfries

RAFFE. *See* Rolf

RAFFLES. *G.* Raffelt; or *Fl.* Raphaels; p.n.
RAGG. *N.* Ragi; *A.S.* Wraca; *D.* Rager; *Dch.* Rack; p.n.
RAGGETT. *Fr.* Ragot; *G.* Rackette; p.n.
RAIKES. A loc. n., Lincs
RAILTON. *See* Relton
RAIN. *N.* Hreinn; *Fr.* Raine, Reine; *G.* Renn; p.n.
RAINBIRD. *N.* Hrein-bjártr; *G.* Reinbardt; *D.B.* Rainbert; p.n.
RAINBOW. *G.* Reinboth; *Fr.* Rainbaux; p.n.
RAINHAM. A loc. n., Ess.
RAINS, RAINES. A loc. n., Ess.
RAINSFORD. From Rainford; a loc. n., Lancs
RAIT. *D.* Raith; a p.n.
RAITHBY. A loc. n., Lincs
RAKE. A loc. n., Devon
RALEIGH. From Rayleigh; a loc. n., Ess. Or *Fr.* Ralet; a p.n.
RALF. *See* Rolf
RAMAGE. *D.* Rames; *Fl.* Ramuz; *G.* Rambach; p.n.
RAMM. *N.* Ramr; n.n. (strong). *D.B.* Ram; *D.*, *G.* Ramm; p.n.
RAMPLEN. *Fr.* Rampillon; a p.n.
RAMSAY. A loc. n., Ess., I. of Man, S. Wales
RAMSBOTHAM. *See* Ramsbottom
RAMSBOTTOM. A loc. n., Lancs. Comp. *Fl.* Ransbotyn; a p.n.
RAMSDEN. A loc. n., Ess., Herts, Oxf.
RAMSHAW. A loc. n., Northbd.
RAMSHAY. *See* Ramshaw
RAMSTEAD. *D.* Ramstad; a loc. and p. n.
RAND. A loc. n., Lincs. Or *N.* Rand-verr; *D.* Rand; a p.n.
RANDALL. *D.*, *G.* Randel; a p.n. *See* Randulph
RANDOLF. *See* Randulph
RANDS. From Raunds; a loc. n., Northants
RANDSFORD. *See* Rainsford
RANDULPH. *D.* Randulff; *G.*, *S.* Randel; *D.B.* Randulf; a p.n.
RANGER. *D.* Rannje; a p.n.
RANKIN. *Fl.* Renkin; p.n.
RANNEY. *N.* Hrani; or *Fr.* René; p.n.
RANSDALE. From Ravensdale (Raunsdale); a loc. n., Derbysh.
RANSOME. *See* Ranson
RANSON. *Fr.* Rançon; a p.n.
RANT. *Dch.*; p.n.
RANTELL. *See* Randall
RANTON. A loc. n., Staffs.
RAPER. *See* Rope
RAPKIN. *G.* Rappke; a p.n. *See* Rapson
RAPLEY. *Fr.* Raparlier (?); a p.n.
RAPP. *D.*, *Dch.*, *G.* Rapp; *Fl.* Rappe; p.n.
RAPPARD. *Dch.*; p.n.
RAPSON. *D.* Rapp; a p.n.
RARP. *Fr.* Rappe; *G.* Rapp; p.n.
RASH. *D.* Rask; *Fl.* Rasse; *G.* Rasch; p.n.
RASHLEIGH. A loc. n., Devon
RASP. *G.* Rasper; a p.n.
RASTALL. From Rusthall; a loc. n., Kent
RATTEE. *D.* Rathje; *G.* Ratay, Rathay; *Dch.* Ratté; p.n.
RATTRAY. A loc. n., Aberdeensh.
RAVEN. *N.* Hræfn; *S.* Ravn; *D.* Rafn, Raun; *Dch.* Raven; *D.B.* Raven, Rauen; p.n.
RAVENSCROFT. A loc. n., Ches.
RAVEY. *Fr.* Revet; a p.n.
RAW. *Fr.* Raux, Réaux; *D.*, *Fl.*, *G.* Rau; p.n. *See* Roe, Rowe
RAWCLIFF. A loc. n., Yorks, Lancs
RAWDON. A loc. n., Yorks
RAWKINS. *G.*, *Dch.* Rauch, Raucke; p.n.
RAWLE, RAWLL. *Dch.* Rohol; a p.n. *See* Ralph
RAWLENCE. *Dch.* Roelants; a p.n. *See* Rawlinson
RAWLEY. *See* Raleigh or Rowley
RAWLINGS. *Dch.* Rohling; a p.n. *See* Rawlinson

RAWLINSON. *N.* Hroðland; *S.* Roland; *Dch.* Roelants, Rolling, Rohling, Roland; *D.* Rolund; *Fl.* Roulandt; *D.B.* Rolland; p.n.

RAWSON. *N.* Rauðssynir; *Fl.* Raussens; p.n. Or *see* Rawlinson

RAY. *See* Reay

RAYBOULD. *N.* Rögnvoldr; *D.B.* Rainbald; *G.* Rebohl; p.n.

RAYCRAFT. *See* Ryecroft

RAYDEN, RAYDON. A loc. n., Suff. Or *Dch.* Reeden; a p.n.

RAYMENT. *See* Raymond

RAYMOND. *N.* Hrómundr; *D.* Reymann; *Dch.* Reiman; *G.* Rehmann; *D.B.* Raimund; p.n. Raimond in Roll of Battell Abbey.

RAYNER. *N.* Hreinnarr; *D.* Reinhard, Reiner; *G.* Rennert, Renner; *Dch.* Renard; *Fr.* Renaud; *Fl.* Rener; *D.B.* Rayner; p.n.

RAYNHAM. A loc. n., Norf.

RAYNOR. *See* Rayner

RAYSON. From Rasen; a loc. n., Lincs. Or *see* Ray

READ. A loc. n., Yorks. Or *see* Reid

READY. *Dch.* Riede; a p.n.

REAM. *N.* Hreimr; n.n. *S.* Reimers; *Dch.* Riem, Reimers; p.n.

REAP. *Dch.* Reep; a p.n.

REARDEN. From Ruardean; a loc. n., Glost.

REASLEY. *See* Risley

REASON. *Dch.* Riessen; a p.n. Or *see* Rayson

REAVELEY. A loc. n., Northbd.

REAVELL. *Dch.* Rietveld; a loc. and p. n.

REAY. A loc. n., Caithness, Kirkcudbright. Or *N.* Hroi; *D.* Reeh; *S.*, *Dch.* Ree; *Fl.* Rey, Reh; *D.B.* Rauai; *Fr.* Ray, Rayé; p.n.

REBBECK. *Dch.*, *G.* Rehbock; a p.n.

RECKITT. *Fr.* Requette, Richet; *G.* Richert; *Dch.* Reket; p.n.

REDAWAY. A loc. n., Devon

REDDAN, REDON. *Fr.* Redant; a p.n.

REDDIE, REDDY. *See* Ready

REDDING. From Reading; a loc. n., Berks. Or *see* Reid

REDDISH. A loc. n., Ches. Or Redditch, Worcest.; or *G.* Rettisch; a p.n.

REDFORD. From Retford; a loc. n., Notts

REDGRAVE. A loc. n., Norf., Suff.

REDHEAD. From Rudyard; a loc. n., Staffs. Or *G.* Rudert; a p.n.

REDMAN, REDMAINE, REDMOND. *N.* Raðmaðr or Raðmann; *D.* Raadman; *Fl.* Redeman; *A.S.* Rederman; *G.* Rathmann; p.n.

REDPATH. A loc. n., Northbd.

REDWOOD. A loc. n., Devon

REECE, REESE. *D.* Rüs; *Fl.* Reisse; *G.* Riess; *Dch.* Rees; Welsh, Rhys; p.n.

REED. A loc. n., Suff. Or *see* Reid

REEDER. *N.* Hreidarr; *D.* Redder; *D.B.* Reder, Reider; *G.* Reder; *Dch.* Reeder; p.n.

REEKIE. *Fr.* Ricquier; *D.* Rieck; p.n.

REEKS. *G.* Ricke, Rieck; *Dch.* Rieke; *Fl.* Rykers; p.n.

REEMAN. *Dch.* Rieman; a p.n.

REEVE. *G.* Riewe; *Dch.* Rieuwe; p.n.

REFFELL. *Fl.* Revael; a p.n. *See* Raffle

REGAN. From Irish O'Regan; a p.n.

REGESTER. A local corruption of Rochester (Lower)

REID. *G.* Ried; *Dch.* Riede; *D.* Read; p.n.

REILLY. From the Irish Radheolagh or Raghalach; p.n. Comp. Reuilly; a loc. n., France. *D.B.* Ruhilie; a p.n.

RELPH. *N.* Hrólfr, abbrev. of Ródulfr; *G.* Rudolf; *F.* Rôlf; *S.* Roll; *Dch.* Reelfs; *D.B.* Redalp, Rolp, Ralf; p.n.

RELTON. From Wrelton; a loc. n., Yorks

REMINGTON. *See* Rimmington

REMNANT. *Fr.* Remont (?); a p.n.

RENDALL, RENDEL. A loc. n., Orkney. Or *see* Randall

RENNISON. *N.* Hreinn; *Fl.* Renson; p.n.

RENSHAW. From Renishaw; a loc. n., Derbysh.

RENTON. A loc. n., Dumbarton. Or Rennington, Northbd.

RENWICK. A loc. n., Camb.

REPINGTON. From Repton; a loc. n., Derbysh. *D.B.* Rapendune

REPUKE. *Fr.* Reboux (?); a p.n.

RESTALL. *See* Rastall

RETALLACK. *See* Retallick

RETALLICK. A loc. n., Cornw.

REVELEY. *See* Reaveley

REVILL. *Fr.* Revel, Revelle; a p.n. From Revel; a loc. n., France

Revel in Rot. Obl. et Fin., K. John.

REW. A loc. n., Devon. Rue, Dorset

REYNOLDS. *N.* Rögnvoldr; *D.*, *S.* Reinhold; *Dch.* Reinold, Renuel; p.n.

RHIMES. *See* Ream

RHIND. A loc. n., Perth

RHODES. A loc. n., Lancs

RIBBANS, RIBBONS. *Dch.* Ribbink; *G.* Rippin; p.n.

RIBICK. *See* Rebbeck

RICHARDSON. *See* Rix

RICHBELL. *N.* Reikall (a rover); *D.* Ritschel; *G.* Richel; *Fr.* Richelle; p.n.

RICHES. *See* Rix

RICHFIELD. From Richeville; a loc. n., France

RICHFORD. From Rickford; a loc. n., Somers.

RICHMOND. A loc. n., Surr., Yorks

RICKET. *Fr.* Richet; a p.n.

RIDALL, RIDDEL, RIDDLE. *D.* Riedel; *S.* Rydall; *Fr.* Ridel, Ridelle; a p.n.

Richard Ridel in Rot. Obl. et Fin., K. John.

RIDDETT. *See* Ridet

RIDDLESWORTH. From Roddlesworth; a loc. n., Lancs

RIDER. *See* Ryder

RIDET. *Fr.*; p.n.

RIDGE. A loc. n., Devon, Glost., Salop, Wilts

RIDGWAY. A loc. n., Devon, Somers.

RIDGWELL. A loc. n., Ess.

RIDLEY. A loc. n., Kent

RIDOUT. *Fr.* Redouté; a p.n.

RIDPATH. *See* Redpath

RIDSDALE. A loc. n., Northbd.

RIGBY. A loc. n., Yorks. *D.B.* Rigbi

RIGG. A loc. n., Dumfries

RIGGLESWORTH. *See* Riddlesworth

RIGGS. *See* Ridge

RILEY. *See* Reilly

RILLETT. *Fr.* Rouillet; *Fl.* Rielaert, Rillaert; p.n.

RIMMINGTON. A loc. n., Yorks. *D.B.* Renitone

William de Rimington was Prior of Sawley Abbey and Chancellor of Oxford, A.D. 1372.

RING. *N.* Hringr; *Dch.* Ring, Rincker; *G.* Ring, Ringer; p.n.

RINGER. *G.*; p.n.

RION. *N.* Hreinn; *D.* Ryan; *G.* Rein; *Dch.* Reijn; *Fl.* Rion; p.n.

RIORDAN. *See* Rearden

RIPLEY. A loc. n., Derbysh., Ess., Surr., Yorks

RIPPER. *Dch.* Rippe; *Fl.* Ripet; p.n.

RIPPIN. *G.* Rippin; *Dch.* Ripping; a p.n.

RIPPINGILLE. From Rippingale; a loc. n., Lincs

RIPPON. From Ripon; a loc. n., Yorks

RIPSHER. *G.* Rippke; a p.n.

RISELEY. A loc. n., Derbysh.

RISING. A loc. n., Norf. Or *S.* Rising; a p.n.

RIST. *N.* Reistr; *G.* Rister; *D.*, *Fl.*, *Dch.* Rist; p.n.

RITCHIE. *Fr.* Richet; a p.n.

RITSON. A loc. n., Devon

RIVERS. *Fr.* Rivez; *D.* Rievers; p.n.

Rivers in Roll of Battell Abbey. *D.B.* Riveire, a tenant in chief.

RIVETT. *Fr.* Rivet; *Fl.* Riffaert; p.n.

RIVINGTON. A loc. n., Lancs

RIX. *N.* Rikard; *D.B.* Richeri, Ricard, Ricar, Richer; *G.* Rietsch; *Dch.* Rikke, Rikkers; *Fl.* Richez; p.n.

ROBB. *Fl.* Robbe; a p.n.

ROBBINS. *Fl.* Robyns; a p.n.

ROBEY, ROBY. A loc. n., Derbysh., Lancs, Yorks

ROBIN. *Fr.*; p.n.

ROBINETT. *Fr.* Robinet; dimin. of Robin

ROBINSON. *N.* Robbi, from Hróbjartr (Robert); *Fl.* Robyns, Robson, Robisson; p.n.

ROBSON. *Fl.*; p.n.

ROCHE. *Fr.*; p.n.

ROCKE. *Dch.*, *G.* Rock; *Fr.* Roche, Rocque; p.n.

Roger Roc in Rot. Obl. et Fin., K. John.

ROCKETT. From Rogate; a loc. n., Suss. Or *Fr.* Rochette, Roquet; p.n.

ROCKLEY. A loc. n., Herts, Notts, Wilts

RODGERS. *N.* Hroð-geirr; *D.* Roedeger, Rodgers; *Fl.* Roger; *Fr.* Rogier; *G.* Roger; *D.B.* Roger; p.n.

RODWELL. *See* Rothwell

ROE. A loc. n., Herts. Or *see* Raw, Rowe

ROFFE. *See* Rolf

ROGERS. *See* Rodgers

ROGERSON. From Rogerstone; a loc. n., Monmouth

ROKEBY. A loc. n., Yorks

ROLFE. *N.* Hrólfr; *G.* Roll, Rolle, Rolof, Roff, Ruff; *D.B.* Ralf, Roulf, Rolf; *F.* Rôlf; *D.* Rohlf; *Fl.* Roll; *Dch.* Roll, Rolff, Rol; p.n.

ROLL, ROLLE. *See* Rolfe

ROLLES. *See* Roll

ROLLESTON. A loc. n., Staffs. *D.B.* Roolfeston

ROLLING. *Fr.* Rollin; a p.n. Or *see* Rawling

ROLLINSON. *See* Rawlinson

ROLPH. *See* Rolf

ROMER. *N.* Raumr (?); *G.*, *Dch.* Römer; *Fl.* Romer; a p.n.

Romieu is on the Huguenot Roll. In ancient times, one who had made the pilgrimage to Rome was called a Romer.

ROMILLY. A loc. n., Normandy. Romiley; a loc. n., Ches.

William de Romillé was the first Baron of Skipton, Yorks.

ROMNEY. A loc. n., Kent

ROOFE. *See* Rolf

ROOK. *N.* Hrúkr; p.n.

ROOM. *G.* Ruhm; *Fl.* Rooms; p.n.

ROOPE. *N.* Hrappr; *G.* Rupp; *D.* Rupe; *Fl.* Roup; a p.n.

ROOT. *See* Rout

ROPE. *See* Roope

ROPER. *See* Rope

ROSCOE. A loc. n., Yorks

ROSE. *D.*, *G.*, *Dch.*, *Fr.* Rose; a p.n.

Rose is among the list of naturalized Protestant exiles from the continent.

ROSHER. *Fr.* Rocher; *Dch.* Rosier; *D.* Roscher; p.n.

ROSKILL. From Rosskell or Hrosskell; a loc. n., Cumb.

ROSLYN. A loc. n., Edinburgh

ROSS. A loc. n., Heref., Scotl., Yorks. *Dch.* Ross; a p.n.

ROSSALL. A loc. n., Lancs, Yorks

ROSSER. From the *Fr.* Rousseau; a Huguenot n. Or *Fl.* Rosaer; a p.n.

ROSWELL. *Fr.* Rousselle; a p.n. *See* Russell
ROTHERHAM. A loc. n., Yorks
ROTHWELL. A loc. n., Lincs, Northants, Yorks. *D.B.* Rodowelle
ROTTER. *Dch.* Rotte; *Fr.* Routier; p.n.
ROTTON. *Dch.* Rooten; a p.n. Or *see* Roughton
ROUCH. *G.* Rausch; a p.n.
ROUGH. *G.* Ruff; a p.n.
ROUGHTON. A loc. n., Lincs, Norf., Salop
ROUNCE. *See* Rands
ROUND. *See* Rant
ROUNTREE. From Rowantree; a loc. n., Cumb.
ROUPEL. *G.* Ruppel; a p.n.
ROUSBY. A loc. n., Yorks. *D.B.* Rozebi
ROUSE. A loc. n., Cornw. Or *Dch.* Rous; *G.* Rausch; *Fr.* Rousse, Rouse; p.n.
ROUT. *N.* Rauðr, Rútr or Hrútr; *G.* Rutha, Roth, Rauter; *D.B.* Rot; *D.* Rauth; *Dch.* Root; *Fl.* Rowet; p.n.
ROUTH. A loc. n., Yorks
ROUTLEDGE. A loc. n., Cumb.
ROUTLEY. From Rothley; a loc. n., Leics. Or *see* Routledge
ROW, ROWE. From the Irish *ruadh*, red. A loc. n., Dumbarton, Somers., Yorks. *See* Raw, Roe
ROWAN, ROWEN. *Dch.* Rouwen, *Fr.* Rouen; p.n.
ROWARTH. A loc. n., Ches.
ROWDON. From Rowden; a loc. n., Devon, Leics.
ROWELL. A loc. n., Glost.
ROWING. *See* Rowen
ROWLAND. A loc. n., Derbysh. Or *Dch.* Rowland; *Fl.* Roulandt; *Fr.* Rouland; p.n.
ROWLATT. From Rowlett; a loc. n., Kent. Or *Fr.* Roulet; a p.n.
ROWLES. From Rolles; a loc. n., Ess.
ROWLEY. A loc. n., Staffs., Wilts
ROWLING. *See* Rawlinson
ROWNEY. *Fr.* Rouneau; a p.n.
ROWORTH. A loc. n., Derbysh.
ROWSELL. *Fl.* Roussel; a p.n. *See* Russell
ROWSON. From Rowston; a loc. n., Lincs
ROWTON. A loc. n., Salop, Yorks
ROXBURGH. The county town
ROXBY. A loc. n., Yorks
ROY. *N.* Hroi; *Dch.* Rooij; *Fr.*, *G.* Roy; p.n.
ROYAL. *Fr.*; p.n.
Galfrid Roille in Rot. Obl. et Fin., K. John.
ROYCE. *G.*, *Dch.*, *Fl.* Reuss; a p.n.
ROYLE. *See* Royal
ROYSTON. A loc. n., Herts, Yorks
ROYTHORNE. From Rowthorne; a loc. n., Derbysh.
RUBERY. A loc. n., Worcest.
RUBIE. *D.* Rubow; *Dch.* Rube; *G.* Rubie; *Fr.* Ruby; p.n.
RUDALL. *Dch.*, *G.* Rudolf, Rudel; p.n.
RUDD. *D.* Rud; a p.n.
RUDDLE. *G.* Rudel; a p.n. Comp. Rudolf
RUDDOCK. Dimin. of Rud
RUDGARD. *See* Rudyard
RUDGE. A loc. n., Devon, Somers., Staffs., Wilts
RUDLAND. From Rutland
RUDRUM. From Rotherham; a loc. n., Yorks. *D.B.* Rodreham
RUDYARD. A loc. n., Staffs.
RUFF. *G.*; p.n.
RUFFELL. *Fr.* Rouval; a p.n.
RUFFLES. *G.* Rouvel; a p.n. Or *see* Raffles
RUGGLES. From Rugles; a loc. n., Normandy
RULE. *Fr.* Ruelle; *Dch.* Rühl; p.n. Or Rueil; a loc. n. in France
RUMBALL. *G.* Rumpel; *N.* Rympill; n.n. *D.B.* Rumbold; *Fl.* Rummel; p.n.

RUMBELOW. *Fr.* Rambouillet (?); or *D.*, *G.* Rummeler, Rummelhoff; *S.* Romell; *Fl.* Rummel, Rommelaere; p.n.

The name was found in England at an early period, for Stephen Rummelowe or Rumbilowe was governor of Nottingham Castle, A.D. 1369. The sailors' 'Heave, oh, rumbylow,' is a coincidence, and refers probably to the grog in prospect.

RUMBLE. *See* Rumball

RUMMINGS. *Dch.* Roumen; *S.* Rumin; *Fl.* Rumens, Rummens; p.n.

RUMP. *D.* Rump; *G.* Rumpe, Rumpf; *Dch.* Rumpff; p.n.

RUMNEY. *Dch.* Rummenie; a p.n. Or *see* Romney

RUMSEY. From Romsey; a loc. n., Ess.

RUNACRES. *Fl.* Runacher; a p.n.

RUNDELL, RUNDLE. *S.* Rondahl; *Dch.* Rouendal; a loc. and p. n.

RUNHAM. A loc. n., Kent, Norf.

RUNNACLES. *G.* Runkel; *Dch.* Runckel; *Fl.* Runacher; p.n.

RUNNALL. From Runhall; a loc. n., Norf.

RUNNECKLES. *See* Runnacles

RUNNICUS. *See* Runacres

RUNNIFF. *D.* Roennov; a p.n.

RUSBY. *See* Rousby

RUSCOE. *See* Roscoe

RUSE. From Roose; a loc. n., Lancs. Or *see* Rouse

RUSH. A loc. n., Dublin. Or *D.*, *G.*, *Dch.* Rusch; a p.n.

RUSHBROOK. A loc. n., Suff.

RUSHBURY. A loc. n., Heref.

RUSHTON. A loc. n., Ches., Dorset, Northants, Salop, Staffs.

RUSHWORTH. From Rishworth; a loc. n., Yorks

RUSKIN. *Fl.* Raskin; *Fr.* Rasquin; p.n.

RUSS. *G.*, *Dch.*, *Fl.* Russ, Russe; *Fr.* Rousse; p.n.

RUSSELL. *Fr.* Roussel. From Ruiseil (a stream, a brook); a loc. n. in Normandy

Rushell or Rosel is in the Roll of Battell Abbey, and Huges de Rozel occurs as one of the benefactors of the abbey of St. Étienne at Caen, founded by William the Conqueror. Rozel, a tenant in chief in *D.B.*

RUST. *D.*, *G.*, *Dch.*; p.n.

RUSTON. A loc. n., Norf.

RUTHERFORD. A loc. n., Roxburgh

RUTHERGLEN. A loc. n., Lanark

RUTLAND. The county

RUTLEY. A loc. n., Worcest.

RUTT. *Dch.* Ruth; a p.n. Or *see* Rudd

RUTTEN. *Dch.*; p.n.

RUTTER. *N.* Hrútr; *Dch.* Rutter; p.n.

RYALL. From Ryhall; a loc. n., Worcest.

RYAN. *D.* Ryan; *Fr.* Royon; a p.n. From Royan; a loc. n., Normandy

RYDER. From Ryther; a loc. n., Yorks. Or *D.* Ryder; *Dch.* Ruijter; p.n.

RYE. A loc. n., Suss. Or *D.* Rye; a p.n.

RYECROFT. A loc. n., Lancs, Yorks

RYGATE. From Reigate; a loc. n., Surr.

RYHOPE. A loc. n., Dur.

RYLAND. A loc. n., Lincs. Rylands; loc. n., Notts

RYLE. A loc. n., Northbd.

RYMAN. *G.* Riemann; a p.n.

RYMER. A loc. n., Suff. Or *G.* Reimer; a p.n.

S.

Saberton. From Sapperton; a loc. n., Derbysh. Or Soberton, Hants

Sabey. *Fr.* Sabbe; *D.* Saaby; p.n.

Sabin. *Fl.* Saapin; a p.n.

Sach. *N.* Saxi; *G.* Sacha, Sack; *Dch.* Saacke, Sak; *D.* Sack; *D.B.* Sac; p.n.

Sacret. *Fr.* Secret; a p.n.

Sacristan. From Sacriston; a loc. n., Dur.

Sadd. A loc. n., Devon. Or *Fr.* Saddée; a p.n.

Saddington. A loc. n., Leics.

Saddle. A loc. n., Argyll

Sadgrove. *See* Sitgreaves

Sadler. *G.* Sattler; a p.n.

Saffery. *See* Savery

Safford. From Salford; a loc. n., Lancs

Sage. *Fr.* Saget; a p.n.

Saggers. *Fl.* Sagaer, Segers, Sager; p.n. *See* Segar

Sainsbury. From Saintbury; a loc. n., Worcest.

St. Clair. A loc. n., Normandy

Sent Clere in Roll of Battell Abbey. *D.B.* de Sent Cler.

St. John. *Fl.* Vansintjan; a p.n.

Three local names in Flanders are Saint Jean (lez-Ypres), Saint-Jean-Geest, Saint-Jean-in-Erems. Sent John in Roll of Battell Abbey.

St. Leger. *Fr.* Saint-Léger; a p.n.

Sent Legere in Roll of Battell Abbey.

St. Quintin. A loc. n. in Normandy

Sent Quintin in Roll of Battell Abbey and *D.B.*

Sainty. *Dch.* Sante; *D.* Santin; *Fl.* Senty; *Fr.* Saintais; p.n.

Sair, Sairs. *See* Sayer

Sale. A loc. n., Ches.

Sales. *See* Sallows

Salinger. *G.;* p.n.

Salisbury. The city of that name

Salkeld. A loc. n., Cumb.

Sallis. From Sallys; a loc. n., Heref. Or *Dch.* Salis; *Fr.* Salles; p.n.

Sallows. From Sallowes; a loc. n., Norf.

Salmon. *N.* Sölmundr; *Fl.* Salman, Salmain, Solmon; *G.* Sallmann; *Scotl.* Salmond; *D.B.* Saloman; *Fr.* Salmon; p.n.

Salt. A loc. n., Staffs. Or *Dch.* Solt; a p.n.

Salter. *S.* Solter; *Dch.* Selter; p.n.

Salthouse. A loc. n., Lancs, Norf.

Saltwell. A loc. n., Lincs

Salvidge. *D.* Selvig; a loc. and p. n.

Sambridge. *See* Sambrook

Sambrook. A loc. n., Salop

Same. From Seaham; a loc. n., Dur.

Samers. *See* Sames

Sames. From Seames; a loc. n., Yorks. Or *D.;* p.n.

Sammars. From Samarés; a loc. n., Jersey. *See* Samers

Sammon. *See* Salmon

Sammons. *See* Salmon

Sams. *See* Sames

Sanday. From Sandy; a loc. n., Beds. Or *Dch.* Sandee; p.n.

Sandbach. A loc. n., Ches. Or *D.* Sandbech; a loc. and p. n.

Sandbrook. *See* Sandbach

Sandell. From Sendall; a loc. n., Yorks. Or *D.*, *S.* Sandell; a p.n.

Sandeman. *Dch.* Sandman; a p.n.

Sanderson. *S.* Sanderson. *See* Sands

Sandford. A loc. n., Devon, Salop, Somers., Westmd.

SANDHALL. *See* Sandell

SANDHAM. From Sandholme; a loc. n., Lincs, Yorks

SANDIFER. From Sandiford; a loc. n., Staffs.

SANDILANDS. A loc. n., Lanark

SANDLANT. *S.* Sandlund; a loc. and p. n.

SANDS. *See* Sandys

SANDWELL. A loc. n., Devon, etc.

SANDWITH. A loc. n., Cumb.

SANDYS. *N.* Sandi; n.n. *G.*, *D.*, *S.* Sand, Sander; *Dch.* Sande, Sanders; *Fl.* Sannes, Sanders; *S.* Sanderson; *D.B.* Sand, Sandi, Sandig, Sendi; p.n.

SANGER. From Saniger; a loc. n., Glost. Or *Fr.* Sangier; *Dch.* Sanger; p.n.

SANGSTER. *Dch.* Sangstier; a p.n.

SANKEY. A loc. n., Lancs. Or *Fl.* Sancke; *Fr.* Sanchez; *Dch.* Sanches; p.n.

SANN. *See* Sandys

SANQUHAR. A loc. n., Dumfries

SANSOM. *Fr.* Sanson; *D.B.* Sanson and de St. Sansone; p.n.

SANXTER. *Dch.* Sangster; a p.n.

SAPEY. *See* Seapey

SAPSED, SAPSEID. From Shepshed; a loc. n., Leics.

SAPSWORTH. *See* Sopworth

SAPWELL. From Sopewell; a loc. n., Herts

SARE. From Sarre; a loc. n. in Kent. *See* Sayer

SARLL. *See* Serle

SARSON. A loc. n., Hants

SARTAIN. *Fr.* Sarton; a p.n.

SASSE. *D.* Sass; a p.n.

SATCHELL, SATCHWELL. A loc. n., Hants. *See* Setchell

SATTERLEIGH. A loc. n., Devon

SATTERTHWAITE. A loc. n., Lancs

SATTLEY. *See* Satterleigh

SAUL. *N.* Sjölfr, contr. of Sæ-úlfr; *G.* Schaul, Schaller, Saul, Sauler; *D.B.* Saulf, Seulf, Sawold, Saul; *Dch.* Scholl, Saul; *Fl.* Swolf, Soualle; p.n.

SAUMAREZ. *See* Sammars

SAUNDERS. *See* Sandys

SAURY. *See* Sawrey

SAVAGE. *Fr.* Sauvage; a p.n.

Le Sauvage in Rot. Obl. et Fin., K. John.

SAVERY. *Fr.* Savary, Sevrey; a Huguenot and p. n.

SAVILLE. *Fr.* Savalle; *D.* Sevel; p.n.

SAVORY. *See* Savery

SAW. *Fr.* Saut; a p.n.

SAWBRIDGE. A loc. n., Warw., Westmd.

SAWER. *D.*, *G.*, *Fl.* Sauer; *Dch.* Sauër; p.n.

SAWREY. A loc. n., Lancs

SAWYER. *See* Sawer

SAWYERS. A loc. n. in Essex

SAXBY. A loc. n., Leics., Lincs

SAXELBY. A loc. n., Leics.

SAXTON. A loc. n., Yorks

SAY. *Fr.* Saye; *Fl.* Saey; *Dch.* See; p.n.

SAYCE. *Fr.* Sayes; *Dch.* Seys; p.n.

SAYER. *N.* Syr; n.n. (?). *G.* Sehr, Seher, Sy; *D.B.* Sired, Sirof, Seiar; *Dch.* Soer, Sierse; *Fl.* Sehier; *D.*, *Fr.* Seyer; p.n.

SAYLE. *See* Sale

SAYMER. *N.* Sig-mundr; *D.B.* Semar, Samar; *Dch.* Seemer, or St. Maur (?); p.n.

SCADDING. *D.* Schad, Skade; p.n.

SCAGELL. *See* Scargill

SCAIFE. *Fl.* Scaff; *G.* Skiefe; *D.* Skife; p.n.

SCALES. A loc. n., Lancs

Or from Hardwin de Scalers or D'Echellers, a follower of the Conqueror, and tenant in chief in *D.B.* William de Escales in Rot. Obl. et Fin., K. John.

SCAMMELL. *G.* Schammel; a p.n.

SCANES. *Dch.* Schans; a p.n.

SCARBOROUGH. A loc. n., Yorks

SCARCE. *N.* Skari; *G.* Schirrsch; *Dch.*, *Fl.* Scheers; p.n.

SCARD. *G.* Scharte (?); a p.n.

SCARE. *N.* Skari; *G.* Schar; *Dch.* Schier; p.n. *See* Scarce

SCARFE. *G.*, *D.*, *Dch.* Scharf; a p.n. *See* Sharpen

SCARLES. *See* Scurll

SCARLETT. *G.* Scharlot; a p.n.

SCARLL. From Scarle; a loc. n., Notts

SCARNELL. *G.* Scharn, Scorna; p.n.

SCARSBROOK. From Scarisbrick; a loc. n., Lancs

SCARTH. A loc. n. (a mountain pass). Or *N.* Scarði; n.n. (hare-lip). *D.* Scard; *G.* Scharte; p.n.

SCHICKLE. *N.* Skekill; *G.* Schichel, Schick, Schickler; p.n.

SCHOFIELD. *Fl.* Schoenfeld; a p.n.

SCHOLES. *See* Skelt

SCHOOBERT. *G.* Schubart; a p.n.

SCHUSTER. *D.* Schuster; a p.n.

SCOBEL. A loc. n., Devon

SCOGGINS. *N.* Skaggi; *D.* Schackinger; *Dch.* Schokking; *Fl.* Schaekens, Shoukens; p.n.

SCOONES. *Dch.* Schoen; a p.n.

SCOPES. *G.* Schoppe; a p.n.

SCORER. From Scorrer; a loc. n., Cornw.

SCOTCHER. *Dch.* Schotse; a p.n. Or *see* Scotter

SCOTCHMER. From Scotchman; or *Dch.* Schottemeijer; a p.n.

SCOTT. *N.* Skati, Skotti; n.n. (a ghost). *G.* Schotte; *Dch.* Schot; *Fr.* Scotti; *S.*, *D.* Skotte; p.n.

Jordan Scot in Rot. Obl. et Fin., K. John.

SCOTTER. A loc. n., Lincs

SCOTTOW. A loc. n., Norf.

SCOURFIELD. *See* Schofield

SCOVELL. From Escoville (now Ecoville); a loc. n., Normandy

Radulph de Scovill held land in Wilts, *temp.* K. John.

SCRACE. *See* Scrase

SCRAFIELD. From Scrayfield; a loc. n., Lincs

SCRAGGS. *See* Scroggs and Scroggie

SCRASE. *Fl.* Schreyers (?); a p.n.

SCRIME. *G.* Schrimmer; a p.n.

SCRIMGOUR. *See* Skrymsher

SCRIMSHAW. *See* Skrymsher

SCRIMSHIRE. *See* Skrymsher

SCRIVEN. A loc. n., Yorks. Or *Fl.* Schrievens; a p.n.

SCRIVENER. *See* Scriven

SCROGGIE. From Scrogie; a loc. n., Perth

SCROGGS. A loc. n., Cumb., Dumfries

SCROGHAM. A loc. n. From *N.* Scröggr; *D.* Scrog; p.n. (*heimr*, home). Or from Scrwgan; a loc. n., Denbigh (?)

SCROTTOW. *N.* Skrauti; *D.B.* Scrotin; *G.* Schröder, Schrödter, Schröter, Schrötter; *D.* Skroeder; *Fl.* Schroeder; *Dch.* Schroeter; p.n.

SCRUBY. From Scrooby; a loc. n., Lincs

SCRUTON. *See* Scrutton

SCRUTTON. A loc. n., Yorks

SCRYMGEOUR. *See* Skrymsher

SCUDAMORE. From Saint Scudamore; a loc. n., Normandy

Sent Scudamore in Roll of Battell Abbey. It is not in *D.B.*, unless Scudet, a tenant in chief, be the same. Lower thinks the name is derived from the old French Escu d'amour.

SCULLY. *N.* Skuli; *G.* Schylla; *D.B.* Scule, Scula; p.n.

SCULPHER. *Fl.* Schulpen (?); p.n. Or Skulthorpe; a loc. n., Norf.

SCURLL. *N.* Skirvill (?); *G.* Skeurell; p.n. Or *see* Scarll

SCURRAH. *See* Scorer

SCURRY. *See* Scorer

SCUTT. *D.* Skytt; *Dch.* Schutt; p.n. *See* Skeat

SEABER. *Fr.* Sibert; a p.n. *See* Seppings

SEABOURNE. A loc. n.

SEABRIGHT. From *N.* Sig-bjartr; *G.* Seibert, Siebert; p.n.

SEABROOK. A loc. n., Kent

SEADON. *Fr.* Sidon; a p.n.

SEAFORD. A loc. n., Suss.

SEAGER. *See* Segon

SEAGO. *See* Segon

SEAGRAVE. A loc. n., Leics.

SEAKER. *See* Seagar

SEAL. A loc. n., Kent, Leics., Surr. Or *G.* Siele; *Dch.* Siell; p.n.

SEALBY. From Selby; a loc. n., Yorks

SEALEY. *See* Seeley

SEAMAN. *Dch.* Seeman; a p.n. Or *see* Symonds

SEAMON. *See* Seaman

SEAPEY. *N.* Sibbi, pet n. of Sigbaldr; *F.* Sebo, Sibo; *D.B.* Sibi, Sib, Sibold; *G.* Siber, Seppe; *Dch.* Siep, Sepp, Seepe; p.n.

SEAR, SEEAR, SEER. *G.* Zier; a p.n. *See* Sayer

SEARLE. *See* Serle

SEARS. *See* Sayers

SEATLE. A loc. n. near Staveley, Lancs

SEATON. A loc. n., Cumb., Devon, Dur., Northbd., Ross, Yorks. *D.B.* Seton

SEAVERS. *Dch.* Sieverts; *D.*, *G.* Sievers; *Fl.* Severs, Seyffers; p.n. *See* Seward

SEAWARD. *See* Seward

SECCOMBE. A loc. n., Devon. Or Seacombe, Ches.

SECKER. *See* Segon

SEDDING. *Fr.* Sedyn; a p.n.

SEDGER. *Fr.* Segers; a p.n. *See* Segon

SEE. *See* Say

SEELEY. From Sillé; a loc. n., Normandy. Or *G.* Siele, Sille; *Fr.* Sillyé; p.n.

SEEVILL. *See* Saville

SEFTON. From Sephton; a loc. n., Lancs

SEGON. *N.* Siggi, dimin. of Sigurðr; *D.B.* Sigar, Sagar, Sighet, Sichet, Suga; *Dch.* Segar, Seger, Sieger; *F.* Sikke; *D.* Sekker, Seeger; *S.* Seger; *Fl.* Segher, Seghin; *G.* Sieg, Siegel, Siegert; p.n.

SEGRAVE. From Seagrave; a loc. n., Leics.

SEILY. *See* Siely

SELBY. A loc. n., Yorks

SELDEN. From Seldon; a loc. n., Devon

SELF. *N.* Sjölfr, a contr. of Sæ-ulfr (sea-wolf); *Fl.* Swolf; *D.B.* Seulf; p.n.

SELKIRK. A loc. n., Scotl.

SELLERS. *Dch.*, *G.* Selle, Zeller; *Fl.* Selders, Sell, Sellier; *Fr.* Sellau; p.n.

SELLEY. *Fr.* Sailly; a p.n. Or from Selly; a loc. n., Salop

SELLICK. From Sellack; a loc. n., Heref.

SELWY, SELWYN. *Fl.* Sallewyn; a p.n.

William Selveyn held land in Oxon *temp.* K. John.

SEMMENCE. *See* Symonds

SEMMENS. *See* Symonds

SEMON, SEMAIN. *Fr.* Sement; a p.n. *See* Simmons

SEMPER. *G.*; p.n.

SEMPILL, SEMPLE. *Fl.* Sempels; a p.n.

SENDALL. *D.* Sandell; *Fl.* Sendall; p.n.

SENIOR. *Fr.* Sengier; *Dch.* Senger, Senner; p.n.

SENNETT, SENNITT. From St. Neot; a loc. n., Cornw.

SENTANCE. From St. Anne's; a loc. n., Cornw.

SEPPINGS. *See* Seapey

SERJEANT. *F.* Sergeant; a p.n.

SERLE. *Fr.* Serlé, Serlui; *D.B.* Serlo; *Dch.* Sarlie; *S.* Serling; p.n.

Magister Serlo in Rot. Obl. et Fin., K. John (Devon), A.D. 1205.

SERMON. *Fr.;* p.n. Also Sermain; a p.n.

SERRES. From Serez; a loc. n., Normandy. *Fr.* Serès; *Fl.* Serruys; p.n.

SERVANT. *Fr.* Serviant; a p.n.

SERVICE. *Fr.* Servais; a p.n.

SESSENS. *See* Sisson

SETCHELL. From Setchell; a loc. n., Camb.

SETON. *See* Seaton

SETTERINGTON. A loc. n., Yorks

SETTLE. A loc. n., Yorks

SEWARD. *N.* Sigvatr; *D.* Sivert; *S.* Sivard; *G.* Sievert, Siewert; *Fl.* Liffert; *Dch.* Sieuwerts; *D.B.* Siward, Seward, Suert; p.n.

SEWILL. *See* Saville

SEXTON. *See* Saxton

SEYMOUR. *Fr.* St. Maur. Or *see* Saymer

SHACKLE. *Dch.* Schakel; a p.n.

SHACKLETON. From Shakerton; a loc. n., Dur. (?)

SHACKSON. *D.* Schack; *Dch.* Schaik; *G.* Schach; p.n.

SHADDICK. *G.* Schadeck; a p.n.

SHADDOCK. *See* Shaddick

SHADE. *See* Sheedy

SHADFORD. From Shadforth; a loc. n., Dur.

SHADRAKE. *G.* Schadrich; a p.n.

SHADWELL. A loc. n., Middlx., Salop, Yorks

SHAFT. *N.* Skapti; *D.* Skafte; *G.* Schaffert; p.n.

SHAFTO. From Shaftoe; a loc. n., Northbd.

SHAKERLEY. A loc. n., Lancs

SHAKESPEARE. From Skegby (?) (*D.B.* Schegebi); a loc. n., Notts. This word is derived from *D. Schacke; Fl.* Schack, Schaeck, Shaek; *Dch.* Schach, Schaick, Schake; *G.* Schäche; *S.* Scheike; p.n.

D. bær or *býr*, a dwelling. Compare Shakerley, Shackerston, Exbear, Ailesbeare, Shebbear, etc. In Rot. Obl. et Fin., K. John, it is spelt Scheggeby.

SHALDERS. *Fl.* Scholders; a p.n. *See* Skelt

SHALE. *Fl.* Schall; *Dch., G.* Schell; *D.* Scheel; p.n.

SHALLESS. *Dch.* Schallies; *G.* Schallisch; p.n.

SHAMBROOK. *See* Sambrook

SHAND, SHANDY. From Chanday; a loc. n., Normandy

SHANKS. *D., Dch.* Schank; *Fl.* Schangh; p.n.

SHANNON. *D.* Schanning; a p.n.

SHAPCOTT. A loc. n., Devon

SHAPLAND. From Shopland; a loc. n., Ess.

SHARDALOW. *See* Shardlow

SHARDLOW. A loc. n., Derbysh.

SHARLAND. From Shirland; a loc. n., Derbysh. (?)

SHARMAN. *G.* Scharmann; *Dch.* Schürman; *D.* Schauman; *D.B.* Sceman (?); p.n.

Lower gives it Shearman, one who shears worsteds, fustians, etc., such a trade being once known in Norwich.

SHARP. *Dch.* Scharp; a p.n. *See* Sharpen

SHARPEN. *N.* Skarpheðinn, Skarpin; *G.* Scharf, Scharfen; *Dch.* Scharp; *D.* Skaarup; p.n.

SHARPINS. *See* Sharpen

SHARPUS. *Dch.* Schaapes; a p.n.

SHARR. *N.* Skari; a p.n. Or *see* Shaw

SHARWOOD. *See* Sherwood

SHATTICK. *See* Shaddick

SHATTOCK. *G.* Schattke; a p.n. *See* Shaddick

SHATTON. A loc. n., Derbysh.

SHAUL. *See* Saul

SHAVE. *D.* Schevers; *Fl.* Scheyven; *G.* Schäfer; *Fr.* Chave; a Huguenot n. *D.B.* Chevre. *See* Chafy

SHAW. A loc. n., Lancs, Oxf., Wilts. From *N.* Skógr, a wood; or *S.* Skog; *D.* Schau, Shaw; *Dch.* Schouw, Schowe; *Fl.* Schaugh; p.n.

SHAWFIELD. A loc. n., Lancs
SHAWNEY. *See* Shorney
SHEAR. From Shere; a loc. n., Surr. Or *see* Scarce
SHEARHOD. From Shereford; a loc. n., Norf.
SHEARS. *Dch.* Schier; *G.* Schierse; p.n. *See* Scarce
SHEAVYN. *S.* Schevin; *Fl.* Scheyvin; a p.n.
SHEEDY. *N.* Skiði; *G.* Schiedeck; *Dch.* Scheijde; *D.* Schythe; p.n.
SHEEKEL. *See* Shickle
SHELDON. A loc. n., Derbysh., Devon
SHELDRACK. *See* Sheldrick
SHELDRAKE. *See* Sheldrick
SHELDRICK. From Sheldwick; a loc. n., Kent
SHELFORD. A loc. n., Warw.
SHELLEY. A loc. n., Yorks
SHELTON. From Skelton; a loc. n., Yorks (*D.B.* Scheltun). Or Shelton, Norf.
SHENSTONE. A loc. n., Staffs.
SHEPHERD. *See* Sheppard
SHEPPARD. From Chebbard; a loc. n., Dorset. Or *Dch.* Schappert; a p.n.
SHEPPEY. A loc. n., Kent
SHERBORNE. A loc. n., Devon, Dorset, Glost., Hants, Somers.
SHERBROOKE. From Shirebrook; a loc. n., Derbysh.
SHERIDAN. From Shrawardine; a loc. n., Salop. Or *S.* Scherdin; a p.n.
SHERIFF. *N.* Greifi; n.n. *A.S.* Gerêfa; *Engl.* Reeve, Shirereeve; *G.* Schriefer; *D.* Schreve; p.n.
SHERINGHAM. A loc. n., Norf.
SHERINGTON. A loc. n., Wilts
SHERRARD. *See* Gerard
SHERRATT. *See* Gerard
SHERREN, SHERRIN. *See* Sherwin
SHERRINGTON. A loc. n., Bucks, Wilts
SHERRY. From Sherridge; a loc. n., Worcest.
SHERSBY. From Shearsby; a loc. n., Leics.
SHERVIL. From Sherwill; a loc. n., Devon
SHERWIN. *D.* Scherwin; *Fl.* Scheyvin; *Dch.* Scherren; *G.* Scherwing; p.n.
SHERWOOD. A loc. n., Notts
SHEW. *See* Shaw
SHEWILL. *Dch.* Schewel; a p.n.
SHEWRING. From Shering; a loc. n., Ess. Or *Dch.* Schuring; a p.n.
SHICLE. *See* Shickle
SHIELDS, SHIELLS. From Shields; a loc. n., Dur.
SHILDRICK. *See* Sheldrick
SHILLCOCK. *G.* Schilke; a p.n.
SHILLING. A loc. n., Dorset. Or *D.*, *G.*, *Dch.* Schilling; a p.n.
SHILLINGFORD. A loc. n., Devon
SHILLITOE. From Shillington; a loc. n., Herts. Or Schildau, Prussia; or *Dch.* Schilte; *G.* Schilter; p.n.
SHILTON. A loc. n., Northants, Oxf., Worcest.
SHIMMIN. *D.* Schieman; a p.n. Or *D.B.* Schemin; a loc. n., Lincs
SHINGLE. *Dch.* Schenkel; a p.n.
SHINGLETON. *See* Singleton
SHINN, SHINNER. From the Irish Shinan, originally O'Shanahan; a p.n. (Lower)
SHIPLEY. A loc. n., Derbysh., Salop, Yorks
SHIPP. *D.* Schipke; *Dch.* Schipper; a p.n.
SHIPPARD. *See* Sheppard
SHIPPEY. From Shiphay; a loc. n., Devon
SHIPPING. From Shippon; a loc. n., Oxf.
SHIPTON. A loc. n., Oxf., Salop, Yorks
SHIPWASH. From Sheepwash; a loc. n., Devon
SHIPWAY. *See* Shippey
SHIRES. *Fl.* Scheyers; a p.n.

SHIRLEY. A loc. n., Derbysh., Hants, Kent, Surr., Worcest.

SHOEBRIDGE, SHOOBRIDGE. From Shewbridge; a loc. n., Lancs

SHOLL. *G.*, *Dch.* Scholl; a p.n.

SHONE. *Dch.* Schoen; a p.n.

SHOOLBRED. From Shulbred; a loc. n., Suss.

SHOPPEE. *D.* Schoppe; a p.n.

SHORE. *See* Sharr

SHOREY. *Fr.* Chourrier; a p.n. (?)

SHORING. *Dch.* Schuring; a p.n.

SHORLAND. A loc. n., Devon

SHORMAN. *See* Sharman

SHORNEY. *Fl.* Schournoy; a p.n.

SHORT. *D.* Schorti; *G.* Scharte, Schorter; p.n.

SHORTEN. *See* Shortins

SHORTER. *G.* Schorter; a p.n.

SHORTING. *See* Shortins.

SHORTINS. *N.* Skati; *G.* Scharte, Schorter, Schote; *D.B.* Suartin, Swartim; *D.* Schorti; *Dch.* Schoutens; *Fl.* Scharten; p.n.

SHOTTER. *G.*, *Dch.* Schotte; a p.n.

SHOTTIN. From Shotton; a loc. n., Dur.

SHOUT. *Dch.* Schout; a p.n.

SHOVE. *Fr.* Chauveau; *Dch.* Schouw, Schuver; *D.* Schow; p.n.

SHOVELLER. *D.* Schovelin; a p.n. Or *see* Shuffle

SHOWEL. *Dch.* Schewel; a p.n. *See* Shuffle

SHOWERING. *See* Shewring

SHOWLER. *Fr.* Chaulet; a p.n.

SHREEVE. *See* Sheriff

SHRIGLEY. A loc. n., Ches.

SHRIMPLING. *G.* Schrempel; a p.n.

SHROSBREE. From Shrewsbury; a loc. n., Salop

SHRUBSOLE. A loc. n., Staffs.

SHUBROOK. From Shobrook; a loc. n., Devon

SHUCKBURGH. A loc. n., Warw.

SHUFFLE. *Fr.* Chauvel, Chouville; p.n.

SHUGAR. *See* Segon

SHUM. *G.* Schumm; a p.n.

SHURMAR. *G.* Schirmer; *Dch.* Schermer; p.n.

SHURY. *See* Shorey

SHUTE. A loc. n., Devon. Or *Dch.* Schoot, Schut; *G.* Schütt; *N.* Skáti; *D.* Skytte; p.n.

SHUTER. *Dch.* Schuter; a p.n.

SHUTLER. *G.* Schüttler; a p.n.

SHUTTLEWORTH. A loc. n., Yorks. *D.B.* Scitelesuuorde

SIBBETT. *Dch.*, *G.* Siebert; a p.n. *See* Sigbert

SIBBIT. *See* Sigbert

SIBEL. *N.* Sig-baldr (Sibbold); *D.B.* Sib, Sibi, Sibbold; *F.* Sibo; *G.* Sibe, Siebe, Sieber, Siebert, Siebler, Seppelt, Sebald; *Dch.* Sibbelee; *Fl.* Siebels, Sibille; p.n.

SIBERT. *See* Sibbett

SIBLEY. From Sible; a loc. n., Ess. Or *Dch.* Sibbelee; a p.n.

SIBTHORPE. A loc. n., Notts

SIBUN. *Fl.* Sibon; a p.n.

SICH. *G.* Sich, Siech; p.n.

SICKLEMORE. From Sicklemere; a loc. n., Suff.

SIDDALL. A loc. n., Lancs. Or *G.* Siedel; a p.n.

SIDDERS. *Dch.* Sieders; a p.n.

SIDDON. *See* Seadon and Seaton

SIDE. *G.* Seite; a p.n.

SIDLE. From Siddall; a loc. n., Lancs. Or *see* Sydal

SIDNEY. From St. Denis; a loc. n., France

SIDWELL. *N.* Siðu-Hallr; a p.n.

SIELEY. *See* Sealey

SIGGE. *See* Segon

SIGGERS. *N.* Sig-urðr; *D.* Seyghers; *Dch.* Seegers; p.n. *See* Segon.

SIGGINS. *See* Segon

SILCOCK. *Dch.* Sielcken; a p.n.

SILENCE. *D.* Seiling, Sillin; p.n. (?)

SILITOE. *See* Shillitoe

SILK. *See* Silcock

SILL. *D.* Sillo; *S.* Sillow; *G.* Siele, Sille; p.n.

SILLETT. *See* Sillitoe

SILLIS. *Dch.* Silles; p.n.

SILVER. *N.* Silfra; n.n. *D.* Silfver; *Dch.* Silva; *Fl.* Silver; p.n.

SILVERLOCK. *D.* Silberloh; a p.n.

SILVERSTONE. A loc. n., Northants

SILVERTON. A loc. n., Devon

SILVERTOWN. A loc. n., Ess.

SILVESTER. *Fl.*, *G.* Silvester; *Fr.* Silvestre; p.n.

SILVEY. *N.* Silfri; n.n. *Dch.* Silva; *S.* Silfven; p.n.

SIMCOCK, SIMCOE. Dimin. of Simmund, Simmon, Simon. From *N.* Sigmundr

SIMKIN. *See* Symonds

SIMMENS. *See* Symonds

SIMMONS. *See* Symonds

SIMMS. *See* Symonds

SIMPER. *G.* Semper, Simba; a p.n.

SIMPLE. *G.* Zimpel; a p.n. Or *see* Semple

SIMPSON. *N.* Simbi, dimin. of Sigmundr; *G.* Simba, Simm; *D.* Simeson; *S.* Simson; p.n.

SIMSON. *See* Simpson

SINCLAIR. *See* St. Clair

SINGLETON. A loc. n., Yorks

SIRER. *Fr.* Sirier; a p.n.

SIRR. *Dch.* Suur; a p.n.

SISLEY. *Dch.* Sisselar; *G.* Cichla; p.n.

SISON. From Syston; a loc. n., Leics.

SISSENS. *See* Sisson

SISSON. From Siston; a loc. n., Glost. Or *Fl.* Sisen; *Dch.* Sisseren; p.n.

SITCH. *See* Sich

SITDOWN. From Seatown; a loc. n., Dorset

SITGREAVES. From Seagrave; a loc. n., Leics. *D.B.* Satgrave

SITWELL. *See* Sidwell

SIVIL. *See* Saville

SKAIFE. *See* Scaife

SKAKEL. *N.* Skakki; *G.* Schachschal, Schactel; p.n.

SKEAT. *N.* Skáti or Skiði; *D.* Skatt, Skytte; p.n. (A shooter, marksman.)

SKEDGE. *See* Skegg

SKEELS. *See* Skelt

SKEEN. *See* Skene

SKEET. *See* Skeat

SKEFFINGTON. A loc. n., Leics.

SKEGG. *N.* Skaggi; *D.* Schek; *Dch.* Scheick; *G.* Schech; *Fl.* Schaek; p.n.

SKELLS. *See* Skelt

SKELT. *N.* Skjöldr; *D.B.* Schelin, Scule; *Fl.* Schoels, Scholders; *D.* Skeel, Skjold; *Dch.* Schall, Schell, Scheltes, Scholl; p.n.

SKELTON. A loc. n., Cumb., Yorks.

SKENE. *G.*, *Dch.* Skene; a p.n.

SKERRITT. From Skirrid; a loc. n., Monmouth; Skerwith, Cumb. Or *G.* Skerhut; *Dch.* Scherwitz; p.n.

SKERRY. A loc. n., Antrim. Or *see* Skerritt

SKETCHLEY. A loc. n., Leics.

SKETT. *See* Skeat

SKEVINGTON. *See* Skeffington

SKEWES. A loc. n., Cornw. Or *Dch.* Schüss; a p.n.

SKEY. *Dch.* Schey; a p.n.

SKIDMORE. *See* Scudamore

SKIFFENS. *Dch.* Schiewink; *G.* Skiefe; p.n.

SKILES. *See* Skoyles

SKILLINGTON. A loc. n., Lincs

SKILLITO. *See* Shillitoe

SKILTON. *See* Skelton

SKINNER. *N.* Skinni; a n.n.

SKIPPER. *Dch.* Schipper; a p.n.

SKIPPINS. *G.* Skiba, Skiebe; *D.B.* Scipti; *D.* Schipke; p.n.

SKIPTON. A loc. n., Yorks

SKIPWITH. A loc. n., Yorks

SKIPWORTH. *See* Skipwith

SKIRROW. *See* Scorrer

SKITT. *D.* Skytt; a p.n. *See* Skeat

SKONE. *See* Scone

SKOULDING. *Dch.* Scholten. *See* Skelt

SKOYLES. *Dch.* Schuil; a p.n. *See* Skelt

SKRINE. From Skreen; a loc. n., Sligo

SKRYMSHER. *G.* Schremser; a p.n.

SKUCE. *Dch.* Schüss; a p.n. *See* Skewes.

SKUDDER. *See* Shutter

SKULL. *N.* Skuli; *Dch.* Schule; *Fl.* Schul; *D.B.* Scule; p.n.

SKULTHORPE. A loc. n., Norf.

SKUSE. *See* Skewes

SKY. *See* Skey

SLACK. A loc. n., Derbysh., Yorks

SLADDEN, SLADEN. From Slaidburn; a loc. n., Yorks

SLADE. A loc. n., Devon, Suff. Or from Slad; a loc. n., Glost.

SLAPP. *N.* Slappi; *G.* Schlappe; *Fl.* Sleyp; p.n.

SLARK. *G.* Slach; a p.n.

SLATCHER. *See* Slaughter

SLATER. *D.* Schlytter; *Dch.* Schlette, Sluyter, Sluiter; p.n.

SLATFORD. From Slaughterford; a loc. n., Wilts

SLATTER. *See* Slaughter

SLAUGHTER. A loc. n., near Sherborne, Glost. Or *G.* Slotta; *Dch.* Slooter; *Fl.* Slotte; p.n.

SLEDDALE. A loc. n., Yorks

SLEEP. From Sleepe; a loc. n., Heref.; or Slepe, Dorset. Or *Dch.* Schlipp, Sloep; *Fl.* Sleyp; *D.* Schlippe; a p.n. *See* Slipper

SLEIGH. *D.* Schlie; *Dch.* Sluy; p.n.

SLEIGHT. A loc. n., Wilts

SLINGSBY. A loc. n., Yorks

SLIPPER. *N.* Sleppi; n.n. *D.* Schlippe; *G.* Schleppe; p.n. *See* Sleep

SLOCOMBE. A loc. n., Devon

SLOMAN.

Lower thinks this is a disguise of the Jewish name Solomon.

SLOPER. *Dch.* Sloeper; a p.n.

SLOUGH. A loc. n., Berks

SLOW. From Sloo; a loc. n., Devon. Or *see* Slough

SLUCE. *Fl.* Sloos, Sluys; p.n.

SLUGG. *Dch.* Sloog; a p.n.

SLY. *See* Sleigh

SLYPER. *See* Slipper

SMAIL, SMALE. *Fl.* Smal; *Dch.* Smale; *G.* Schmehl; p.n.

SMALLEY. A loc. n., Derbysh.

SMALLFIELD. A loc. n., Yorks

SMALLWOOD. A loc. n., Staffs.

SMART. *D.* Smart; *D.B.* Smert; p.n.

SMEATON. A loc. n., Cornw., Yorks

SMEDDLES. *See* Smethills

SMEE. *G.* Smy; a p.n.

SMELLIE. From Smeley; a loc. n., Ess. Or *D.* Schmelling; a p.n.

SMELT. *Dch.*; p.n.

SMETHILLS. A loc. n., Lancs

SMILES. *See* Smail

SMILEY. *See* Smellie

SMIRKE. *Fl.* Smerche; a p.n.

SMITH. *N.* Smiðr; *D.* Schmidt, Schmith, Smidt, Smidth, Smit, Smith; *Dch.* Smid, Smiet, Smith, Smitt; *Fl.* Smet, Smit; *G.* Schmidt, Schmitt; p.n.

SMITHERS. *See* Smithies

SMITHIES. A loc. n., Yorks. Or *Dch.* Smithuis; a p.n.

SMITHSON. From Smithstone; a loc. n., Devon

SMOUT. *Fl.*; p.n.

SMURTHWAITE. From Smirthwaite; a loc. n., Cumb.

SNAPE. A loc. n., Devon, Norf., Suff., Yorks. Or *Dch.* Sneep; *Fl.* Schnepp; p.n.

SNAPPER. *Dch.*; p.n.

SNARE. *D.* Snaaijer; *D.B.* Snerri; *G.* Schnier; *Dch.* Snoer, Schnaar; *Fl.* Sneyers; p.n.

SNASDALL. A loc. n.

SNAZLE. From Snedshill; a loc. n., Salop. Or *G.* Schnegula; a p.n.

SNEAD. A loc. n., Worcest.

SNEE. *G.* Snay; a p.n.

SNEEZUM. From Snettisham; a loc. n., Norf. Or *Fl.* Sneesens; a p.n.

SNELL. *N.* Snjallr; n.n. *G.* Schnell, Schnelle, Schneller; *D.B.* Schnelling; *Dch.* Snel, Snellen; p.n.

SNEPP. *See* Snape

SNEYD. A loc. n., Staffs., Worcest. Or Snaith, Yorks

SNOOK. *N.* Snákr; n.n. *Dch.* Schnücke; *Fl.* Snoek; *D.B.* Snoch; p.n.

SNOOKS. A loc. n., Devon. Or *Fl.* Snoeckx; a p.n.

Lower thinks it is a corruption of Sevenoaks, Kent.

SNORE. *See* Snare

SNORING. A loc. n., Norf.

SNOWDEN. A loc. n., Yorks

SNOWDON. A loc. n., Staffs.

SNUGGS. *See* Snooks

SNUSHALL. From Snowshill; a loc. n., Somers.

SOAM. From Soham; a loc. n., Camb. Or *N.* Sámr (swarthy, Finnish); *G.* Same; *D.B.* Samar; *Dch.* Sam; *S.*, *Fl.* Somme; p.n.

SOAMES. *Fl.* Somers; a p.n.

SOANE. *G.* Sohn; *Dch.* Son; p.n.

SOANES. *D.B.* Soian; *G.* Sohns; *Dch.* Son; *Fl.* Soons; p.n.

SOAR. A loc. n., Lincs. Or *Dch.* Soer; *G.* Sohr; p.n.

SOBEY. *Dch.* Sobbe; a p.n.

SODDY. *See* Soder

SODEN. *Dch.* Soeding; a p.n.

SODER. *Fr.* Sodeau; *Dch.* Soede; p.n.

SOFFE. *Fr.* Soffie; a p.n.

SOFLEY. *See* Softley

SOFTEY. *See* Softley

SOFTLEY. A loc. n., Dur.

SOLE. *D.* Sohl; a p.n.

SOMERFIELD. *D.*, *S.*, *G.* Sommerfeld; a p.n. *See* Summerville

SOMERFORD. A loc. n., Hants, Wilts

SOMERS, SOMES. *Fl.* Somers; a p.n.

SOMERSET. The county

SOOBY. From Sotby; a loc. n., Lincs

SOOLE. *See* Sole

SOONS. *See* Soanes

SOPER, SOPPER. From Sober; a loc. n., Yorks. Or *G.* Sopart; *Fl.* Sopers; p.n.

SOPPET. *See* Sopwith

SOPWITH. From Sopworth; a loc. n., Wilts

SORBEY. *See* Sowerby

SORBY. A loc. n., Yorks

SORE. *See* Soar

SOREL. *Fr.*; p.n.

SOTHAM. From Southam; a loc. n., Warw.

SOTHEBY. From Sotby; a loc. n., Lincs

SOTHERN. From Sotherton; a loc. n., Suff.

SOTHERS. From Southease; a loc. n., Suss.

SOUL. *See* Sole

SOULBY. A loc. n., Westmd.

SOULSBY. *See* Soulby

SOUNDY. From Sandy; a loc. n., Beds

SOUPER. *G.* Sober; a p.n.

SOUTHALL. A loc. n., Middlx.

SOUTHAM. A loc. n., Glost., Warw.

SOUTHARD. *See* Southward

SOUTHBY. *See* Sotheby

SOUTHCOMBE. A loc. n., Devon

SOUTHCOTT. A loc. n., Cornw. Or from Southcote; a loc. n., Yorks

SOUTHERN. From Southton; a loc. n., Wilts

SOUTHERWOOD. *See* Southwood

SOUTHEY. A loc. n., Devon. Or *Fr.* Souday; a p.n.

SOUTHGATE. A loc. n., Middlx.

SOUTHWARD. From Southworth; a loc. n., Lancs. Or *see* Southwood

SOUTHWELL. A loc. n., Dorset, Notts

SOUTHWOOD. A loc. n., Somers.

SOWARD. *See* Southward

SOWELS. *See* Saul

SOWERBUTTS. A loc. n., Lancs

SOWERBY. A loc. n., Lancs, Yorks. *D.B.* Sorebi

SOWTER. *N.* Sóti; *D.B.* Sota; *G.* Sotta, Sowade, Sauter; *Dch.* Soeter, Souter; *Fl.* Suttor; *Fr.* Sutter; p.n.

SOWTON. A loc. n., Devon

SPAIN. *Dch.* Spaan; a p.n.

SPALDING. A loc. n., Lincs

SPALL. From Sporle; a loc. n., Norf. Or *Dch.* Spall, Spoel; p.n.

SPANKIE. *Fl.* Spanoghe; or *G.* Spanger; p.n.

SPANTON. From Spaunton; a loc. n., Yorks

SPARHAM. A loc. n., Norf.

SPARKE. *S.*, *Fl.* Spaak; *Dch.* Sporck; *G.* Spauke; p.n.

SPARROW. *S.* Sparre; a p.n. *See* Spurr

SPARSHOTT. From Sparsholt; a loc. n., Hants

SPAULL. *See* Spall

SPEAIGHT. *See* Speight

SPEAK, SPECK, SPEKE. From Speke; a loc. n., Lancs

SPEAKMAN. *Dch.* Spiekerman; a p.n.

SPEAR. *G.* Speer; *Dch.* Spier; p.n.

SPEARING. *Dch.* Spiering; a p.n.

SPEECHLY. From Spetchley; a loc. n., Worcest.

SPEED. *See* Spitty

SPEEDY. *See* Spitty

SPEER, SPEIR. *Dch.* Spier; *Fl.* Spiers; p.n.

SPEIGHT. *S.* Spethz; *D.* Speich; *Dch.* Spigt; *Fl.* Specht; *D.B.* Spec, Spech; p.n.

SPELLER, SPELLS. *Fl.*, *Dch.* Spellers; a p.n.

SPELLMAN. *Dch.* Speelman; *G.* Spielmann; *Fl.* Spelmans; p.n.

SPENCER. From Despenser (*Lat.* Dispensator); a steward

Dispensator, a tenant in chief in *D.B.*

SPERLING. *G.*; p.n. *See* Spurr

SPICE. *D.* Speich; a p.n.

SPICER. *Old Fr.* Espicier (?)

Benedict le Spicer in Rot. Obl. et Fin., K. John.

SPIKINGS. *D.* Speich; *Fl.* Speck; *Dch.* Spek; *D.B.* Spec, Spech; p.n.

SPILL. *Dch.*; p.n.

SPILLER. *G.*; p.n.

SPILLING. *D.* Spelling; a p.n.

SPILSBURY. A loc. n., Worcest.

SPINK. *D.* Spincke; *Dch.* Spaink; *Fl.* Spinnock; *G.* Spinde; p.n.

SPITTA. *D.B.* Spieta; p.n. *See* Spittal

SPITTAL. A loc. n., Derbysh., Ess., Lincs, Northbd., S. Wales

SPITTLE. *See* Spittal

SPITTY. A British loc. n., Spyddid or Spytty. From the Latin *hospitium*, a hospital, as in Yspytty Ystwith (Card.) and Llan-spyddid (Brecons). Also *Fl.* Spits; *D.* Spit, Spitters; *Dch.* Spit, Spits, Spitters; *S.* Spitz; *D.B.* Spieta; p.n.

SPOER. *See* Spurr

SPOFFORD. *See* Spofforth

SPOFFORTH. A loc. n., Yorks

SPOKES. *Dch.* Spook; a p.n.

SPONG. *D.* Sponneck; a p.n.

SPOONER. *G.* Sponer; a p.n.

SPORE. *See* Spurr

SPORLE. A loc. n., Norf.

SPOTTISWOODE. A loc. n., Berwick

SPRANGE. *Dch.* Sprang; a p.n.

SPRATLEY. From Sproatley; a loc. n., Yorks

SPRATT. *Dch.* Spruit; *G.* Sprotte; p.n.

SPRAY. *Dch.* Spree; a p.n.

SPRECKLEY. *D.* Spechler; a p.n.

SPRIGGS. *Dch.* Sprik; a p.n.

SPRING. *G.*, *Dch.*, *D.* Springer; a p.n.

SPRINGALL, SPRINGHALL. From Springhill; a loc. n., Lancs. Or *Fl.* Springael; a p.n.

SPRINGBELT. *Dch.* Springveldt; a p.n.

SPRINGETT. *See* Springbelt

SPRINGTHORPE. A loc. n., Lincs

SPRINKS. *G.* Springst; a p.n.

SPRINZ. *G.* Sprinzel; a p.n.

SPROAT. *See* Sprott

SPROD. *See* Sprott

SPROSTON. From Sprowston; a loc. n., Norf.

SPROTT. *G.* Sprotte; a p.n.

SPRUCE. *Dch.* Spross; *G.* Sprosse, Spruch; a p.n.

SPRUNT. *D.* Sprunck; *G.* Sprung; p.n. (?)

SPRY. *G.* Spreu; a p.n.

SPUNNER. *See* Spooner

SPURGE. *See* Spurgeon

SPURGEON. Dimin. of Sporre (Sporrechen). *See* Spurr

SPURGIN. *See* Spurr

SPURR. *N.* Spörr; n.n. (a sparrow). *D.* Sporré; *G.* Spörel; *Dch.* Spoor; *D.B.* Spur, Sperri; p.n.

SPURRELL. *G.* Spörel; a p.n. *See* Spurr

SPYER. *G.* Speier; *Dch.* Spijer; p.n.

SQUANCE. *G.* Schwanitz; a p.n.

SQUIRE. *Fr.* Esquier; a p.n.

John le Squier in Rot. Obl. et Fin., K. John. Also a Huguenot n.

STABLE. From Staple; a loc. n., Kent. Or. *D.* Stabel; *Dch.* Stapel; *Fl.* Stabel; *D.B.* Stable; *G.* Stebel; p.n.

STABLEFORD. A loc. n., Staffs.

STACEY. *Fr.* St. Eustace; a loc. n.

STACPOOLE. A loc. n., Pembrokesh.

STADDON. A loc. n., Devon

STADEN. A loc. n., Devon. Or *Dch.* Staden; a p.n.

STAFF. *D.* Staw; *S.* Staaf; *G.*, *Fl.*, *Dch.* Staff; p.n.

STAFFORD. The county town

STAGG. *D.* Stage; *Fl.* Stache; *G.* Stach; p.n.

STAGOLL. *See* Steggall

STAINER. *N.* Steinnar; *Fl.* Stanier; *G.* Steiner; p.n.

STAINES. A loc. n., Middx.

STAINNS. *See* Staines. Or *N.* Steinn; *G.* Stein; *Dch.* Steen; p.n.

STAINTON. A loc. n., Cumb., Dur., Lancs, Yorks

STAIR. A loc. n., Ayrsh. Or *D.* Stæhr, Sthyr; *G.* Stähr, Stehr; p.n.

STALEY. A loc. n., Ches.

STALKER. *Dch.* Stolker, Stolkert; p.n.

STALLABRASS, STALLEBRASS. From Stallingbusk; a loc. n., Yorks

STALLARD. *Fl.* Stallaert; a p.n.

STALLER. *Dch.* Staller; p.n. *Fr.* de Stalleur; Huguenot n.

STALLION. *S.* Stahlin; *Fl.* Staelens; *G.* and *Dch.*, Stalling; p.n.

STAMER, STAMMERS. *G.* Stammer; *Dch.* Staamer; p.n.

STAMFORD. A loc. n., Lincs

STAMP. *D.B.* Stam; *G.* Stampe; p.n.

STAMPER. *D.* Stampe; *Dch.* Stamperius; *Fl.* Stampaert; *D.B.* Stamp; p.n.

STANBOROUGH. From Stainborough; a loc. n., Yorks

STANBRIDGE. A loc. n., Dorset, Ess., Yorks

STANBURY. A loc. n., Devon, Yorks

STANCLIFFE. From Staincliffe; a loc. n., Yorks

STANCOMBE. A loc. n., Devon, Dorset

STANDEN. A loc. n., Wilts

STANDIDGE. *See* Standish

STANDISH. A loc. n., Glost., Lancs

STANDFAST. *G.* Standfuss; a p.n.

STANESBY, STANSBY. From Stonesby; a loc. n., Leics.

STANFORD. A loc. n., Norf.

STANGER. *D.* and *G.* Stanger; *S.* Stange; p.n.

STANHAM. *See* Stoneham

STANHOPE. A loc. n., Dur.

STANIFORD. A loc. n., Devon, Salop

STANIFORTH. From Stainforth (*D.B.* Stenforde); a loc. n., Yorks. Or *N.* Steinfirðr; a p.n.

STANLEY. A loc. n., Staffs.

The name of this manor was assumed by the Norman knight Valescherville. *D.B.* de Valuille. Also a loc. n., Dur., Glost., Lancs, Lincs, Yorks.

STANNARD. *N.* Steinuðr; *G.* Steinert, Steinhardt, Stanner; *Fl.* Standaert; *D.B.* Stanard, Stanhert, Stanart; p.n.

STANNERS. *G.* Stanner; a p.n. *See* Stannard

STANNETT. *See* Stannard

STANPFLY. From Stanfree; a loc. n., Derbysh. (?)

STANSFIELD, STANFIELD. A loc. n., Camb., Lancs, Suff., Yorks. *D.B.* Stanesfelt

STANSHAW. A loc. n. Or *see* Stanger

STANTON. A loc. n., Derbysh., Heref., Salop, Somers, Wilts

STANWAY. A loc. n., Ess., Salop

STANWELL. A loc. n., Middlx.

STANYON. A loc. n., Northants

STAP. *Fl.* Staps; *Dch.* Stappes; p.n.

STAPLES. From Staplers; a loc. n., Hants. Or Staple, Devon

STAPLETON. A loc. n., Glost., Salop, Somers., Wilts

STAPLEY. A loc. n., Devon

STAREY. *See* Sterry

STARKEY. *Fr.* Staquet; *G.*, *D.*, *Fl.*, *S.*, *Dch.* Stark, Starke, Starck; p.n.

STARLEY. From Stawley; a loc. n., Somers. (?)

STARLING. *S.* Stahlin; a p.n. *See* Starr

STARNE. *N.* Stjárn; *G.*, *D.*, *Fl.*, and *Dch.* Stern; p.n.

STARR. *N.* Starri; *D.B.* Stari, Stori, Stare; *Dch.* Storre, Starre, Stower, Stuhr; *G* Stöhr, Stör, Stahr; *S.* Stahre, Star, Stare; *D.* Stahr; p.n.

START. A loc. n., Devon

STARTIN. From Starton; a loc. n., Warw.

STARTUP. *D.*; loc. and p.n.

STATHAM. A loc. n., Ches.

STATHER. *See* Stathern

STATHERN. A loc. n.

STATTER. *See* Stather

ST. AUBYN. From St. Aubin; a loc. n., Normandy

STAUNTON. A loc. n., Glost., Heref., Leics., Worcest.

STAVELEY. A loc. n., Derbysh., Yorks, Westmd.

STEABBEN. From Stebbing; a loc. n., Ess.

STEAD, STEED. From Stidd; a loc. n., Lancs. Or Stydd, Derbysh.

STEANE. *Dch.* Steen; a p.n.

STEARN. *See* Starne

STEBBENS. *See* Stebbings

STEBBINGS. *N.* Steypir; *D.B.* Steypi, Stepiot; *Fl.* Stepan, Steppe; *Dch.* Step, Stephan; *D.* Stephens; p.n. Or *see* Steabben

STEBLE. *S.* Stiebel; *D.* Stibolt; *G.* Stiebahl; a p.n.

STED. *See* Stead

STEDALL. *G.* Steidel; a p.n.

STEED. *See* Stead

STEELE. *Dch.* and *G.* Stiel; a p.n.

STEER. *N.* Styrr; *D.* Stühr, Stæhr; *S.* Stühr; *G.* Steer, Stehr, Stier; *Fl.* Stiers; *Dch.* Steer; *D.B.* Sterr, Sterre, Stori, Stur; p.n.

Styr, a thane at the court of Ethelred II., mentioned in royal letters patent. Also in Hardicanute's reign.

STEGGALL. *N.* Stag-näl; n.n. *S.* Stagnell; *G.* Steckel, Steg, Steigler, Stiegler; *D.* Stage, Stege; *Dch.* Steege, Stechel, Stiggel; p.n.

STEGGLES. *See* Steggall

STEGGOLD. *See* Steggall

STEMBRIDGE. A loc. n., Somers., S. Wales

STENSON. A loc. n., Derbysh. Or *D.* Stensen; *S.* Stennsson; p.n.

STEPTOE. *G.*, *Fl.* Steppe, Stiphoudt; a p.n.

STERLING, STIRLING. A loc. n., Scotl.

STERRY. *Dch.* Sterre; a p.n.

STEVENSON. *See* Stiffin

STEWARD, STEWART. *D.* Stigaard; *S.*, *Dch.* Stuart; *Fl.* Steyaert, Stuywaert; p.n.

STIBBARD. *N.* Styr-baldr (?); *D.* Stibolt; *Dch.* Stibbe, Stiphout; *G.* Stibor, Stibale; p.n.

STIBBON. *N.* Styr-björn; *D.* Stybe; *G.* Stibane; p.n.

STICHBURY. *See* Stutchbury

STICHLEY. From Stirchley; a loc. n., Salop

STICHLING. From Stickillin; a loc. n., co. Louth. Or *D.* Stick; *G.* Stich; a p.n.

STICKLAND. A loc. n., Dorset

STIFF. *S.* Styffe; *G.* Steffe, Stief; *Dch.* Stiev, Stiffij; *Fl.* Steuve; *D.B.* Stefan; p.n.

In the Midland counties Stiff is used as a contraction for Stephen. Compare Staff and Stofer.

STIFFIN. *D.* Steffens, Steffin; *Dch.* Stieven; a p.n.

STIGGANT. *N.* Stigandi; n.n. (a stepper). *D.B.* Stigand; a p.n.

STIGGINS. *N.* Stigandi; n.n. *D.* Stikken; p.n.

STIGGLE. *Dch.* Stiggel; a p.n. *See* Steggall

STIGGLES. *See* Steggall

STIGLE. *See* Steggall

STILES, STYLE, STOYLE. From Styal; a loc. n., Ches. Or *G.* Steil; a p.n.

STILL. *G.*, *Dch.* Stille; a p.n.

STILLINGFLEET. A loc. n., Yorks

STIMSON. *Dch.* Stemes; *Fl.* Steemans; *D.* Steman; p.n.

STIRK. *Dch.* Sterk; *Fl.* Sterck; *G.* Stercke; p.n.

STIRRUP. From Styrrup; a loc. n., Notts. Or *D.* Stürup; a p.n. *See* Steer

Stürup is the Danish form of Styrthorp, a loc. n.

STOBBS. *See* Stubbs

STOCK, STOCKS. A loc. n. *D.*, *Fl.*, *G.* Stock; *Dch.* Stok; *D.B.* Stochi, Stoches; p.n.

De Stok and De Stokes occur several times in Rot. Obl. et Fin., K. John.

STOCKBRIDGE. A loc. n., Dorset, Hants

STOCKDALE. A loc. n., Cumb.

STOCKEN. From Stockend; a loc. n., Warw., Worcest.

STOCKER, STOKER, STOKEY, STOKOE. *G.* Stöcker; *Fl.* Stocquart; p.n.

STOCKFORD. From Stokeford; a loc. n., Dorset

STOCKHAM. A loc. n., Devon

STOCKING. A loc. n., Herts. Or *Dch.* Stokkink; p.n. *See* Stock

STOCKINGS. *See* Stocking

STOCKTON. A loc. n., Dur., Salop, Warw., Worcest.

STOCKWELL. A loc. n., Devon, Surr.

STOFER. *Fl.* Stoove, Stouffe, Stoffin, Stoffyn; *Dch.* Stoffers, Stöver, Stuffers, Stuiver; *G.* Stöffer; p.n. *D.B.* Stov

Compare Staff.

STOKE. A loc. n., Devon, Heref., Kent, Salop, Somers., Staffs., Surr.

STOKELY. A loc. n., Cornw.

STOKES. A loc. n., Devon

STOLLERY. *G.* Stolareyck; a p.n

STONARD. *D.* Stonor; a p.n. *See* Stannard

STONE. A loc. n., Kent, Staffs., etc.

STONEHAM. A loc. n., Hants. Or Stonham, Suff.

STONEHOUSE. A loc. n., Devon, Hants, Glost.

STONELAKE. From Stoneleigh; a loc. n., Warw.

STONELEY. A loc. n., Warw.

STONES. *N.* Steinn; *D.* Steen; *S.* Stein, Sten; *Fl.* Steens; p.n. Also a freq. loc. n.

STONEX. *N.* Steinn-öx; *G.* Steinike, Steinig, Steinke, Steinacker; p.n.

STONEY. A loc. n., Warw.

STOOP, STOPP. *Dch.* Stub, Stoop; p.n.

STOPHER. *See* Stofer

STOPS. From Stopes; a loc. n., Lancs

STOREY. *Fl.* Storie, Story; *Fr.* Stora; *D.B.* Stori; p.n.

STORK. A loc. n., Yorks. *D.B.* Estorch

STORR. *D.* Stahr; *Dch.* Stor; p.n. *See* Starr

STORRS. A loc. n., Westmd.

STORRY. *See* Storey

STOTE. *Fl.* Stoht; *Dch.* Stout; p.n.

STOTESBURY. From Stottersbury; a loc. n., Northants

STOTT. *N.* Stóti; *Dch.* Stoete; p.n.

STOUT. A loc. n., Devon, Somers. Or *Dch.* Stout; *G.* Staudte; p.n.

STOVELL. *See* Stowell

STOVING. From Stoven; a loc. n., Suff.

STOW. A loc. n., Ess., Salop, Staffs.

STOWELL. A loc. n., Somers., Wilts

STOWER. A loc. n., Dorset. Or *Dch.* Stower; a p.n.

STOWERS. *See* Stower

STRACHAN. A loc. n., Kincardine

STRAHAN. *See* Strachan

STRAKER. *Dch.* Stracké; a p.n.

STRANGE. *N.* Strangi; *Dch.* Strange; p.n.

John le Strange held land in Staffs. *temp.* K. John.

STRANGER. *See* Strange

STRANGWAYS. A loc. n., Lancs

STRANGWICH. *See* Strangways

STRAPP. *D.* Starup; or *Dch.* Straub; p.n.

STRATFOLD. From Stratfield; a loc. n., Hants

STRATFORD. A loc. n., Oxf., Suff., Warw., Wilts

STRAWBRIDGE. A loc. n., Somers.

STRAWSON. *G.* Strauss; a p.n.

STRECKLE. *G.* Streckel; a p.n.

STREET. A loc. n., Devon, Hants, Somers., Suss.

STREETER. *D.* Stræter; *G.* Streda; p.n.

STREETON, STRETTON. A loc. n., Derbysh., Staffs., Warw., etc.

STRELLEY. A loc. n., Notts

Walter de Straley in Rot. Obl. et Fin., K. John.

STRETCH. *G.* Streich; a p.n. Stric in *D.B.*

STRIBLING, STRIPLING. Dimin. of *D.* Stripp; a p.n.

STRICKLAND. A loc. n., Cumb.

STRICKSON. From Strixton; a loc. n., Northants. Or *see* Stretch

STRIDE. *G.* Streit; a p.n.

STRINGER. *Dch.* Strenger; *G.* Stringer; p.n.

STRIP, STRIPP. *D.* Stripp; *Dch.* Streep; p.n.

STRODE. *See* Stroud

STRONG. *See* Strange

STRONGITHARM. *See* Armstrong

STROTHERS. A loc. n., Dur.

STROUD. A loc. n., Dorset, Glost., Hants, Middlx.

STROVER. *G.* Struwe; *Dch.* Stroeve, Struwer; p.n.

STROWGER. *See* Strowyer

STROWYER. *D.* Stroeyer; *D.B.* Strui; *G.* Struwe, Stry; *Fl.* Strohouwer; p.n.

STRUMPSHAW. A loc. n., Norf.

STRUTT. *Fl.* Stroot; *G.* Struttmann; p.n.

STUART. *Fl.* Styaert; *Dch.* Stuart; *G.* Sturtz; p.n. *See* Stewart

STUBBS. A loc. n., Yorks (*D.B.* Stubuzan, Stubbsham). Or *N.* Stubbi; n.n. *D.B.* Stubart; *G.* Stöbe; *D.* Stub; *Dch.* Stübbe; p.n.

Adam de Stubber in Rot. Obl. et Fin., K. John.

STUBBINGS. *See* Stubbs

STUCK. *See* Stuckey

STUCKEY. *Dch.* Stucki; a p.n.

STUDD. *D.* Stuhde; *G.* Studer, Studt; p.n. *See* Stead
STUDHOLME. From Studham; a loc. n., Herts
STUKELEY. From Stewkley; a loc. n., Bucks
STURCH. *See* Sturge
STURGE. *D.*, *G.* Storch; *Fl.* Storck; *Dch.* Sturk; a p.n.
STURGEON. *Fr.* Lestourgeon; a p.n.
STURMER. *N.* Styrmir; *G.* Stürmer; p.n.
STURT. *See* Stuart
STUTCHBURY. A loc. n., Northants
STUTFIELD. From Estouteville; a loc. n. near Yvetot, Normandy (?)
STUTTER. From Stutton; a loc. n., Suff. Or *G.* Stutzer; a p.n.
STUTTLE. *See* Stutfield
STYAN. *N.* Steinn; a p.n.
STYGLE. *See* Steggall
STYLES. *Dch.* Stijl; *D.* Steil; p.n.
SUART. *See* Seward
SUCKER. *G.*; p.n.
SUCKLING. *F.* Sikke, Sikko; *A.S.* Sycling; *S.* Syk; *Dch.* Suchtelen, Sukkel; *G.* Suche, Suckel; p.n.
SUDBURY. A loc. n., Middlx., Suff.
SUDLOW. *G.* Suderla; a p.n.
SUFFELL. *See* Suffield
SUFFIELD. A loc. n., Norf.
SUFFLING. *A.S.* Swefling; a p.n.
SUGARS. *See* Segon
SUGDEN. A loc. n., Salop
SUGG. *G.* Suge; a p.n.
SUGGATE. From Southgate; a loc. n., Derbysh., Middlx.
SUGGETT. *See* Suggate
SUGGITT. *See* Suggate
SULLOCK. *See* Sellick
SULLY. A loc. n., S. Wales. Or *Fr.* Soulé; a p.n.
SUMMERBEE. From Somerby; a loc. n., Lincs
SUMMERFIELD. *See* Somerfield
SUMMERS. A loc. n., Ess. Or *Fl.* Somers; a p.n.
SUMMERSBY. *See* Summerbee
SUMMERSUN. From Somersham; a loc. n., Hants. *D.B.* Summersham
SUMMERVILLE. *Fr.* Sommerville; a p.n.
SUMNER. An apparitor, a summoner

Halliwell, quoting Nominale MS. Nomina dignitatum clericorum, gives '*Aparator*, a summunder.'

SUMPTER. From Sumpting; a loc. n., Ess. Or Sometour, a sumpterman
SUMPTON. From Summerton; a loc. n., Camb., Norf., Oxf., Somers.
SUNMAN. *Dch.*; p.n.
SURFLIN. *See* Suffling
SURREY. The county. Or *Fr.* Surée, Sury; p.n.
SURRIDGE. A loc. n., Devon
SURTEES. A loc. n. derived from the river Tees, Durham

An ancient family long resided there.

SUSSAMS. *G.* Süssmann (?); p.n.
SUSSENS. *See* Sisson
SUTCH. *G.* Suche; a p.n.
SUTER. *See* Sowter
SUTHERLAND. The county
SUTLIFF. From Southcliffe; a loc. n., Lincs, Yorks
SUTRE. *See* Sowter
SUTTABY. *See* Sutterby
SUTTERBY. A loc. n., Lincs
SUTTLE. *See* Southwell
SUTTON. A loc. n., Ches., Devon, Lancs, Notts, Yorks, etc.
SWABY. A loc. n., Lincs
SWAIN. *N.* Sveinn; *Dch.* Swen; *D.* Svenne; *Fr.* Suin; *Fl.* Svenne; *D.B.* Swen, Swain; p.n.
SWAINSON. *S.* Svenson; *D.* Svenssen; p.n.
SWALLOW. A loc. n., Lincs
SWAN. *N.* Svanr; *D.* Swane, Svane; *D.B.* Suuan, Suan; *Dch.* Swaan; *S.* Svan; p.n.
SWASH. *N.* Svasi; *D.B.* Suauis; *G.* Swazina; p.n.

SWAYNE. *See* Swain

SWEENEY. *See* Swiney

SWEET. *Dch.* Swidde; a p.n.

SWEETAPPLE. *Dch.* Zoetappel is the corresponding word, but there is not the certainty of its being a p.n., as Lightvoet is for Lightfoot

SWEETING. *Dch.* Swieten; *D.B.* Sueting; p.n.

SWEETLAND. A loc. n., Devon. Comp. Swithland

SWEETMAN. *N.* Sig-vatr; *A.S.* Seward, Siwart; *D.B.* Suetman, Sueting, Suertin; *Dch.* Soetman; *G.* Swidom; p.n.

SWEETSER. *G.* Schweitzer; *Fl.* Switser; p.n.

SWEPSTONE. A loc. n., Leics.

SWETENHAM. From Swettenham; a loc. n., Ches.

SWIFT. A river, Leics.

SWINBORNE. *See* Swinburn

SWINBURN. A loc. n., Northbd. Or *N.* Sveinbjörn; a p.n.

SWINDELL. From Swindale; a loc. n., Cumb.

SWINDLEY. *See* Swindell

SWINEY. A loc. n., Salop

SWINFEN. A loc. n., Staffs.

SWINGER. *G.* Schwinger; a p.n.

SWINGLER. *G.* Schwingel; a p.n.

SWINHOE. From Swinhope; a loc. n., Lincs

SWINNERTON. From Swynnerton; a loc. n., Staffs.

SWINSTEAD. A loc. n., Cumb., Lincs

SWIRE. *See* Swyre

SWORD. *N.* Svertingr; *F.* Sweerd; *Dch.* Sweertz; *Fr.* Sourdes; p.n.

SWYRE. A loc. n., Dorset

SYDAL. *N.* Siðu-Hallr; *D.* Seidel; *G.* Sydow, Siedel; p.n.

SYDENHAM. A loc. n., Devon, Kent

SYDER. From Syde; a loc. n., Glost. Or *see* Sydal

SYER. *See* Sayer

SYFERT. *N.* Sighvatr; *D.* Sievert; *D.B.* Sighet; *G.* Seiffert, Seyffert; *Fl.* Seyffers; *Dch.* Seyffardt; p.n. *See* Seward

SYKES. A loc. n., Yorks

SYME. *Dch.* Seijm; a p.n. *See* Simms

SYMES, SYMS. *See* Sims

SYMINGTON. A loc. n., Ayrsh.

SYMONDS. *N.* Sigmundr; *D.B.* Simond, Seman, Scemund, Semar; *G.* Siegmund, Siegmann, Siemens, Siemon, Siems, Simmon; *Dch.* Semeins; *Fl.* Symon; p.n.

SYPHER. *See* Syfert

SYRES. *See* Syers. Or St. Cyres; a loc. n., Devon.

SYRETT. From Sarratt; a loc. n., Herts

T.

TABB. *G.* Taube (?); a p.n.

TABBERER. *N.* Tabarðr; *Fr.* Tabouréau; p.n.

TABER. *Fr.* Tabur; a p.n. Or *see* Tabb

TABERNACLE. *Dch.* Tabbernal; a p.n.

TABNER. *Dch.* Tabbernée; a p.n.

TABOR. *See* Taber

TABRAM. A loc. n.

TABRAR. *See* Tabberer

TACK. *D.*, *Fl.* Tack; *Dch.* Tak; *S.* Tack, Tacke; p.n.

TACKLEY. A loc. n., Lancs. Or Takeley, Ess.

TACON. *Dch.* Takken; a p.n.

TADD. *See* Taddy

TADDY. *Fr.* Thadée; a p.n. from Thaddeus

TAFF. A loc. n., S. Wales

TAGART. From Scot., McTaggart; p.n.

TAGG. *See* Tack

TAILBY. *N.-Fr.* Taille-bois; *Fl.* Talgebosch; *D.B.* Tailgebosc, Tallliebosc; p.n.

TALBOT. *Fr.* Talbot; *Fl.* Talabot; *D.B.* Talebot; p.n.
In Roll of Battell Abbey.

TALER. *G.* Thaler, Tallert; p.n.

TALL. *Dch.* Tal, Tall; p.n.

TALLBOYS. *See* Tailby

TALLEMACH. *See* Tollemache

TALLENT. From Talland; a loc. n., Cornw.

TALLON. *S.* Talén; *Fr.* Talon; p.n.

TALMADGE, TALMAGE, TALMIDGE. *See* Tollemache

TAMBLYN. *Fr.* Tamberlain; a p.n.

TAME. From Thame; a loc. n., Oxf.

TAMLYN. *See* Tamblyn

TAMMADGE. *See* Tollemache

TAMMAGE. *See* Talmage

TAMPEN, TAMPIN. *See* Tamblyn

TAMPLIN. *See* Tamblyn

TANCRED. *N.* Þakk-raðr; *D.* Tang-gaard; *D.B.* Tornerd; *G.* Tancred; *Dch.* Tanker (?); p.n.
Latinised in Norman times into Tancredus.

TANDY. *Fr.* Tantais; a p.n.

TANEY. *See* Thain

TANGYE. *N.* Þenja; n.n. (an axe). *D.* Tang, Tange, Teng; *Dch.* Tang, Tanker, Tenge, Tenger, Tinga, Tinke; *Fl.* Tanghe; *Fr.* Tanguy; p.n.

TANK. *See* Tangye

TANKLIN. Dimin. of *D.* Tang; a p.n.

TANN. *N.* Tanni; *F.* Tanno; *G.* Tanne, Tanner, Tannig; *Fr.* Tanne; p.n.

TANNER. *G.* Tanner; p.n. *See* Tann

TANSLEY. A loc. n., Derbysh.

TAPHOUSE. A loc. n., Devon

TAPLEY. A loc. n., Devon

TAPLIN. Dimin. of Tabb or Tapp

TAPLOW. A loc. n., Bucks

TAPP. *Dch.* Tappe; a p.n.

TAPPER. *Dch.* Tappé; *D.* Tappert; *G.* Tapper; p.n.

TAPPIN. *See* Tapp

TAPSON. From Tapton; a loc. n., Derbysh.

TAPSTER. The Scotl. and N. Engl. form of Tapper

TARBART, TARBET, TARBUTT. From Tarbat; a loc. n., Ross

TARDY. *Fr.*; p.n.

TARGETT. *See* Tagart

TARLTON. A loc. n., Glost.

TARN. From Thearne; a loc. n., Yorks

TARR. A loc. n., Somers.

TARRANT. A loc. n., Dorset

TARRAS, TARRIS. *G.* Tarras; a p.n.

TARRY. *See* Terry

TARTAR. *See* Tate

TARTE. *See* Tardy

TARVER. From Torver; a loc. n., Lancs

TASH. *G.* Tasche; *Fl.* Tesch; p.n.

TASKER. From Tascott; a loc. n., Devon. Or *Dch.* Teske; a p.n.

TASSELL. From Tessall; a loc. n., Worcest. Or *Fr.* Tassel; *D.B.* de Taissel; a p.n.

TATE. *N.* Teitr; *F.* Tade; *D.B.* Tate, Teit; *G.* Theda; p.n.

TATHAM. A loc. n., Yorks

TATTENHALL. A loc. n., Staffs.

TATTERSHALL. A loc. n., Lincs

TATTON. A loc. n., Ches.

TAUNTON. A loc. n., Somers.

TAVERNER, TAVINER, TAVNER. *Fr.* Tavernier; *Dch.* Taverne; p.n.

TAY. *Fl.* Tay; *Fr.* Téhy; p.n.

TAYLOR. *Fr.* Tailleau, Taillir; p.n.
Silvester Taillor in Rot. Obl. et Fin., K. John.

TAYNTON. A loc. n., Glost.

TEAGER. *G.* Tiecke; *Dch.* Tieger, Tieke, Tiggers; *S.* Tiger; *D.B.* Tiger; *Fr.* Tigé; p.n.

TEAGLE. *G.* Tiegel; a p.n.
TEAGUE. *See* Teager
TEAKLE. *See* Tickle or Teagle
TEALE. From Theale; a loc. n., Somers.
TEAPE. *Dch.* Teepe, Tip; p.n.
TEAR, TEER. *Fr.* Thier, Thiers; *Dch.* Thier; p.n.
TEARLE. *Dch.* Terlet; a p.n.
TEASDALE. A loc. n., Dur.
TEASDELL. *See* Teasdale
TEASDILL. *See* Teasdale
TEASEL. *G.* Tiesler; *D.* Thysel; *S.* Tisell; *Dch.* Tessel, Teeseling; p.n.
TEATHER. *See* Tedder
TEBAY. A loc. n., Westmd.
TEBB, TEBBS. *See* Tibbetts
TEBBATTS. *See* Tebbut
TEBBITT. *See* Tebbut
TEBBUT. *A.S.* Tedbert; *Fr.* Thibaut; p.n.
TEDDER. *D.* Thede; a p.n. *See* Tate
TEE. *Fr.* Thys; *D.* Thye; p.n.
TEED. *See* Tidd and Tate
TEELE. *G.* Tille, Tilo, Tylle; *D.B.* Tihel, Tehel; *S.* Tilly; *D.* Tilge; *Fl.* Tilley; *Dch.* Tiele, Til; *Fr.* Thil; p.n.
TEEVAN. *See* Tiffen
TEGART. *See* Taggart
TEGG. *Dch.*; p.n.
TELFER. From Telford; a loc. n., Kent. Or *N.-Fr.* Taillefer; a p.n.
TELLET. *See* Tillett
TELLING. *Fl.* Telen, Tellin; *D.*, *Dch.* Telling; p.n.
TEMME. *G.* Themme; a p.n.
TEMPANY. *D.* Trempenau; a p.n.
TEMPERLEY. From Timperley; a loc. n., Ches.
TEMPEST. *Fl.* Tempst; a p.n.
TEMPLE. A freq. loc. n. Also *Dch.*, *G.* Tempel; *Fl.* Tempels; p.n.
TEMPLETON. A loc. n., Devon
TENCH. *Dch.* Tenge; a p.n.
TENNENT. *G.* Thenen; a p.n.
TENNET. *See* Dennett
TEPPER. *Dch.* Tepe; *G.* Tepfer; p.n.
TERRELL. *Fr.* Tirel; *D.* Turrell; *D.B.* Tirel; p.n. *See* Tyrrell
TERRINGTON. A loc. n., Norf.
TERRY. *Fr.* Terris, Therry, Thery, Thierry; p.n.
TESTER. *Fl.* Testaert, Testar, Teste; p.n.
TETLEY. *See* Titley
TETLOW. *See* Tetley
TETSALL. *See* Tattersall
TETT. *See* Tate
TEULON. From Toulon; a loc. n., France
TEVERSON. From Teversham; a loc. n., Camb.
TEWELS. *Fl.* Tevels; a p.n.
TEWKESBURY. A loc. n., Glost.
TEWSON. *See* Tyson
TEXTOR. *Dch.*; p.n.
THACKER. *Fl.* Dacker; *Dch.* Dekker; p.n.
THACKERAY. A loc. n. Comp. Dockwray, Cumb.
THACKWRAY. *See* Dockwra
THAIN. *N.* Thegn; *D.* Thiene; *Fl.* Thein; *Dch.* Theyn; *G.* Thien, Thenen; *D.B.* Tain, Taini, Teini, Teigni; p.n.
THAIRLWALL. *See* Thirlwall
THAKE. *See* Thacker
THANE. *See* Thain
THARP. *See* Thorpe
THATCHER. *See* Thacker
THAXTER. *See* Thacker
THAYNE. *See* Thain
THEAKSTON. A loc. n., Yorks
THEED. *See* Tidd
THELWALL. A loc. n., Ches.
THEOBALDS. *See* Tipple
THEW. *See* Twoo
THEXTON. *See* Theakston
THICK. *G.* Dicke; a p.n.
THICKNESSE. *Fr.* Xhignesse; a p.n.
THIN. *Dch.* Thijn; *D.*, *G.* Thien; *Fr.* Thin; p.n.
THING. *See* Thynne

THIRGOOD. *See* Toogood

THIRKETEL. *N.* Þórketell; *D.B.* Torchetel, Torchil, Turchil; *S.* Torkels; *D.* Therchil, Terkel, Thorkel; p.n.

THIRKETTLE. *See* Thirketel

THIRLWALL. A loc. n., Northbd.

THIRST. *G.* Durst; a p.n.

THIRTLE. *See* Thirketel

THISTLE. *D.* Thysel; *S.* Thiesel; *Dch.* Dissel; p.n.

THISTLETHWAITE. A loc. n.

THISTLETON. A loc. n., Cumb., Lincs, Rutland

THODAY. *D.* Thode; a p.n. *See* Todd

THOM. *See* Thompson

THOMPSON. *N.* Tumi; pet n. for Thomas. *S.* Tomasson; *D.* Thomassen; *Dch.* Thomson; *D.B.* Tumie, Tumme, Tombi; p.n.

THORBURN. *N.* Þór-björn; *S.* Torbiörn; *D.* Thorbjoern; *Dch.* Torbein; *G.* Turbin; *D.B.* Thurbern, Torbern; p.n.

THORLEY. A loc. n., Dorset, Hants, Herts

THORNBOROUGH. A loc. n., Cumb., Northbd., Oxf., Yorks

THORNE. A loc. n., Yorks and Suff. *D.B.* Torn. Or *N.* Thórny; *D.* Thorning; *Dch.* Thorn; a p.n.

THORNHILL. A loc. n., Derbysh., Dorset, Wilts, Yorks

THORNICROFT. A loc. n., Ches.

THORNLEY. A loc. n., Lancs

THORNS. *See* Thorne

THORNTON. A loc. n., Devon, Lancs, Leics., Yorks

THOROLD. *N.* Þóraldr; *D.B.* Tored, Torold, Tori, Torol, Toi, Thori; *Fr.* Thorel; p.n.

THORPE. A freq. loc. n., Lincs, Yorks, etc.

THORRINGTON. A loc. n., Ess.

THOULESS. *See* Thurlows

THOYTS. *See* Thwaites

THRASHER, THRESHER. *D.* Drescher; a p.n.

THREADGALE. *See* Trudgil

THREADKELL, THREADKILL. *See* Trudgil

THRELFAL. From Threlfield; a loc. n., Yorks. *D.B.* Threlfeld, Trelefelt

THRIDGOLD. *See* Trudgil

THRIFT. *Dch.* Drift; a p.n.

THRING. *D.*, *S.* Thorin; *Fl.* Thurin; *G.* Thöring; p.n.

THRIPP. *See* Thrupp

THROOP. A loc. n., Dorset, Hants, Somers., Wilts

THROSSEL. *G.* Drossel; a p.n.

THROWER. *See* Trower

THRUPP. A loc. n., Glost.

THURBURN. *See* Thorburn

THURGAR. *N.* Thorgeirr; a p.n. Comp. Thurgarton, Norf.

THURGUR. *See* Thurgar

THURKETTLE. *See* Thirketle

THURKLE. *See* Thirketel

THURLAND. From Thurgoland; a loc. n., Yorks

THURLES. *See* Thurlows

THURLEV. From Thurleigh; a loc. n., Beds

THURLOW. A loc. n., Suff.

THURLOWS. A loc. n., Suff.

THURRELL. *Fr.* Thorel; a p.n. *See* Thirketle

THURSBY. A loc. n., Cumb.

THURSFIELD. A loc. n., Staffs.

THURSTON. A loc. n., Lancs, Norf., Suff.

THURTELL. *See* Thirketel

THWAITES. A loc. n., Cumb., Yorks

THYER. *D.* Thyre; a p.n.

THYNNE. *See* Thin

TIARKO, TIARKS. *F.*; p.n.

TIBB, TIBBS, TIBBY. *See* Tibbetts

TIBBALD. *Fr.* Thibault; a p.n. from Theobald. *See* Tipple

TIBBETTS, TIBBITTS. *Dch.* Dibbetts; a p.n. *See* Tebbut

TIBBITT. *Fl* Tybaert; a p.n.

TIBBLES. *See* Tipple

TIBBS. *See* Tibbetts

TIBNAM. From Tibbenham; a loc. n., Norf.
TICE. *Fl.* Thyes; *Dch.* Theijs; *Fr.* Thiess; *G.* Thys; p.n. A contr. of Mathias
TICHBON. *See* Tichborne
TICHBORNE. A loc. n., Hants
TICKELL. *See* Tickle
TICKETT. From Tecket; a loc. n., Northbd.
TICKLE. From Tickhill; a loc. n. in Yorks. Or *Dch.* Tikkel; a p.n.
TICKNER, TICKNOR. From Ticknall; a loc. n., Derbysh.
TIDBALL. *See* Tibbald
TIDBURY. A loc. n., Hants
TIDD. A loc. n., Camb., Lincs. *See* Tate
TIDDER. *See* Tiddy
TIDDY, TIDEY, TIDY. From Tydee; a loc. n., Monmouth
TIDMAN. *D.* Thideman; *G.* Thiedemann; *Dch.* Tiedeman; p.n.
TIDSWELL. From Tideswell; a loc. n., Derbysh.
TIFFEN. *Fr.* Thifane, Tiphaigne, Typhaigne; a p.n.
TIGHE. *See* Teager or Tye
TIGHT. *G.* Ticht; *Dch.* Tuit; *D.* Teitge; p.n.
TIGWELL. *See* Tugwell
TILBROOK. *See* Tilbury
TILBURY. A loc. n., Ess.
TILDESLEY. From Tyldesley; a loc. n., Lancs
TILKE. *D.* Tillge; *G.* Tilke; p.n.
TILL. *D.*, *G.*, *Fl.* Thiel; *Dch.* Til, Till, Thiel; p.n.
TILLARD. *See* Tilleard
TILLCOCK. *See* Tills
TILLEARD. *D.* Theilgaard, Theilade; *G.* Tillert; *Dch.* Tillaard; *Fr.* Thillard; p.n.
TILLETT. *G.* Tillert; *Fr.* Tillot; p.n. *See* Tilleard
TILLEY. A loc. n., Somers. Or *see* Tilly
TILLING. *Fl.* Thielen; a p.n.
TILLS. *See* Teele
TILLY. *Fr.* Thillais, Tilley; p.n.
Geoffroy de Tilly occurs as one of the benefactors of the abbey of St. Étienne, Caen, Normandy, founded by William I. Henry de Tilly held Marshwood, Somers., *temp.* K. John.
TILLYER. *See* Tilleard
TILNEY. A loc. n., Norf.
TILSON. *See* Tills
TILYARD. *See* Tilleard
TIMBERLAKE. From Timperley (?); a loc. n., Ches. (?)
TIMBERS. *Dch.* Timmers; a p.n.
TIMBRELL. From Timble; a loc. n., Yorks
TIMBS. *See* Tims
TIMES. *See* Tims
TIMEWELL. A loc. n., Devon
TIMMS. *See* Tims
TIMS. *D.*, *S.* Thim, Timm; *Dch.* Tim, Tims; *G.* Thimm; p.n.
TINDALL, TINDALE, TINDELL. *Dch.* Tindal; *S.* Tengdahl; p.n.
TINGEY. *See* Tangye
TINGLE. A loc. n., Yorks
TINK. *See* Tinker
TINKER. *Dch.* Tinke, Tuinker; p.n.
TINKLER. *Dch.* Dinkelaar; a p.n.
TINKLEY. From Dingley; a loc. n., Northants
TINN. *Fl.* Tinne; *Dch.* Tijn; *Fr.* Thin; p.n.
TINSLEY. A loc. n., Yorks
TINWORTH. From Timworth; a loc. n., Suff.
TIPP. *See* Tibb
TIPPELL. *See* Tipple
TIPPER. *G.* Tippner; a p.n.
TIPPETT. *See* Tibbett
TIPPETTS. *See* Tibbetts
TIPPING. *Dch.* Tieben, Tippen; a p.n *See* Tiffen
TIPPLE. From Tiphill; a loc. n., Somers. Or *D.* Theobald; *Fl.* Thiebauld; *Fr.* Thibault; *G.* Thepold, Tiepolt, Thiebau; *D.B.* Tidbold, Tebald; p.n.

TIPTOD. From Thibtot; a loc. n., France
Tibtote in Roll of Battell Abbey.

TIREBUCK. *G.* Tirbach; a p.n.

TISSINGTON. A loc. n., Derbysh.

TITCHEN. *G.* Titsche; *Dch.* Titsingh; p.n.

TITCHMARSH. A loc. n., Northants. *See* Titmas

TITCOMB. A loc. n., Wilts

TITFORD. From Thetford; a loc. n., Camb., Norf.

TITLEY. A loc. n., Heref.

TITLOW. *See* Tetlow

TITMAS. From Tidmarsh; a loc. n., Oxf. Or *see* Titchmarsh

TITT. *D.* Thiede; *G.* Tita; *Dch.* Tiedt, Tito; *Fl.* Tits; p.n. *See* Tate

TITTERTON. From Titterstone; a loc. n., Salop

TOALE. *See* Toll

TOAS. *See* Tosar

TOATS. *D.* Thott; *Fl.* Toto; *D.B.* Toti; p.n.

TOBIN. *See* St. Aubyn

TOBY. *Fr.* Tobie, Toby; *Dch.* Tobi, Tobé; p.n.

TODD. *N.* Todda; n.n. *G.*, *Dch.* Tode; *D.* Thode; *D.B.* Todi, Toti; p.n.

TOFTS. A freq. loc. n. *See* Tuffs

TOGHILL. From Taghill; a loc. n., Derbysh.

TOGWELL. *See* Tugwell

TOINTON. From Torrington; a loc. n., Devon, Lincs

TOLD. *D.*; p.n.

TOLER. From Toller; a loc. n., Dorset

TOLFREE. *See* Tolfrey

TOLFREY. From Tollervey; a Cornish p.n.

TOLL. *Dch.*, *D.*, *S.*, *G.* Toll; p.n.

TOLLADY. From Tolladine; a loc. n., Worcest. Or *Dch.* Toledo; or *S.* Tholander (?); p.n.

TOLLEMACHE. From Tollmarsh; a loc. n., Buckfastleigh, Devon
Tollemach in Roll of Battell Abbey. Richard Talamag, Talamasch, or Talemasch, held lands in Ess. and Oxon *temp.* K. John, Rot. Obl. et Fin. Talmach, a benefactor to Ipswich Priory in the thirteenth century.

TOLLER. *See* Tooley

TOLMASH. *See* Tollemache

TOLVER. *N.* Thorolfr; *D.B.* Tolf, Torolf; p.n.

TOMBE. *See* Toombs

TOMBLESON. *See* Tombling

TOMBLIN. *See* Tombling

TOMBLING. From Tombelain; a loc. n., Normandy. Or *N.* Þumli, Thumalin; n.n. (Tom Thumb). *G.* Tümler, Tümpling; p.n.

TOMLINE. *See* Tombling

TOMLINSON. *See* Tomling

TOMPKINS. *See* Toombs

TONGUE. A loc. n., Sutherland. Or Tonge, Leics.; Tong, Yorks

TONKIN. Dimin. of Antonius. *F.* Tönjes; p.n.

TONKS. *F.* Tönjes; a p.n. *See* Tonkin

TOOBY. *See* Tubby

TOOGOOD. *N.* Thorgautr; *D.* Thuge; *G.* Tückert; *Dch.* Tuke; *D.B.* Turgod, Turgot; p.n.

TOOHEY. *Dch.* Tahey, Tooy; p.n.

TOOKE. *N.* Tóki; *D.* Tyge or Thuge; *Lat.* Tycho; *G.* Tuch; *Dch.* Tuck, Tuk, Tuke, Tukker; *Fl.* Tyckaert; *D.B.* Tochi, Toche, Tochil, Toch, Toc; *Fr.* Touq; p.n.
Touke in Roll of Battell Abbey.

TOOLE. From the Irish O'Tuathail; a p.n. Or *D.* Thule; *Dch.* Tulle; *S.* Tul; p.n.

TOOLEY. *N.* Thor-ólfr (?); *D.* Thule; *D.B.* Turolf, Torol, Toulf, Tol, Toli, Tholi, Toul, Thole; *Fl.* Toullet; *Dch.* Tulle; *S.* Toll; p.n.

TOOMBS. *N.* Tumi; *Dch.* Toom, Thoms; *D.* Thom; *G.* Thomas, Tomisch; p.n.

TOOMEY. *N.* Tumi; pet n. for Thomas. *D.B.* Tumie, Tumme, Tombi; p.n.

TOONE. *N.* Tunni; *Dch.* Tuin; *D.* Thun; *S.* Tuné; p.n. *See* Town

TOOP. *See* Topp

TOOT. *See* Tooth

TOOTAL, TOOTEL, TOOTLE. *See* Tuthill

TOOTH. *N.* Toti; n.n. *Fr.* Touté; *D.B.* Toti; p.n.

TOOVEY. *N.* Tófi; *S.* Thufva, Dufva; *Fl.* Dufey; *Fr.* Tuvée, Tuffay; *D.B.* Tovi, Tuffa; p.n.

TOP. *See* Topps

TOPHAM. From Topsham; a loc. n., Devon

TOPLER. *See* Topley

TOPLEY. From Topcliffe; a loc. n., Yorks

TOPLIS. From *G.* Toplitz; a loc. and p. n.

TOPP. *Dch.*, *Fl.* Top; *S.*, *D.* Topp; *D.B.* Tope, Topi; p.n.

TOPPING. *Fr.* Taupin; a p.n.

TOPPLE. *See* Topley

TOPPS. *Fr.* Topasse (?); a p.n. Or *see* Topp

TOPSOM. From Topsham; a loc. n., Devon

TORBET. *See* Torbitt

TORBITT. *N.* Tabarðr (?); *G.* Taubert; p.n.

TORR. A loc. n., Cornw., Devon

TORRANCE. A loc. n., Stirling

TORRENS. *Dch.*; p.n. Or *see* Torrance

TORRINGTON. A loc. n., Devon

TORROP. *D.* Thorup, Torup; p.n.

TORRY, TORRIE, TORREY, TORY. *Dch.* Torres; a p.n.

TOSAR. *Fr.* Touzé, Touzet; *Dch.* Tuser; *D.B.* Tosard; p.n.

TOSH. *See* Touch

TOUCH. *G.* Tusch; *Fr.* la Touche; p.n. *See* Took

Touke in Roll of Battell Abbey.

TOUGH. A loc. n., Aberdeen. Or *Dch.* Tuff, Touw; p.n.

TOULD. *D.B.* Torold, Touilt; p.n. *See* Thorold

TOULMIN. *Fl.* Tolleman; a p.n.

TOSSELL. *See* Tassell

TOSSELYN. *D.B.* Tascelin, Tezelin; *Dch.* Teeseling; p.n. *See* Teasel

TOTHERICK. From Todridge; a loc. n., Northbd.

TOTHILL. A loc. n., Lincs

TOTTENHAM. A loc. n., Middlx.

TOTTLE. *See* Tothill

TOVELL. From Tourville (?); a loc. n., Normandy

TOW. From Thou; a loc. n., Normandy. Or *Dch.* Touw; *G.* Thau; p.n.

TOWELL. A loc. n., Devon. Or *see* Tovell

TOWERS. From Tours; a loc. n., Normandy

W. de Tours had the manor of Lowick or Lofwick, Lancs, from W. de Taillebois, baron of Kendal, after the conquest, and assumed the name of de Lofwick.

TOWLER. *See* Tooley

TOWN. *N.* Tónn; n.n. *D.* Tonn; *S.* Tuné; *Dch.* Tuin; *D.B.* Ton, Tone, Toni; p.n. Or *Dch.* Toon, dimin. of Anthony; a p.n.

TOWNS. *Fl.* Teuns; a p.n. *See* Townson

TOWNSEND. A loc. n., Devon

TOWNSON. *D.* Tonnesen; a p.n. *See* Town

TOWSE. *See* Tosar

TOWSEY. *Fr.* Toussaint, Tousseyn; p.n.

TOY, TOYE. *See* Tye

TOZE. *See* Tosar

TOZER. *See* Tosar

TRACEY. From Trazeignes (?); a loc. n. in Flanders. Or from the Irish O'Treassaigh; a p.n. (*treas*, the third)

Tracy in Roll of Battell Abbey. De Traci and de Trascy in Rot. Obl. et Fin., K. John.

TRAFFORD. A loc. n., Lancs

TRAISE. *See* Tracey

TRAPP. *Fl.*, *D.*, *Dch.*, *S.*, *G.*; p.n.

TRASK. *G.* Treske; a p.n.

TRASS. *Dch.* Traus; a p.n.

TRATT. *See* Troutt

TRAVELL, TRAVIL. From Traffell; a loc. n., Cornw.

TRAVIS. *Fr.* Travers; a p.n. *D.B.* Travers

TREACHER. *Dch.* Treiture; *G.* Tresser; p.n.

TREADWELL. From Tredgarville; a loc. n., S. Wales

TREANOR. From Trenear or Trenower; loc. names, Cornw.

TREBECK. *Dch.* Traarbach; a p.n.

TREBLE. A loc. n., Devon

TREBY. From Trebigh; a loc. n., Cornw.

TREDGETT. From Treguth (?); a loc. n., Cornw.

TREE. *Fr.* Tré; a p.n.

TREEBY. *See* Treby

TREEN. A loc. n., Cornw.

TREETON. A loc. n., Yorks

TREFFRY. A loc. n., Cornw.

TREFUSIS. *Fr.* Tréfousse; a p.n.

TREGARTHEN. A loc. n., Cornw.

TREGEAR. A loc. n., Cornw.

TREGELLAS. A loc. n., Cornw.

TREGENZA. From Tregenna; a loc. n., Cornw.

TREGIDGO. From Tregidhoe; a loc. n., Cornw.

TREGO. From Tregue; a loc. n., Cornw.

TREGONING. A loc. n., Cornw.

TREGURTHA. From Tregotha; a loc. n., Cornw.

TREHARNE, TREHEARNE, TREHERNE. From Trehane; a loc. n., Cornw.

TRELAWNY. A loc. n., Cornw.

TRELEASE. A loc. n., Cornw.

TRELEAVEN. From Trelaven; a loc. n., Cornw.

TRELIVING. *See* Treleaven

TRELOAR. From Trelow; a loc. n., Cornw.

TREMAIN, TREMAYNE. A loc. n., Cornw.

TREMBETH. From Trembath; a loc. n., Cornw.

TREMBLE. *Fr.* Tremblay; a p.n. From le Tremblay; a loc. n., Normandy; or from Tremeale; a loc. n., Cornw.

TREMELLEN. From Tremellin; a loc. n., Cornw. (the mill-town)

TREMENHEERE. A loc. n., Cornw.

TREMLETT. From Trembleth; a loc. n., Cornw.

TRENAM. *See* Trenaman

TRENAMAN. From Trenmaen; a loc. n., Cornw.

TRENCH. From La Trenche; a seigneurie in Poitou, France. A loc. n., Salop

TRENDELL. From Trendeal; a loc. n., Cornw.

TRENGROUSE. A loc. n., Cornw.

TRENGROVE. A loc. n., Cornw.

TRENNER. *See* Treanor

TRENOW. From Trenower; a loc. n., Cornw.

TRENT. A loc. n., Somers. *D.B.* Trend, Trent; p.n.

TRENTHAM. A loc. n., Staffs.

TRENWITH. A loc. n., Cornw.

TREPESS. A loc. n., Cornw.

TRESHAM. A loc. n., Glost.

TRESIDDER. From Tresaddern; a loc. n., Cornw.

TRESIZE. From Tresayes; a loc. n., Cornw.

TRETHEWY. A loc. n., Cornw.

TRETT. *Fr.* Tréhet; a p.n.

TREVALDWYN. A loc. n., Wales. Baldwin's dwelling

TREVALLION. *See* Trevelyan

TREVASKIS. A loc. n., Cornw.

TREVATT. From Trevarth; a loc. n., Cornw. Or *see* Trevitt

TREVELYAN, TREVILLION. From Trevelgen or Trevellan; loc. n., Cornw.

TREVENEN. From Trevennen; a loc. n., Cornw.
TREVERTON. *See* Trevethan
TREVETHAN. A loc. n., Cornw.
TREVETT, TREVITT. *Fr.* Trevette; a p.n.
Trivet in Roll of Battell Abbey.
TREVOR. A loc. n., N. Wales
TREW. *G.* Trew; *Dch.* Trouw; *D.* Thrue; p.n. Or *see* True
TREWBY. *See* Treby
TREWINNARD. From Trewinard; a loc. n., Cornw.
TREWREN. From Trewern; N. Wales. Or Truren; a loc. n., Cornw.
TRIA. *Dch.* Trier; a p.n.
TRIAIRE. From Trehire; a loc. n., Cornw.
TRIBE. *Dch.* Treub; *G.* Treiber; p.n.
TRICK. *See* Trickett
TRICKER. *See* Trickett
TRICKETT. *Fr.* Triquet; a p.n.
TRICKEY. *See* Trickett
TRIFFITT. *See* Trevitt
TRIGG. *Fr.* Trigot; *D.* Thrige, Trygg; *S.* Trygger; *Dch.* Tright; *D.B.* Trec; p.n.
TRIGGER. *N.* Tryggvi; *D.* Trygg, Træger; *Dch.* Drieger; *Fl.* Trigot; *G.* Troeger; *S.* Trygger; p.n.
TRIM. *Dch.*; p.n.
TRIMER. *See* Trimmer
TRIMMER. From Tremeer; a loc. n., Cornw. Or Trimber, Yorks
TRINDER. A Cornish p.n.
TRINGALL. From Trinkeld; a loc. n., Lancs
TRINGHAM. From Trimingham; a loc. n., Norf.
TRIPLOW. A loc. n., Camb.
TRIPP. *Dch.* Trip, Triep; p.n.
TRITTON. *Dch.* Tritten; a p.n. Or *see* Treeton
TRIXON. *See* Trigg
TROLLOP. A loc. n. From *D.* Trolle; a p.n.
TROMP. *Dch.*; p.n.
TROOD. *Fr.* Troude; a p.n.
TROST. *G.* Trost; *Dch.*, *Fl.* Troost; a p.n.
TROTMAN. *G.* Trautmann; a p.n.
TROTT. *N.* Trúdr; *Dch.* Trots; *S.* Trotz; p.n.
TROTTER. *Dch.* Trottier; a p.n.
TROUBRIDGE. *See* Trowbridge
TROUGHTON. From Trohoughton; a loc. n., Dumfries. Compare Trawden, Lancs; Troedythin, Llandaff; Trotton, Suss.
TROUNCE. *Fl.* Truyens; a p.n.
TROUP. A loc. n., Banffs. Or *see* Throop
TROUSDALE. A loc. n., Yorks
TROUTBECK. A loc. n., Westmd.
TROUTT. *Dch.* Traude; a p.n.
TROW. *See* True
TROWBRIDGE. A loc. n., Wilts
TROWELL. A loc. n., Notts
TROWER. From Troway; a loc. n., Derbysh.
TROWSE. *G.* Trautsch (?); *Fr.* Troussé; a p.n.
TROY. *G.* Treu; a p.n.
TRUDGETT. *Fr.* Trugard (?); a p.n. Or *see* Tredgett
TRUDGILL. *Dch.* Tregele (?); a p.n.
TRUE. A loc. n., Devon
TRUEFITT. *Fr.* Truflet (?); a p.n. Or *see* Trevitt
TRUELL. From Trull; a loc. n., Somers. Or *see* Trowell
TRUELOVE. A loc. n., Devon
TRUETT. *Fl.* Truyt; a p.n.
TRUMAN. *Dch.* Trijman; *G.* Trauman; *D.B.* Trumin; p.n.
TRUMBLE. *Fl.* Trumpel; a p.n. Or *see* Tremble
TRUMM. From Drum; a loc. n., Aberdeen. Or *Dch.* Tromm; a p.n.
TRUMMER. From Drummore; a loc. n., Wigtownsh.
TRUMPER. *Fl.* Trumper; *Dch.* Trompee; *G.* Trümper; p.n.
TRUMPLER. *See* Trumper
TRUMPP. A loc. n., Glost.

TRUNDEL. *N.* Trandill; n.n. *S.* Tranell; *Fl.* Trentels; a p.n.

TRUSCOTT. From Trescott; a loc. n., Staffs. Or Tresscoit, a manor in St. Mabin, Cornw.

TRUSLER, TRUSLOW. From Trusley; a loc. n., Derbysh.

TRUSSON. *S.* Trysen; a p.n.

TRUSWELL. From Tresawell; a loc. n., Cornw.

TRUWHITT. From Trewhitt; a loc. n., Northbd.

TRY. *D.* Thrye; a p.n.

TRYON. *Dch.* Trion; a p.n.

TUBB. *See* Tubby

TUBBS. *See* Tubby

TUBBY. *N.* Thórbjörn; *D.B.* Turbern, Tubern, Tubi, Tube; *G.* Dube, Töpper; *Dch.* Torbein, Tubbing, Tupkin; *Fr.* Toubeau; p.n.

TUBMAN. *G.* Taubmann; a p.n.

TUCK, TUCKEY. *See* Tooke

TUCKER. *Dch.* Tukker; *G.* Tuckert; *Fl.* Tyckaert; p.n. *See* Tooke

TUCKNESS. *See* Thicknesse

TUCKWELL. *See* Tugwell

TUDBALL. *See* Theobald

TUDDENHAM. A loc. n., Suff.

TUDGE. *G.* Tuch, Tusch; *Fr.* Touche; p.n.

TUDHOPE. From Tudhoe; a loc. n., Dur.

TUDOR. The Welsh form of Theodore

TUFF. *Dch.* Duif, Toff; p.n. *See* Toovey

TUFFEN. *N.* Dufan; *S.* Dufven; p.n. Or *see* Tiffen

TUFFIL. *See* Tuffnell

TUFFIN. *See* Tuffen

TUFFLEY. A loc. n., Glost.

TUFFNELL. *N.* Dufnial; a p.n.

TUFFS. *N.* Tófi; *D.B.* Tovi, Tuffa, Tofig, Tof; *G.* Tüffert; *Dch.* Toff; *S.* Tufveson; p.n. Or *see* Tufts

TUFNAIL. *See* Tuffnell

TUFTON. A loc. n., Hants

TUFTS. From Tofts; a loc. n. in Norf.

TUGWELL. From Tughall; a loc. n., Northbd. (?)

TUKE. *See* Tooke

TULEY, TULLEY, TULLY. *See* Tooley

TULL. *See* Toole

TULLETT. From Tult; a loc. n., Devon. Or *Fr.* Toullet; a p.n.

TULLIDGE. From Tullich; a loc. n., Aberdeen

TULLIS. *See* Tullidge

TULLOCK. From Tullagh; a loc. n., co. Cork

TUMPENNY. *See* Tempany

TUNALEY. *See* Tunley

TUNBRIDGE. A loc. n., Kent

TUNGATE. From Tundergarth (?); a loc. n., Dumfries

TUNKIN. *See* Tonkin, Tonks

TUNKS. *See* Tonks

TUNLEY. A loc. n., Somers.

TUNMER. *See* Tunmore

TUNMORE. A loc. n. Eight places in Ireland and Scotland

TUNNEY. *N.* Tunni; n.n. *S.* Tuné; *D.B.* Tunne; *Dch.* Tunninga; p.n.

TUNNICLIFFE. From Tonnacliff; a loc. n., Lancs

TUNSTALL. A loc. n., Kent, Staffs., Suff.

TUPHOLME. A loc. n., Lincs

TUPMAN. *See* Tubman

TUPP. *See* Tubb

TUPPER. *G.* Töpper; a p.n.

TUPPING. *Dch.* Tubbing; a p.n. *See* Tubby

TUR. *See* Torr

TURBAND. *N.* Þorbrandr; *D.B.* Torbrand, Turbrand, Turbrant; *G.* Turbin; p.n.

TURBEFIELD. *Fr.* Turberville; *D.B.* Turberville; p.n.

TURBETT. *D.B.* Torbert, Turbert; p.n.

TURBEY. *G.* Turbe; a p.n.

TURK. *Fl.* Turck; *Dch.* Turk; *D.* Türck; *G.* Tourke, Türk; p.n.

TURNADGE. *See* Turnidge

TURNBULL. *Dch.* Turngebouw (?); a p.n.

TURNER. *Fr.* Tournaire, Tourneur, Turnier; *Fl.* Turner; p.n.

Reginald le Turnur held land in Oxon *temp.* K. John.

TURNEY. From Tournay; a loc. n., France. *D.B.* de Torny; a p.n.

TURNHAM. A loc. n., Devon, Middlx.

TURNIDGE. From Turnditch; a loc. n., Derbysh.

TURPIN. *G.* Turbin; *Fr.* Turpin; p.n. *See* Thorburn

Walter Turpin held lands in Dorset *temp.* K. John.

TURRELL. *See* Tyrrell

TURTILL. *See* Thirketle

TURTLE. *See* Thirketel

TURTON. A loc. n., Lancs

TURVEY. A loc. n., Beds

TURVILLE. A loc. n., Bucks. Or Tourville, Normandy

TUSHAW. *G.* Tusche; a p.n.

TUSON. *See* Tyson

TUTCHER. *Fr.* Tousjours (?); a p.n.

TUTE. *See* Tooth

TUTHILL. From Toothill; a loc. n., Hants, Lincs

TUTILL. *See* Tuthill

TUTING. From Tooting; a loc. n., Surr.

TUTT. *See* Tooth

TUTTELL. *See* Tuthill

TUTTIETT. *Fl.* Tytgat; a p.n.

TUTTLE. *See* Tuthill

TWADELL. From Tweeddale; a loc. n.

TWAITS. *See* Thwaites

TWAMLEY. From Twemlow; a loc. n., Ches.

TWEDDEL. From Tweed-dale; a loc. n.

TWEED. *See* Tweedie

TWEEDIE. *D.* Tvede; a p.n.

TWEEN. *Dch.* Tuijn, Tuyn; p.n.

TWELLS. Originally Atte-Wells. *See* Wells

TWIDDY. *See* Tweedie

TWIGG. *See* Twight

TWIGHT. *Dch.*; p.n.

TWINBERROW. A loc. n., Worcest.

TWINER. *See* Twinn

TWINING. *See* Twyning

TWINN. *See* Tween

TWISDEN. From Twisten; a loc. n., Lancs

Twisten was called Twysilton *temp.* K. John, at which period the family of that name were owners there.

TWISLETON. *See* Twisden

TWISS. *Dch.*; p.n.

TWITCHELL. *See* Twitchwell

TWITCHIN, TWITCHING. From Twitchen; a loc. n., Norf.

TWITCHWELL. From Titchwell; a loc. n., Norf.

TWITE. From Thwaite; a loc. n., Norf., Yorks

TWOGOOD. *See* Toogood

TWOO. *See* Tow

TWYCROSS. A loc. n., Leics.

TWYDELL. *See* Tweddle

TWYFORD. A loc. n., Derbysh., Hants, Lincs, Norf., Salop

TWYNAM. From Twineham; a loc. n., Suss.

TWYNING. A loc. n., Glost.

TYACK. *F.* Tiarko, Tiarks; *Fr.* Taiche; p.n.

TYARS, TYAS. *See* Tice

TYCE. *See* Tice

TYDEMAN. *Dch.* Tydeman; a p.n. *See* Tidman

TYE. *D.* Thye; a p.n. *See* Dye

TYERMAN. *Dch.* Tieman; a p.n.

TYLECOTE. From Tulket; a loc. n. on the Ribble near Preston, Lancs (Brit. Tylcoed (?)). Or Holecote, Ullcote, Northants

Philip de Ulecot and Hugh de Bailiol, in 1216, sided with King John against his brother Richard. Persons of the name of Talkatt, Tallcot, Taylcote, Taylcott, were living at Braintree, Essex, in 1623. John Tallcott occurs in a list of emigrants to America in 1632.

TYLER. *Fr.* Thuillier, Tuilleau; *Fl.*, *G.* Theiler; *Dch.* Theile; *D.* Theill, Theillard; p.n.

TYNDALE, TYNDALL. *See* Tindal

TYRER. From Tyrie; a loc. n., Aberdeen (?)

TYRRELL. *D.* Turrell; *Fr.* Thirel, Tirel; p.n.

Tirell in Roll of Battell Abbey, and Tirel in *D.B.*

TYRWHITT. From Tywardreth; a loc. n., Cornw.

TYSON. *See* Tyssen

TYSSEN. *D.* Thuessen, Thyssen; *Dch.* Thijssen, Tijssen; *Fl.* Tison, Tyssen; *D.B.* Tison, Tisun; p.n. *See* Tye

Gislebert Tison, a tenant in chief, *D.B.* (Notts, Yorks, Lincs), had twenty-nine manors forfeited upon the ravaging of Yorks by William I. Teison or Thisun in Rot. Obl. et Fin., *temp.* K. John.

U.

UBANK. *See* Ewbank

UDALL. *Fr.* Oudalle; a p.n. Or from Yewdale; a loc. n., Cumb. Or *S.* Uddvall; a loc. and p. n.

UDEN. *Dch.* Uden; *S.* Uddén; p.n.

UFF. *D.* Uffe; a p.n.

UFFINDEL. From Uffendal; a loc. n. *D.* Uffe; a p.n.

UGLOW. *S.* Uggla; a p.n.

ULLETT. *See* Hullett

ULLMER. *D.*, *Dch.* Ulmer; a p.n.

ULP. *See* Ulph

ULPH. *N.* Ulfarr or Ulfr; *F.* Ulferd; *D.B.* Ulf, Ulfere, Ulfi; *G.* Uhl, Uhlfig, Ulfert; p.n.

ULYATT. *See* Ullett

UNCLE. *Dch.* Unkel; a p.n.

UNDERDOWN. A loc. n., Cornw.

UNDERHILL. A loc. n., Devon

UNDERWOOD. A loc. n., Derbysh., Devon, Notts

UNGOOD. From Hengoed; a loc. n., Salop

UNSWORTH. A loc. n., Lancs

UNTHANK. A loc. n., Cumb. and Northbd.

UNWIN. *Fl.* Unwin; a p.n.

UPCHER. *See* Upsher

UPCOTT. A loc. n., Devon, Somers.

UPFILL. From Uphill; a loc. n., Devon (?)

UPHAM. A loc. n., Hants

UPJOHN. Welsh, Apjohn (?); a p.n.

UPPERTON. A loc. n., Devon

UPSALL. A loc. n., Yorks

UPSHER. From Upshire; a loc. n., Ess.

UPTON. A loc. n., Berks, Cornw., Devon, Dorset, Hants, Kent, Somers., Wilts, Yorks

UPWARD. *See* Upwood

UPWOOD. A loc. n., Hunts

URE. From Urr; a loc. n., Kirkcudbright

UREN. *D.* Euren; a p.n.

URIE. *G.* Ury; a p.n.

URMSTON. A loc. n., Lancs

URQUHART. A loc. n., Elgin

URRY. *See* Hurry

URWICK. From Urswick; a loc. n., Lancs

Adam de Urswick, 6 Edw. III. (1332), was chief forester of Bowland. Sir Robert, knight of the shire, 5 to 20 Rich. II., and 1 and 2 Henry IV. Sir John de Urswick, 14 Rich. II., sheriff. Christopher, chaplain to Henry VII., the 'Sir Christopher' of Rich. III., Act V., § 5, buried in Hackney Church.

USBORNE. From Husborne; a loc. n., Beds

USHER, From Ushaw; a loc. n., Dur.

USHERWOOD. *See* Isherwood

USILL. *Dch.* Husel; a p.n.

UTTERMARE. From Udimore; a loc. n., Kent

UTTERTON. From Otterton; a loc. n., Devon

UTTING. *N.* Udr; *F.* Udo, Ude, Uden; *G.* Olte, Oettinger; *Dch.* Ouden; *Fl.* Utten; *S.* Udden; *D.B.* Eudo, Udi, Othingar; p.n.

UWINS. *See* Ewens

UZZELL. *See* Usill

V.

VACHELL. *Dch.* Wachtell; a p.n.

VAGG. *D.* Waage; a p.n.

VAIL. *See* Vale

VAISEY. *See* Veasey

VAIZEY. *See* Veasey

VALE. *Fl.* Vale; *Dch.* Weel; p.n.

VALENTINE. *Fr.* Valentin; *Dch.* Valentien; p.n.

VALIANT. *Fr.* Vaillant; a p.n.

VALLER. *Fl.* Wallaert; *Dch.* Waller; p.n.

VALLINGS. *D.* Wahlin, Wallin; *Dch.* Walen; *Fl.* Wallens; p.n.

VALPY. From *D.* Valby; a loc. n.

VANDELEUR. *Fl.* Vande Laer, Vanderloo; p.n.

VANE. *See* Fane

VANNECK. *Fl.* Van Eck, Vanneck; p.n.

VARDEN. *D.* Warding; *G.* Wardein; *Dch.* Vaarting, Fardon; *Fl.* Verdeyen; *D.B.* Werden, Fardan, Fardein; p.n. *See* Farthing and Verdon

VARDIGANS. *See* Vertigan

VARLEY. A loc. n., Ess. Also *Fr.* Varlez; a p.n.

VARLO. *See* Varley

VARNAM. *See* Farnham

VARNELL. *Fl.* Fannell; a p.n.

VARNEY. *Fl.* Warny; a p.n.

VARNHAM. *See* Farnham

VARVILL. From Varaville; a loc. n., Normandy. *Fr.* Vauville; a p.n.

Varuurile in Roll of Battell Abbey. De Warwell in *D.B.*

VASEY. *See* Veasey

VASS. *Dch.* Vas, Vasse, Vassy; *Fl.* Fas, Fasser; p.n. *See* Vassar

VASSAR. *Fr.* Vasseur; *Fl.* Vassert; *G.* Wasser; *D.B.* Waz, Waso; p.n.

VAUGHT. *See* Faught

VAUS, VAUSE, VAWSE. *See* Vaux

VAUX. A loc. n., Normandy. Or *see* Faulke

VAVASSOUR. *Fr.* Vavasseur, Le Vavasseur; p.n.

VAWSER. *Dch.*, *Fl.* Wassard; a p.n. *See* Vassar

VEAL. *G.* Wiehle; *Fl.* Wiel; *Fr.* Ville; a p.n. *See* Viall

VEARS. *Dch.* Weers; a p.n.

VEASEY. *See* Fessey

Vessay or de Vesci in Roll of Battell Abbey; *D.B.* de Veci.

VEITCH. *G.* Vietsch; a p.n.

VELLUM. *See* Welham

VENABLES. A loc. n., Normandy

D.B. Gislebert de Venables, an under-tenant (Ches.) at the time of the Survey. Richard de Venables in Rot. Obl. et Fin., K. John. The barony of Kinderton continued in this family till 1676.

VENESS. *Fl.* Van Esse, Vanesse; a p.n.

VENIMORE. *See* Fennimore

VENN. A loc. n., Cornw. *See* Fane

VENNING. *See* Fane

VENTRIS. From Ventry; a loc. n., Kerry, Ireland. A *D.* Wendrick; *Dch.* Vendrick; *Fl.* Vendry; p.n.

VERDON. From Verdun; a loc. n. in France

Verdoune in Roll of Battell Abbey. Bertram de Verdun, a tenant in chief in *D.B.* (Staffs.). In 1273, John de Verdun held lands in Belton, Leics. Bertram de Verdun founded Croxden Abbey, 23 Henry II., 1176.

VERE. From Ver; a loc. n., Normandy. *D.B.* de Ver; a p.n.

VERLANDER. *Fl., Dch.* Verlant, Verlinde; p.n.

VERLEY. *See* Varley

VERNON. From Vernon; a loc. n. in Normandy

Vernoun in Roll of Battell Abbey; *D.B.* de Vernon.

VERRY. *Fr.* Wéry; *Fl.* Werry; *Dch.* Verre; p.n.

VERSCHOYLE. From Vascœuil; a loc. n., Normandy. *Fl.* Veerschuijl; a p.n.

VERTIGAN. *B.* Vortigern (?)

VERTUE. *G.* Werther; a p.n. Or *see* Virtue

VERVILL. *See* Varvill

VESEY. *See* Veasey

VESPER. *Dch.* Weesper; a p.n.

VESTEY. *D.* Westi; a p.n.

VIALL. From Vile; a loc. n. in Normandy. Or *N.* Veili; *D.* Viehl; *G.* Wiehle; *Fl.* Wiel; *Fr.* Ville; a p.n. *See* Veal

Vile and De Vile are in the Roll of Battell Abbey.

VIAN. *Fr.* Viane; *D.* Wiene; p.n.

VICARAGE. *Fl.* Wichterich; a p.n.

VICKERMAN. *D.* Wickman; a p.n.

VICKERS. *N.* Víkarr; *D.* Wick, Vickers; *Fl.* Wyckaerts; *Dch.* Wichers, Wiggers; *G.* Wickert; p.n.

VIDLER. *D.* Fiedler; a p.n.

VIGORS. From the *Fr.* Vigor; a Huguenot n. Or Vigeoise; a loc. n., France

VILLIERS. From Villers; a loc. n., Normandy. *Fl.* Villers; *D.* Willer; *Dch.* Willaars; p.n.

VIMER. *N.* Vémundr; *D.B.* Wimund, Wimer; *Dch.* Weyman, Wijman; *G.* Wimmer, Weimann; *S.* Weman; *Fl.* Wyman, Weman; p.n.

VINCE. *Fl.* Vinche, Wyns; *Dch.* Wins; *G.* Vins; p.n. Or from St. Vincent (?)

VINCENT. *Fr.* St. Vincent; a p.n. *See* Vince

VINE, VINN. *Fr.* Vin; *Fl.* Wion, Wyn; *Dch.* Vinne; p.n.

VINEY. From Vinhay; a loc. n., Devon. Or Vinney, Somers.

VINT. *Fl.* Windt; *D.* Wind; p.n.

VIPOND, VIPONT, VIPAND. *Fr.* Vipout; a p.n.

Thomas Vipout was Bishop of Carlisle 1255.

VIRGIN. *S.* Virgin; *Fl.* Wirtgen; p.n.

VIRGO, VIRGOE. *Fl.* Vergote; *D.* Vergo; *Dch.* Vergouw; p.n.

VIRTUE. From Verton; a loc. n., France

VISE. *See* Wise

VISGERS. *Fl.* Visschers; a p.n. *See* Whisker

VITTERY. *Fr.* Vitré; a p.n.

VIVEASH. *See* Vivish

VIVISH. *Fr.* Fievez; a p.n.

VIZARD. *Fr.* Visart; a p.n.

VIZER. *Fr.* Viseur; *Dch.* Visser; p.n.

VOISEY. *Fr.* Voisin; a p.n.

VOKES. *See* Faulke

VORES. *G.* Voras; *Dch.* Voous; *D.B.* de Waras (?)

VOS, VOSE. *D., Dch., Fl., G.* Voss; a p.n.

VOYCE. *Dch.* Voijs; a p.n.

VYE. *Fr.* Vuy, Vuye; p.n.

VYNER. *Fr.* Vigneux (?); a p.n.

VYSE. *See* Wise

W.

WACE. *G.* Weese, Wehse; *Dch.* Wees; p.n.

WACEY. *G.* Weese; a p.n.

WACKETT. *G.* Weckert; a p.n.

WADD. *N.* Vadi; *D.* Wad; *D.B.* Wada, Wade, Wado; p.n.

WADDELL. *D.* Wadel; *S.* Wadell; *D.B.* Wadel; p.n.

WADDELOW. *D.* Wadel; *D.B.* Wadelo; p.n.

WADDESLEY. From Wadsley; a loc. n., Yorks

WADDILOVE. *See* Waddelow

WADDING. From Waddon; a loc. n., Wilts, Dorset. Or *S.* Wadén; a p.n.

WADDINGTON. A loc. n., Devon, Lincs, Yorks

WADDUP. From Whadub; a loc. n., Cumb.

WADDY. *N.* Vadi; *D.B.* Wada, Wade; p.n.

WADE. A loc. n., Hants

WADHAM. From Waddingham; a loc. n., Lincs. Or *Dch.* Wadum; a p.n.

WADLEY. A loc. n., Berks, Devon

WADMAN. *S.*; p.n.

WADSWORTH. A loc. n., Lancs, Yorks

WAGER. *G.* Wager; a p.n.

WAGG. A loc. n., Somers. Or *N.* Vágr; *D.* Waage; *Dch.* Waag; *D.B.* Waga; p.n.

WAGGETT. *S.* Vagt; a p.n. Or *see* Wackett

WAGGON. *Fl.* Wagon; a p.n.

WAIGHT. *See* Waite

WAILING. *See* Wylie

WAIN. *G.* Wehn; a p.n.

WAINER. *G.* Wehner; a p.n.

WAINWRIGHT. *D.* Weinrich; *G.* Wahnrich (?), Weinerich, Weinert, *D.B.* Weniet, Wenric; p.n.

WAITE. *D.* Vet, Wiet; *Fl.* Vets; *F.* Wiet; *G.* Weth; *D.B.* Wiet; p.n.

WAKE. *N.* Vékill; *D.* Weeke; *G.* Weck; *S.* Wacklin; *Fl.* Weeck; *D.B.* Weghe (?); p.n.

WAKEFIELD. A loc. n., Northants, Yorks

WAKEHAM. A loc. n., Dorset

WAKELIN, WAKELING. *S.* Wacklin; a p.n. *See* Wake

WAKELY. A loc. n., Herts

WAKLEY. *See* Wakely

WALCOTT. A loc. n., Lincs, Norf., Salop, Worcest.

WALDEGRAVE. From Walgrave; a loc. n., Northants

Anciently, Waldegrave.

WALDEN. A loc. n., Yorks

WALDON. *See* Walden

WALDRON. A loc. n., Suss. Or *Dch.* Woelderen; a p.n.

WALDUCK. *Dch.*, *G.* Waldeck; a p.n.

WALE. *D.* Wehl; *Fl.* Weyll; p.n.

WALES, WAILES, WAYLES. From Wales; a loc. n., Yorks. *D.B.* Walise

WALESBY. A loc. n., Lincs, Notts

WALEY. *See* Whalley

WALFORD. A loc. n., Staffs.

WALKDEN. A loc. n., Lancs

WALKER. *N.* Valgarðr; *Dch.* Walkart, Walker; *Fl.* Walckiers; *G.* Walke, Walker; *D.B.* Walcher; p.n.

WALKERLEY. From Walkley; a loc. n., Yorks

WALKINGSHAW. A loc. n., Renfrew

WALL. A loc. n., Staffs.

WALLACE or WALLIS. *N.* Valir; *A.S.* Valas or Wealas, the Welsh, *i.e.*, foreigners or strangers. *Fl.* Wallays; a p.n.

There was an influx of Anglo-Normans into Scotland in the reign of David I. Among these was Richard Waleys, the ancestor of the great Wallace. He has left his name at Richardtun in Ayrshire. Valers is in the Roll of Battell Abbey; and de Vals, de Wals, Walo, Walise, Walscin, are in *D.B.* The north-western part of France was called by the Norsemen, Walland.

WALLACH. *Dch.*; p.n.

WALLBRIDGE. A loc. n., Glost.

WALLEDGE. *D.* Wallich; a p.n.

WALLER. *S.*, *Dch.*, *Fl.* Waller; a p.n. Wallers; a loc. n., Devon

WALLETT. *Dch.* Walet; a p.n.

WALLING. *D.* Wallin; *S.* Wallen; p.n.

WALLINGTON. A loc. n., Hants, Norf., Surr.

WALLIS. *See* Wallace

WALLMAN. *See* Whall

WALLOP. A loc. n., Hants

WALMSLEY. A loc. n., Lancs, Staffs.

WALPOLE. A loc. n., Norf., Somers., Suff.

WALRON. *See* Waldron

WALSH. From Wallash; a loc. n., Staffs. Or *Dch.* Walsch; a p.n. *See* Wallach

WALSHAM. A loc. n., Norf., Suff.

WALSINGHAM. A loc. n., Norf.

WALSOM. *Dch.* Walsem; a p.n. Or *see* Walsham

WALTERS. *Dch.* Wolters; *Fl.* Wauters, Wouters; p.n.

WALTHEW. *N.* Valthóf; *G.*, *Dch.* Walther; *A.S.* Waltheof; *D.B.* Wailoff, Wallef, Waltef; p.n.

WALTON. A loc. n., Berks, Derbysh., Herts, Lancs, Norf., Somers., Staffs., Suff.

WANKLYN. *S.* Wancke; *D.* Wang; p.n. A dimin.

WANNOP. From Wandhope; a loc. n., Cumb.

WANSBOROUGH. From Wanborough; a loc. n., Surr., Wilts

WANT. *N.* Vandill (?); *D.B.* Wand, Wanz, Wants; *G.* Wander; *Dch.* Wandt; *Fl.* Wanet; p.n.

WARBEY, WARBY. From Warboys; a loc. n., Hunts

WARBRICK. From Warbreck; a loc. n., Lancs

WARBURTON. A loc. n., Ches.

WARD. A loc. n., Devon. Or *Dch.* Waard, Warde; a p.n.

WARDALE, WARDELL. *See* Wardle

WARDEN. A loc. n., Kent, Northants, Northbd.

WARDLE. A loc. n., Lancs

WARDLEY. A loc. n., Rutland. Or Weardley, Yorks

WARE. A loc. n., Devon, Herts

WAREHAM. A loc. n., Dorset

WARFORD. *See* Walford

WARHURST. *D.* Warhus; *Fl.* Verhust; p.n.

WARING. *See* Wearing

WARLAND. *Fl.*; p.n.

WARLEIGH. A loc. n., Somers.

WARLOW. From Wardlow; a loc. n., Derbysh.

WARMAN. *D.* Warming; *G.* Warmer; p.n.

WARMER. *See* Worm. Or Walmer; a loc. n., Kent

WARMINGTON. A loc. n., Northants, Warw.

WARN, WARNE. From Waghen or Wawne; a loc. n., Yorks

WARNEFORD. A loc. n., Hants

WARNER. *D.B.* Warner; a p.n. *See* Warren

WARNES. *D.* Warns; a p.n.

WARR. *D.* Warrer (?); a p.n. Or *see* Ware

WARRAM. From Warham; a loc. n., Norf.

WARREN, WARRENER. *N.* Væringr; *D.B.* Warin, Wareng, Warenger; *Fr.* Warin, Verenne; p.n. *See* Wearing

Gundred de Warren or Warrenna held lands in Wilts *temp.* K. John, 1201.

WARRINGTON. A loc. n., Ches.
WARRY. *D.* Warrer (?); a p.n.
WARSAP. *See* Worsop
WARTER. A loc. n., Yorks
WARTH. *See* Ward or Worth
WARWICK. A loc. n., Cumb., Hants, and the county town
WASE. *See* Wace
WASEY. *See* Wace
WASHBOURN. A loc. n., Devon
WASHINGTON. A loc. n., Suss.
WASPE. *See* Warsap
WASTELL. A loc. n., Worcest.
WATCHAM. From Watchcombe; a loc. n., Devon
WATERALL. From Waterfall; a loc. n., Staffs.
WATERHOUSE. A loc. n., Staffs.
WATERLOW. *Fl.* Waterloos; a p.n.
WATERS. *Fl.* Wauters; a p.n. *See* Walters
WATERSON. *See* Walters
WATERSTONE. A loc. n., Pembroke
WATFORD. A loc. n., Derbysh., Herts, Northants
WATKINS. *See* Watts
WATLER. *Fr.* Watelet; a p.n.
WATLING. *See* Watts
WATLOW. *See* Waterlow
WATMORE. *See* Whitmore
WATTON. A loc. n., Norf.
WATTS. *N.* Hvati; *D.* Watt; *A.S.* Watling; p.n.
WAUCHOPE. From Warcop; a loc. n., Westmd. (?)
WAUD. *D.* Waad; a p.n.
WAUGH. *See* Waughn
WAUGHN. *See* Warne. Or *N.* Vagn; *D.B.* Warns, Vagan, Waga, Wana; *G.* Wahn, Wahner; *Dch.* Waan; *Fl.* Warnau; *D.* Wohn; p.n.
WAWN. *See* Waughn
WAY. A loc. n., Devon, Kent
WAYBORN. From Waybourne; a loc. n., Norf.
WAYCOTT. *G.* Weckert (?); a p.n.
WAYLAND. A loc. n., Dorset. Or *Fl.* Weyland; a p.n.
WAYLES. *N.* Veili; n.n. *G.* Wels; *Fl.* Weil; *D.B.* Welle; p.n.
WAYMAN. *See* Wyman
WAYMOUTH. *See* Weymouth
WEAGER. *See* Widger
WEAKLEY, WEAKLIN. *See* Wakelin
WEAL. *Dch., Fl.* Wiel; *G.* Wiehl; p.n.
WEARE. A loc. n., Somers.
WEARING. *N.* Væringi; the name of the Warings or northern warriors who served as body-guards to the Byzantine Emperors. *Fl.* Vering; *D.B.* Warenger, Werinc, Wareng, Warinc, Warin; p.n.

The Varangian Guard was originally composed of this Scandinavian tribe, but was afterwards recruited from Northern Europe and England. There is a Varengafjord in Norway.

WEATHERALL. A loc. n., Camb. *See* Wetherall
WEATHERBURNE. *See* Wedderburn
WEATHERLEY. A loc. n., Warw.
WEATHERS. *See* Withers
WEAVER. A loc. n., Ches., Devon. Or *D.* Wæver; a p.n.
WEAVING. *Dch.* Wieffering; a p.n.
WEBB. *Fl.* Webb; a p.n.
WEBBER. *D., Dch., G.* Weber; a p.n.
WEBSDALE. A loc. n.
WEBSTER. The Scot. and N. Engl. form of *D., G., Dch.* Weber; a weaver
WEDD. *See* Weeds
WEDDERBURN. A loc. n., Berwick
WEDDING. *D.* Weden; *S.* Wedin; p.n. Or *see* Wheddon
WEDDUP. A loc. n.
WEDGEWOOD. A loc. n., Staffs.
WEDLAKE. *See* Widlake
WEDLOCK. *See* Widlake
WEDMORE. A loc. n., Somers.
WEEDE. *Fl.* Widy; *S.* Wid; p.n.
WEEDEN. From Weedon; a loc. n., Northants
WEEDING. From Weeting; a loc. n., Norf. Or Weedon, Northants. *See* Weed

WEEDS. *N.* Viðarr; *F.* Wiets; *D.B.* Wido, Wed, Wider, Widard, Widr, Wiet, Widius; *G.* Wieder; *S.* Wid; *D.* Wied; p.n.

WEEKS. A loc. n., Ess.

WEEVILL. *N.* Vívill; *D.* Wivel; *Dch.* Wiwel; p.n.

Richard de Wivill held lands in Yorks *temp.* K. John, A.D. 1200.

WEGG. *Dch.* Wegge; *D.B.* Wege, Weghe; p.n.

WELBORN. A loc. n., Lincs, Norf. Or *G.* Wilborn; a p.n.

WELCHER. *See* Wilscher

WELDON. A loc. n., Northants

WELFORD. A loc. n., Berks, Glost., Northants, Warw.

WELHAM. A loc. n.

WELLAND. A loc. n., Devon, Worcest.

WELLBY. A loc. n., Leics., Lincs

WELLINGHAM. A loc. n., Norf.

WELLINGTON. A loc. n., Salop, Somers.

WELLS. A loc. n., Somers. Or *G.* Wels; a p.n.

WELLSPRING. A loc. n., Devon

WELLUM. *See* Welham

WELTON. A loc. n., Lincs, Northants, Somers., Yorks

WEMBORN. From Wimborne; a loc. n., Dorset

WENBORN. *See* Wemborn

WENDEN. A loc. n., Ess.

WENHAM. A loc. n., Suff.

WENLOCK. A loc. n., Salop

WENT. *D.*, *G.*, *S.* Wendt; *Fl.* Vent; *Dch.* Went; p.n.

WENTWORTH. A loc. n., Camb., Yorks

WESLEY. *N.* Vestliði; *S.* Westlau, Wessling; *Dch.* Wesler, Wesseling; *G.* Wesely; *Fl.* Wesly; p.n. Or from the Irish MacUaislaidh; a p.n. *See* Westley

WEST. *N.* Vestarr; *D.*, *Dch.*, *Fl.* West; *D.B.* Westre; p.n.

WESTACOTT. A loc. n., Devon

WESTBEAR, WESTBEER. A loc. n., Devon, Kent

WESTBROOK. A loc. n., Berks, Norf., Wilts

WESTCOTT. A loc. n., Devon, Warw.

WESTERBY. *D.*; loc. and p. n.

WESTGATE. A loc. n., Dur., Kent, Yorks

WESTHORPE. A loc. n., Lincs, Northants, Notts, Suff.

WESTLEY. A loc. n., Camb., Salop, Suff.

WESTON. A loc. n., Herts, Staffs., Suff., Yorks

WESTRAY. A loc. n., Orkney. Or *N.* Vestarr, Vestre; *D.S.* Wester; *Dch.* Westra; *D.B.* Westre (Saxon tenant); p.n.

WESTREPT. From Westhorpe; a loc. n., Norf. *See* Westropp

WESTROP. A loc. n., Wilts. *D.* Westrup; a loc. and p. n.

WESTWATER. From Wastwater; Cumb.

WESTWOOD. A loc. n., Devon, Kent, Notts, Wilts, Yorks

WETHERALL. A loc. n., Cumb.

WETHERLEY. From Wetherby; a loc. n., Yorks

WETHERSETT. *S.* Wetterstedt; a loc. and p. n.

WETMORE. *See* Whetmore

WETTERN. *Dch.* Wetten, Wetteren; p.n.

WETTERTON. From Wetherden; a loc. n., Suff.

WEY. *N.* Véi or Vé-geirr; *D.* Weyhe; *D.B.* Weghe, Wege, Waih; *Fl.* Wey; *Dch.* Weih; p.n.

WEYMOUTH. A loc. n., Dorset

WHADCOAT. *See* Whatcott

WHAITES. *N.* Veðr or Vettir; *F.* Wêt, Wêts; *D.* Wetje, Vett, Vetter; *G.* Weth; *Fl.* Wets; *D.B.* Wiet; p.n.

WHALE. *See* Wale

WHALEY. A loc. n., Derbysh., Hants

WHALL. *N.* Vali; *D.B.* Walo, Walle, Wala; *G.* Walla, Walle; *Dch.*, *S.* Wall; p.n. *See* Wall

WHALLEY. A loc. n., Derbysh., Lancs

WHARMBY. From Warmanbie; a loc. n., Dumfries

WHARTON. A loc. n., Heref., Lancs, Lincs

WHATCOTT. From Whatcote; a loc. n., Warw.

WHATELEY. A loc. n., Warw.

WHATLEY. A loc. n., Somers.

WHAYMAN. *See* Wyman

WHEALS. *See* Veals

WHEATBREAD. *See* Whitebread

WHEATER. *Dch.* Witte; a p.n. *See* White

WHEATLEY. A loc. n., Devon, Lancs, Notts, Oxf., Yorks

WHEATON. A loc. n., Staffs.

WHEATSTONE. From Whetstone; a loc. n., Leics., Middlx.

WHEDDON. From Whaddon; a loc. n., Glost.

WHEELER. *N.* Víl-raðr; *Dch.* Wielaerts; *G.* Wiehle; *D.* Vieler; p.n. *See* Veals

WHEEN. *See* Wynn

WHELAN. *Dch.* Wielen; a p.n.

WHELHAM. From Whelnetham; a loc. n., Suff.

WHELPDALE. From Wheldale; a loc. n., Yorks

WHENT. *S.*, *D.* Wendt; *G.*, *Dch.* Went; p.n.

WHERRY. *Fl.* Wéry; a p.n.

WHETMORE. From Wetmoor; a loc. n., Staffs.

WHETTAM. *Dch.* Wettum; a p.n.

WHEWELL. *See* Weevill

WHIBLEY. From Weobley; a loc. n., Heref.

WHICHCOTE. A loc. n., Salop

WHICHER, WHICKER. *See* Widger

WHIDBORNE. From Whitburn; a loc. n., Linlithgow, Heref.

WHIDDEN. From Whiddon; a loc. n., Devon. Or *S.* Widen; a p.n.

WHIDDINGTON. *See* Whittington

WHIFF. *D.* Wiuff; a p.n.

WHIGHAM. From Whickham; a loc. n., Dur.

WHILEY. From Wyley; a loc. n., Ess.; or Wylye, Wilts. Or *N.* Veili; *G.* Weil; *Dch.* Weil; *Fl.* Weiler; *D.* Weile; *D.B.* Welle; p.n.

WHIMPER. From Whymple; a loc. n. in Devon. Or Wimpole, Camb.

WHIN. *D.* Wiene; *D.B.* Wine; *Dch.* Win; *Fl.* Wyns; p.n.

WHINCOP. A loc. n., Cumb.

WHINERAY. A loc. n.

WHINNERAH. *See* Whineray

WHINYATES. From Wingates; a loc. n., Northbd.

WHIPHAM. From Wipham; a loc. n., Suss.

WHIPPLE. *S.* Wibell; a p.n.

WHIPP. *N.* Vippa; *D.B.* Wiber; *G.* Wippert; p.n.

WHIPPS. *G.* Wippich; a p.n.

WHIPPY. *G.* Wippig; a p.n.

WHISH. *See* Hewish

WHISKER. *N.* Viga-styrr (?); *D.B.* Wiscar, Wisgar; *Dch.*, *Fl.* Visscher; *G.* Wiskos, Wiskott; p.n.

WHISSELL. From Wysall; a loc. n., Notts. Or *see* Whistler

WHISTLECRAFT. *G.* Wesselhöft; a loc. and p. n.

WHISTLER. *N.* Vestliði (?); *D.B.* Wislaw, Wislac; *G.* Wissell; *Dch.* Wissel, Wisselaar; p.n.

WHISTON. A loc. n., Cornw., Northants, Staffs., Yorks

WHITBREAD. *See* Whitebread

WHITBURN. A loc. n., Dur., Heref.

WHITBY. A loc. n., Yorks

WHITCHER. *G.* Wiche, Wichers, Wichert; *Dch.* Wichers, Wiggers; *D.* Wiggers; p.n. *See* Widger

WHITCHURCH. From Whitechurch; a loc. n., Yorks

WHITCOMBE. A loc. n., Devon, Dorset, I. of Wight, Somers.

WHITE. *N.* Hvítr; *S.* Witt; *Dch.* Witte; *D.B.* Wit, Wite; p.n.
WHITEAR. *See* Whiterod
WHITEBREAD. *Fl.* Wittebord; *D.B.* Witbert, Wibert; p.n.
WHITEHEAD. *F.* Withard; a p.n. *See* Whiterod
WHITEHEART. *See* Whitehead
WHITEHORN. A loc. n., Devon
WHITEHOUSE. *Dch.* Withuis; a p.n.
WHITEHURST. A loc. n., Staffs.
WHITELAW. From Whitlow; a loc. n., Northbd.
WHITELEY. A loc. n., Devon, Yorks
WHITELOCK, WHITLOCK. *S., Dch.* Witlok; a p.n.
WHITEMAN. *Dch.* Witman; *D.B.* Wihtmar; p.n.
WHITEROD. *F.* Witerd, Witherd, Withert, Withers; *Dch.* Wittert; *D.B.* Widard; p.n.
WHITESIDE. A loc. n., Cumb.
WHITEWAY. From Whitway; a loc. n., Hants
WHITFIELD. A loc. n., Dorset, Kent, Northants, Salop
WHITHAM, WITHAM, WHITWHAM. From Witham; a loc. n., Ess., Lincs
WHITHARD. *See* Whitehead and Whiterod
WHITING, WHITTING. *D.* Witten; *S.* Witting; p.n.
WHITLEY. A loc. n., Northbd., Wilts, Yorks
WHITMARSH. From Whitnash; a loc. n., Warw.
WHITMORE. A loc. n., Staffs.
WHITNEY. A loc. n., Bucks, Heref.
WHITTAKER. From Whitacre; a loc. n., Worcest. Or Wheatacre, Norf.
WHITTALL. *See* Whitwell
WHITTENBURY. From Whittlebury; a loc. n., Heref.
WHITTERIDGE. *See* Witheridge
WHITTET. *See* Whiterod
WHITTICK. From Whitwick; a loc. n., Leics.
WHITTINGHAM. A loc. n., Haddingtonsh.
WHITTINGTON. A loc. n., Norf., Salop, Staffs., Warw., Worcest.
WHITTLE. From Whittle; a loc. n., Lancs. Or Whitle, Derbysh. *See* Whitwell
WHITTLESEY. A loc. n., Camb.
WHITTOME. From Whittenham; a loc. n., Oxf.
WHITTON. A loc. n., Norf., Salop, Staffs., Yorks
WHITRICK. *See* Witheridge
WHITWELL. A loc. n., Derbysh., Hants, Herts, Leics., Norf., Yorks
WHITWORTH. A loc. n., Dur., Lancs
WHUR. *See* Wyer
WHYART. *See* Whyatt
WHYATT. *D.* Wiegardt; *Dch.* Wijaarda, Wyatt; *F.* Wiaarda; *Fl.* Wuyts; *D.B.* Wiet; p.n.
WHYBORN. *See* Wayborn
WHYBREW. *See* Whybrow
WHYBROW. From Wyeborough or Wyebrow; a loc. n. on the Wye. Or *see* Wybrow
WHYLE. *See* Wylie
WHYTLAW. *See* Whitelaw
WIBBERLEY. *See* Whibley
WICK. *See* Wigger
WICKENDEN. From Wichingdine; a loc. n., Rutland
WICKETT. *Fr.* Wicot; a p.n.
WICKHAM. A loc. n., Berks, Ess., Hants, Kent, Suff.
WICKS. *See* Wigger
WIDDICOMBE. A loc. n., Devon
WIDE. *D., Dch., G.* Weide; *S.* Wide; p.n.
WIDGER. *D.* Wiegart; *S.* Wigert; *G.* Wiediger; p.n.
WIDGERY. *G.* Wichary; a p.n. *See* Whitcher
WIDLAKE. From Widelake; a loc. n., Cornw.
WIDNALE. From Widdenhall; a loc. n.

WIFFIN. *Dch.* Wijvering; a p.n. Comp. *N.* Vífill; *D.B.* Wifle, Wifere, Vivara; p.n.

WIGER. *See* Widger

WIGG. *See* Wigger

WIGGAN. From Wigan; a loc. n., Lancs

WIGGER. *N.* Vikarr; *D.B.* Wigar, Wigot, Wicgar, Wiga; *G.* Wick, Wicke, Wickert; *Dch.* Wiggers; *D.* Weeke, Wegge, Wich, Wiecke, Wigh, Wijg, Wick; *S.* Wickert, Wik, Wigert; p.n.

WIGGETT. *S.* Wigert; *D.B.* Wigot; p.n. *See* Wigger

WIGGIN. *N.* Víkingr; *S.*, *Fl.* Wiking; *Dch.* Wijking; *D.B.* Wiking, Wighen; p.n. *See* Wigger

WIGGINTON. A loc. n., Herts, Yorks

WIGHT. *S.* Wigert; *D.B.* Wigot; p.n. *See* Wiger or White

WIGHTMAN. *See* Whiteman

WIGLEY. A loc. n., Hants

WIGMORE. A loc. n., Heref., Salop

WIGNAL. From Wiggenhall; a loc. n., Norf.

WILBERFORCE. From Wilberfoss; a loc. n., Yorks

WILBOURN. *See* Welborn

WILBRAHAM. A loc. n., Camb.

Anciently, Wilburgham.

WILBY. A loc. n., Norf., Northants, Suff.

WILCH. *See* Wilscher

WILCOCKS. *Fl.* Wilçockx; *D.B.* Willac; p.n. Dimin. of Will

WILD. *See* Wildee

WILDBORE. *Dch.* Wildeboer; a p.n.

WILDEE. *F.* Wildert, Wilt; *D.B.* Wilde; *G.*, *D.*, *Dch.* Wilde; p.n.

Adam le Wilde in Rot. Obl. et Fin., K. John.

WILDGOOSE. *See* Wilgress

WILDMAN. *Dch.*, *Fl.* Wildeman; a p.n.

WILDONE. From Wilden; a loc. n., Beds

WILEMAR. *N.* Víl-Hjálmr; *F.* Wilhelm, Wilm; *D.B.* Wilmar, Willelm, Wilelmus, Willa; *G.* Wilhelm; *Dch.* Willemar; p.n.

WILES. *Fl.* Weyllas; a p.n.

WILFORD A loc. n., Notts. Or Williford, Staffs.

WILGOSS. *See* Wilgress

WILGRESS. *N.* Vilgeirr; *D.B.* Wilegrip; *Dch.* Willigers; *G.* Williger, Williges; p.n.

WILKE. *F.* Wilko, Wilke; fam. n. *F.* Wilken; *Dch.* Wilke, Wilkes; p.n.

WILKEN, WILKENS. *D.*, *Dch.* Wilken, Wilkens; *Fl.* Wilkain; p.n.

WILKERSON. *See* Wilke

WILKIE. *See* Wilke

WILKINS. *See* Wilkens

WILKINSON. *See* Wilke

WILLEMENT. *N.* Vil-mundr; *D.B.* Wilmer; *G.* Willigmann, Willman; *Dch.* Willeman; p.n.

WILLESEE. From Wilsey; a loc. n., Suff.

WILLETT. Dimin. of Will. *See* Wilemar

WILLEY. *D.* Wille, Willig; *Fl.* Wyllie; *G.* Wiehle, Wille, Willich; *Dch.* Wiele, Wille, Wijle; p.n.

WILLIAMS. *See* Wilemar

WILLIAMSON. *See* Wilemar

WILLIMONT. *See* Willement

WILLIMOT. Dimin. of Wilm. *See* Wilemar

WILLING. *Dch.* Willing; a p.n.

WILLOUGHBY. A loc. n., Leics., Lincs, Notts, Warw.

WILMOT. *Fl.* Wilmart, Wilmet; *Fr.* Wilmotte; p.n.

WILSCHER. *Dch.* Wildschut, Wilschut, Wilshaus; a p.n. Or *see* Wilsher and Wiltshire

WILSHAK. *G.* Wilschek; a p.n. Or Wilsick; a loc. n., Yorks

WILSHEE, WILSHER. From Wilshaw; a loc. n., Staffs., Yorks. Or *see* Wiltshire

WILSON. *D.* Will, Wilson; p.n.

WILTON. A loc. n., Cornw., Norf., Northants, Somers., Wilts, Yorks

WILTSHEAR, WILTSHIRE. The county

WIMBLE. From Wimpole; a loc. n., Camb.

WIMBUSH. From Wimbish; a loc. n., Ess.

WIMHURST. *Dch.*, *G.* Wimmers; a p.n.

WINCE. *See* Winch or Vince

WINCH. A loc. n., Norf. Or *S.*, *D.* Winge; *Dch.* Wins; *D.B.* Winge; p.n.

WINCHCOMBE. A loc. n., Glost.

WINCKELS. *Dch.* Winkels; a p.n.

WINCKLEY. From Winkleigh; a loc. n., Devon

WINCKWORTH. From Wingerworth; a loc. n., Derbysh.

WINCOP. *See* Whincop or Winkup

WINCUP. *See* Winkup

WINDALL. *S.* Windahl; a loc. and p. n.

WINDER. *D.* Winder, Winter; p.n.

WINDISH. *G.* Windisch; a p.n.

WINDLE. A loc. n., Lancs

WINDLEY. A loc. n., Derbysh.

WINDOVER. From Wendover; a p.n., Hants

WINDSOR. A loc. n., Berks, Dorset

WINDUS, WINDUST. From Windrush; a loc. n., Glost. Or *see* Windish

WINEARL. *See* Winecarl

WINECARLS. *Dch.* Winkels; a p.n.

WINFIELD. *See* Wingfield

WING. *See* Winch

WINGATE. From Windygate; a loc. n., Fife

WINGFIELD. A loc. n., Derbysh., Suff.

WINGROVE. From Wingrave; a loc. n., Bucks

WINKEL. From Winkhill; a loc. n., Staffs. Or *Dch.* Winkel; a p.n.

WINKFIELD. *See* Wingfield

WINKLE. *See* Winkel

WINKUP. *Dch.* Winkoop; a p.n. Or *see* Wincop

WINMILL. A loc. n., Devon

WINN. *See* Whin and Wynne

WINNALL. A loc. n., Warw.

WINSER, WINZAR. *See* Winsor

WINSLOW. A loc. n., Bucks, Heref., Yorks

WINSON. *See* Whin

WINSOR. A loc. n., Cornw., Hants. Or *see* Windsor

WINSPEAR. From Winceby; a loc. n., Lincs. *D.B.* Winzebi

Winsbær or Winsbýr is the Danish form.

WINSTANLEY. A loc. n., Lancs

WINSTON. A loc. n., Dur., Suff.

WINTER. *D.*, *S.*, *Dch.*, *Fl.*, *G.* Winter; a p.n.

WINTERBORN, WINTERBOURNE. A loc. n., Glost.

WINTERBOTHAM, WINTERBOTTAM. *See* Winterbourne (?)

WINTERTON. A loc. n., Lincs, Norf.

WINTHROP. A loc. n., Lincs

WINTLE. *See* Windle

WIRE. *See* Wyer

WISBY. From Wiseby; a loc. n., Lincs

WISDOM. *D.* Wisbom (?); a p.n.

WISE. *G.* Weis, Weiss; a p.n.

WISEMANN. *Dch.* Wiseman, Wisman; *G.* Weissmann; p.n.

WISKER. *See* Whisker

WITCOMB. A loc. n., Somers.

WITFORD. A loc. n., N. Wales

WITH. From Withy; a loc. n. Somers.

WITHALL. *See* Whittall. Or from Withiel; a loc. n., Cornw.

WITHERBY. A loc. n., Worcest.

WITHERIDGE. A loc. n., Devon

WITHERINGTON, WITHRINGTON. From Widdrington; a loc. n., Northbd.

WITHERN. A loc. n., Lincs

WITHERS. *N.* Viðarr; *F.* Withers; *Fl.* Wittert; *G.* Wieder; *D.B.* Wider, Widard; p.n. *See* Whittet

WITT. *Dch.* Witt; a p.n. *See* White

WITTON. *See* Whitton

WITTY. *Fl.* Wittigh; a p.n.

WIX. A loc. n., Ess.

WIXLEY. From Whixley; a loc. n., Yorks

WOAKES. *D.* Woges; a p.n.

WOBBE. *Dch.* Wubbe (?); a p.n.

WOLLARD. From Walworth; a loc. n.

WOLNO. *See* Woolnough

WOLSELEY. A loc. n., Staffs.

WOLSEY. *See* Wolesley

WOLSTENHOLME. A loc. n., Lancs

WOLTON. *See* Walton

WOLVERTON. A loc. n., Hants, Kent, Wilts

WOMACK. *D.B.* Wimarch, Wimer; p.n.

WOMBWELL. A loc. n., Yorks

WONNACOTT. From Onecote; a loc. n., Staffs.

WOOD. *N.* Uðr; *D.* Uhde; *F.* Udo, Ude; *D.B.* Udi; p.n.

WOODALL. From Woodhall; a loc. n., Lincs, Worcest., Yorks

WOODARD. *D.* Wad, Wodder; *G.* Woders; *D.B.* Wadard; p.n.

WOODBERRY. *See* Woodbury

WOODBRIDGE. A loc. n., Camb., Suff.

WOODBURN. A loc. n., Northbd.

WOODBURY. A loc. n., Cornw., Devon, Hants

WOODCOCK. Dimin. of Ude. *See* Wood

WOODEND. A loc. n., Staffs., and other counties

WOODERSON. *D.* Wodder; a p.n.

WOODESON. *See* Wooderson

WOODFALL. A loc. n., Kent, Wilts

WOODFORD. A loc. n., Ess., Glost., Somers.

WOODGATE. A loc. n., Lancs, Staffs.

WOODGER. *See* Woodyard

WOODHAM. A loc. n., Ess.

WOODHEAD. A loc. n., Ches., Northbd.

WOODHOUSE. A loc. n., Derbysh., Hants, Lancs, Staffs., Somers.

WOODIN, WOODING. *Dch.* Wouden; *Fl.* Wodon; p.n.

WOODLAND. A loc. n., Devon, Lancs

WOODLEY. A loc. n., Devon, Hants

WOODMASON. From Woodmanstone; a loc. n., Surr.

WOODROFFE, WOODRUFF. *See* Woodrow

WOODROW. A loc. n., Dorset

WOODSTOCK. A loc. n., Oxf.

WOODTHORPE. A loc. n., Derbysh., Lincs, Oxf., Yorks

WOODWARD. *See* Woodard

WOODYARD. *See* Woodard

WOOF. *D.*, *G.* Wulff; a p.n.

WOOKEY. A loc. n., Somers.

WOOL. A loc. n., Dorset. Or *G.* Wolle; *D.* Uhl, Woll; p.n.

WOOLAGE. From Woolwich; a loc. n.

WOOLARD, WOOLLARD. *S.* Wollert; a p.n.

WOOLASTON. A loc. n., Heref., Northants, Salop, Staffs., Worcest.

WOOLLATT, WOOLLETT. *See* Woollard

WOOLCOCK. *G.* Wolke; a p.n.

WOOLCOTT. From Woolscott; a loc. n., Staffs.

WOOLDRIDGE. *See* Worlledge

WOOLERSON. From Woolverstone; a loc. n., Norf. Or *see* Woolaston

WOOLFENDEN. A loc. n.

WOOLISCROFT. From Woolescroft; a loc. n., Staffs.

WOOLLEY. A loc. n., Derbysh.

WOOLMAN. *D.* Vollmann; *G.* Wollmann; p.n.

WOOLMER. *D.* Vollmer; a p.n.
WOOLNOUGH. *N.* Ulf-njótr; *A.S.* Ulnod; *D.B.* Ulnoth; p.n.
WOOLRYCH. *See* Worlledge
WOOLSTON. A loc. n., Hants, Oxf.
WOON. A loc. n., Cornw.
WOOR. *See* Whur
WOOSNAM. *See* Wolstenholme
WOOSTER. From Worcester; the county town
WOOTON. *See* Wootton
WOOTTEN. A loc. n., Suff.
WOOTTON. A loc. n., Hants, Heref., Northants, Salop, Somers.
WORBOYS. A loc. n., Camb., Hunts
WORBY. *See* Worboys
WORD. A loc. n., Kent, Suss.
WORDLEY. From Wordsley; a loc. n., Staffs.
WORDSWORTH. *Fl.* Wadswerth; a p.n.
WORLEDGE. *See* Worlledge
WORLEY. *See* Whalley
WORLLEDGE. From Warlage; a loc. n., Northbd.
WORM. *N.* Ormr; *D.B.* Orm, Ormar; *D.* Worm; *Dch.* Wormer; *G.* Wormt, Wurm; p.n.
WORMALD. *See* Wormull
WORMER. *See* Warmer
WORMSLEY. A loc. n., Heref.
WORMULL. From Wormhill; a loc. n., Derbysh.
WORN. *See* Warne
WORNER. *See* Warner
WORNUM. From Warnham; a loc. n., Suss.
WORPOLE. From Warpole; a loc. n., Devon
WORRALL. A loc. n., Yorks
WORROW. *D.* Worre; a p.n. Or *see* Worrall
WORSDELL. From Worsall; a loc. n., Yorks
WORSEY. *D.* Worsaae; a p.n.
WORSHIP. From Warsop; a loc. n., Notts
WORSLEY. A loc. n., Lancs
WORSTER. From Worstead; a loc. n., Norf. or from Worcester
WORTH. A loc. n., Ches., Suss., Yorks
WORTHAM. A loc. n., Suff.
WORTHING. A loc. n., Suss.
WORTHINGTON. A loc. n., Lancs, Leics.
WORTLEY. A loc. n., Glost., Yorks
WORTON. A loc. n., Middlx.
WOTTON. A loc. n., Glost.
WRAGG. *N.* Ragi; *Fr.* Ragot; *D.* Rager; p.n. *See* Ragg
WRATE. *D.* Wriedt; *S.* Wrede, Wret; p.n.
WRATTEN. From Wratting; a loc. n., Camb., Norf., Suff.
WREN. *See* Rennie
WRENCH. *G.* Wrensch; a p.n. Or *see* Renishaw
WRENFORD. From Rainford; a loc. n., Lancs
WRETHAM. A loc. n., Norf.
WRIGHT. *D.* Wright; a p.n. Or Wryde; a loc. n., Camb.
WRINCH. *See* Wrench
WRISTBRIDGE. *D.* Wrisberg; a p.n.
WRITER. *G.* Reiter; a p.n.
WRODT. A loc. n., Lincs
WROTTESLEY. A loc. n., Staffs.
WURR. *See* Wyer
WYAND. *Dch.* Weijand; a p.n.
WYARD. *See* Whyatt
WYATT. *Dch.*; p.n. *See* Whyatt
WYBROW. *D.* Wibroe; a p.n. *See* Whybrow
WYBURN. *See* Wayborn
WYCHE. A loc. n., Lincs
WYER. *Dch.* Weijer; *G.* Wier, Wirrwa; *D.B.* Wiuar, Wiuara (?); p.n.
WYETH. *D.* Wiethe; a p.n.
WYGARD. *See* Wigger
WYKE. A loc. n., Yorks
WYKEHAM. A loc. n., Hants, Lincs, Northants, Yorks
WYKES. A loc. n., Northants, Salop, Surr.

WYLDE. *See* Wildee

WYLIE. *See* Whiley

WYMAN. *N.* Vémundr; *D.B.* Wimund, Wimer; *Dch.* Weyman, Wijmen; *G.* Wimmer, Weiman; *S.* Weman; *Fl.* Wyman, Weman; p.n.

WYNDHAM. From Windham; a loc. n., Norf. Or Wymondham, Leics.

WYNNE. *Welsh* Gwynn

WYNYARD. *Fl.* Wyngaard; *Dch.* Wijngaart; p.n.

WYON. *Fl.* Wion; a p.n.

WYRE. *See* Wyer

WYTHE. *D.* Wiethe; a p.n.

WYTTON. *D.* Witten; a p.n.

WYVILL. A loc. n., Lincs. Or *N.* Vívill; *D.*, *Dch.* Wivel; a p.n. *See* Weevill

Y.

YALDEN. From Yalding; a loc. n., Kent

YALE. *Fl.* Jell; a p.n.

YALLOP. *N.* Hjálp; *G.* Hallupp, Halop; p.n. *See* Gallop

YAPP. *F.* Jabbo, Jabbe; *G.* Jaap; *Fl.* Jabé; *D.* Jappe; p.n.

YARDE. A loc. n., Somers.

YARDLEY. A loc. n., Northants, Worcest.

YARHAM. From Yarm; a loc. n., Yorks

YARINGTON. A loc. n.

YARLEY. From Yardley; a loc. n., Northants, Worcest.

YARMUTH. A loc. n., I. of Wight, Norf.

YARRAD. *See* Yarrod

YARRANTON. From Yarnton; a loc. n., Oxf.

YARROD. *N.* Geir-röðr; *G.* Jerathe, Jerothe; p.n. *See* Jarrett

YARROW. A loc. n., Scotl., Somers. Also Jarrow, Dur.

YATE. A loc. n., Glost. Or *see* Yates

YATES. *N.* Geitr (?); *G.* Jaty, Jaite; *Fr.* Jette; p.n. *See* Gates

YAXLEY. A loc. n., Camb., Norf., Suff. From *F.* Jak

YEAMES. *D.* Gjems; *G.* Jambert, Gems; *Dch.* Jampart, Jemkes, Gemert; *Fl.* Jamar, Jamart, Jambers, James; *D.B.* James; p.n.

YEAMON, YEOMAN. *Fl.* Jemayne; a p.n.

YEARSLEY. A loc. n., Yorks

YEILDING. A loc. n., Worcest.

YELD. From Yelt; a loc. n., Cornw.

YELDHAM. A loc. n., Ess.

YELL. *Fl.* Jell; *S.* Yell; p.n.

YELLAND. From Yealand; a loc. n., Lancs

YELLOLY. A loc. n., Scotl.

YELLON. From Yelling; a loc. n., Hunts

YELLOPP. *See* Yallop

YELVERTON. A loc. n., Norf.

YEO. *Fr.* Jehu; a p.n.

YEOMAN. *G.* Jochmann; a p.n.

YEOWELL. From Yeovil; a loc. n., Somers. Or *see* Jouel

YERBURY. From Yearby; a loc. n., Yorks

YERLING. *See* Yirling

YETTON. *See* Yatton

YEULETT. *See* Ullett

YEWDALL. From Yewdale; a loc. n., Lancs. Or *see* Udall

YEWENS. *Fl.* Juveyns; a p.n.

YEXLEY. *See* Yaxley

YIRLING. *N.* Erlingr; *S.* Gjerling; *D.B.* Erlenc; a p.n.

YONGE. *D.*, *Dch.*, *Fl.*, *G.* Jong, Jung, Junger; p.n.

YORK. A loc. n

YORSTON. From Yorton; a loc. n., Salop

YORWARTH. From Yoadwath; a loc. n., Yorks

YOUARD. *See* Howard

YOUART. *See* Huart

YOUD. *Dch.* Joode; *D.* Jud; p.n.

YOUELL. *See* Jouel

YOUELS. *See* Jouel

YOUENS. *See* Yewens

YOUHILL, YOUILL. *See* Jouel

YOULDEN. *See* Youlton

YOULES. *See* Jouel

YOULTON. A loc. n., Yorks

YOUNG. *See* Yonge

YOUNGER. *D.* Junker; a p.n.

YOUNGMAN. *D.*, *Dch.*, *G.* Jungman; a p.n.

YOUNGS. *Fl.* Junges; a p.n.

YOXALL. A loc. n., Staffs.

YOXLEY. *See* Yaxley

YULE. *See* Jouel

YULL. *See* Jouel

Z.

ZOUCH. From Sauchay (?); a loc. n., Normandy

APPENDIX.

THE following names are under consideration. Many of them are local names, but as they cannot be found in any existing gazetteer or county directory, they are very likely those of manors, which are not necessarily parishes, or small estates situated in different parts of the country.

Any information respecting them will be thankfully received by the author, as will any other suggestions for the improvement of this work, in a second edition, should such be called for.

Adlam, Akenhead, Alefounder, Allerdyce, Allshorn, Ancient, Argles, Arrowsmith, Atchley, Atyeo, Ayerst.

Badman, Banthorpe, Bardrick, Battam, Batters, Beames, Beardshaw, Beardsworth, Bearcroft, Beecroft, Bestman, Bickerdyke, Biddlecombe, Bidmead, Bidwell, Birchmore, Bissicks, Blackbeard, Bradbeer, Bradstock, Broadbent, Brodribb, Budibent, Bulport.

Cade, Call, Carwithen, Cavafy, Chenerey, Chinnery, Chrimes, Chuckerbutty, Circuit, Clerihew, Click, Clothier, Clucas, Collingridge, Copestake, Critchfield, Cruickshank, Cudby, Cuff, Culpeper, Culperwell, Cutforth.

Dadfield, Dashwood, Daunt, Denley, Dewsnap, Dibb, Dibley, Dockerill, Doidge, Doig, Drakeford, Drinkwater, Dowding, Dudd.

Enticknap, Everest, Eversfield.

Faddy, Fairservice, Faithful, Fastnedge, Faulding, Faultless, Felgate, Fensham, Fensom, Fentum, Fessenden, Few, Fewtrell, Filgate, Firk,

Firkins, Firmstone, Fishenden, Fladgate, Flavell, Flear, Flindall, Flinders, Flintoff, Flogdell, Fothergill, Foxcroft, Frakes, Frew, Fripp, Frogley, Furmstone.

Gabbesey, Gace, Galbraith, Gamgee, Gape, Garnham, Gatfield, Gathercole, Gaukroger, Gellatly, Gepp, Getgood, Gillington, Gillitlie, Girdlestone, Gisby, Gladwell, Glover, Golightly, Goodge, Gorham, Goudge, Grabham, Greagsby, Greely, Greensmith, Greenwood, Gridley, Grigsby, Grindrod, Grinham, Grinslade, Grisenthwaite.

Habgood, Hadgraft, Hainbon, Hanlon, Harkaway, Hastelow, Hathornthwaite, Havergal, Haylock, Heavyside, Helpman, Herapath, Heritage, Hickory, Hignell, Hobday, Hogsflesh, Horlack, Horlick, Horsfall, Hostome, Huxtable.

Imray, Imrie, Inn.

Jeffcoat, Joyner.

Keeping, Kefford, Kethro, Kidney, Kinglake, Kinstruck, Kirty, Kistrick, Knew.

Lasken, Lattey, Laverick, Leadbeater, Leadbitter, Learoyd, Lightbody, Lightowler, Lilliecrap, Linklater, Linnington, Linscott, Lippincott, Lipscombe, Littlechild, Lofting, Longbourne, Lovebond, Lovibond, Lovegrove, Lovejoy, Lovelady, Lovelock, Loverock, Lovesey, Loxdale, Lushington, Lythaby.

Maidment, Mainprice, Makemade, Manchip, Marrable, Maxlow, Mellows, Melsom, Mends, Merryweather, Middlebrook, Middleditch, Monksfield, Monypenny, Murch.

Nall, Narraway, Neary, Need, Needes, Nettleship, Newcomb, Nind, Noad, Nodes, Noldwritt, Norsworthy.

Orbell, Ortner, Outram, Overall, Overell, Overill, Oxtoby.

Pagriff, Paramore, Paveley, Pedgrift, Penderleigh, Penlington, Pentecost, Perriam, Petley, Pettifer, Pettiford, Pieby, Pim, Pym, Popplewell, Prentice, Prentis, Pummel, Purgold.

Rackley, Ractstray, Raffety, Ransley, Ranstead, Ravenscliffe, Ravenscourt, Remblance, Reside, Resther, Rickarby, Ridgely, Ridler.

Scattergood, Search, Serwech, Shadbolt, Shalders, Sherlock, Shipsides, Shives, Shoard, Shoesmith, Shoosmith, Shorrock, Shortridge, Shrapnell, Shrimpton, Shuffrey, Sidebottom, Silence, Sillence, Silverside, Singlehurst, Sirgood, Sirkett (see Circuit), Smallbone, Smallman, Smallpage, Smallpiece, Smethurst, Snelgrove, Snoad, Snoxall, Snoxell, South, Spanswick, Spearman, Spearpoint, Spenceley, Spendlove, Sperring, Spon, Sporton, Spours, Spouse, Spragg, Sprague, Sprake, Spratling, Sprules, Squibb, Stallwood, Stallworthy, Standeven, Staniland, Stent, Stillwell, Stopford, Stradling, Strickstock, Strudger, Strudwick, Struggler, Stunt, Sturdy, Sullivan, Sunnuck, Supple, Swarbrick, Sweetapple, Swindlehurst, Swinglehurst (see Singlehurst), Swithinbank, Swivel, Sworn.

Tadhunter, Tapscott, Tapsfield, Tarling, Taswell, Thickbroom, Thresh, Thunder, Timgate, Timlet, Tinckham, Tingcombe, Tinham, Tinson, Tiplady, Todhunter, Tolhurst, Toplady, Tordoff, Tosswill, Totman, Totterdell, Towndrow, Trant, Tranter, Trapnell, Treasure, Treinen, Trimming, Trimy, Trinder, Trinen, Tringham, Triphook, Trollope, Truckle, Trundley, Tumblety, Tupp, Tustain, Tustin, Twelvetrees, Twentyman, Twisaday, Twyman.

Uffindel, Ullathorne, Umphleby, Underhay, Ungless, Uniacke, Unite, Unwin, Upsdall, Upsom.

Verity, Vinnecombe, Vinrace, Visick, Vousden.

Wabe, Wagstaff, Wakeford, Wapshere, Warlock, Waterfield, Waygood, Wayham, Waylet, Weatherstone, Wedderspoon, Wellbeloved, Wellstead, Wharnsby, Whatling, Whichelow, Whitehand, Widnell, Wigfall, Wigfull, Wigram, Wimperis, Wimpey, Wimpory, Wincott, Windebank, Windybank, Wisedell, Wisden, Witherspoon, Wolstencroft, Wolveridge, Wooderspoon, Woodfield, Worland, Worsfield, Worssam, Wotherspoon, Wrangham, Wrentmore, Wrigley.

Yabsley, Yarnall, Yarnel, Yarr, Yearren, Yeatman, Yetman, Yellowlee, Yellowlees, Yendon, Yeves, Yockney, Yount.

Lightning Source UK Ltd.
Milton Keynes UK
UKHW010702090223
416681UK00007B/1743

9 789353 809362